The Asian American Experience

Series Editor
Roger Daniels, University of Cincinnati

PLEASE
Return
to
Don Nunamaker

D1073281

THE
HOOD RIVER
ISSEI

THE HOOD RIVER ISSEI

An Oral History of Japanese Settlers
in Oregon's Hood River Valley

LINDA TAMURA

Foreword by Roger Daniels

UNIVERSITY OF ILLINOIS PRESS
Urbana and Chicago

First Illinois Edition, 1993
© 1993 by the Board of Trustees of the University of Illinois
Manufactured in the United States of America
P 8 7 6 5 4

This book is printed on acid-free paper.

Library of Congress Cataloging-in-Publication Data

Tamura, Linda, 1940–
   The Hood River Issei : an oral history of Japanese settlers in
Oregon's Hood River Valley / Linda Tamura : foreword by Roger
Daniels.
       p.   cm. — (The Asian American experience)
   Includes bibliographical references and index.
   ISBN 978-0-252-06359-6
   1. Japanese Americans—Oregon—Hood River Valley (River)—History.
   2. Hood River Valley (Or. : River)—History. 3. Oral history.
I. Title.   II. Series.
F882.H9T36   1993
979.5'61004956—dc20   92-34546
CIP

To: the ideals of the Issei
the spirit of my grandparents
the ever-present faith of my parents

Beikoku ni
Hyakunen o mukaeshi
Iminra no
Tsuzuru rekishi ni
Ashiato nokosu

The immigrants are celebrating
The centennial in America.
As one of them,
I leave a trace in history.

Tanka written by Mrs. Shizue Iwatsuki and
translated by Mrs. Michiko Kumashiro

Contents

Foreword

The Issei—the first generation of Japanese immigrants to the United States—are almost all gone. They came between the 1890s and 1924, when Congress forbade any further immigration from Japan. Most kept few written records, and much of what they did write was destroyed or lost when the U.S. government uprooted them from their homes in 1942. If oral history of so-called ordinary people had been in vogue in the later 1940s and 1950s, or even in the 1960s and 1970s, the story of much of that generation could have been captured. Now, most of it is lost forever. Thanks to Linda Tamura, a Sansei (third-generation Japanese American), some of what Proust called "the search for lost times" has been brought to a happy fruition. She has patiently and skillfully constructed a mosaic of rural Japanese American life.

Hood River, Oregon, the small community that is the locus of Linda Tamura's book, became notorious for a few weeks in 1945. Its American Legion Post—still largely composed of World War I veterans—removed the names of all sixteen of the valley's Japanese American servicemen from the community's public roll of honor. *Life* magazine devoted several pages to the incident, and the action itself was condemned in many liberal and not so liberal publications as a sign of gross intolerance. But Tamura is not writing about that aspect of Hood River or about the politics of discrimination and antidiscrimination. Instead, her book focuses on the lives of its Issei generation as the survivors chose to remember it.

Minoru Yasui, a son of the leading Japanese American family of the valley, told a Portland newspaperman early in 1940 how proud the local Japanese were of their community's achievements in agriculture: "Today the Japanese of Hood River County produce an annual crop of $500,000. This includes 90 percent of the county's asparagus, 80 percent of the strawberries, 35 percent of the pears, and 20 per cent of the apples." Just over two years later the proprietors of that small agricultural empire and the rest of the Japanese American community were exiled by the U.S. government. Yasui himself, the first Japanese American to pass the bar examination in Oregon, was by then languishing in jail, a victim of his notion that the Constitution of the United States protected even U.S. citizens of Japanese ancestry from being subjected to curfews and other restraints imposed solely on the basis of their parents' nationality. Eventually Yasui's case was briefly considered by the Supreme Court, but no high court opinion bears his name.

Some of the Hood River Japanese, including Yasui who resettled in Denver, never came back. Many did, and it is the survivors of the pioneer generation that Tamura has interviewed and whose lives she has reconstructed. Her group is a tiny one, but it is not a sample. It is instead the totality of the survivors of the Issei who still lived in Hood River in the early 1980s and were well enough to be able to participate. She was obviously a knowledgeable and sympathetic interviewer, who had a great deal of respect for and empathy with her subjects, an empathy they seemed to have returned.

What can we learn from her work? Certainly her subjects are not representative of their generation. In the first place, the female predominance among the survivors is unrepresentative of the heavily male immigrant generation. In the second place, the Hood River Japanese—462 persons, 162 of them Issei, according to the 1940 census—were more prosperous than most West Coast Japanese, and, I suspect but cannot demonstrate, those who returned—largely landowners or leaseholders—were among the more prosperous in the community. In the third place—although no one can be sure about this given the current state of our knowledge—the women Tamura interviewed seem to have had more education and other advantages in Japan than did most America-bound Japanese women.

What her book shows us—as nothing else in the English language literature about Japanese Americans does—is how a group of largely female, elderly Japanese residents of an American agricultural community remembered their lives. She has helped them do this and has woven their individual narratives into a loose but meaningful structure. It may well be that their memories have rounded off some of the harsher edges of their experiences and understated the discrimination and scorn that was one of the common denominators of their existence. Although Tamura's informants do not seem to regard themselves as, in Linda Gordon's phrase, "heroes of their own lives," that is surely what they were.

ROGER DANIELS

Preface

On the glistening mid-Columbia River, dozens of colorful sails glide across the wind-whipped waters, with snowcapped Mt. Hood towering just twenty-six miles to the south. Nestled at the base of the majestic mountain as it slopes to meet the rugged, basaltic columns of the Columbia River gorge lies the secluded valley of Hood River, Oregon. Along the tree-covered Cascade Mountains, the fertile valley basin is punctuated by occasional volcanic bluffs and is studded with fourteen hundred acres of orchards that bear its renowned pears and apples. The town, home to 4,600, burgeons during the summer, when it transforms into a windsurf mecca and recreation site.

Beginning in the early 1900s, hundreds of Issei, or first-generation Japanese, were also attracted to this picturesque and isolated valley. Forerunners of the current wave of Pacific Rim immigrants, the Issei ventured across the Pacific Ocean with lofty dreams that they would quickly become wealthy. Economic pressures had plagued them in Japan, where the new Meiji regime had replaced the feudal system with a Western-style government and an industrial society. To raise revenue for modernizing education, banking, law, the military, the telegraph, and railway travel, the Japanese government had heavily taxed the peasant farmers. Faced with poor harvests, famine, burdensome taxes, and the need for additional work to support their families, many had been motivated to migrate overseas. Japanese newspapers had publicized the successes of those who had purchased land in the United States, where one could earn twice as much money per day. Stories had even been told that money was so plentiful it could be scooped from the ground.

Issei debarked in San Francisco, Tacoma, Seattle, and Portland and immediately sought jobs, primarily as laborers in agriculture, small businesses, the fishing industry, sawmills, and railroads. "Birds of passage,"[1] they considered themselves sojourners in this country. Issei envisioned working diligently and earning enough money to return to Japan and lead stable lives. Their numbers increased rapidly. In 1890, just 2,039 Japanese lived in the United States; ten years later, the number of Issei had expanded to 24,326. Although the majority resided in California and Washington, the number in Oregon increased as this state's railroad companies began to recruit Japanese contract laborers. From 1890 to 1900, Oregon Issei numbers grew from 25 to 2,501[2] (see Appendix A).

Issei who encountered Oregon's Hood River Valley saw that this lush area offered not only scenic reminders of their native Japan but also labor opportunities in the developing lumber and agricultural industries. The site of the expanding Oregon Lumber Company of eastern Oregon, it was also beginning to gain a national reputation for the quality of its apples. As more logged-off stumpland was cleared and transformed into orchards, more laborers were in demand. Many Issei thus settled in Oregon's tiny Hood River Valley, just ten miles wide and twenty-six miles long.

Despite low wages and strenuous labor in the United States, the frugal Issei saved their meager earnings. They began to purchase or, in exchange for their labor, receive small tracts of uncleared timber, swamp, or brush land. Gradually, they transformed this marginal land into productive strawberry and asparagus fields and apple orchards. At the same time, they struggled to adjust to the strange language and customs of this new land and began to raise their own families. Separated by the rough valley terrain and poor roads, Issei and their families lived in separate communities—Parkdale and Dee in the upper valley close to Mt. Hood; Odell, Pine Grove, and Oak Grove in the rolling hills near the town of Hood River. Despite the physical distance between their farms and their focus on cultivating their crops, Issei in this relatively isolated valley developed a community of strong social bonds, sharing both economic and social support. By 1910, this tiny valley's Japanese population of 468 was the largest in Oregon outside Portland.[3] The Japanese constituted almost 6 percent of the 8,016 Hood River residents, which also included twenty-one Native Americans and Chinese (see Appendix A).[4]

Ominously, as the Issei's orchards were beginning to mature and become productive, local and state anti-Japanese sentiments also began to escalate. The first bill in Oregon to prevent land purchases by immigrants was introduced in 1917 by a Hood River senator. Two years later, thirty-eight community members formed an Anti-Alien Association, vowing to deny landownership to valley Japanese. By 1920, a state investigation of the "Japanese situation in Oregon" reported that " 'the Japanese question' is more acute in Hood River than in any other place in Oregon."[5]

Twenty years later, shortly after Pearl Harbor was bombed in 1941, all West Coast Issei and their American-born children were removed by the U.S. government to concentration camps, where they spent as long as three years behind barbed-wire enclosures. Finally permitted to return home in 1945, they were met by a community campaign discouraging their return. Local sentiment had so intensified that names of Japanese American servicemen who had fought in World War II with U.S. forces were removed from a county war memorial, bringing nationwide censure to the valley. At the same time, a small but unheralded group organized to counteract propaganda and offer support to Issei who chose to return to Hood River. After more than thirty years of peaceful coexistence following the war, a local newspaper acknowledged that "those of Japanese ancestry and their Caucasian compatriots have shared their special talents and skills to build a better fruit center, a thriving community and a good place in which their children can grow up."[6]

Issei today still seem to retain the inner strength that enabled them to withstand such strenuous physical labors, financial hardships, and racial persecution during those difficult years. Only twenty of the Issei who returned to Hood River were still alive at the time I began this oral history project in 1985. (Fourteen have since died.) In 1986, five of the returning Issei were men who averaged 90 years of age (ranging from 83 to 97), and fifteen were women with an average age of almost 89 (ranging from 82 to 102). Few had shared their experiences with friends or even family members, choosing instead to reminisce privately. Why this reticence about lives so rich in ethnic heritage and the pioneering spirit? One had to wonder. Perhaps one reason was that their pasts were enmeshed in painful memories that they might simply have preferred to forget. Perhaps another reason was that Issei were inclined to avoid calling attention to themselves and preferred instead to focus humbly on others. Perhaps because those of us from later generations, being Americanized, had been unable to converse with them in Nihongo, or Japanese, we may have appeared disinterested in their life histories. Or perhaps, in our efforts to spare Issei the pain of those difficult times, we had discouraged them from expressing their own thoughts and feelings.

Given these possibilities, would the Issei, as private as they were, be willing to overcome that reserve and share their personal experiences, their thoughts, and their feelings so others might better understand their life stories? That became a major question as I began my inquiry into their lives for this oral history portrait.

Fortunately, fourteen of the twenty Hood River Issei agreed to be interviewed. (Among the others, several Issei could not participate because of declining health.) Their tape-recorded interviews became a revelation:

they reminisced, they laughed, they shed tears, they rejoiced. This oral
history of the Hood River Issei is thus largely preserved because of these
sixty-nine interview sessions, which have been transcribed on 366 single-
spaced pages.

This inquiry into the pasts of the Issei begins by examining their early
years in Japan, their views of America, and their travels across the Pacific
Ocean. It continues by relating, in their own styles and in responses to
numerous questions, their adjustments to arduous labor in a strange land
and their descriptions of how they raised their families and developed
close ties within their own Japanese communities. Remembering the
bombing of Pearl Harbor, they each shared their reactions and their fears
and doubts as they were subjected to public scrutiny, were uprooted from
their homes, and then spent almost three years confined in concentration
camps. Anxieties increased when they gradually returned to their homes
in 1945, worried about public reactions and often devastated by the conditions of their property and belongings. Finally, they each gave messages
to future generations of Japanese, their own thoughts on the Issei, and
their views of themselves. They have thus provided the story of the Hood
River Issei in their own words.

Typical of Issei who resided in Hood River, almost 60 percent of the
interviewees for this project came from southwestern Japan, with eight of
the fourteen from the prefectures of Hiroshima and Okayama. Their families had, by and large, been farmers, with ten raising rice (or rice and
wheat) and two raising silkworms. They were educated for their time,
with the men averaging nine years of school in Japan and the women
seven and a half years. The average age of both women and men was
eighty-seven, with ages ranging from eighty-two to ninety-five years. Issei
women tended to arrive on the West Coast later, between 1915 and 1921,
after the middle-aged men determined that they would remain in this
country longer than expected and therefore sought wives. Six of the
eleven women followed their husbands to the United States after ceremonies in Japan; four were picture brides who met their husbands-to-be
for the first time on U.S. soil; and two men followed the common Japanese practice of marrying into heirless families and becoming adopted
sons who assumed the family name. Women, when they married, were
relatively young, averaging nineteen years, with ages ranging from seventeen to twenty-two. Their spouses, however, were considerably older,
averaging twenty-eight years, with a range from twenty-two to thirty-two
years. One ninety-five-year-old male interviewee, who arrived in 1907,
was typical of the early male Issei settlers. (Others, much older than their
wives, have since died or were in poor health at the time of this project.)
The two younger male interviewees arrived in 1917 and 1919 to join fam-

ily members already settled in Oregon. Both became adopted sons when they married at the ages of twenty-four and twenty-six. As for the religious faiths of the interviewees, six Issei were Buddhists and four were Methodists, the primary religions of the valley Japanese before their children gradually joined their own community churches. All but one couple were engaged in fruit farming, the primary occupation of Issei in Hood River.

I introduced the project to Issei and their families during visits in the summer of 1985. A few I knew personally, since I was born in the valley and graduated from high school there. My paternal grandparents had been orchardists and had been active in the local Japanese Methodist church, where Grandpa Tamura played both piano and organ and assisted Issei through his fluency in English. My maternal grandparents, after a picture-bride marriage, had become orchardists as well. They had maintained their devotion to Buddhism, and Grandpa Noji became a leader in the Hiroshima prefectural organization. Despite having family ties and having been raised in the valley, I personally knew few of the Issei. In each case, I explained to them, through my parents' translation, that the purpose of this oral history project was to record their memories. Together with those of other participants, they would form a collective story of the Hood River Issei, to be shared with their grandchildren and other generations. Since I had just completed my own grandmother's biography, I was particularly eager to record stories of others. After discussing procedures for tape-recorded interviews, I invited Issei to take part and encouraged them to gather any photos, documents, or records that might assist in documenting their pasts. Then I mailed participating Issei letters (translated into Japanese) that summarized the project and outlined topics to be discussed. Eleven Issei women and three Issei men participated in interviews from October 1985 through May 1986.

Individual interviews took place in the homes of respective Issei. Three lived alone (each with family members nearby), two were the only living Issei couple, another was married to a native-born Japanese woman who arrived in the 1960s, and the others lived with family members. Most of the interviews were tape recorded, and each session lasted approximately one and a half hours. The number of recorded interview sessions per Issei ranged from one to eight. There were also numerous follow-up contacts in person and by phone.

Because I neither spoke nor understood Japanese at the time of the interviews, I engaged a translator. The translator was a Nisei, a second-generation Japanese, who, because of his fine reputation within the Hood River Japanese community, quickly became an asset. Generally, interviews became three-way conversations. After I asked my question in English, the translator restated it in Japanese, whereupon the Issei pondered the question and responded in Japanese, which again was translated into English. Because of the nature of this exchange, the process of gathering information became lengthy and, at times, complicated. In two cases, Issei chose to answer some questions in broken English. A few Issei understood my English questions and were able to respond immediately, eliminating the middle step. Sometimes, however, it was evident from their responses that they had misunderstood the question. Often Issei related their stories in a mixture of English and Japanese. Sometimes they launched into lengthy stories, often not pausing long enough for adequate translations. Then my translator and I made a polite request: "Chotto matte kudasai" (please wait). Occasionally, however, when a story was particularly emotional or difficult to interrupt, we simply allowed Issei to continue and replayed the tape later for translation.

When they became comfortable with the format, most Issei seemed to take pleasure in talking about the past. For some, in fact, once they were aware of our interest and their memories began to flow, the floodgates of their emotions and experiences opened and their recollections came spilling through. Some freely expressed both pain and pleasure. All told stories that were fresh and unpretentious. Several admitted that the information they shared would be surprising to their own families.

During interviews, most Issei were very careful to avoid making negative comments about others. One stated, in response to a question about internment camps, "I do not recall any pleasant experiences in camp—not even one"; however, when asked what unpleasant memories she had, she quickly added, "I do not recall any negative things at this time." Yet this same woman openly expressed remorse about her own experiences, shedding tears when recalling her loneliness in the United States and the FBI's abduction of her husband during the war. Many times, Issei seemed surprised by further requests for details, such as "What kinds of vegetables did you grow in Japan?" or "Which items were you unable to buy because of the language barrier?" As might be expected, questions involving recollections were simpler to answer than those requiring analysis or evaluation, such as "How were American women different from Japanese women?" We often broke these down into a series of smaller queries that led to the ultimate question. Some issues were particularly sensitive, most notably the loyalty questionnaire required of Japanese during World War II, which asked whether they would "swear unqualified allegiance" to the United States and whether they would volunteer for service to this country. The questionnaire provoked much dissension, and Issei body language during my interviews indicated that this was an extremely uncomfortable subject. One of the most difficult questions came near the conclusion of each set of interviews when I asked each Issei for a self-description. Almost half of them made self-effacing comments, while the rest seemed to evade the question. They all possessed very humble natures.

Each succeeding interview began with follow-up questions, sometimes to check facts or translated statements, other times in an attempt to gather more specific information. At the end of each interview, I customarily noted a topic about which the interviewee had given me particularly helpful information. I also outlined the topics we would discuss at the next session. Invariably, Issei apologized for being unable to answer some questions or for possessing poor memories. Considering the ages of my interviewees, however, I was quite amazed and most appreciative of their abilities to recall details from the past. Two, in fact, prepared for interviews by writing notes, while two others referred to diaries to refresh their memories and check facts. All seemed to have thought carefully about the topics. Many provided records, photographs, and documents, including minutes of a Japanese community organization in Hood River dating back to 1925 (see Appendix B).

Although family members willingly assisted, the interviews were most successful when there were only three main participants. When family members were present, Issei tended to rely on them or, quite naturally, reacted self-consciously if the accuracy of their information was questioned. Thus, instead of sitting in, family members of the Issei were asked to help in other ways—by reviewing transcripts to confirm information or to answer additional questions at a later time. Most were very conscientious, frequently asking questions of the Issei again or, in one case, orally translating transcripts for the Issei. Often they remarked on how much new information they had gained. Family members who were able to assist in this way thus provided a necessary and much appreciated service.

Since most of the interviews were held during morning hours, they were transcribed the same day. I transcribed the majority, receiving welcomed assistance from members of my own family on ten of them. The auditing process became lengthy as well, for, in addition to checking the accuracy of each transcript, I often relied on my mother's valuable ear to interpret Japanese statements. In the transcribing and editing process, we tried to reproduce the Issei statements in English as accurately as possible. This was complicated by the fact that many Japanese expressions are not literally translatable into English. Also, Issei statements often came after I asked follow-up questions to clarify and expand the topic. In such cases, I often combined comments made during different portions of the interview or in response to follow-up questions. In all cases, Issei expressions and speech patterns were followed as closely as possible. The editing process included deleting repetitions, misunderstandings of questions or translations, and misinterpretations because of hearing difficulties; substituting for contractions used to translate Japanese expressions; changing verb tenses for consistency; altering points of reference (e.g., "here" was edited to refer to the United States, "there" to refer to Japan); resequencing information to clarify their points; eliminating some names, with the consent of the interviewees; and rephrasing some translations for clarity, often in cooperation with the translator.

Once we had concluded interviews with an Issei, I began the process of arranging comments by topics, according to outlines used for the interviews. I reviewed each transcript for appropriate information related to subjects in the outline (e.g., school experiences in Japan) and sometimes expanded the outline based on novel statements. Then I extracted the comments and combined them with those made by other Issei. After we had concluded all the interviews and I had arranged comments in topical sections, I sequenced the sections in logical or chronological order. I then added introductions, explanations, and transitions to cement the comments of Issei and provide a historical perspective to their experiences. Every effort was made to verify the Issei's information by checking written resources and, when records were unavailable (particularly regarding some local situations), contacting other knowledgeable people.

The purpose of this book is threefold: to allow the Hood River Issei to tell their own life stories about emigrating from Japan and settling in the United States; to document their collective stories of perseverance in a country where they faced an unfamiliar language and culture, physical hardships, discrimination, and wartime persecution; and to illustrate the development of rural Hood River's Japanese American community. I hope these oral histories will provide a window to the nature and experiences of Hood River Issei and those characteristics that enabled them to survive racial persecution, language barriers, strenuous labor, and financial hardships, while still maintaining their dignity and a loyalty for their new homeland. Copies of the tapes of Issei interviews will be deposited at the Oregon Historical Society and the Hood River County Museum.

Acknowledgments

I am most grateful to the Hood River Issei and their families for welcoming me into their homes, earnestly sharing their stories, assisting in the collection of photos and memorabilia, and reviewing transcripts for accuracy. Without their cooperation, this project would have been impossible. In particular, thanks to my own family for their inspiration and support: my mother and father, not only for their faith in me but also for their assistance in auditing, cataloging, and acquiring materials; Uncle

Mam Noji, for his enthusiastic and tireless efforts as translator during my interviews; my sister Judi, for her willingness to assist at the word processor; and most of all, Grandma Noji, for her ever-present dedication and good humor.

I owe special thanks to those who provided invaluable assistance by reviewing drafts of the manuscript and offering both suggestions and encouragement: Roger Daniels, Jane Mohraz, Ralph Falconeri, Gordon Dodds, Charles Morrissey, Tom Griffith, Linda Dodds, and Rick Harmon.

The library staffs at the following institutions were very helpful in locating documents: Alex Toth, Pacific University; Oregon Historical Society; Portland State University; Hood River County Museum; Hood River Historical Society; Commission on Archives and History of the United Methodist Church; and Forest Grove City Library.

There were many who assisted me in acquiring valuable documents and photographs. In addition to the Issei, I would like to thank Kinu Akiyama, Shig and Grace Yamaki, Ayako Iwatsuki, the late Yori Tambara, Harry Inukai, Ben Kino, Consul Shigenobu Suzuki, Alice Ito, the late Chiye Sakamoto, Ray Sato, Toru Noji, the late Ray Yasui, George Akiyama, the late George Kinoshita, Rev. Don Colburn, Rev. Chester Earls, Lee and Naomi Schick, Rev. Everett Gardner, Glada Kays, Ruth Guppy, Polly Timberman, Ray Mainwaring, David McKeown, Margaret Brower, Lindsay Buckner, Clem Pope, Dale Wonsyld, Yoko Gulde, Kazuko Ikeda, Stephen Kohl, Michiko Kumashiro, and Jim Flory.

Special appreciation is also extended to the Mid-Columbia Japanese American Citizens' League and to Pacific University, for granting my sabbatical leave.

Issei Profiles

Mrs. Itsu Akiyama,[1] Oak Grove
Eighty-nine years old[2] .
Born March 25, 1896, in Okayama, Japan

Mrs. Itsu Akiyama immigrated to the United States as a nineteen-year-old picture bride in 1915 and immediately faced disappointing living conditions in a tiny, barren hut and ten-hour workdays hoeing strawberries. After her husband, president of the local Japanese American Relations/Cultural League, was taken by the FBI during World War II, Mrs. Akiyama ran the family's thirty-five acre orchard and became head of the family for thirteen months. When the Akiyamas returned to the valley from the wartime concentration camps, they found about five acres of weeds one and a half feet tall, requiring the entire family to work long hours to restore their farm. A deeply religious woman, Mrs. Akiyama is a member of the Japanese Methodist church and now lives in a Hood River retirement center.

Despite initial misgivings about having her words recorded on tape, Mrs. Akiyama, for the sake of her grandchildren, was very motivated to talk about her life. Petite with close-cropped, silvering, curly hair, she sat compliantly on her living room sofa during all of our interviews. While answering questions, she typically folded her hands in her lap, often drawing them out gracefully for emphasis. Her face, very expressive, emoted joy and laughter as well as suffering, all of which she willingly shared. When discussing particularly painful subjects, however, her face often appeared drawn and her eyes reddened, evidencing a far-away look as she seemed transplanted into times past. Then she quickly attended to the question at hand. So obliging, she whisked out of the room twice during one interview, quickly returning with photos or craftwork to explain her comments more clearly. On one occasion, after she had been ill, I asked her if she was tired. "No," she said, "it is relaxing to talk." Clearly, this sensitive and honest woman reveled in telling of her past, while displaying an ability to re-create scenes and emotions vividly. At the end of the interviews, she commented, "It pleased me so much to recall these past events that I am now writing to my sister in Japan. I intend to share some of my history with her."

Mrs. Tei Endow, Odell

Eighty-five years old

Born August 22, 1900, in Tokyo, Japan

Mrs. Tei Endow, the daughter of grocery store owners in Shimizu, saw marriage as an opportunity to live in the United States without the burden of overbearing in-laws. Envisioning a glamorous life in America, where even the flies would be different, she wore fashionable, custom-made suits on the ship when she left Japan in 1918. When she arrived, she was aghast at the difficult and lonely life she faced farming on twenty acres of hilly terrain. During the war, the Endows left the concentration camp in September 1943 to work in the Montana sugar beet fields before returning to Hood River. The education of her children was one of her foremost goals.

Smiling and laughing constantly, Mrs. Endow was exuberant as she relived her past. Often she became so involved in her stories that we gently reminded her, "Chotto matte kudasai" (Please wait), in order to translate her answers. Mrs. Endow was familiar enough with English that she often combined English with Japanese. Eager to cooperate, she often prompted the language translator as he interpreted, ensuring that each segment of her answer was included. Most of all, she delighted in talking about her children, for she was obviously very proud of them. In her spirited responses throughout the interviews, she generally gave impressions and details that were fresh and uninhibited. Extremely generous, when she learned we could not stay for tea after our first visit, she immediately emptied the candy dish of its miniature chocolate bars and gave them to us.

Mrs. Endow died on April 21, 1992.

Mrs. Shigeko Fukui, Dee

Eighty-five years old
Born March 27, 1901, in Okayama, Japan

Mrs. Shigeko Fukui's family in Okayama harvested and weaved straw for tatami (floor mats). In 1919 she married and came to the United States. She assisted on the family farm, clearing land, sorting fruit, and harvesting strawberries. During the war, the Fukuis were interned at camps in Pinedale, Tule Lake, and Heart Mountain. Mrs. Fukui lives in Dee with a son and a daughter-in-law and enjoys handcrafts, including embroidering and knitting.

An April snow had fallen early the morning of our first interview with Mrs. Fukui, bringing concerns for blossoming fruit trees. Yet inside the Fukui home, the black wrought-iron stove radiated warmth in the small living room. Photos of great-grandchildren were displayed on the television set, and brightly colored afghans and pillows (knitted by Mrs. Fukui) decorated the two living room sofas. Since she was reluctant to be recorded on tape, her answers to questions were written by hand. Quite often during the interview, she smiled and giggled, clasping her hands together between her knees and periodically leaning forward. Mrs. Fukui also obliged us by retrieving her two latest articles of handwork, an embroidered wild duck and a colorful, latch-hooked barnyard scene.

Mrs. Maki Hamada, Milwaukie

Eighty-nine years old
Born October 3, 1896, in Bingo (outside Hiroshima), Japan

Mrs. Maki Hamada, raised on a rice and wheat farm outside Hiroshima, enjoyed farming because it meant she did not have to attend school. Her husband, the younger brother of Mrs. Asayo Noji's husband, returned to Japan in 1914 to marry her. In Hood River, the Hamadas and Nojis shared a home for several years with another family and property co-owner.

A woman with a very happy disposition, Mrs. Hamada resided in Milwaukie with a daughter and her family at the time she was interviewed. Thin and frail, she spent her days seated in a living room recliner, watching television, napping, and taking pleasure in rereading letters from her sister-in-law in Japan. Incapacitated by cerebellum ataxia (a gradual deterioration of the cerebellum) and several small strokes, she had difficulty with coordination and forming words. Yet, when she understood questions and was able to respond, she immediately broke into wide, satisfied grins.

Mrs. Hamada died on August 18, 1987, at the age of ninety-one.

Mr. Masaji Kusachi, Dee
Eighty-two years old
Born March 1, 1903, in Okayama, Japan

Mr. Masaji Kusachi joined his father in the United States in 1919 and, ten years later, became a yoshi (a young man who becomes an adopted son after marrying the daughter in an heirless family), marrying into the family of a young widow in Dee. During his early years in America, he worked at various jobs, including a railroad gang, sawmill labor, and strawberry cultivation. After Pearl Harbor was bombed, his family first lived in the Portland Assembly Center, an odious, former livestock yard. When his wife died of cancer at the Minidoka camp, he became a single father of seven young children. After the war, the Kusachi family returned to a ransacked home, an orchard that had received inadequate care, and a caretaker's bill for $1,700. In 1985, Mr. Kusachi married a woman from Okayama, his birthplace. He served as president of the Japanese Society in Hood River for almost twenty years and received the Sixth Class Order of the Sacred Treasure of the Emperor of Japan in 1981.

Despite the beginning of snow flurries when we arrived in March for our first interview, Mr. Kusachi, still wearing his insulated boots and work clothes, confessed he had just returned from pruning trees and spent some time warming himself by the stove. Folding his hands against his plaid, flannel shirt and striped suspenders, Mr. Kusachi kept our conversation at a leisurely pace. While pondering a question, he was likely to lean his head against the back of the sofa, cross his hands behind his head, and utter under his breath, "So-na," the Japanese equivalent of "I wonder." In each case, he demonstrated the capacity to illustrate his answers with thoughtful examples. While he was caring for his seven children alone for twenty years, he developed a reputation as a fine cook and baked three-layer birthday cakes for them to take to school. Although he admitted to having lost interest in cooking, we reminded Mr. Kusachi of a particularly tasty apple pie we had sampled after an earlier visit. "Oh," he murmured with an amused look, "I accidentally made the pie taste good."

Mr. Kusachi died in September 1986, shortly after returning from a weekend of fishing, one of his favorite pastimes.

Mrs. Misuyo Nakamura, Odell
Eighty-two years old
Born June 5, 1903, in Hiroshima, Japan

Mrs. Misuyo Nakamura ran away from her brother's home in Japan at the age of eight rather than face the prospect of life as a geisha. After family members requested that she marry, she complied and came to the United States with her new husband in 1921. Her new life on a strawberry farm was particularly difficult, for she worked ten-hour days even while suffering morning sickness and later consented to sole responsibility for five acres of strawberries. Mrs. Nakamura attributed the death of one of her children to her preoccupation with work and finances. During the war, the Nakamuras left a concentration camp to work on farms in Idaho. Mrs. Nakamura continues to reside in the valley next door to a son and daughter-in-law.

Mrs. Nakamura and Andy, a tiny, gray poodle who was her constant companion during the interviews, lived in an immaculate, tastefully decorated home. The three velveteen living room sofas displayed crocheted backings and cross-stitched floral pillows made with Mrs. Nakamura's loving touch. In multiethnic tradition, a wood-carved Buddha stood next to a bronze bust of John Kennedy and a spread-winged eagle on the mantel. At the beginning of the interviews, Mrs. Nakamura made it clear she would not divulge information injurious to others, although she proceeded to talk openly about her own life. Having faithfully kept a diary, she was able to relate exact dates and numerical figures. Despite this, she chided herself for not remembering more and for being unable to speak English. Extremely conscientious, she once requested time to check the accuracy of a Buddhist fable with her minister. On another occasion, she told of rising in the middle of the night when she realized that Emmett, instead of Payette, had been her home in Idaho. Nuzzling Andy's curly coat of gray hair while she spoke, Mrs. Nakamura spoke so vibrantly that one listening might have guessed her voice belonged to a young girl, not an eighty-two-year-old woman.

Mrs. Hatsumi Nishimoto, Pine Grove
Eighty-five years old
Born September 3, 1900, in Hiroshima, Japan

Mrs. Hatsumi Nishimoto imagined that by marrying and coming to America she could avoid farmwork. In 1918 she worked as a cook for fifteen Japanese men at a railroad repair station in eastern Oregon. Afterward, she and her husband labored on five different farms for seven years and then leased one hundred acres for another five years before purchasing their own twenty acres in 1930. When her husband was taken by the FBI during World War II after they found a small bullet in the woodshed, Mrs. Nishimoto became head of the family for five months. Upon the family's return to Hood River after the war, she lost six pounds in one week working to restore the family's neglected orchard and home. Mrs. Nishimoto still lives on the family farm with her daughter-in-law.

Listening thoughtfully, Mrs. Nishimoto eyed me carefully as I fashioned my questions in English. Then she typically turned to face the translator as he spoke in Japanese. After pondering the topic with furrowed brows, she gazed intently into my eyes as she responded, seemingly very concerned that I understood the exact nature of her experiences. Her answers were concise, and she waited patiently while they were translated. During some of her more sentimental recollections, her eyes watered and she dabbed at tears. But, at the conclusion of the first interview, she explained that, since difficult experiences remained with her forever, she did not mind sharing them. Several weeks before our interview, she had reminded me eagerly that she had reviewed my outline of topics and was ready to begin. Because of her preparation and careful consideration of the questions, we covered a number of topics quickly. Although she took the interview process seriously, she also laughed often as we traversed her memories. Sometimes her laughter followed questions requesting more details, almost as if she were wondering, "You really want to know more?" Her good-natured laughter became so spirited and infectious that it was easy to become involved in her stories.

Mrs. Asayo Noji, Parkdale

Eighty-nine years old
Born February 20, 1897, in Hiroshima, Japan

Mrs. Asayo Noji, my maternal grandmother, came to the United States in 1916 as a picture bride. Initially finding nothing that she liked about America, she learned to cook and sew from her enterprising husband. She worked as a domestic for a neighboring Caucasian family and later helped with the family's strawberry fields. For several years the Nojis, Hamadas, and another family co-owned property and lived together in one house. Mrs. Noji's husband served as president of the local Hiroshima prefectural association, a mutual aid society and social organization. During the internment years she learned to create ikebana (Japanese flower arrangements) and shell jewelry. The Nojis were the first family to return to the Hood River valley after the war and became a test case for determining attitudes of the American Legion toward parents of Nisei serving in the armed forces. She continues to live in Hood River with her eldest son, Mamoru.

When I had first sought to write my grandmother's life story five years before, she had been adamant that her life would remain private. Humbled by the belief that only celebrity grandmothers, such as Rose Kennedy, should be memorialized, she had stated emphatically that she was "just a poor old woman." Finally, after other family members interceded, she had consented. After months of "FBI questioning"—as she called it—her biography was written for family access only. For the present set of interviews, I asked my grandmother about only selected topics—stories unique among the Issei whom I had already interviewed. Despite her initial hesitancy about being recorded on tape and feeling that she had already divulged sufficient information, she was very cooperative, seemingly earnest in her desire to cooperate in her granddaughter's project. In fact, as soon as the first question was asked, she launched into detailed explanations. Very animated in her storytelling, she spoke quickly, expressive in her tone of voice, facial expressions, and hand and body movements. Immediately upon request, she also sang a rice planting song from her early years in Japan. Other answers seemed obvious to her. When asked for descriptions, several times she offhandedly remarked in Japanese, "Oh, you know—you've seen it" or "Just like the photo you have."

Mrs. Miyoshi Noyori, Dee, Oregon and Sacramento, California
Eighty-five years old
Born February 15, 1901, in Okayama, Japan

Mrs. Miyoshi Noyori, an ambitious young woman, viewed travel to America as a learning experience and a chance to gain financial success. When she arrived in 1919, however, she was gravely disappointed to find an isolated hovel infested with rats and living conditions worse than she could possibly have imagined. Mrs. Noyori assisted in hoeing strawberries even while pregnant and deformed her hand while manipulating the heavy stump puller used for clearing land. The dilemma of raising children and constantly working almost brought the tragic loss of her son. During her internment she learned to cut hair, though admittedly haphazardly at first. Now she divides her time living with family members in Hood River and Sacramento.

Very petite and outgoing, Mrs. Noyori seemed exceedingly spry for her eighty-five years. A very gracious hostess, she welcomed us into her living room and quickly motioned us to be seated. Concerned about my comfort as the interview progressed, she set a cushion on the stool where I was seated and later brought me a padded dining room chair. Midway through the interview, as her words were being translated, she hurried into the kitchen, where the popping and fizzing of a soda pop bottle could be heard. When urged not to worry about refreshments, she called out "Just water!" and quickly returned with a tray of snacks. Very alert, she responded to questions clearly and immediately, often without needing translation. At one point, she delightedly paused to reflect in Japanese, "Isn't it fun to delve into history?" At the end of another interview, she enthusiastically remarked, "Today I talked a lot, so weren't you pleased with the stories?" She added that she had many stories to relate, since at one time she had had an ambition to write her autobiography. On another occasion, after expressing some deep thoughts, she admitted, "I feel good about explaining my own feelings." When we had concluded our interviews, she related that some might say "Too much talk!" But, she added, "I enjoyed this, and I do not believe I have said anything bad about anyone."

Mr. Chiho Tomita, Odell

Ninety-five years old
Born March 20, 1890, in Fukushima, Japan

Mr. Chiho Tomita completed eleven years of school in Japan and came to the United States in 1907 to earn money for his family. After working as a mission boy for the prominent Frank family in Portland, he became a fruit laborer in the valley, where his five years of English classes proved invaluable. He married his wife, selected from picture-bride photos, in 1918, and they eventually purchased a twelve-acre farm. Although Mr. Tomita intended to return to Japan with his family, his American-born children convinced him to stay. For four years after the war, Mr. Tomita was head of the local Japanese Society, and in 1974 he received an imperial award from the emperor for promoting relations between the United States and Japan.

When he was interviewed, Mr. Tomita resided on his Willow Flat farm with his eldest son, Taylor, in a home highlighted with Japanese decorations: a fan-shaped clock on the shelf, a Japanese male doll on the television, scrolls and Oriental scenes on the wall, and Japanese vases and candy dishes set on the tables. During the interviews, Mr. Tomita wore a *yukata* (cotton robe) and sat upright on his recliner, using a heating pad to comfort his ailing foot. He had made notes on the outline of topics mailed to him and often referred to them. Knowing Mr. Tomita was more fluent in English, I attempted to conduct the first interview by myself but found need for a translator for the rest of the interviews. Actually, Mr. Tomita chose to give most of his answers in broken English, relying on translation only when necessary. He gave some answers emphatically, while at other times he admitted "pretty hard to tell" and apologized for being unable to remember. After the second interview, while we were talking informally, Mr. Tomita asked me a personal question, which brought an immediate reprimand from his daughter. I assured her that, since her father had answered my many questions, I would answer his too. Then, before I left on a trip to Japan, he bid me good-bye and added a protective warning, "Don't drink the water."

On April 2, 1988, two weeks after his ninety-eighth birthday, Mr. Tomita died at the Hood River Care Center.

Mrs. Hisa Wakamatsu, Oak Grove
Ninety-two years old
Born July 1, 1893, in Nagahama, Japan

Mrs. Hisa Wakamatsu assisted her father in his business of repairing night-soil buckets in Japan and eventually dropped out of school, which she has since regretted. When she arrived in the United States as a picture bride in 1915, she was surprised to meet people of different skin and hair color and disappointed to be unable to converse with them. At various times she and her husband raised dairy cattle and hops and found, as did most Issei, that finances were a constant concern. She was also compelled by her family to make sake, a favored Japanese drink.

Leaning forward in her cane-backed rocker, Mrs. Wakamatsu frequently broke into fits of halting laughter as she retold incidents from her past. Once, too, she seemed temporarily overcome with grief as she wiped away tears that welled in her eyes. On each of our visits, Mrs. Wakamatsu's curly, white hair was always coiffed in a becoming, bouffant style. She smiled frequently, taking comfort in her pet dachshund, a gift from daughter Hana, who lived next door. Extremely free in sharing details of her life, Mrs. Wakamatsu often talked without pause but also expressed *kinodoku* (regret) that she was unable to give more information. Several times she repeated the story of how her youngest son found "stones from the sky" (meteorite fragments) at Tule Lake and attributed her long life to the luck of the stones. So very kind, she gave each of us one of the dense, rounded basaltlike stones, reminding us repeatedly to take good care of them.

Mrs. Wakamatsu died on February 8, 1989.

Mrs. Hama Yamaki, Pine Grove

Ninety-four years old

Born October 10, 1891, in Fukushima, Japan

Mrs. Hama Yamaki's family raised silkworms in Fukushima. After completing sewing school, she received two marriage proposals but envisioned a life in America that would be much easier. She married in 1913, and she and her husband lived in Portland for five years before moving to Hood River and purchasing a farm. During the war, the Yamakis left the concentration camp to lease an eleven-acre truck farm in Idaho for three years and returned to their Hood River farm in 1946. A devout Methodist, she lived with the family of her son Shig.

Mrs. Yamaki had carefully prepared for our meeting, having written lengthy notes, and dutifully asked when she should begin talking into the tape recorder. As she explained events in her life, she frequently paused to smile warmly at me, then continued the conversation at a lively pace. During the interview, her son and daughter-in-law were most cooperative, even whispering a "Shh" warning to the cat when it meowed. Later they mentioned that these sessions were good mental stimulation for Mrs. Yamaki and that she was enjoying them. Extremely talented at knitting, Mrs. Yamaki seemed to complete an afghan or pillow every two or three days. She admitted to having knitted several hundred creations, many in patterns she designed from simple observation. A gifted writer of haiku, Mrs. Yamaki also willingly shared several of her poems. At the end of each interview, it was always heartwarming to see Mrs. Yamaki, despite the winter elements, smiling and waving from her screen door as we drove away.

Mrs. Yamaki died on August 2, 1988, at the age of ninety-six.

Mrs. Masayo Yumibe, Dee, Oregon, and Sacramento, California
Eighty-two years old
Born February 21, 1904, in Fukuoka, Japan

Mrs. Masayo Yumibe lived with relatives on a rice farm in Fukuoka until her parents called her to the United States when she was eighteen. She worked as a domestic for an affluent family in Dee and was in awe of their extravagant life-style. In 1913 she and her husband married in a simple ceremony. Both returned immediately to their jobs and, for five months, to separate homes. Mrs. Yumibe took pride in early financial sacrifices that enabled her eldest son to achieve his goal of becoming a physician. She now resides in Sacramento.

Mrs. Yumibe's curly black hair evidenced only traces of gray, despite her eighty-two years. During the interview, she responded eagerly to questions, clasping her hands and rubbing her fingers back and forth. Although she had had cataract surgery less than a month before, she managed to maintain good eye contact. Often she turned to her husband for assistance in answering a question, just as he sought her help during his own interviews. During the final two interviews, covering the period of life after their marriage, Mr. and Mrs. Yumibe were interviewed together.

Mr. Miyozo Yumibe, Dee, Oregon, and Sacramento, California
Eighty-four years old
Born July 1, 1901, in Fukuoka, Japan

Mr. Miyozo Yumibe was raised on a rice farm in Fukuoka. In 1917 he immigrated as a *yoshi*, an adopted son who eventually married into the Yumibe family in Hood River. As a seventeen-year-old, he began chain work at the Dee Sawmill and continued employment at the sawmill for forty-one years, until he retired in 1959. During the family's internment, Mr. Yumibe worked as a camp janitor. Upon his return to the valley, he became one of the organizers of the Buddhist church group.

Mr. Yumibe and his wife shared the distinction of being the only living Issei couple in Hood River. That was to change, however, for they had decided to sell their two acres and move to Sacramento, California, to be near their children. Very pleasant and mild-mannered, Mr. Yumibe's characteristic greeting was a broad smile that flashed across his ruddy cheeks. Seemingly very happy-go-lucky, he appeared to take in stride those setbacks that might have been considered more traumatic by others. His reaction to most incidents was simply "pretty good." During our interviews, because of his hearing difficulties, his wife intervened quite often to interpret or add information. Of particular pride to Mr. Yumibe was his driving record. Despite his age, he received rebates from his insurance company for remaining accident-free.

Mr. Yumibe died in October 1990.

Chronology of Important Events

1638   Tokugawa shogunate forbids Japanese from traveling abroad.

1853   July 8—Commodore Perry anchors at Edo (Tokyo) Bay.

1854   March 31—U.S.-Japan treaty opens selected Japanese ports to U.S. ships.

1866   Japanese nationals are permitted to travel abroad for schooling.

1868   Tokugawa shogunate is overthrown; Meiji era shifts from an agricultural to industrial economy.

1872   Japanese Education Code devises plan for universal education.

1884   Emigration of working classes from Japan is permitted.

1890   Twenty-five Japanese reside in Oregon.

1891   One thousand Japanese reside in Oregon.

       Japanese bachelors are employed as railroad section hands in Oregon.

1893   Japanese Methodist Mission (currently the Epworth United Methodist Church) is opened in Portland.

1900   2,501 Japanese reside in Oregon.

1902   First Japanese in Hood River are employed in Mt. Hood Railroad labor gangs.

1905   Six hundred Japanese in Hood River are employed clearing land.

       Niguma Variety Store opens on First and Oak Street in Hood River.

1906   Oregon Lumber Company in Dee hires Japanese mill workers.

1907–8   U.S.-Japan Gentlemen's Agreement limits U.S. immigration to nonlaborers, those already settled in the United States, and their families.

1908   Japan increases mandatory education from sixteen months to six years.

Yasui Brothers' Store opens after Yasuis purchase Niguma Variety Store in Hood River.

August 3—First recorded property deed to a Hood River Japanese is issued to Hiyakuichi Watanuki.

1910   Hood River County's Japanese population of 468 is the largest in Oregon outside Multnomah County.

Issei operate seven farms in Hood River.

1913   Apple Growers' Association is established in Hood River.

1914   Japanese Farmers' Association of Hood River is organized.

1915   Japanese men in the United States with savings of eight hundred dollars are eligible to summon wives from Japan.

1917   First Oregon bill to prohibit alien ownership of land is introduced by George Wilbur, state senator from Hood River.

1919   Anti-Alien Association is organized in Hood River.

1920   Frank Davies's report to the governor states that the "Japanese question" is most acute in Hood River.

1921   February 25—Japanese government voluntarily stops issuing passports to picture brides.

1923   Anti-Alien Land Law of Oregon prohibits persons not eligible for citizenship from owning or leasing land.

1924   U.S. Immigration Act prohibits immigration to those ineligible for citizenship.

December 1—Japanese law prevents automatic dual U.S.-Japanese citizenship of Nisei, second-generation Japanese.

1925   Japanese Community Hall in Hood River is erected.

1926   Japanese Methodist church is organized with five members in Odell, Oregon.

1941   March 19—Bill Yamaki becomes first Hood River Nisei to enter armed services.

Spring—U.S. Army begins training Japanese language translators.

December 7—Japanese bombers attack Pearl Harbor, Hawaii; the United States enters World War II.

December 12—Mid-Columbia Japanese American Citizens' League (JACL) announces pledge of loyalty to the United States.

1942 January 8—Hood River Issei send Oregon's Governor Charles Sprague a pledge to support the United States.

February 5–6—FBI conducts two-day contraband search of 151 Hood River Japanese homes.

February 7—All Issei are required to carry identification certificates.

February 19—Executive Order 9066 is signed by President Franklin Roosevelt, giving the War Department authority to remove "any and all persons" from designated military areas.

February 26—Hood River delegation testifies before the Tolan Committee (a congressional committee to investigate defense migration), urging evacuation of Japanese.

March 2—Lt. Gen. John DeWitt, commander general of the Western Defense Command, establishes military areas on the West Coast.

March 7—All local Japanese are required to be in their homes between 8:00 P.M. and 6:00 A.M.

March 27—Voluntary evacuation ends, and Japanese are barred from moving out of Military Area No. 1.

March 28—Minoru Yasui intentionally violates 8:00 P.M. to 6:00 A.M. curfew in Portland and is jailed.

May 13—Hood River Japanese depart by train to Pinedale Assembly Center in central California.

July–August—Hood River Japanese are transferred to Tule Lake Relocation Center in northern California.

October—Ten thousand Japanese participate in the government's agricultural leave program.

November 16—Minoru Yasui is convicted in district court for curfew violation based on his status as an "enemy alien."

1943 February—Government administers loyalty questionnaires to all internees seventeen years and older.

April 2—Poll conducted by the *Hood River Sun* indicates 84 percent of Hood River residents do not wish Japanese to return.

June 21—U.S. Supreme Court upholds Minoru Yasui's conviction for curfew violations.

September–October—Tule Lake is designated as a segregation camp for "disloyals"; other Japanese are transferred to other relocation centers.

October—Hood River American Legion unveils war memorial on county courthouse displaying names of county residents serving in the armed forces. 442nd Regimental Combat Team is formed from Japanese volunteers.

1944 November 29—Names of sixteen Nisei servicemen are removed from memorial plaque on Hood River Courthouse.

December 17—Public Proclamation Number 21 ends mass exclusion order of Japanese.

1945 January—Three Nisei men are the first Japanese to return to Hood River.

January 3—Sgt. Frank Hachiya of Hood River is killed in the Philippines.

January 26—First of a series of ads is printed in local newspaper urging Japanese not to return to valley.

April—Hood River American Legion Post votes to restore names of Nisei to county memorial plaque.

May—Hood River League for Liberty and Justice organizes to support Japanese.

August 15—Japanese government surrenders; World War II ends.

1947 February—Rev. Sherman Burgoyne receives Thomas Jefferson Award in New York from the Council Against Intolerance in America.

Alien Land Law of Oregon is declared invalid by the Oregon Supreme Court.

1948 July 2—Japanese-American Evacuation Claims Act offers evacuees limited compensation for material losses.

1952 McCarran-Walter Act abolishes racial qualifications for citizenship; Issei become eligible for American citizenship.

1974 Mrs. Shizue Iwatsuki is named Hood River's Woman of the Year.

1983 June—Commission on Wartime Relocation and Internment of Civilians recommends that the U.S. government apologize

for World War II detention of Japanese and pay appropriate redress money.

1987 October 5—U.S. Supreme Court denies the petition of Minoru
Yasui's widow to continue his *coram nobis* case.

1988 August 10—Civil Liberties Act of 1988 extends a government
apology to Japanese for World War II internment and autho-
rizes $20,000 payments for each eligible person.

1992 September 27—Civil Liberties Act amendments authorize $400
million to complete redress payments and to fund historical research and education programs.

THE
HOOD RIVER
ISSEI

Prologue

FOR OVER TWO HUNDRED YEARS, beginning in the seventeenth century, Japan virtually closed its doors to the rest of the world. This self-imposed isolation, from 1638 to 1854, was an effort to maintain peace while protecting its feudal institutions and value systems from the influence of foreigners.[1] During this era, descendants of the Tokugawa family ruled as shogun over a centralized feudal system. In essence, daimyo (feudal lords) were overseers of samurai (the military class), which in turn ruled over vassal peasants, who were somewhat respected then as a productive agricultural class.[2] Within their rigid class system, the Japanese thus developed a respect for military leadership based on the ethics of the samurai class, a sense of unquestioning loyalty, a strong feeling of group identity, and a willingness to follow prescribed behavioral rules.[3]

Japan's policy of exclusion was dramatically challenged when U.S. Commodore Matthew Perry and his formidable fleet of four warships arrived in 1853. After anchoring at the mouth of Edo (Tokyo) Bay, Perry requested a formal reply to a letter he delivered from President Millard Fillmore, which proposed friendship and commerce between the two countries. When he returned early in the following year with an imposing squadron of eight ships, the overpowered Japanese agreed to enter into the Treaty of Kanagawa. The 1854 treaty opened the harbors of Hakodate and Shimoda to American ships, and later negotiations by newly appointed Consul Townsend Harris allowed Americans to reside in Japan.[4] By 1866 certain Japanese nationals were permitted to travel abroad for schooling, because the government had begun to appreciate the value of Western technology.[5]

Sentiment opposing this new open policy, however, compounded growing dissension from samurai, fears of impinging foreign powers, and an increasing belief in the need for unity under centralized leadership. Thus, after more than two and a half centuries of rule, the Tokugawa shogunate was overthrown. In 1868, with imperial power restored through the teenage emperor Meiji, the country abolished feudal domains.

Japan quickly took initiatives to modernize its government and economy. Following selected models of Western countries, it introduced broad changes: a modern court and legal system, a banking and monetary system, a telegraph network, railroads, port facilities, a military system, a modern factory system, and universal education. The developing country also created the first Japanese constitution, dual assemblies, a civil service, and limited male suffrage. Through improved technology, it also increased silk production and produced weapons and ammunition.

With its newfound economic and military strength, Japan demonstrated its prowess in two successive wars. In the Sino-Japanese War of 1894–95, the developing military power soundly defeated China and gained control of Taiwan. Following the Russo-Japanese War of 1904–5, Japan annexed Korea and asserted its authority over the southern parts of Manchuria. With its victory over Russia, Japan emerged as not only the foremost Eastern power but also a prestigious colonial power recognized among Western nations.

Concurrent with its increasing military prowess, Japan also continued rapid industrialization, although improvements were unevenly distributed through its population. While new, urban industries benefited from modern technology, the agricultural sector continued to depend on manual labor. Although farmers, the former peasant tenants of the feudal domains, had become owners of their farmland during the Meiji era, they were heavily taxed to ensure continuous revenue for the increasing modernization of the Japanese state. This, coupled with years of unpredictably poor harvests and low prices for their products, increased the plight of the Japanese farmers.[6] It was on this land and under these harsh, rural conditions that the early chapters on the Hood River Issei begin.

PART ONE

Living in Japan

Natsukumo ya
Kage Otoshiiku
Mugibatake

Summer clouds
Shadows on the field
On the wheat farm.

Haiku written by Mrs. Hama Yamaki and
translated by Mr. Ben Kino

1

Early Life

MOST ISSEI SPENT their early years in rural Japan. Barely 15 percent of Japan's land was arable, however, and that small portion was not especially fertile. Japanese farmers thus depended on long growing seasons, plentiful rainfall, dutiful and hard-working family members, and intensive irrigation and cultivation methods to produce maximum yields per acre. Barley, wheat, millet, beans, and sweet potatoes were staples, but rice production, equal to their total output, outranked them. Along parts of the west coast, warmer climates permitted double cropping, where summer rice and winter grains or vegetables alternately grew on the same soil.[1]

Gohan, or steamed rice, was such a staple of the Japanese diet that it was also the term for *meal.* Yet all except the very wealthy considered plain rice a delicacy. Mr. Miyozo Yumibe described life on the farm in Fukuoka in southwestern Japan, where he lived for sixteen years:

> Rice was planted in June to be harvested in October, and wheat was planted on the same plot of land and harvested from April to May. Our rice grew in terraced rice paddies.[2] We owned two to two and a half acres altogether, and our farm was probably small to medium-sized. We also raised sweet potatoes on the side for the family to eat. In those days, it was common for farmers to mix a little bit of ground wheat with rice, so we would have more to eat. With seven kids, father, mother—we needed lots of food! We exchanged any surplus food for other foodstuffs. Brokers from the store came to our farm to buy our rice. We stored it inside the house in sacks made from rice straw. Each sack weighed maybe 130 pounds,

so loading was heavy work. But I just threw the sack on my back and carried it to the wagon (drawn by a horse) of the rice broker. At that time I think one acre of land produced about twenty sacks of rice.

In the beginning stages, the carefully cultivated rice plants grew in nursery beds. During May, rice seeds were planted in blocks of soil, where they were more easily supervised while winter crops matured in the fields. After approximately forty days, when the shoots stood about twelve inches tall, they were transplanted to flooded fields, assuring more uniform growth.[3] Generally, the entire family was involved in this tedious work. Mrs. Masayo Yumibe, whose parents had left for the United States when she was seven years old, lived with her grandparents, aunt, and uncle, and she recalled with distaste her arduous duties on the family farm in Fukuoka:

Growing up on a rice farm was a hard life! The whole family worked in the rice paddy. We had to bend over barefoot in the mud to transplant four or five plants together. These were placed every six inches along rows lined with string. Hard work! I carried the rice shoots in baskets hanging from both ends of a pole I balanced on my shoulders. Then I scattered the plants along the rows. After I had transplanted all of them, I again had to balance the pole to bring back more plants. I had never performed such difficult and heavy work! I could not say no, because I was taking orders from my aunt. I felt it was my obligation to help. Although my father had sent a hundred dollars from America for my upkeep, my relatives were giving me food and living quarters, so I did whatever they asked. I felt *enryo* [self-imposed restraint], which means you do what you are asked. I do not remember how long I worked each day. Everyone started at the same time—and when they quit, I quit, too.

The annual transplanting often became a communal operation and was viewed as a festive occasion by some. Mrs. Asayo Noji from Hiroshima admittedly spent little time working on the farm but fondly remembered the frivolity, good humor, rhythmic singing, and tasty refreshments:

Omoshirokata! [That was a lot of fun!] We hired a crew of about ten men and twenty women—enough to finish in one day. Women came before dawn to bundle rice plants with *wara* [rice stalks]. At about ten o'clock the men arrived to level the ground. They led oxen—perhaps six or eight—which pulled pronged implements around and around the swampy field. Later the men marked the planting rows with rope. Then they placed the rice bundles in baskets which dangled front and back from long poles on their shoulders. "*Pan-pan-pan-pan,*" they threw the bundles at intervals around the field for transplanting. After we women transplanted one row together, we all stepped backward at the same time and planted the next row. The mud sank above our ankles, so we secured our kimono [Japanese dresses] or *yukata* [cotton robes] above our knees with *koshiobi* [girdles]. Young girls wore reds and pinks with *tasuki* [cords used to gird the sleeves of kimonos, allowing free movement of arms]. Middle-aged women wore bluish or greenish colors. (As we grew older, we wore more subdued colors.)[4] And we all wore broad-brimmed straw hats. Some new brides wore clean, fresh clothes, so everyone tried to flick mud on them. We had so much fun!

Since our crew was large, we hired singers. The leader beat a drum, and another man kept time with a big circular gong. We all sang together and had a great time transplanting in rhythm with the music. Young children worked between the adults—that way we could learn the songs. There were many rice planting songs! In the morning we sang morning songs; in the afternoon, afternoon songs; in the evening, evening songs. There was even a song to sing when we planted by the side of the road. First the drum leader sang:

"This is by the side of the road.

Let the plantings be picture perfect."

Then everyone answered, singing, "Lovely as a picture!" When the drummer pounded "*ten-ten-ten-ten,*" we knew it was time to straighten up and rest. Then when he sang again, it was time to get back to work. Toward the end of the day, the men mingled with the women. They joined the singing and transplanting. And they playfully bumped the women so that when they fell, they knocked others over, too. Everyone got dirty that way, for we all tried to soil each other's clean clothes! That was just so much fun! I cannot forget it.

We ate a lot of good food, too: *yotsu-ja* [morning snacks] at nine o'clock, then lunch, and another snack around 2:30. At those times workers ate in the veranda and entryway of our house. Later in the day, men carried huge trays out to the fields and served vinegared cucumber and seaweed topped with slices of *tako* [octopus]—all arranged on persimmon leaves. That was especially tasty outside! When work was finished, everyone went home to bathe and returned for *gochiso* [good food], including sashimi [sliced raw fish] and sake [rice wine].

To fertilize their newly planted rice shoots, farmers depended on human wastes, which were aged, diluted (often with bathwater to conserve
the precious water), and poured around the plants. The malodorous yet
beneficial night soil was collected in wooden buckets positioned directly
beneath the holes in bathroom floors. This was so valuable that it was
purchased from townspeople as well.[5] Mrs. Hisa Wakamatsu's father,
in addition to caring for his small rice farm, repaired these night-soil
buckets:

> My father's and brother's jobs were to repair night-soil *oke*
> [wooden buckets] and *geta* [wooden clogs]. My father would go up to
> the hills to get a soil mixture (much like cement) to plug the leaks
> in the *oke*. During good weather, he repaired night-soil containers
> at people's homes. When the day was rainy, he repaired *geta* at
> home. My brother and I helped my father by collecting the *oke* and
> *geta*. My brother carried them in baskets dangling from a straw pole
> slung across his shoulders, and I carried them by hand. We walked
> to eight different villages. I felt I was pleasing my father by helping
> him.

In their efforts to remain self-sufficient, small farming families, in addition to raising rice, provided as many of their own necessities as possible
and often gained extra income from outside sales. Mrs. Shigeko Fukui's
parents in Okayama also wove tatami, thick straw mats that covered the
floors of every Japanese home:

> *Yu*, the straw plant used to make tatami, was planted once a year,
> when it was cold outside.[6] Late in the summer they were harvested,
> and the green stalks were dipped in a two-and-a-half-foot mud
> puddle[7] and then spread out to dry. Every day for about a week, we
> turned the straw twice on each side. (I do not know whether dip-
> ping strengthened the straw, but they seemed to last a long time.)
> We sorted the straw into three different sizes—most were taller than
> me, and I am almost five feet tall! To string the straw together, we
> spun threads from *kawa* [bamboo husks] on a wheel manipulated by
> foot. I helped to weave the straw and threads on our looms. Tatami
> may have lasted as long as two years, although wealthy people
> changed their tatami every year. In Japan they were a standard size
> [six feet by three feet]. Rooms were measured by how many tatami fit
> in the room, for example, a six-tatami room or an eight-tatami
> room.

Villagers in the central and northern provinces of Japan increasingly
shifted from subsistence farming to growing commercial cash crops,

among them the production of silk. In Fukushima, the Yamaki family engaged in silkworm breeding, which Mrs. Hama Yamaki described:

My family was one of the earliest to raise silkworms for seeds and used to gather them before the time of trains.[8] These *tane* [seeds, a term used for silkworm eggs] were sold all over Japan, but the Fukushima area had a particularly good quality of seeds. They were graded highly by inspectors.

Silkworms were bred by placing male and female moths for half a day on trays covered with an oily film to prevent them from flying. After they had mated, they produced their seeds and died. My grandpa and grandma gathered the *tane*. They separated them on a small white paper and threw away the imperfect ones. If there was an illness in the seeds, they all ruptured. But if they turned creamy white and moved *piku-piku-piku-piku* [wiggle, wiggle], that was the sign of a good seed. It took about one month to raise silkworms. In the woods, we gathered clean *kuwa* [mulberry] leaves to feed them. That was a big job.

Our house was so large that we were able to raise silkworms in one section of the house and live in the other side. Every available space, even the *engawa* [narrow veranda between the rooms and outer wall of the house] was used for incubating the eggs. We needed so much help during the ten days of silkworm breeding that we ate a one-hundred pound sack of rice every two days!

For one Issei destined for a comfortable childhood on a large rice and wheat farm, life would dramatically change. After the death of Mrs. Misuyo Nakamura's father when she was thirteen months old, she and her mother moved to a brother's home in Hiroshima. At the age of eight, repulsed by family intentions for her future, Mrs. Nakamura surprised even herself with her newfound courage:

I really hated living with *ani-san* [older brother].[9] His wife, a former geisha [female entertainer], tried to prepare me for that kind of life by teaching me arts such as *shamisen* [three-stringed guitar]. In my view, though, geisha were very lowly. You see, geisha entertained men and helped them to relax before going home. They danced, played *shamisen*, sang, and served sake. This actually meant catering to male pride, and I considered this neither a very clean nor righteous life. My brother's wife intended to instruct me in geisha ways and then to sell me to a man who would employ me in geisha service and keep my earnings. This is not something I wanted to do! Because I was still a young child in the first grade, I would have been sold as a *maiko* [dancing girl], in training to become a geisha. Geisha were hired by the hour, based on their appearance, so if you had a pretty face and stylish figure, you would probably be worth more money.

I still find it difficult to believe that, at the age of eight, I was so desperate I escaped from my brother's clutches! I ran away to my mother's home.[10] Both my brother and his wife came after me, but I was not there. I was playing *karuta*, a card game, at the home of my neighbor. At the front door, my brother's wife grabbed me and tried to force me to return. But, because I detested that sort of life, I refused. I am still amazed at the *dokyo* [courage] I had then! There was a scuffle with the lady of the house, who was successful in protecting me, but not without becoming somewhat injured in the chest. This is an embarrassing story to tell, but this did happen; and it was a traumatic time for me.

Stories the Hood River Issei tell about their early lives generally reflect their humble beginnings in rural Japan. They are representative of early Issei on the West Coast, three-fifths of whom came from agricultural settings.[11]

2

School

In a village there shall be no home without learning,
and in a house no individual without learning. . . .
—Education Code, Department of Education,
Japan, 1872

IN 1872 the Japanese Education Code, issued by the newly formed Department of Education, devised plans for universal education. Through
this policy, Japanese education progressed from a class-based system,
where 43 percent of the boys and 15 percent of the girls attended school,
to one where all children, regardless of class or gender, were expected to
become literate.[1] By 1900, 98 percent of children of primary school age
attended school.[2] Beginning in 1908, mandatory education in Japan
gradually increased from sixteen months to six years for all children between six and fourteen years of age, unless exempted by the mayor for
such reasons as physical or mental incapacity or extreme poverty.[3] Many
of the Hood River Issei were to achieve the equivalent of an eighth grade
education. Yet, as Mrs. Asayo Noji remembered, students in her first class
in primary school were various ages: "When I started school, only four of
us in a class of thirty-six were six years old[4]—the others were actually
seven, eight, and even nine years old. My mother had recorded all her
children's births at the *yakuba* [town office] within a week of our births,
but some did not remember to record their first births until they were
pregnant with their second child."

Despite being one of the youngest, Mrs. Noji (barely five feet tall today) stood as the third tallest girl in her class. She enjoyed her school
days, which began with opening ceremonies outside the school:

After the morning bell rang, we assembled outside in rows. To take attendance, we stood erect with our left hands on our waists and counted off "one," "two," "three"—. Then, in turn, we snapped our heads to the left. After the principal greeted us, we filed into our classrooms, where girls sat on one side and boys sat on the other. I guess my head did not like arithmetic, but I liked singing, history, and reading. My favorite drill came when someone read aloud and made a mistake. The rest of us jumped from our seats to correct that person! Whoever stood first got to read aloud next, and the teacher really praised that person, saying, "You did well!"

Beginning in 1890, the foundation for public schools was the Imperial Rescript of Education. Anchored in the Confucian teachings of the Tokugawa feudal period, the rescript promoted loyalty to the emperor, filial piety, fidelity, harmony, and self-dedication as principles of moral conduct. Japanese were admonished not only to be "good and faithful subjects but [to] render illustrious the best traditions of your forefathers."[5]

Shushin (moral training) became a vehicle for teaching moral conduct by using historical events and legends to instill reverence for the emperor, loyalty to superiors, and personal pride.[6] Classes emphasized nationalism, and hours were devoted to memorizing lists of emperors and famous battles, performing a variety of physical exercises in response to instructions, singing patriotic songs, and discussing the rescript. Mrs. Misuyo Nakamura, who had defied a family scheme to secure her future as a geisha, was treated much like a "teacher's pet" for her tendency to obey instructions and master lessons. She explained the influence of moral education: "*Shushin* instruction was devoted to developing moral character. We were taught: 'Your behavior toward others must never be harmful. Show respect to your elders and parents. Show gratitude for favors by saying thank you. Behave properly and never lie.' We learned that even though you might not do well in other subjects, it was most important to excel in *shushin* class to be considered successful."

After the mandatory first six years of school, scheduled Monday through Saturday each week, tuition was required from those who continued their schooling. For some, the financial burden on their families made further education difficult or altogether impossible, as Mrs. Misuyo Nakamura pointed out: "Families were rated 'first class,' 'second class,' 'third class,' or 'destitute.' In most cases, children from destitute families did not attend further. Families from other classes paid tuition based on their economic standings. In our own area, those at the top level paid thirty sen a month per child, the next level twenty sen. I used to take twenty sen. Very poor families would pay in the neighborhood of ten sen. (At that time, in comparison, one sen would buy a small *manju* [rice flour cake] or ten *ame* [rice jelly candies].)"

Another consideration was the entrance examination required for the more academically oriented middle schools and high schools. During eleven years of school, Mr. Chiho Tomita acquired skills in conversational English, compulsory in middle school, and years later explained in English:

> We had examinations to go to high school. Teacher said to look for a character and do reading and writing and arithmetic. Very simple. I studied before I go to examination so get through fast. When I go to high school, have just 150 children. But 300 children go for examination. About half drop.[7] I was very smart at that time! My mother could not go to school very many years so she send me to high school. She thought need high education if you can. It cost more money—about one yen (fifty cents) for three months— but more education. All her eight children in school. In Japan most farm children just go grammar school, that's all. No high school. No college. I had six years grammar school then go to high school five years. Some farmers said, "What for you go to high school?"

Many farming families echoed these farmers' sentiments because they depended on all available hands to work in the fields. Mrs. Hisa Waka-matsu, whose father repaired wooden buckets and raised three daughters alone after the death of her mother, lamented her own childhood predicament: "I fell far behind the other students at school, because my mother insisted I do household work rather than homework. I suppose my help was needed on the farm because we were very poor. My father had assumed I attended school while he was at work. He urged me to return, telling me, 'If you do not go to school, people will make a fool of you.' But I had not passed my first year of school. It embarrassed me so much to attend the same class for a second year that I refused to go to school— now I wish I had followed my father's instructions."

Others had their own reasons for disliking school:

> I guess I liked farming because then I did not have to go to school! I did not like anything about school—and I did not like to study. [Mrs. Maki Hamada]

> The worst part of school was attending during winter. We had only a tiny hibachi in the center of the room. Long time ago! I did not like school. [Mrs. Hatsumi Nishimoto]

After six years of primary school in Japan, twenty-one-year-old Hama Yamaki (*lower left*) attended sewing school, since sewing skills were essential for marriage. Her class took a trip to a hot springs in 1912. (Courtesy of Hama Yamaki)

After primary school, boys and girls received their general education separately. Boys had opportunities to continue their education at the more academically oriented *kotogakko* (high school). Few girls enrolled in high school, and only about 8 percent continued through *koto-jogakko*, a four- or five-year secondary school for girls. Academic standards were lower than those for boys, with fewer hours spent on language, science, math, history, and geography and greater emphasis placed on social and homemaking skills.[8] As an alternative, many young girls attended girls' schools that offered practical, domestic crafts. "Let's see" Mrs. Masayo Yumibe recounted, "six, seven, eight—nine years: I had six years of primary school and three years of girls' school. My practical girls' school offered courses to teach life skills to girls: cooking, sewing, silkworm culture, weaving on a loom, writing, *sumi* [writing with ink], arithmetic, *shishu* [embroidery]."

Other girls were encouraged by their families to attend *saiho*, or sewing school, usually held in churches. For young women, dexterity in sewing was considered essential in womanhood and as bridal training.[9] Among those attending was Mrs. Hama Yamaki, who recalled:

> Most girls quit school after six years, but I wanted to continue my education. So I went to sewing school right after I graduated from primary school. My family was insistent that I attend, because sewing was considered important for marriage. If you went to regular girls' school, you might be able to write and read better—but, for a girl, sewing was most important. So I went both to sewing school and to a special school where I finished two years' classes in one year. I learned sewing, flower arrangement, tea ceremony, and weaving. It was my desire to become a seamstress and a teacher. I made *hakama* [full, ankle-length, pleated trousers], *haori* [loose cloak], and wedding gowns of silk.

Education beyond primary school in Japan thus was affected by one's financial standing, ability, and gender. For Issei, the ethical values ingrained in their early schooling would guide behavioral patterns throughout their lives.

3

Japanese Women

BEYOND MASTERING the practical, domestic crafts they had learned in school, Japanese women were expected to conduct themselves according to strict rules of propriety. "Young women should be *yasashii* [gentle, ef-feminate] with quiet dispositions and beautiful etiquette," Mrs. Hama Yamaki explained. "My family was very strict. We had two maids, so I was expected to behave. If I did not, I was scolded. I was instructed: 'Do not embarrass the family when you go out. Do not be like Americans.[1] Be quiet. Behave like a lady and not like a tomboy. Do not be *ranbo* [rowdy].' They stressed that all the time! (Perhaps I was a little on the *ranbo* side, because I played tennis at school!)"

Beginning in the seventeenth century, a Confucian-based treatise en-titled *Onna Daigaku* (*The Greater Learning for Women*) set principles for the behavior of Japanese women. According to *Onna Daigaku*, the only qualities befitting women were obedience, chastity, mercy, and a quiet manner. The chief duty of girls was to practice filial piety, reciprocating their obligations to their own parents. This was, however, viewed merely as preparation for the submissive status they would later hold in married life. While boys were pampered and protected, girls had to follow their parents'—and society's—more rigid expectations. Girls learned early of their inferior status to boys, were served meals after their brothers, and were rebuked for aggressive impulses[2], as Mrs. Misuyo Nakamura remem-bered so well:

> We girls were taught that our behavior should be decorous—al-ways quiet and reserved. Boys were able to express themselves more freely and were not reprimanded as much for any improper or bois-terous behavior. I recall an instance when my mother slapped me:

A friend had come to our house while my mother was styling my hair in *momoware*, a stylish chignon of seventy years ago. Long hair was divided into half above the forehead, rounded, and pulled to the top of the head; then each section was pulled to the back, wound in circular fashion, and topped with a decoration. This took a long time—maybe as long as thirty minutes. In my eagerness to join my friend, I tossed my head and told my mother, "I would like to go now." Pschat! This upset her so much that she slapped me across the face quite hard. My stepfather, considered by my friends to be gentle and almost saint-like, observed us while he smoked by the hibachi. "Misuyo, you are wrong," he scolded me. "Your mother is trying to fix your hair, so be still." That was the only time I was ever slapped.

At the time I was raised in Japan, it was unusual for a man and woman to walk side by side—normally the woman followed the man. At mealtime the man would be served the most favored portions. In the case of fish, he was served the main body while the woman received the head and tail. And whenever a woman expressed her opinion, which was infrequently, her views were considered of little value. *Shujin*, or husband, means *master*, so men were given an elevated position in life. This was a custom in Japan so we did not give it too much thought.

Women were reconciled to serving their husbands in the most courteous, humble, and conciliatory manner. After all, *Onna Daigaku* dictated, "The great life-long duty of a woman is obedience. . . . When the husband issues his instructions, the wife must never disobey them. . . . A woman should look on her husband as if he were heaven itself, and never weary of thinking how she may yield to her husband. . . . "[3]

Three laws of obedience had also been defined for women: first, obedience to their fathers; second, obedience to their husbands when they married; and third, obedience to their sons when they aged. In his parable about the seven types of wives, Buddha was said to have likened a wife to a murderer, thief, master, mother, sister, and friend. He professed, however, the ideal of the wife who conducted herself like a maid-servant. She served her husband well and with fidelity, obeyed his commands, expressed no resentment or wishes of her own, and endeavored to make him happy.[4] A woman's needs were always to be considered secondary, especially as a new bride. "When you married," Mrs. Itsu Akiyama observed, "you automatically became subservient to the husband's family. You had to agree to everything that was asked of you, and you could never say no. My niece would often tell of her difficult moments as a farmer's bride.

Since she was not a farmer's daughter, she was not able to do the work expected. In many homes, if [a bride] did not fit into the family life, she would either be asked to leave or she might leave on her own. But then she would lose her dowry."

Marriages, like births, were not legal until registered at the village office. As in the case Mrs. Akiyama described, wives were unprotected by law and had no recourse if driven out of the husband's home. After 1914, the courts did require the husband to give a small monetary compensation in such circumstances.[5]

In joining the unfamiliar household of her husband, however, a young bride typically took on the demanding role of attending to not only her husband's needs but those of her mother and father-in-law as well. She was expected to submerge herself in the family's traditions, worship their ancestors, and observe their mode of life. In her ordeal to follow the prescribed manner of her new mother-in-law, the relationship often became strained. Yet it was expected that, through hard work, circumspect behavior, and bearing children, the newcomer to the household should prove her worth and loyalty.[6] For girls who had received modern educations emphasizing broader, more progressive ideas, following traditional customs often proved difficult. Mrs. Tei Endow pointed out the dilemma:

> Young people would learn new ideas. Old people, especially those who stayed away from town and had no contact with others, would keep their older habits. If a new bride came into that family, those old customs would be imposed upon the bride. It was customary that women, particularly young brides, should rise first in the morning, then prepare the meal and clean up before they went to work in the field. I used to hear that, even when some families sat down to dinner, the women and children ate separately from the men. In my family, the women took baths after the men. And we usually did exactly what our elders told us.

The five worst maladies to affect women's minds were indocility, discontent, slander, jealousy, and silliness. These, according to the moralist Kaibara, affected 70 to 80 percent of all women and were curable only through self-inspection and self-reproach. For this reason, women were expected to distrust themselves and always obey their husbands.[7]

4

Thoughts of America

EXAGGERATED STORIES of financial success in the United States lured many Japanese who dreamed of the country four thousand miles across the ocean where one could "get rich quick." Beset with problems of population growth and widespread unemployment, the Japanese government as well as the prefectures (local governing units, or *kens*) encouraged citizens to seek jobs in America. Emigration companies widely advertised the advantages of traveling overseas.[1] Guidebooks published by the Japanese Enterprising Association and other organizations included such titles as "Up-to-date Policy for Going to America" and "How to Succeed in America."[2] Newspapers and magazines publicized the exploits of those who had become landowners and entrepreneurs in America. Mrs. Itsu Akiyama expressed the enthusiasm typical of the times: "I thought America was such a wealthy place that all you had to do was scoop money from the ground! When I was a child, my relatives in America sent a gift of wide ribbon with many colors and designs. They told me how grand America was and how much more money you could earn! In Japan I put in long hours from breakfast until dark, and I earned just thirty cents a day. In America I could earn two dollars a day! I was thrilled about America!"

Some, like Mrs. Hatsumi Nishimoto, erroneously envisioned an escape from the tedium of farm labor: "Even as a child, I had the ambition of coming to America, because I had heard that it was a large and wealthy country. Rice farming in Japan was *erai* [difficult]! I did not like it at all! I thought that if I came to America, I would not have to farm."

In Japan, the Meiji transformation from an agricultural to an industrial economy had seriously burdened farmers. Heavy land taxes, combined with market fluctuations and poor harvests, often forced farmers to sell their land. Some sought partial or full-time employment as factory workers in the cities, which soon swelled with displaced laborers. Others were enticed by opportunities in sparsely settled Hokkaido and migrated to the northern island. Job opportunities remained scarce as the population increased and soldiers returned from war (the Sino-Japanese War from 1894 to 1895 and the Russo-Japanese War from 1904 to 1905).[3] After 1884, members of the working class were permitted by the government to leave Japan as contract laborers.[4] Mr. Miyozo Yumibe recalled the continuing economic pallor when he left Japan in 1917:

> Japan's economic conditions at that time were very bleak, and there were few jobs. A working man earned only about fifty cents for a ten-hour day. Pretty cheap, huh? Too many people and no land in Japan! On the average there may have been two or two and a half acres per farmer, but there was no way to expand. We heard that life in America was much better—a dollar would buy two yen! So, many people desired to escape the economic problems of Japan. I heard that some stowed away on boats to America or, failing that, became stowaways to Mexico and then at night crossed the border into America. When they were caught by the authorities, they were sent back to Japan.

A high proportion of Issei emigrated from the southwestern prefectures of Japan. More than forty thousand of those agricultural laborers had come via Hawaii, for the Hawaiian Board of Immigration had recruited them as a supply of cheap, experienced labor for sugarcane fields.[5] Some Issei had then continued across the ocean to the West Coast, where wages and working conditions were better. During the 1880s, in southwestern Japan, the combination of growing population, economic pressures, and the attraction of the United States provided strong incentives for emigration. Moreover, observed Yosaburo Yoshida, inhabitants of those districts, which had previously contributed pirates and warriors, tended to be particularly "venturesome and enterprising."[6] In addition, the average farm in Japan was less than three acres, considered insufficient to support a family at that time. Hiroshima, with 2.7 acres of farmland per capita, was notable in its number of emigrants. The prefecture in Japan with the smallest amount of farmland per person, it issued the highest number of passports in Japan between 1899 and 1903. During that period, the ten prefectures with the greatest number of Japanese emigrants were Hiroshima (21,871), Kumamoto (12,149), Yamaguchi (11,219), Fukuoka (7,698), Niigata (6,698), Wakayama (3,750), Nagasaki (3,548), Hyogo (3,532), Okayama (2,176), and Miyagi (1,613).[7] The majority of Hood River Issei came from Hiroshima

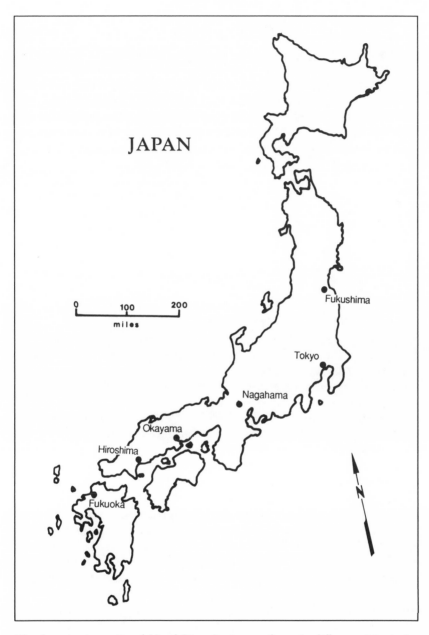

JAPAN

Fukushima

Tokyo

Nagahama

Okayama

Hiroshima

Fukuoka

0 100 200
miles

N

The fourteen interviewed Hood River Issei came from six different cities in Japan. The majority were born in the southwestern prefectures, where people were considered "venturesome and enterprising." (Map by Bob Abrams) and Okayama.[8] Of the fourteen inverviewed, four were born in Hiroshima, four in Okayama, and two in Fukuoka.

Most of the early West Coast Issei were ambitious young bachelors who considered themselves "birds of passage" in the United States,[9] intending to earn money quickly and return to Japan as wealthy men in three to five years. Optimistic Issei intended to earn from one to three thousand dollars, which they believed would enable them to buy land and provide secure lives in Japan. Three-fifths came from rural areas and were raised in agricultural families.[10] Some were younger sons whose opportunities in Japan were limited by the practice of primogeniture, where the eldest son inherited the family name and most of the property. A high proportion who left were eldest sons who were determined to help pay off family debts in Japan. Mr. Chiho Tomita, the eldest of eight children, explained in English: "My neighbor friend come to America for one year and wrote me a letter once in awhile. One dollar American money worth two dollars in Japan. That's why people come to this country to work. My father pretty poor at that time, so I like to come to America and send him money."

In 1907, the year Mr. Tomita left Japan for the United States, the two countries were initiating the "Gentlemen's Agreement." Prompted by President Theodore Roosevelt's concern that discriminatory actions in California could affect diplomatic relations with Japan, the agreement was intended to curb Japanese immigration diplomatically. Roosevelt had agreed to negotiate with Japan to restrict immigration if the San Francisco School Board would rescind its segregation of Japanese school children and if California refrained from passing more anti-Japanese legislation.[11] A year later, Japan agreed to issue passports only to laborers returning to the United States and to their wives, children, and parents. Under those terms, only those joining relatives had the option to travel to America. The number of men, which had exceeded women seven to one, began to move into balance with the number of women after 1908; yet thousands of Issei were destined to remain bachelors.[12] For Mr. Masaji Kusachi, like many others, the opportunity to go to the United States solved a dilemma about the future: "After I graduated from eight years of school in Okayama, my future was somewhat uncertain. I was not fond of farming in Japan, so I had a choice of either going into the military or continuing school. About that time, my father, who was already in America, asked if I would like to join him. I thought, 'Well, this might be a good opportunity to go to America for two or three years.' "[13]

5

Marriage

THE LAND ACROSS the Pacific soon became the destination of many Japanese newlyweds. Men working in the United States had discovered that they would realize their dreams of financial security only by extending their years of labor. A number had purchased property and established roots in American farmland. Now approaching middle age, some men returned to Japan, joining tour groups or enlisting the aid of family and friends in search of suitable wives who would join them in America.

Arranged Marriages

In a society where family and household took precedence over the individual, marriages for love were distrusted as rash, romantic choices that could compromise an entire family's reputation. Instead, marriages became family affairs that were formally arranged by family heads. Family lineage was considered so important that prospective marriage partners were screened by *baishakunin* (marriage go-betweens, also referred to as *nakodo*), respected citizens of the community. *Baishakunin* carefully scrutinized bloodline as well as social standing, character, wealth, education, health, and even signs of the zodiac. After satisfactory investigations and an exchange of photos, members of the households met during *o-miai* (marriage interviews). If the families consented, marriage followed.[1] Customarily, young women in Japan complied with their parents' marriage choices, since, as Mrs. Hatsumi Nishimoto reminisced, refusing to do so was considered filial disobedience:

I wanted to see America, and the chance came when Nishimoto returned from America with the object of matrimony. In wedding matters, the Japanese girl went to whomever her parents selected, whether she liked it or not. I did not question this, because that was most natural in Japan. Generally one expressed a desire to have a mate; and the *baishakunin* made introductions. Then, on behalf of each family, he conducted an investigation. As soon as matters became serious, our family asked friends about the prospective groom: his family lineage and desirability as a husband.

We met for the first time when Nishimoto and the *baishakunin* called on us at our home. Following the custom of the old days, we were not able to talk; we simply faced each other while the *baishakunin* for both families intervened. And, until we had the approval of our parents, we would not be permitted to go anywhere. Later my parents asked if I approved of him. Since my ambition was to go to the United States, I approved!

After we received the approval of our parents, our wedding plans proceeded. The wedding took place on January 10, 1918, at the groom's family home. I was eighteen and my husband was thirty-two years old. In those days, customs were very strict. If a girl married without family approval, she was literally removed from the family.

A young woman's situation could also remain precarious after the marriage, when she lived in the home of her husband and his parents. Expected to devote herself to the traditions of her new family, she was obliged to leave if she could not adapt.[2] *Onna Daigaku* (*The Greater Learning of Women*, the Confucian treatise on women) had proclaimed seven reasons for divorce: disobedience, failure to bear children, lewdness, jealousy, disease, excessive talking, and stealing.[3] As a result, some women, like Mrs. Tei Endow, may have seen young married life in America as an escape from the prospect of overbearing mothers-in-law in their native land:

> Mr. Endow was not my boyfriend, but I considered marriage because I wanted to come to America. My parents decided on marriage. That was the way marriages were arranged in Japan. Endow's parents were deceased. I thought that this way I would not have to live with his family. There could be many complaints, especially about housecleaning, when the bride lived with the husband's family. We would wonder: did it have to be done just the way we were told? Anyone like me, who had not done housework, would probably be put out! We were married in December 1917, and the next March we came to America. I was eighteen and my husband was twenty-eight.

Thoughts of a lucrative but temporary stay in America also entered young women's minds when they saw the well-dressed Japanese men who had returned. In the unusual position of making her own marriage decision, Mrs. Miyoshi Noyori found humor in the first stolen glimpse of her husband-to-be:

> "Looks like *kane-mochi* [wealthy man]! Nice navy blue suit, you know." What I remember most was that he presented himself formally to my parents, kneeling on the floor with his hands on the tatami [straw floor mat] and bowing low. (For one returning from America, this may have been his first time bowing low on tatami.) My sister and I were peeking through a hole in the *fusuma* [sliding door]. We were very amused! Then my mother asked me to come out and meet him. I was extremely embarrassed. Later my parents asked if I had any desire to marry this man. In my own mind, I had motives of making money in America. Since my older sister had hearing problems, it was up to me to make money to help my parents expand their grocery store. It appeared that America would provide me with financial success! So it was my wish to marry him. My parents did not press me, for they said the decision was up to me. "If you do not want to go, that is okay. If you do, then that would be fine, too." I was sort of an ambitious person, and I could see that my future in a country village was limited. I wanted to learn, and I had great aspirations to go to Okayama city. This opportunity I did not have, so the other option, to go to America, seemed better. After seeing pictures of America, this seemed a grand opportunity for me.

For another bride who was given a voice in the selection of her marriage partner, practical considerations were also heavily weighed. Mrs. Hama Yamaki reconstructed her moments of indecision after receiving two marriage proposals:

> Like most men then, Yamaki returned to Japan for marriage purposes. Although he looked around, he was not able to find anyone who suited him. He was ready to return to America a single man. But a close friend urged him, "At your age, you should go back to America married." Although Yamaki apparently wanted me, he was hesitant to ask, because we had been raised like brother and sister.[4] I also had a marriage proposal from a large shoyu [soy sauce] producing family. I could not make up my mind between Yamaki and the other man! The *baishakunin* was getting a bit frustrated. It was most difficult to turn the other proposal down. But since my health

was not very good, I questioned my ability to help manage the many women shoyu factory workers. Choosing that man would have meant a lot of hard work, and it seemed that I would have an easier life with Yamaki. My other reason was that I had two brothers already in America. *Ani-san* [older brother] said we could all live together if I came to America!

For Mrs. Misuyo Nakamura, who had previously fled geisha training, a marriage proposal brought family intervention and a surprise wedding, not entirely uncommon for the times:

Hitoshi Nakamura was anxious that I join him in America. When his father returned to Japan from America, Hitoshi had asked him to seek a suitable bride, saying, "I would be agreeable to anyone you suggest." By chance I had occasion to meet Hitoshi's brother and sister when I paid my respects at the cemetery.[5] Afterward they suggested to their father that I would be an ideal wife, saying, "She's the one!" Soon after that, *o-jiisan* [Grandfather Nakamura, Hitoshi's father[6]] visited my family to discuss wedding possibilities. I was asked my opinion, but I did not say yes. Immediately after Hitoshi returned to Japan, he wrote me a letter, telling me he had only a one-month stay in Japan. If he were to remain longer, he would be subject to military draft. Since he was short of time and I was not answering, Hitoshi sent a telegram to my second brother in Korea,[7] asking him to intervene in the matter. My brother was a soybean buyer in Korea, and he returned to Japan to discuss the matter. He expressed concern that all other family members were married and that I should be married too. He reminded me that, since our parents knew Hitoshi's parents and it was urgent that Hitoshi marry soon, we could avoid the customary research into family backgrounds. In fact, he felt so deeply moved that he begged me: "I request that you marry this person, for I would be greatly relieved." So I replied, "If it is this much of a concern to you, I wish to relieve your worry. I will marry this person."

A strange thing happened when my mother and I visited the family of my husband-to-be. We presumed we had been invited to plan the wedding. But when we arrived, the family was busily preparing for a ceremony that very evening! They had even laid out the wedding kimono of Hitoshi's sister for me to wear. We were definitely not prepared for this, and a quarrel resulted. Mother said, in effect, "You have deceived us into an early marriage." Here we were—just my mother and me—my stepfather was not even with us! But, since I did not want to become a burden to my stepfather, who had adopted me when he married my mother, I felt obliged to agree with the plans."

The wedding ceremony on January 12, 1921, at the Nakamura home involved an exchange of sake in small cups. This ritual of nine sips bound the couple in marriage:

> While kneeling next to each other, Hitoshi and I were served in a private room by a lady wearing a fine kimono. First she offered sake to Hitoshi, who went through the motions of drinking it. Then the cup was refilled and given to me. I took just a sip—mostly for ceremony. *San san kudo* means "three, three, nine times" ceremony, because three teacups of graduated sizes were stacked. No words were spoken—not even a yes or a no—just the exchange of sake.[8] For the ceremony, I wore a white silk kimono,[9] but I considered it very odd that Hitoshi only wore everyday *nihongi* [Japanese clothes] instead of *montsuki* [formal, black silk kimono ornamented with five circular, white *mon*, or family crests]. He did not even wear a suit!
>
> Afterward, in lively celebration, Hitoshi and I exchanged drinks in front of the Nakamuras' forty or fifty invited guests. The guests sang while they ate and drank. After changing from my wedding kimono, I returned to the banquet area and was asked to serve sake. (It was customary that the bride serve the guests.) On my knees, I faced each guest in turn, bowed, and recited, "Dozo yoroshiku one-gai shimasu" [Please continue your good will toward me. I am happy to make your acquaintance]. This I repeated all the way around the room. I was excited, but I was also embarrassed to serve all those people! The guests were all from the Nakamura side, because my family did not know about the wedding.

Picture-Bride Marriages

For many men, a return trip to Japan to seek brides was considered too costly, both in terms of money and time. In addition to the month required for the round-trip, another two months could be spent searching for a mate, entering a formal engagement, and planning a ceremony. The added costs for fare, living expenses, and extravagant weddings could drain a laborer's savings.

Shashin-kekkon, picture-bride marriages, thus evolved as a practice that conformed to both Japanese social custom and U.S. legal requirements. After July 1, 1915, any Japanese male in the United States could summon a wife if he could verify that he had acquired eight hundred dollars in savings at least five months prior to application.[10] (Before that time,

Japanese farmers were required to demonstrate they could support families by showing annual profits of four to five hundred dollars, plus a thousand dollars in savings.) That same year, in an effort to promote harmonious marriages, a requirement was added to limit the age difference between spouses to thirteen years. In addition, the bride's name was to be entered in the husband's *koseki* (family register) six months prior to her passport application, a time limit designed to impede prostitutes.[11]

Following the procedures of a typical arranged marriage in Japan, immigrant men sought help from parents or relatives, after sending photos and information about their lives in America. They selected their lifelong mates with care, as Mr. Chiho Tomita explained in English: "My father told me I better marry, so I think okay. But I can't go to Japan—no money. At that time lots of Japanese like me married with picture. I wrote letter, 'I have no money and I working for a *hakujin* [Caucasian] family and staying in a little cabin. If okay, then come over to America.' First time my father send picture, I don't like it so I send it back. Third time I told him, 'This picture all right.' So my father understand which one looked good. Which one best? Best one for me!"

Although the decision was out of her hands, Mrs. Itsu Akiyama affirmed the appeal of a picture-bride marriage:

> The picture-bride custom may be laughed at now, but arranged marriages were proper in those days and love marriages were considered most improper. (There was a teacher who married for love at the time, and she became a victim of ridicule.) So I had faith in my relatives making the marriage arrangements. I do not know how I was chosen—I did not question the decision. Both sides of the family heartily encouraged the marriage, and my future husband and I exchanged letters. He was considered to be *shinbo* [persevering] and was highly recommended by my sister-in-law. I was young and innocent, so I thought I might just as well come to America and see what a rich country it was.

After arrangements had been made to the satisfaction of both families, an extravagant nuptial dinner was held in Japan with a family member substituting for the absent groom. Formal attire was the rule, and bridal preparations took hours, as Mrs. Asayo Noji described:

> When you became a bride, it was customary to have a hairdresser pile your hair on your crown in *maru-mage* [the round chignon of a married woman].[12] I did not want this done, but everyone insisted. I did not like it at all! It took practically all morning to style my hair and apply white makeup and lipstick. Three lines were also painted on my neck. A black line behind each of my ears extended down

As a picture bride, nineteen-year-old Asayo Noji's marriage was arranged through an exchange of photos. Her future husband had been praised for his perseverance and for studying hard in school. (Courtesy of Asayo Noji)

the nape of my neck, as well as one black line down the back.
Then a white line was drawn vertically between the black ones.
When the kimono was pulled back from the neck, the lines looked
very pretty. *Sanbon suji* [three lines] was an old tradition for formal
weddings. Then my face was cleanly shaven except for my eyebrows
and a little hair left at the top of my forehead in the shape of Mt.
Fuji. This was done to make me look pretty.[13]

Then, once the groom's parents had registered the marriage in the *koseki*, the marriage was considered valid.

Adopted Sons

Continuing the family name, its lineage, and its traditions was of
prime importance in Japan, for each generation was linked to the next
through its male successors. Families without sons therefore acquired male
heirs through simple adoption. A *yoshi*, an adopted and often related
young man, then married the eldest daughter, took the family name as his
own, inherited the family property and position, and perpetuated the
family line. Like Mr. Miyozo Yumibe, some *yoshi* were called to America:

> I was born a Tanaka, but I was adopted by Mr. Yumibe when I
> was eleven years old. Mr. Yumibe, my father's cousin in America,
> had no sons to succeed him. So the Yumibe parents returned to Ja-
> pan and asked to adopt the oldest son in our family. But "can't do,"
> because in Japan the oldest son "must follow the papa" [tradition-
> ally becomes the head of the family]. So I was next in line to be a
> *yoshi*—any place is all right for the second brother! I think the two
> papas made arrangements at the courthouse, but I was not told
> then. I lived with my Tanaka family until I was sixteen, for Japanese
> law said I could not immigrate to the United States for five years
> after becoming a *yoshi*. According to another law, I would have been
> prohibited from immigrating to the United States if I had remained
> in the Tanaka family. Since the Yumibe parents were already in
> America, they could call me overseas as their son.[14] I was a young
> boy, and I wanted to come to America. There were many in our
> family, and we were poor at the time. If one of us could make money
> in America, this would be a relief to my family.

Marriages in Japan were thus time-honored unions of couples and their
families, which were also necessary to continue family lineage. Whether
they began with introductions by *baishakunin*, through an exchange of
photos, or through an adoption of a male successor, all marriages involved elaborate proceedings arranged by the involved families.

PART TWO

Bound for America

Chichi haha to
Wakare wa shitare
Taiheiyoo
Wataru funade no
Osanakarishi ware wa

Leaving my parents behind,
I ventured out to sail across the
Pacific.
Ah, how young I was!

Tanka written by Mrs. Shizue Iwatsuki and translated
by Mrs. Michiko Kumashiro

6

Leaving Japan

FILLED WITH DREAMS of a new life in America and buoyed by such guide-books as *How to Succeed in America*,[1] Japanese men and women prepared for their overseas trips. Influenced by printed materials and stories that tended to exaggerate opportunities abroad, Mrs. Tei Endow, among others, anticipated glamorous lives in America:

> Some people came back to Japan with stories about Americans wearing strange clothes. I wanted to see this for myself! I had wonderful visions of America! I pictured that even the flies would be different! My husband told me not to bring any excess baggage, so my parents had Western clothes custom-made for me in Yokohama. The tailor sewed fashionable clothes worldwide, and everything was measured to fit my body. I had custom-made suits, silk blouses, coat, and hat. I remember I wore a brown suit with square shoulders on my trip to America, and I could see that other people envied me. Now that I had my wardrobe, I was prepared to come to America!

For sixteen-year-old Mr. Miyozo Yumibe, packing was quite simple when he left in 1917: "I did not really have too much to prepare. I put on my coat, packed my suitcase, and left. We were also required to bring at least one hundred yen or fifty American dollars; otherwise we would not be able to land. This was probably necessary, because, if we were rejected in the United States, we would need money for our trip back to Japan."

An immigration law of 1903 required that steamship logs indicate whether alien passengers possessed fifty dollars or, if less, the amount. Apparently, though, laws did not actually require them to hold a specific amount of money. Those intending to live in the United States were asked whether they could read or write, and a yes answer was accepted as proof of literacy.[2]

The Japanese Foreign Ministry also required emigrants to obtain passports and pass physical examinations at their ports of departure. "Emigrant houses" located in both Yokohama and Kobe gave tests for trachoma (a contagious virus of the eye), hookworm, and syphilis, since emigrants would be expected to pass the same tests once they arrived in the United States.[3] Because of the widespread use of human wastes for fertilizing fields, intestinal worms and trachoma flourished, requiring treatment and postponing departures for many.[4] But the optimistic Mr. Miyozo Yumibe was not particularly perplexed by the turn of events: "I was detained at Kobe for a whole month because of my stool inspection. I lived in a hotel there until I waited for my next examination, and my Tanaka papa sent me more money. There were lots of people who did not pass the test, so I was not worried. I thought, 'If I do not pass it now, I will surely pass it later.' Since I had a whole month, I spent a lot of my time sightseeing!" Mrs. Masayo Yumibe was also detained when she left in 1921: "I brought *futon* [thick quilt] and I wore *nihongi* [Japanese clothes]. In Kobe I was given stool and eye examinations. I had to stay at a hotel there for a month, because I needed an operation for *torahomu* [trachoma] on both eyes. It was a pretty bad disease—we had to use separate towels. (If the infection was severe, a person could become blind.) I had a light infection diagnosed at a school eye inspection, but medicine had not immediately cleared it. Even after my operation, though, I had no bandages and no pain. I stayed one month at a hotel in Kobe."

Then, as they embarked on their journeys, family members came to bid them farewell, offering words of encouragement while ever mindful of the purposes of the trips. Mr. Chiho Tomita recounted his departure in English: "I was seventeen years old. I brought one blanket and shirts. Have to take a passport from the Fukushima government and examination for health. Cost about sixty dollars to ride on boat, so my father borrowed money and gave to me. I thought maybe this is the last time I see my father, my mother, my family. My mother said, 'Keep good health and send money.' "

Families were reluctant to consider that their separations might become permanent. "My parents said, 'If you do go to America, be sure to come back within three years. But if you cannot return in three years, definitely come back in ten years!'[5] My father took me to Kobe where I caught the ship. I cried together with my sister," Mrs. Itsu Akiyama remembered.

Whatever the conditions or words of advice, leaving was difficult. Yet there were always thoughts of what lay ahead. "I was happy to be coming

INSPECTION CARD.

(Immigrants and Steerage Passengers.)

Port of departure, Yokohama, Japan.   Date of departure, OCT 10 1908

Name of ship, "JOS... M... RU..."   Yokohama,

Name of immigrant, Mr. Yeitaro Wakamatsu

Last residence, Shiga Ken

Inspected and passed at Yokohama, Japan.	Passed at quarantine, Port of	Passed by Immigration Bureau
	..............., U. S.	Port of...............
	(Date.)	(Date.)

(The following to be filled in by ship's surgeon or agent prior to or after embarkation.)

Ship's list or manifest 1   No. on ship's list or manifest 7

Berth No...	Steamship Inspection	15 16 17 18 19 20 21 22 23 24 25 26 27	To be punched by ship's surgeon at daily Inspection

E. Wakamatsu

VACCINATED

(Signature or Stamp.)

F. mukai

Keep this Card to avoid detention at Quarantine and on Railroads in the United States.

Diese Karte muss aufbewahrt werden um Anfenthalt an der Quarantäne, sowie auf den Eisenbahnen der Vereinigten Staaten zu vermeiden.

Quarantaine, ainsi que sur les chemins de fer les Etats-Unis.

Deze kaart moet bewaard worden, ten einde oponthoud aan de Quarantijn, alsook op de ijzeren wegen der Vereenigde Staten te vermijden.

Conservate questo biglietto onde evitare detenzione alla Quarantina e sulle Ferrovie degli Stati Uniti.

Tento listek musite uschovati, nechcete-li ukaranteny (zastaveni ohledně zjistěni zdraví) neb na dráze ve spojených stětech zdrzeni byti.

Tuto kartocku treba trimat' u sebe aby sa predeslo zderzovanu v karantene aj na zeleznici ve Spojených Statoch.

此札ヲ保存所持セラルベシ   道等ニテ停留スル免カルベク、タメ   合衆國ニ於ケ此検疫所又ハ鉄

Hisa Wakamatsu's boarding ticket ensured that she had passed strict physical examinations when she left Japan in 1908.

to America," Mrs. Asayo Noji said, "but parting was very sad. My relatives told me, 'Take good care of yourself, *shinbo* [persevere], hurry home—and good-bye!' I told them *sayonara!* [good-bye] and cried. This was especially hard for my parents, for I was their first daughter to leave for such a distant place. And, in those days, few people we knew traveled to America as picture brides. Yet, I had heard that America was a land of richness and a large country, so I was happy to be coming."

7

Sailing to America

EMBARKING ON the two-week voyage to America, Issei could take one of three courses. Some gained passports to travel first to Hawaii, Mexico, or Canada. This occurred until 1908, when the final provision of the Gentlemen's Agreement between the United States and Japan prevented "secondary immigration" into the United States.[1] An unknown number of Japanese stowed away or became crewmen on cargo boats bound for America and then "jumped ship."[2] The most acceptable and common means was to obtain passports from the Japanese Foreign Ministry as U.S. immigrants.

Before 1900, circumstances on the boats often bordered on the inhumane. A San Francisco newspaper cited an incident where Issei were stowed without water on top of sugar sacks in dark hatches of a cargo vessel.[3] Later, conditions, though cramped, improved. Yet those two-week voyages, for many, became an initiation to strange American foods, Western-style beds, and—worst of all—seasickness, as recounted by a number of passengers:

Awa Maru[4] was probably a six-thousand-ton ship, and it rocked quite a bit. I came on second class, and I was seasick all the time. I was so sick I felt as if I were dead! On New Year's Day we were served ozoni [rice cake stew] and Japanese goodies, but they did not last long because I threw them up. Occasionally we were served Western food and bread and butter, but I could not stand the smell of butter![5] I did long for good drinking water. [Mrs. Itsu Akiyama]

The big waves crashed together and raised our boat twenty feet high. Through the window, the approaching waves resembled mountains! I rode third class on the eight-thousand-ton *Mexico Maru*. I got seasick and could not eat on the ship. [Mrs. Miyoshi Noyori]

From Yokohama we traveled third class on *Kashima Maru*, a middle-sized ship. It was such a dreadful journey, I vowed that I would never return to Japan by ship! Our boat rocked back and forth—even my trunk moved. I was seasick, so I lay in bed most of the time. Even after I got out of my bunk bed, it was difficult to walk around. [Mrs. Hatsumi Nishimoto]

On the ship from Kobe to Yokohama, waters were kind of rough so I got seasick. Even in the dining room, dishes of food slid on the table. No trouble from Yokohama to Seattle, because the sea was quiet—or perhaps I got used to riding the ship. [Mrs. Masayo Yumibe]

I don't worry because three hundred young people came at the same time on the same boat. I ride on England freight boat. It takes fifteen days in the ocean and I had pretty bad seasick. I couldn't eat nothing. If I had food, all throw out. Most everybody seasick so most sleep in a row on blankets. Pretty hard. [Mr. Chiho Tomita, in English]

As a new wife who had become a victim of seasickness and then had been separated from her husband on the ship, Mrs. Misuyo Nakamura was particularly frightened when her husband seemed to have disappeared:

Manila Maru was the name of the ship. We left Kobe on February 5, 1921, and rode third class for fifty dollars one-way. The trip took about three weeks, and the seas were rough. Oh, both Papa[6] and I suffered from sea sickness! Strangely, even though we were a married couple, we were assigned to different sleeping sections below deck. One section was for men and another was for women. *Kowai* [Frightening]! I shared a room with strangers. I did not know anyone! There may have been anywhere from eight to ten women in my room. We slept in upper and lower bunks along the walls of that small room. In those rough seas, I remember that my luggage slid back and forth across the floor. The rocking of the ship was so severe that I clung to my bed at night! But I was particularly worried when I did not see my new husband at the dining area. He had become so seasick he could not come to meals! I had so many worries that I truly felt like crying! I was young and so very lonesome—I did not know what to do. I was seventeen years and nine months old—poor thing, huh? My husband was not yet twenty-three.

Among the fortunate few who appeared to be unaffected by the swelling of the ocean, Mrs. Asayo Noji adeptly continued her normal routine on board the ship:

> *Canada Maru* was a six-hundred-ton ship. People told me it was small compared to other ocean-going vessels, but it certainly looked big to me! I thought the ship was pretty, because it was newly painted—sort of a tan color. But the smell of fresh paint combined with the "ship smell" for a terrible odor! At Kobe I think thirty to forty of us boarded. Then the ship sailed to Shimizu where they loaded a lot of china; then more boarded at Yokohama. Perhaps there were one hundred passengers in all.
>
> Funny, it seemed that some got seasick as soon as they boarded. Yet, for some reason, when the boat rocked back and forth, that just seemed to make me hungry! The others became ill and could not eat. Me, I ate every meal, took a bath every night, and slept comfortably in the middle level of a triple bunk.
>
> Some men on board had been to America before, so we gathered around them. They told us that we were a select group. "You had to have had good reputations to come to America," they said. We were also told that we were lucky, because women in America were treated at a higher level than men. But they further cautioned picture brides, "Look very carefully at pictures of your prospective husbands to be certain you are meeting the right man." I was not worried, though, because I sort of knew my future husband anyway.

For Mr. Miyozo Yumibe, the ocean waters were calm and the summer trip was pleasant:

> I came third class on *Yusen Kaisha* Shipping Company's five-thousand-ton vessel. There must have been at least 175 passengers, so it was crowded. The boat trip, which cost about ninety dollars, was pretty good! We left in June 1917, and the day was pleasant. Waters were so smooth, it was just like living in a house. I could get up on deck and gaze at the ocean. Nobody got sick. There was a dining room with a lot of tables where we ate Japanese food. The rooms had double-decked beds, much like the sleeping cars on the railroad. Occasionally they showed moving pictures on the boat— mostly Japanese pictures. We spent a lot of time talking with other passengers, guessing where we might be going in the United States. There were lots of people on the boat, and we became friends, so there was really no reason to worry. I wanted to come to America to make money.

For many Issei, the voyage was uncomfortable, disheartening, and much too long. Anxiously awaiting the end of their two-week journeys, Issei were buoyed by the allure of new lives in the so-called land of opportunity.

PART THREE

Arrival in America

Nushoku no
Take no tsubomi o
Hori ateshi

The color of milk—
The bud of a mushroom.
I found them.

Haiku written by Mrs. Hama Yamaki and
translated by Mr. Ben Kino

8

First Impressions

DRESSED IN TRADITIONAL kimono and *geta* (wooden clogs) and with visions of plentiful money and ready-made fortunes, Issei eagerly set foot on American soil. Yet their optimism and carefree notions of everyday American life were quickly crushed. Mrs. Hisa Wakamatsu expressed the surprise and disillusionment typical of the newcomers: "When I arrived in Tacoma, I saw that all the people had white skin and hair of different colors! I thought I had landed here by mistake! And I was troubled when I could not understand them. I truly wondered, 'For what purpose did I come here?' I was so confused that I asked my husband, 'What should I do?' He told me just to keep still—I need not say anything. That brought tears to my eyes."

The newly arrived Issei, most of whom had traveled as third-class passengers, endured meticulous physical examinations upon their arrival at the *iminkan* (immigration center). Those who did not pass their tests were confined. Living conditions were degrading—from the appearance of the building to the quality of food. For Mr. Masaji Kusachi, there was nothing at all to be appreciated about the *iminkan*:

> At the time I came to America in 1919, there were two common afflictions: stool worms and trachoma, a painful and infectious eye condition. So we were subjected to physical examinations both in Japan and at the Seattle *iminkan*. Those cleared were at liberty to leave, but a large number of us were detained—mostly for stool worms—and had to take medication until the problems cleared. We had a weekly inspection at the *iminkan*, and I had to remain for four weeks.

Arriving at the Seattle immigration center, kimono-clad Japanese women met their husbands, many for the first time. (Courtesy of Alice Ito)

The *iminkan* was a pretty tough place—just like prison. The five-story building was just north of the railroad depot in Seattle. It was pretty dirty, and all the windows were covered with iron bars. When we went to the dining room one floor down, we were counted as we passed by and counted as we left—then the doors were slammed! Because it was a trying time for us, I remember it very well. We were served Chinese food, and I do remember one meal in particular. They served what looked like straw—of course, I could not eat it! The table was stacked high with slices of bread, so I poured sugar on bread and ate that instead.[1] They did not serve adequate food, as far as I was concerned.

We were confined with many Chinese and spent most of our time in a room filled with rows of bunk beds. Men had a separate room from the women. It certainly was noisy in there, and even at night you could hear snoring all around. There was nothing for us to do except to sit on our beds waiting for the weekly examination. On that day we were not supposed to eat any breakfast. But we were young people who were very hungry—so our friends would always bring us food. And even though our stool problems may not have been cleared in four weeks, everyone was released in four weeks' time anyway.

Language and food were the biggest problems for Mrs. Tei Endow, as she described: "When we arrived in Seattle in 1918, doctors discovered that I had worm eggs, and I was confined to the *iminkan* for two weeks. This was not considered a serious condition, though, because many people had worm eggs in their stools. My greatest difficulty was that I could not speak English, but a *hakujin* [Caucasian] lady who could speak some Japanese volunteered to help me talk to the immigration officials. Food was my biggest complaint. It seemed they served fried cabbage with *iriko* [tiny dried fish] every day."

In some cases the examination process seemed arbitrary, and the inconsistency in releasing immigrants raised speculation about unfair testing procedures:

> I had been so seasick that I was not able to have a stool, so I had to borrow my friend's. The donor of the stool was able to leave, but I was held for another fifteen days. I guess I was detained because of the pallor of my face from seasickness. [Mrs. Miyoshi Noyori]

> After my husband and I landed in Seattle, I was detained at the customhouse for three whole weeks—even though I had passed the physical examinations in Japan! It was rumored that our releases depended on a lottery system, and we guessed we were detained longer to meet expenses.[2] I was given weekly examinations, and they kept postponing my release.

> Life in the customhouse was not too different from being on the ship, because we had the same bunks. I could not buy anything with my Japanese money. My husband had given me a couple dollars to make small purchases, so I remember buying bananas at the cafeteria. My husband had no trouble at customs, so he lived with relatives who were raising loganberries in the Kent, Washington, area. About once a week he visited me. On his first visit, he brought a tiny flower in a pot, which surprised me. But while I was in the customhouse, I often wondered, "Why did I come to America?" I thought about this a lot. I was still a young person thrown in with strangers. I felt very lonesome, for my husband could visit me for only a short time each week. [Mrs. Misuyo Nakamura]

More disappointments, unfortunately, lay ahead for some of the picture brides. Clasping photos of their intended husbands in anticipation of face-to-face meetings, some voiced regrets. An interested onlooker, Mrs. Hatsumi Nishimoto described what she observed: "When we gathered in the immigration office, we could see people comparing photos with prospective spouses. I remember some of the ladies were in tears, because their husbands were not anything like their photos. 'Everybody young pictures,' so the photos looked much better than the real people! Later I heard that some women wished to return to Japan instead of going through with marriage."

Picture brides were often shocked to meet husbands much older than they had expected or who bore no likeness whatever to their photos. It was not uncommon for Issei men, many in their middle years, to send either much more youthful photos of themselves or photos that had been retouched to eliminate blemishes or baldness. A few simply substituted photos of much more handsome friends. In some cases, personal holdings also had been misrepresented, with the keeper of a boardinghouse portrayed as a hotel operator or a small shopkeeper depicted as a merchant.[3] As a rule, women were ten to fifteen years younger than their husbands,[4] were educated for their time,[5] and had a slightly higher socioeconomic status than their husbands.[6] Each picture bride was required to show a valid passport, a certified copy of her husband's family registry, and a health certificate. In turn, her husband was obligated to bring a certificate of identification and occupation by the Japanese consulate, an additional proof of employment (land title or lease agreement), and a bank deposit book.[7]

Mrs. Asayo Noji recalled the circumstances of meeting her new husband, whom she had not seen since she was three years old:

There was a room where we met our prospective husbands. (I think we had tests the first day, and I probably met Papa on the second day.) Men wore regular suits, and all the women wore kimonos. Fuji-san [Mr. Fuji], who had lived in our neighborhood in Hiroshima, introduced me to Papa. Fuji-san owned a Seattle hotel and also made introductions for four or five other men who stayed at his hotel. He asked me, "Are you satisfied that this man matches your picture?" I said, "Yes." I guess Papa also said, "All right." Papa wore a white summer suit with black stripes. He was much thinner than his pictures, but I supposed this was due to hard work. I stayed in the *iminkan* for two weeks. Visiting hours were from two o'clock to three o'clock so Papa came to see me every other day. He was not allowed to bring food, because we were on medication. But the day we met, he had measured my ring size; and on his next visit, he brought me a gold ring. Not everyone received rings, so this made

Picture-bride Asayo Noji favored the more comfortable Western clothes she wore for her July 14, 1916, marriage to Kichizo Noji at a Seattle Buddhist church. Afterward her husband ordered more tailor-made garments and bought her a Singer sewing machine. (Courtesy of Asayo Noji)

me happy. He asked if there was anything I needed—all I wanted was soap.

Baffled at first when a strange man came to her door, Mrs. Itsu Akiyama, another picture bride, described her ensuing wedding preparations:

> Because I was young, I had complete faith in the man. Another person, though, was sent to pick me up at the *iminkan*. I did not like the looks of him, so I slammed the door! Akiyama and I met later at the *iminkan*. I had no particular feelings about him—the man looked just like his picture. He was wearing a suit, and I was in *nihongi* [Japanese clothes]. I do not remember what we talked about. He did not say welcome, and he did not say anything about his work. I do not even recall saying the usual first-time greeting, "O-hajimete gozai-masu."[8]

> A *nihonjin* [Japanese] clothier dressed me for the wedding. Naturally he did not want me to wear *nihongi*, because he was selling clothing. I wore a white blouse and blue skirt with a lace scarf that I did not really think I needed. I also wore a gold band with red stone that my husband had sent to Japan. I thought Western clothes were much more comfortable than Japan clothes, where you had to wear tight *obi* [wide sash]. The minister performed our wedding ceremony on January 18 or 19, 1915, at the Buddhist church in Seattle.

Although wedding rites had been conducted in Japan, couples were required to remarry in American ceremonies until 1917, the year the U.S. government legally recognized picture-bride marriages.[9] Mr. Chiho Tomita recalled in English his wedding as well as his wife's candid reaction upon their meeting: "I send lots of money to my wife—over one hundred dollars to buy first-class ticket. Cost a lot of money but pretty easy to land and don't need to go to immigration office. I met my wife in Seattle. I asked her about her family. She told me I was sunburned and pretty brown—brown face. Ceremony at a hotel on May 30, 1918—Decoration Day [Memorial Day]. I wore a regular suit, and I took my friend's dress for my wife to wear. A minister read the Bible, and I gave her wedding ring made of gold."

From 1910 to 1920, the number of Japanese women in Oregon between twenty and forty-four years old increased from 201 to 769.[10] According to federal estimates, picture brides constituted more than half of all married Japanese women arriving during those ten years.[11] During the period between 1912 and 1920, a total of 6,988 picture brides arrived.[12] Exclusionists condemned the practice as immoral, a means to increase the Japanese population through high birthrates, and a ploy to import additional laborers in violation of the Gentlemen's Agreement of 1907–8. With the anti-Asian hysteria in California still looming, the Japanese government voluntarily stopped issuing passports to picture brides in 1921. Small numbers of women continued, however, to arrive in the United States through mid-1924. Yet the imbalance of almost two men to each Issei woman destined many adult Japanese males for bachelorhood.[13]

9

The Japanese Methodist Church

MANY OF THE newly arrived Issei, with little knowledge of American language and customs, took comfort in the charitable activities of Christian
churches, for they offered opportunities to learn to speak and adjust to life
in America. Issei soon found that the Christian churches' ethical training
coincided with Buddhism, and the social welfare seemed to fill the void
left by their close family contacts at home.[1] The social scientist S. Frank
Miyamoto affirmed, "Nothing in Japan is more sacred than the help-
fulness of one member of society towards another, and the Christian
missionaries with their practice of benevolent aid to the young immigrants arriving on these shores must have endeared themselves to these
people."[2]

Methodist churches on the West Coast had particularly strong out-
reach programs and, as a result, attracted the largest number of Issei.[3] In
Portland, the Japanese Methodist mission was opened in 1893 by Rev.
Teikichi Kawabe from the San Francisco church. The mission grew rapidly, increasing its membership to over a hundred persons after the first
year. Within two years, the mission had rented its fourth building. By
1903 it founded a church at a newly purchased site on the corner of
Northwest Fifteenth and Glisan. The church formed a Sunday school, a
fujinkai (ladies' society), and a kindergarten, where Japanese children
could learn English.[4]

Mrs. Hama Yamaki, for one, particularly appreciated the social activities of the church: "On Sunday we attended the Portland Methodist
Church. My husband studied English there, and I looked forward to view-
ing movies in the evening. We enjoyed one serial movie so much we went
almost six months to see it. It was about a one-thousand-dollar box that
eluded its searchers each week.[5] The movie was in English and I could

not understand it, but my husband and friends would explain it to me later. After awhile, I could guess what was going on. But I did not get to see the end of the movie, because I was in the last stages of pregnancy."

Similar to other Christian missions, the Japanese Methodist church served as an employment service, helping Issei to gain jobs, recruiting them as dishwashers, windowwashers, waiters, cooks, or gardeners. Daily salaries were said to have ranged from $1.50 in 1900 to $2.00 in 1907 and $3.00 in 1915. Many were hired as "mission boys" (houseboys) to perform domestic duties for private families, enabling them to learn the English language and become more familiar with American customs.[6] Feeling both awe and embarrassment in his attempts to adapt to American ways, Mr. Chiho Tomita recounted in English his arrival in 1910:

> First time I come to the U.S., [I saw a] pretty town: house, buildings, streets all different from Japan, so I thought, "This is America." Houses higher [here]—in Japan, two-story building the highest, not high rises. In town lots of horses. Every street have a car, and first-class trains run through here. In Japan, no ride—just walk by feet. In Portland transported by *densha*—what-you-call "electric car." Just get tickets at ticket office. I don't know anything about train restaurants, so I bought one loaf bread about five cents. I do not know how to eat just one loaf of bread, so cut off with knife and put sugar on top and eat. *Hakujin* [Caucasian] just look around me it's funny. I don't think it's funny—I just eat.
>
> My friend took me to Epworth Methodist Church building on Portland heights, Fifteenth and Glisan.[7] I stayed there [for] twenty cents a night. Regular hotel twenty-five cents night so five cents cheaper. Church have kitchen in the basement so people pay so much for a meal. Lots of Japanese young men—eighteen, nineteen, twenty [years old], mostly young people. I try to get job. Some *hakujin* telephone the church to ask for mission boy to do inside housecleaning, dishwashing, help laundry, all kind of work. I would do any kind work to have chance make money.

Mr. Tomita was hired by Aaron Meier, who, with his son-in-law, Sigmund Frank, owned the Meier and Frank department store, then a single, five-story building located at Morrison and Fifth in Portland. Julius Meier, a brother and the store's president, served as governor of Oregon from 1931 to 1935. Working for this affluent family and being overseen by the stout and firm Mrs. Meier,[8] Mr. Tomita had some awkward moments, as he detailed in English:

> I went first time to the [Aaron] Meier family of Meier and Frank. Quite a family. Man and wife and three boys and one girl. Mr.

Meier rich man so they don't care about how to spend money. [They had] one cook, one waitress, one nurse for little baby, and me—four workers. They said Mrs. Frank is boss and tell me what to do. First mop the porch, then hang carpets on the line and knock off dirt. Big job, pretty heavy. Every room almost—living, dining room— have to be swept by hand. Dishwash after eat and bring dish, cup, everything when they're through eat. (In Japan most of the dish- washing my mother did. I don't do nothing—just eat, that's all.) I got twenty-five dollars a month. I worked about half a day, mostly start in the morning about seven o'clock and stop about twelve o'clock.

One day I used carpet sweeper pretty strong. I hit the table while I cleaning the carpet and I broke the flower vase. Waitress girl [maid] said to go to Mrs. Meier and [say] excuse me. I said no! They tried [to see] if I was honest or not. So they put in the pants pocket money—oh, five cents, ten cents, twenty-five cents, all kind of money—two to three dollar. While I pressing pants, I find it in pockets so I took it to Mrs. Meier. She said okay. She don't count any money. So everything okay.

In Portland and throughout the West Coast, the Japanese Methodist church fulfilled important roles in the practical, social, and spiritual lives of the Issei. As a center for inexpensive lodging, employment, socializing, and spiritual support, the church also helped Issei become familiar with American culture and language as they sought to adjust to life in their new surroundings.

10

Adjustments to American Life

ISSEI BROUGHT to this country their own cultural baggage from rural Japan. Young, naive Japanese women, most in their teens, approached life in America in a thoroughly Japanese fashion—from their attire to the foods they ate to their humble demeanors. Natives of a country insulated by its traditions and ethnic homogeneity, they were challenged not only by meeting those who looked so unlike them but also by the dramatic differences in language and culture. In the hierarchical Japanese society that emphasized "knowing one's place," they had been raised to accept their lower social positions. This meant deferring to superiors, elders, and males; recognizing strong paternal authority within the family; and suppressing their own desires in favor of the group.

The newcomers were distraught then to find that life on this side of the Pacific Ocean could be so startlingly unlike the rigid expectations and traditions to which they had become accustomed in Japan. Many, too, were transplanted from lives of relative leisure to oppressive physical labor in this foreign land. With little experience in either farmwork or in household chores, they were disappointed to find their "land of plenty" was actually the site of strenuous physical labor and dismal living conditions. Yet their Japanese upbringing motivated them to accept and endure, despite disillusionment.

Admittedly an innocent eighteen-year-old who had imagined she would be scooping money from the ground, Mrs. Itsu Akiyama initially admired her new homeland but quickly grew skeptical as she faced a lonely life in America:

> While we were traveling from Seattle to Portland on the train, I could see farm buildings with red roofs appearing between the

mountains. This was lovely to me! And I thought the Caucasian
girls were very pretty, because they were wearing dresses. At that
time—I don't know why—I wore *geta* [wooden clogs] with my
American clothes! (Our feet were broad, so American shoes were
uncomfortable.) I do remember that I walked behind my husband,
because that was the custom in Japan.

I did everything in the Japanese manner, because I did not know
American ways. Firing a wood stove was very difficult, and I was
scolded for having improperly cooked the rice. I remember I was
asked to make *tsukemono* [pickled vegetables]. In Japan Grandma
made the *tsukemono;* and, if she was not there, my mother made it.
My mother had worried about my cooking, but I thought that I
could at least make *tsukemono!* Once, though, I put in too much
salt, and I got scolded.

Life in Japan moved at a slower pace, and we observed all the
matsuri [festivals]. When we came over here, we had to work, work,
work! No time off for anniversaries and celebrations. I had no
friends, and I was always thinking of my parents—it was lonely. I
wanted very much to go back to Japan, but mother always said to
shinbo [persevere] over here. It was difficult but I did. I was young
and innocent and had no religious bent. I did not know much.

We came in a wagon from Portland to live with Papa's brother
and wife in Hood River. There was nothing but timber around, and
I wondered how far we were going to go. Finally we came to a small
house down Lover's Lane Road. I thought, "My goodness! Are we
going to be living in this small hut?" It only had planks for floors,
and there were no rugs. We had to get our water from a free-flowing
flume, and we cooked on a wood stove. There was no electricity—
just oil lanterns. At that time, there were three to four feet of snow
covering the ground. In Japan it only snowed by inches—over here
it snowed by the foot!"

Many Issei women, bitterly disappointed, still attempted to heed the
advice of their families to persevere in this new land. Certainly, at one
time or another, those would seem to be lofty goals. Confronted with the
primitive facilities of her American home, Mrs. Tei Endow found no need
for her fashionable, custom-made wardrobe and tried to keep her distraught feelings to herself:

I thought America would be a beautiful place, and my expectations were great! There were many others who had come with the
same anticipation and found it difficult to adjust—outside the valley, a lot of divorces resulted. I myself was so disappointed and bitter

that many times I cried myself to sleep. When I arrived, I was very lonesome. I had no farm experience, and I found it hard to weed the strawberry plants.

There were many inconveniences: We had no electricity and had to use kerosene lamps, which needed constant cleaning. We had no running water, so twice a day we bucketed our drinking water from a small well. Even in Japan we had the convenience of electricity and running water in our house! Our *o-benjo* [toilet] was outside. The only difference was that in America we sat on a bench—in Japan we had to squat. And our bathroom was just a big washtub in the kitchen. We heated hot water on a stove and poured it into a washtub. Husband took first bath, then we threw the water outside and refilled the tub. During the summer we used irrigation water. But in the winter, we placed the washtub or a bucket under the roof to catch the water that drained. We only took one bath each week. In between we washed ourselves with wet cloths. I was very disappointed to find how backward this section of America was.

I often asked my husband why he bought twenty acres of such hilly land. Endow told me he had disliked the hotel business in Salt Lake so much that he and a friend had decided to look for a more desirable area. When they arrived in Hood River, he had been enthralled with Mt. Adams. It resembled Mt. Fuji so much that he decided, "This is where I want to live." On clear days when he could view the mountain, he would comment on how impressive it was and how he felt he was sleeping at the foot of Mt. Fuji. He did not say anything about Mt. Hood!

Despite lofty expectations of America, Mrs. Miyoshi Noyori freely admitted her error as she recounted her first glimpse of America:

This was not what I had expected! I wondered why I had come! I had seen a picture of a pretty town in America with majestic mountains in the background. And when I arrived I saw lovely homes along the river and thought I would be living there. In reality, we traveled a narrow road with deep ruts that was surrounded by uncleared brushland. I had left a large home in Japan for a small, dark, two-room cabin! I thought, "Did I leave Japan to come to a place like this?" It was much worse than I could possibly have imagined!

In Japan we were accustomed to living among friends. Then to come to an area with few people! Very lonesome! My only company was one cat, although we had a lot of rats running around too. I could hear rats scampering around a storeroom in the back of our

house. Dreadful rats with eight-inch tails! "I'm scared, you know—
don't touch!" And I found rodent droppings all over! The first night
we slept on an old, sagging spring mattress held up on each corner
by apple boxes. When I first saw all those rodent droppings that
filled the seams of the mattress, I did not feel like sleeping! Then
the first time we served tea, we noticed a distinct odor. We guessed
there was a rat at the bottom of the well. So we spent half a day
cleaning the well, and, indeed, we found three rats!

I had goosebumps thinking how lucky we were that we did not
get ill. We had been drinking that water and taking baths in it! I
had no experience with this kind of work in the strawberries. After
being seasick and being detained in customs, I was not healthy. Yet,
I had made the decision on my own—not persuaded by my parents—to come to America. So, in my own mind, I was determined
to face the obstacles of living here. Also I found I was pregnant already. After resting one day, I went out in the field with my husband
and his father to hoe strawberries. I really did not have the strength,
but I was determined. In Japan the custom for young brides was to
help the family, so I presumed this was my lot in America.

Surprises were so numerous they became almost routine. Why did Japanese farmers wear simple work clothes when they worked in their fields
rather than the fashionable suits they had favored during their return trips
to Japan? And why did Americans wear shoes in their homes, when it
simply required more housecleaning? A number of regrettable discoveries
were made by Mrs. Asayo Noji as she settled into her home with its unfamiliar furnishings:

Mr. Barrow—a huge man—came after us on a horse and buggy.
When he said hello, I did not know what to say. Papa told me, "Just
say hello." So I obligingly replied, "Ha-ro." That was easy until he
also held out his big hands. Such a large man to shake hands with
little me—his handshake was big and strong! We rode his buggy
way into the woods down a lonesome, dirt road. The big timber on
both sides was so thick, it was almost dark! Mr. Barrow owned a
large home there, but he showed me a little "boyhouse" [camp-
house] that was my new home. It was a funny, unpainted wood
house with maybe two small windows. I had such a lonesome feeling, because I had never seen such a small house!

I felt like crying when I entered. Inside were a table, wood stove,
two or three chairs, and a bed in the partitioned bedroom. I had
never seen high tables and beds like that! In Japan we sat and slept
on the floor—we did not have chairs. I was afraid I would fall off the

In 1916, after traveling down a lonesome dirt road in Hood River, Asayo Noji encountered the smallest house she had ever seen. The "funny, unpainted wood house" and discomforts of her new life in America led her to conclude there was nothing she liked about America. (Courtesy of Asayo Noji)

bed! Even the stove and pots and pans were strange. There was no *furo* [bath] and the *o-benjo* was outside. Everything was so strange that, when I wrote home, I did not tell my family about the discomforts. I had never suffered anything, and I did not want them to cry over me. But there was nothing I liked about America—and I did not feel very well at all."

Mrs. Noji's inexperience in cooking, however, brought surprising revelations about her new husband:

I learned everything from Papa [her husband]. He taught me to cook, run the machines, and clean. I remember when Papa first made fried potatoes for breakfast. He cooked them with bacon, and they were just delicious with coffee and toast. But at that time, Hirasawa-san [Mr. Hirasawa] lived with us, so I was expected to prepare lunch for him each day while Papa was gone. This presented a problem, because I did not know how to cook! I wondered "What should I do?" Since the rice was already cooked, Papa suggested that I simply serve canned sardines with the rice. Cooking was such a problem for me that Papa usually ended up preparing most of the meals in those early days! You see, when I lived in Japan, I had not really cooked. Even then, the utensils here were unfamiliar. I worried a lot about making mistakes! Papa was very good at every-thing—he even showed me how to bake cakes and bread. But I really disliked cheese and butter! Papa liked to melt cheese in the oven, and I just could not stand that penetrating odor! Papa had also bought a Singer sewing machine and [dress] patterns to fit me. After he showed me how to operate the foot treadle, I sewed my own dresses. Papa was an enterprising person who always said, "There is not anything we cannot do."

Mrs. Hatsumi Nishimoto developed culinary skills too—also thanks to her husband: "My husband had quite a knowledge of Western food, be-cause he had helped a Caucasian family cook. He showed me how to bake biscuits and how to fry strips of meat for *okazu* [cooked meat and vege-tables]. I liked Western food, and I thought cooking in America was easy! But I missed Japan all the time. I missed my parents the most. I wrote to them in such a manner that they would not worry. I tried to avoid un-desirable subjects."

Others, like Mrs. Hama Yamaki, learned to be resourceful in their ef-forts to cook: "It was hard to adjust from Japanese to American customs. I learned to cook from my brother's wife, although she did not know too much herself! We learned together. When we made *o-sekihan* [steamed rice mixed with red beans], we had to ask Dr. Oyamada's wife for help. Our cooking was mostly *nihon-shoku* [Japanese cooking]. We enjoyed making sukiyaki [simmered meat and vegetables]."

By 1921 the Columbia River highway, looping from Portland to Hood River, had been paved, and the newly constructed Columbia Gorge Hotel stood on the rugged bluffs overlooking the Columbia River. Downtown the Butler Banking Company was celebrating twenty-one years of ser-vice, while league bowling at the local alley continued three nights a week, with Ladies' Night on Thursdays. J. C. Penney advertised apron check gingham for twelve cents a yard, and a Simmons bed could be pur-chased for $8.95 at E. H. Franz Company.[1] But for the newly arrived and once optimistic Mrs. Misuyo Nakamura, conditions in the town were un-fathomable. She found one word which aptly described it:

Kitanai [Filthy]! I thought Hood River town was filthy! Compared to the town I knew in Japan, buildings here appeared very old and dirty. Waste material, like cigarette butts and candy papers, were strewn on the concrete streets. There were lots of horses and buggies too. People tied their horses to a special post close to the Hackett's store.

I was sorely disappointed that we did not have a house of our own. Then we found an abandoned pool hall close to the railroad.

In back of the pool hall was a tiny, vacant bedroom with only a heating stove and sink. My impression of living in a place like this? "Gee, do I have to live and eat and sleep in this hovel?" Everything was so filthy! Because this room had only a heating stove with a chimney—much different from a cooking stove—I had to build a large fire. But the pot belly stove stood so tall that the top surface did not warm very easily. Even then, I was expected to cook rice on it. And I was inexperienced in cooking. Again I wondered why I had come to America!

Most of the Issei believed they would live in the United States for only a few years before returning to their birthplaces. Earning the necessary money, however, meant forgoing simple pleasures in their already frugal life-styles. Mrs. Hisa Wakamatsu had ambiguous feelings about some of these sacrifices: "I hoped that, within three to four years, I would be able to return to Japan. Papa would tell me, 'If you eat *funyu* [fermented bean cake], you will not be able to return.' I thought the story was told in jest, because we both liked *funyu*. In fact, I may have eaten more than he did! But *funyu* was so expensive that if we kept eating it, Papa told me all our money would go for *funyu* instead of for our trip to Japan."

A tradition savored by many Japanese in their new land was drinking sake, a beverage of fermented rice with 14 percent alcoholic content. Japanese usually consumed warm sake in tiny cups and followed special courtesies. The host's duty was to keep libations flowing freely, refilling guests' cups and maintaining lively conversation. Each guest then was careful to reciprocate by refilling the host's cup as well. Games and rituals often added to the merriment and pace of drinking, while petty misdeeds were excused if committed when one was intoxicated. This lively practice, however, caused some consternation for Mrs. Hisa Wakamatsu:

Papa dearly loved to drink—he just had to have his sake—and insisted that his guests drink with him. Making sake was not easy, because I was expected to make it throughout the year—summer and winter. I did not like making so much, so I told Papa, "I will not make any more." Then, in jest, I suppose, he said, "If you cannot make sake, you should leave me. I will just make it myself." I had no place to go, so I had to remain and make sake to appease Papa.

We made sake from *koji* [yeast] and rice. Into two fifty-gallon drums we poured a sack and a half of rice, or three one-hundred-pound sacks altogether. After I put *koji* in, we steamed this on the stove. Then the mixture was put into a barrel to be strained and pressed about a month later. But *o-jiisan* [husband's father], who was also hooked on sake, could not wait. He dipped a bowl into the batter and drank it directly. And if it was not suitable, he threw it back into the mixture. Quite often when he did that, the sake turned sour; and we had to dump it in the field. Such a terrible waste! After the sake mixture had been pressed and cleared, we poured it into gallon jugs. Each one hundred pounds produced fourteen or fifteen gallons. Lined up in the basement, the wine became clear—a lovely sight. But *o-jiisan* dipped a chopstick into the sake and gave a taste to my three-year old son. I objected, so he did not do this in front of me. But, he told me, "If a son does not drink sake, he will not become a man."

Issei were bitterly disappointed with their miserable and lonely lives in America. Not only were the customs and language different from Japan's, but their dreams of grandeur and wealth had been squelched. The rustic homes and squalid living conditions were stark contrasts to the high expectations they had brought to the West Coast. Each day brought new frustrations, challenges, and adjustments.

PART FOUR

Labor

Katsukatsu mo
Iwa ni ne wo hari
Kusabana no
Tamotsu inochi ni
Furete omouyu

How touched I am
By wildflowers.
They put down roots
Even in bare rock
And so sustain their tiny existence.

Tanka written by Mrs. Shizue Iwatsuki and
translated by Dr. Stephen W. Kohl

11

Railroads, Stumps, and Sawmills

AT THE TURN of the century, the Pacific Northwest's development of railroads, logging and lumbering, fishing, and agriculture brought opportunities that began to match the dreams of venturesome Japanese. The Chinese Exclusion Act of 1882 had curtailed the West Coast supply of Chinese laborers, who, since their arrival in the mid-nineteenth century, had incurred complaints about cheap labor and racial impurity.[1] By 1897, when the Alaska gold rush drained the Northwest of laborers, the transcontinental railroads began to solicit Japanese workers as an inexpensive labor force.[2] As a result, the number of Issei in the United States increased from 2,039 in 1890 to 24,326 in 1900 and 72,157 by 1910. During those years, approximately three-fifths of the Japanese resided in California, and one-fifth lived in Washington, because of the port cities of San Francisco and Seattle. In Oregon, the numbers grew from 25 in 1890 to 2,501 in 1900 and 3,418 by 1910, or less than 5 percent of the Japanese population in the United States.[3]

Industrious, accustomed to working long hours, trained to be disciplined, and willing to work under severe conditions, Issei tended to perform less desirable work at wages that, according to a report of the Immigration Commission, were lower than those paid other workers. The historian H. A. Millis reported that before 1911 while many Japanese laborers worked for $1.50, $1.60, and $1.75 a day, others earned $1.75, $2.00, and $2.25 for the same work.[4] For Issei, however, those wages were almost double the meager salaries they might have earned in Japan. In 1902, for example, carpenters and roofers in Japan earned 65 sen (less than 33 cents) while unskilled workers received 35 sen. Yet at that time, Japanese workers in the United States could earn 80 cents to one dollar per day. So, despite the harsh reality of daily and intense physical labor, they accepted the lower wages.[5] Living in poverty, they saved their humble earnings with the steadfast belief that, as sojourners in America, their hard work would be rewarded when they returned to Japan.

Typical of those who immediately discarded any carefree notions of life after arriving in the United States was Mrs. Hatsumi Nishimoto: "As a young woman, my desire had been to come to America. Those who had returned to Japan after working in America seemed to have plenty of money. We really had the impression that in America money was freely available. I soon discovered that life here was not that easy—in fact, it was very difficult. 'Too hard work!' Never in America have I picked up a penny from the ground!" Stories had circulated in Japan that money was so abundant one could scoop it from the ground. After arriving, however, Issei immediately discovered the harsh realities of this new land.

Railroads

Young, ambitious Japanese bachelors worked as railroad section hands beginning in 1891. Traveling with crews to build and maintain railroads across the West, they became acquainted with stretches of rural America. By 1892, about four hundred Issei worked on the section of the Union Pacific Railroad from Huntington, Oregon, to Granger, Wyoming.[6] Probably the first railroad in the country to hire a large number of Japanese was the Oregon Short Line, which linked transcontinental lines at Baker, Oregon, for transporting eastern Oregon's rich timber and ore.[7]

Japanese railroad contractors, who recruited Japanese laborers and negotiated wages and working conditions, became important intermediaries between Japanese and the railroad companies. After Issei were hired, labor contractors generally collected fees of one dollar per month as well as a given amount per day or a percentage of the earnings. Often they were also able to supply Japanese goods at a profit.[8] In Portland, Oregon, Shinzaburo Ban provided this service for railroad officials. A former diplomatic official in Tokyo and secretary at the Japanese consulate in Hawaii, he arrived in Portland around 1891 and began hiring Japanese laborers for the Oregon Railroad. Eventually, Ban distributed railroad hands in Oregon, Washington, Montana, Wyoming, North Dakota, Nebraska, and Colorado. As business flourished, he gradually established numerous businesses in Portland, including a mercantile shop, shingle mills, and small businesses catering to Japanese. Selling Japanese goods to laborers and gaining a commission of five to ten cents a day from them,[9] Ban became the most financially prominent Japanese in the state by 1900.[10] Through his contract work, Portland became the leading site in the Pacific Northwest for distributing Japanese railroad workers.[11]

Life for those railroad workers, however, was oppressive, with men working eleven- to fourteen-hour days and frequently almost starving themselves in efforts to increase their savings. From monthly salaries of forty dollars, a fee of four to seven dollars was deducted for meals. The men ate tasteless, nonnutritious meals barely capable of sustaining them. Breakfast might have included seaweed, miso (soybean paste) soup, and rice. Lunch eaten on the worksite consisted of coffee, rice, a tiny bit of sausage or cheese, and bread without butter or jam. The evening fare was frequently dried radish with rice.[12] Destitute as they were, a stray jackrabbit was considered a feast, and a cow killed by a passing train became a "heaven-sent banquet," according to Minoru Yasui.[13] Malnourished workers, in anticipation, were known to have arranged for the untimely presence of a hapless cow on the tracks. Since the railroad accepted responsibility for disposing of the carcass for unfortunate owners, section hands obediently buried it—only to retrieve the valued supply of fresh meat later that evening.[14] The men usually lived in cooperative groups called gangs and slept in boxcars set on the sidetrack. Easy victims of disease and accidents, however, several thousand may have died on the rough frontier.[15]

Japanese section hands earned about a dollar a day[16] and showed a willingness to work for lower wages than Italians, Greeks, and Slavs, although they were paid five cents more per day than their Chinese predecessors.[17] A 1911 report of the Immigration Commission recognized their stature as workers: "They learn more quickly than any other race now employed; they are sober, tractable, and industrious."[18] By 1905, 26 percent of the Oregon Issei were employed by the railroad,[19] and in 1906, approximately thirteen thousand, or one-third of all Issei in the United States, were railroad laborers.[20]

Among those employed by 1918 was Mrs. Hatsumi Nishimoto. A lone woman among fifteen railroad workers, she described her experience as a cook at an eastern Oregon railroad repair station:

> From Portland I accompanied my husband in 1918 to Huntington, Oregon, a hot, dry town just this side of the Idaho border. My husband was recruited to work at a railroad repair station called a roundhouse, and I was hired as the cook. Before I came, the fifteen Japanese workers had been sharing cooking responsibilities, with one man each day quitting work early to prepare the meals. My ingredients were generally dried foods from Japan, because, without irrigation, they were unable to raise vegetables here. I prepared mostly *nihon-shoku* [Japanese food] in a big pot heated by a wood fire. Breakfast was at 6:00 A.M. so I woke at 4:00 to make pancakes.

I poured batter directly on top of the greased, wrought iron stove and had to watch the pancakes all the time so they would cook to a golden brown. For lunch at noon I cooked rice, daikon [white radish], and gobo [burdock root]. I prepared rice and Japanese dried food for dinner at 6:00 P.M., and each man was entitled to one helping. After a few complaints about the lack of vegetables, I planted lettuce and served the thinned shoots with shoyu [soy sauce] and rice. I received fifty-five dollars a month, considered good money in 1918. Some of it I sent home to Japan, and some I mailed to the Sumitomo Bank branch in San Francisco. When I was not cooking, I retired to my room. Our house—much like a cave covered with earth—looked like an Indian dwelling. Huntington was such a hot area that this was the only way to keep comfortable. The one window was so tiny we had to turn our lights on during the day.

We lived in Huntington for four months, and the men worked in the roundhouse cleaning the coal-burning locomotives. It was such a hot, dirty job that they were paid well. Their biggest complaint was the dirt! With soot covering their faces, they looked just like black men! At the end of the day, they followed the Japanese custom of washing themselves first and then immersing themselves in a large barrel of hot water. Most of the men were elderly, about forty years old or more. All had left their wives and children in Japan to come to the United States. They were working so hard to save money that they wore their pencils down to one-inch stubs! I noticed that when they did not have enough money to send to Japan, they frequently borrowed among themselves. Their only luxury was whiskey, for they did enjoy drinking.

This life was truly difficult for me. Having just come from Japan, I was very lonesome. And at night, kowai [frightful]! Our camp was located at the foot of a hill, and I still remember how coyotes howled from above! Many times I pleaded with my husband, "Kaeru, kaeru" [I want to return to Japan]. But he told me we should persevere.

In 1920, teenager Masaji Kusachi joined a railroad gang near Carson, Washington. For one and a half months, his home was a boxcar camped in the mountainous Columbia gorge:

A man named Matoba, the head of the section gang for SPS [Seattle Portland Spokane] line, offered special wages of fifty cents an hour. And, if you worked all day, you could get credit for ten hours instead of eight, which is five dollars a day! This was a very good wage, so Father and I went to work. I was not given any hard, physical labor because I was only seventeen years old. Gang members, though, had a difficult job replacing steel rails. It required skill to drive the steel spikes in such a way that they were flush against the rails. The hardest work was to force the old spikes out of the ground using long levers. When workers knew a train was coming, they had to replace the rails in a hurry, for the train could not afford to wait.

Most of my time was spent furnishing coffee to the thirty Japanese men. I thought, "This is pretty good to be paid for such easy work!" I made the coffee in a b-i-g pot! This was my first time drinking coffee and my first time making it. My biggest problem was getting clean water to make the coffee. Close to Carson we had a water tank car, but when we worked farther away, I found that the river water was dirty. And the coffee grounds had a tendency to float, so my boss told me to pour cold water on top of the coffee so the grounds would settle. This was a good technique!

While we worked for the railroad, we were given lodging in railroad cars on the sidetrack. You have seen freight cars with windows in them? This is where we used to live. There could have been almost ten men sleeping per car. All these cars were furnished with beds, and it was nice and warm inside. There must have been at least five or six cars. Among them were a dining car, a cooking car, and a water tank car. The meals cost us each fifteen to seventeen dollars a month and were very good. In the morning we ate *miso-shiru* [soybean paste soup]. Some days we had *dango-jiru*, soup with dumplings. It was kind of salty and not very tasty. We had to eat it, though, because we got hungry! There was no recreation and, in this camp, gambling was not permitted. I do not remember doing anything. Oh, yeah, I was tired at the end of the day. I worked for the railroad for a month and a half. This was probably in the spring of 1920, for there were red flowers in bloom.

Early Hood River Settlement

With salmon-filled rivers, hillsides covered with salmonberries and huckleberries, and forests inhabited by deer, elk, and bear, the Hood River Valley at one time amply supplied the needs of a group of about six hundred Indians. Members of the Lewis and Clark expedition had noted the tiny valley and its Indian village in 1805, and fur trappers and traders for the Hudson's Bay Company followed. In the 1840s, early pioneer settlers had originally called the stream "Dog River" because they were

Hood River Valley, nestled between towering Mt. Hood and the waters of the
Columbia River, attracted farming and lumbering ventures in the late 1800s and
early 1900s. (Courtesy of Hood River Museum)

driven to add dog meat to their meager stew pots. In 1851, the first permanent settler, Nathaniel Coe, also planted the valley's first fruit trees.
Later settlers befriended the local Waucoma Indians, who worked on
their farms and traded deer and fowl for their goods. While small lumber
operations and cattle and hog farms became profitable by the 1870s, settlers also began to experiment with different varieties of apples, peaches,
strawberries, prunes, and other fruits. By the early 1900s, through trial-
and-error methods in selecting and raising apples, farmers began to increase acreage and specialize in varieties that would gain them national
recognition at horticultural fairs.[21]

Young Issei men, mostly bachelors in their late teens, first arrived in
Hood River around 1902, employed by the Mt. Hood Railroad on labor
gangs. Their task had been to lay a spur line from the town of Hood River
to the small settlement of Parkdale about seventeen miles south. The railroad line, completed in 1906 by the Oregon Lumber Company, eliminated the previous practice of driving logs down the stream to the
railhead in Hood River and coincided with the company's move outside
the town. In addition, it provided reliable transportation not only for passengers but also for fruit shipments from the area's developing apple industry. Railroad labor, though not steady, continued for about ten years.[22]

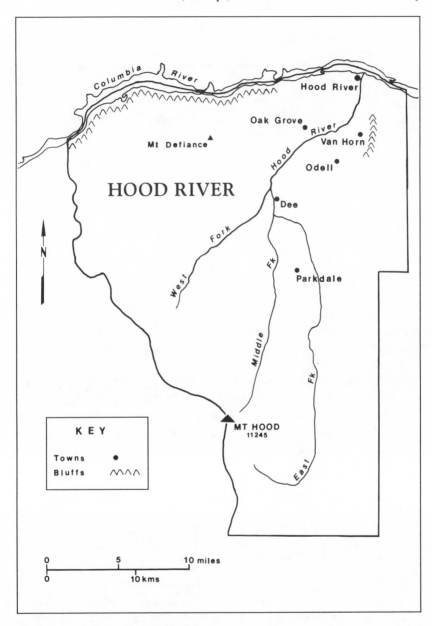

Issei lived south of the town of Hood River in farming communities that included Parkdale, Dee, Odell, and Oak Grove. (Map by Bob Adams)

Clearing Land

In addition to their labor on the railroads, Issei were sought as an inexpensive labor force to clear the heavy stands of fir and pine for private landowners.[23] By around 1905 as many as six hundred Issei were employed felling trees and dynamiting stumps,[24] earning one dollar for a ten- to fifteen-hour day.[25] Most men worked under contract in groups of twenty to twenty-five. Stories were told of dynamite explosions so frequent that they resembled cannonade during war.[26]

Danger was an accepted part of the job, Mr. Chiho Tomita explained in English:

> When harvest over, you find some other job, like clearing land. I worked with other people about ten hours a day. Cut down big pine and fir timber and put dynamite under the root and explode. Pretty dangerous. I don't worry about the danger. One man was clearing land, and, after a long time, no explode. So he liked to go see why not explode and he died. Now when no explode, we wait until next morning to be safe. Then pull tree trunks up with horse. Pile them up, let them dry through the summer. Then light big timber, cut ten to fifteen feet apart, and burn them up. At that time, lots of wood all over.[27]

Japanese soon began clearing their own property as they acquired inexpensive logged-off land from the lumber company. In 1920, after accumulating five hundred dollars, the Noyori family purchased 18.5 acres of stumpland from the Oregon Lumber Company. Husband and wife worked side by side in this physically demanding work. "We had such large stumps," Mrs. Miyoshi Noyori recounted, "it took three men to encircle one with their arms! We cleared just two acres, because the only tools we had were a mattock [digging tool with blade set at right angles] and a pee-pee [peavey, a long-handled leverage tool with a hook on one end]."

After cutting and burning the surrounding brush and removing the small stumps and roots, they piled and burned the debris. Then they inserted dynamite to blow the stumps apart, as Mrs. Noyori further explained:

> For those big stumps, we had to place as many as fifteen sticks in three different holes—or forty-five sticks altogether. We hooked the dynamite to a device; and when we pushed a lever, there was a big explosion! Pieces of stump and dirt rose and created a huge cavity in the ground as large as my living room. Dirt covered everything, so my job was to clean the ground before we set off the charges.

Clean-up work after dynamiting was a big job, too, because the stump broke into at least three pieces. We burned them, but they would not burn by themselves, so we threw on other wood to make a big fire. This clean-up work was a big job! It took as many as two days to take care of one big stump. After it completely burned, you had to fill the big hole. That was exhausting work, and we worked very hard.

The Noyoris eventually acquired a stump puller. Steel cable wound on a large drum was attached to the stump. When rotated by horses hitched to a connecting beam, the cable twisted the drum, pulling the stump upward: "The horse went around a reel, then it became my job to pull the large one-inch cables and carry the big hook that wrapped around the next stump. This deformed my hand, as I can show you now. When I returned to Japan, others told me, 'You do not have to explain life in America, for we can tell from the appearance of your hands.' "

Sawmill Labor

The expanding northwest lumber industry attracted large numbers of Japanese, who found the work more stable than railroad labor. As railroad section hands, not only had Issei suffered from the physically demanding work and rough frontier living conditions but several thousand had become casualties of disease and accidents.[28] Working for lumber companies and sawmills, however, Japanese began to face more racial hostility as they came into increased competition with white workers. Because of opposition from Caucasian employees, many mills refused to hire Japanese. Yet, as the logging industry prospered, demands for labor and the shortage of workers brought continual need for the cheap labor provided by the industrious and adaptable Japanese.[29] In 1909, as many as twenty-five hundred, or 4 percent, of the mill workers in Washington and Oregon were Japanese.[30]

South of the town of Hood River, in a flat area on the river's middle fork, the Oregon Lumber Company began a sawmill operation in 1906, close to its timber source. Here, where the small settlement of Dee had its roots, Japanese hired on as mill workers.[31]

First employed at the Dee Sawmill in 1918, Mr. Miyozo Yumibe found he was well-suited to the work:

My first job was taking slab wood off the chains. Slab wood or edging was the first piece cut from the log before regular boards were cut. Moving chains transported the slab wood to our area, and we loaded it onto a freight car. Locomotives could burn this wood for fuel. Later I was given an inside job sorting different grades and lengths of lumber. We diverted slab wood to one side and the good quality lumber to an edge saw which cut it to certain lengths. My job could probably be described as monitoring the uneven flow of moving lumber and slab wood [running discharge chains]. If too much or too little lumber moved down, I would slow down or speed up the chain equipment. At first I moved the boards using a stick with a hook on one end. Gradually the equipment improved to the point that I could control the flow of wood simply by pushing buttons. Oh, yes, I liked my job! At that time the inside jobs were held by about twenty Japanese. I worked seven days a week—on Sunday I worked as a fireman, cleaning up the boiler room. Before war I was paid sixteen cents an hour. During those depression years, farmworkers were earning only twelve cents an hour.

In the depths of the Great Depression, Mr. Masaji Kusachi's temporary green-chain work helped to sustain his family:

After the logs had been cut up, I pulled cut lumber off the chain according to different dimensions. Working on the green-chain was considered heavy work. But once you got used to it, you developed a certain knack so you were not always fighting the lumber. Instead of pulling it, you moved the lumber with you. That was a trick of the trade. Handling railroad ties was one of the more dangerous jobs I had. If you did not move the two-foot by twelve-foot beams just right, they could drop and crush your feet. I earned thirty-five cents an hour, and I worked six to eight hours a day. The Oregon Lumber Company was largely supported by Mormon church people, so we were treated very well.[32] In this mill there were mostly Japanese workers and a few Chinese and Italians.

Millworkers unionized in 1938—without the support of Japanese laborers, however. In 1933, under President Franklin Roosevelt, Congress had set up the National Industrial Recovery Act (NIRA), which, among its provisions, guaranteed workers the right to organize and bargain collectively. Though the NIRA was declared unconstitutional two years later, the National Labor Relations Act of 1935 also guaranteed the right to organize and bargain collectively. Japanese mill workers, desperate to increase their earnings yet raised in Japan to respect authority, continued working while their coworkers picketed. Mr. Miyoso Yumibe said:

When I joined the union, I received forty cents an hour. President Roosevelt had administered the NRA, [National Recovery Administration] to help the nation recover from the depression. I remember that when the union people first came to the mill, our labor force was divided. Most of the Caucasians went on strike, but all the Japanese and several *hakujin* [Caucasians] in favored positions kept working. Why? The biggest reason was that Japanese wanted to be secure in their jobs, and so it was necessary to keep working. If we had gone on strike, we might have been fired. Pickets stood on the Y-junction of the road, but those of us who lived in the sawmill camp did not have to face them. When the situation was finally settled, the Oregon Lumber Company agreed to accept the union, and everybody joined. "No join union—no job." We had meetings every week and were required to show passcards before being admitted. After that we received time-and-a-half pay for overtime and double-time on Sundays. I worked eight hours a day Monday through Saturday and six hours on most Sundays.

Sawmill Camp

While employed at the Dee Sawmill, Japanese laborers lived in a "camptown" in a clearing along the river's east fork and close to the mill. On the river's east bank stood the Dee Hotel, boardinghouse, post office, store, tavern, and box factory. Scattered along the flats on the west side were two long buildings, each divided into four housing units, and approximately twelve small homes. Connected by a boardwalk, they were constructed simply with shiplap siding and shingle roofs. Each unit was spare, composed of a tiny living room, kitchen, and bedroom and heated by a black wrought iron kitchen stove.[33] Among the Caucasian laborers in the camp resided three or four Japanese workers and their families, including Mr. Miyozo Yumibe, who described their life:

> American single men working at the sawmill lived in a Dee boardinghouse and hotel. All the Japanese men wanted to save money to return to Japan, so we lived in the sawmill camp. We spent money only for food and clothes—nothing frivolous. Life in the camp was pretty good, because there were many young people. I lived alone in a twelve- by twelve-foot room with just a bed and a small tin stove inside. My room was free, but the house was not well-constructed. It was very cold in the winter so I had to use the stove. We had a mess hall and an outside privy closeby. A cook prepared our meals, and I paid a fee each month.

One might not expect lilting strains of violin music in a sawmill camp. Yet, while working at the Wauna Sawmill near Astoria, Mr. Masaji

Kusachi learned to play the violin. The violin strains created a charm that contrasted sharply with the camp conditions he found so offensive:

> That camp was dirty! The rainy season extended over half a year—so "no sunshine but lots of mud." There must have been forty to fifty Japanese men living there, mostly two to a room. Living conditions were poor. The only good thing about our cabins was that they did not leak rain, although wind blew through the cracks. Our privy was just a hole with a bench long enough so four or five could go to the bathroom at the same time. As I think about it now, it was not a place fit for a human to live! And yet, we were all young and had a great time there, not inconvenienced by our lack of English.
>
> I had a Japanese friend who played the violin, so I learned, too, just to kill time. While a group of young men gambled—I guess they played poker—three of us played the violin. At first we practiced in our own rooms, because we got nothing but squeaks! Then we played *hakone no yama* [Japanese children's songs] together. We played by ear and had a good time. On Sundays in the summer we often played baseball with a Japanese crew from Westport Sawmill, so I did not have much time to play the violin.

Issei found that Oregon—and the Hood River Valley—offered multiple opportunities to earn wages. In 1910, the 468 valley Issei constituted almost 14 percent of the Japanese in Oregon and 5.84 percent of the Hood River population, the highest it would achieve.[34]

12

Early Farm Labor

AFTER COMPLETING CONTRACTS with the railroad, many Japanese, enchanted by the valley's beauty and similarity to the Japanese countryside, decided to remain as farm laborers in Hood River. Most Issei had farming experience and a healthy respect for the skills needed to bring sustenance from the soil, for in Japan farmers were more esteemed than those in trade or industry. In rural areas, too, Issei found better pay and more promising job prospects than in the cities. They appreciated work that did not require technical skills and initial cash investments. As unmarried men, they were also willing to conform to seasonal demands of agricultural work and often lived and worked together in labor gangs.[1]

In the small town of Hood River, local Japanese congregated at the Niguma Variety Store on the northeast corner of First and Oak streets. Founded in 1905, the establishment eventually added a boardinghouse and served as mail drop, Japanese social center, and brothel. Three years later, the only Japanese goods store in the valley was purchased by Renichi Fujimoto and his brother Masuo Yasui.[2] The Yasui Brothers' Store, which advertised "Japanese goods from the flowery kingdom," featured both Eastern and Western stock: kimonos, Oriental fans, soy sauce, and Japanese vegetables as well as overalls, cast-iron pans, pocket watches, toys, and hard candy.[3]

Co-proprieter Yasui, who had immigrated to the United States in 1902 at the age of sixteen, had first worked as a cook on a railroad gang and then as "houseboy" for a family in Portland. There he had also studied Christianity at the Methodist church and English at Couch School night classes.[4] Yasui's facility with the English language enabled him, through his store, to act as liaison between Caucasian orchardists and Japanese

In 1890 Hood River's Oak Street included several stores and the Mt. Hood Hotel. The community was served by the Oregon Railroad and by Columbia River steamers. (Courtesy of Hood River Museum)

workers.[5] Among the eager workers was Mr. Chiho Tomita, who also found his five years of English classes indispensable, as his own words in English revealed:

In 1908 Mr. Yasui tell me, "Why don't you go to Hood River [to] pick apples?" I thought, "Yes, I'd like to go." Mr. Yasui and his brother, Renichi Fujimoto, owned a store in Hood River. They had grocery store downstairs and upstairs hotel, so I stay there. When start picking apples, *hakujin* [Caucasians] come to Yasui Store and say, "I like two to three boys to work." Mr. Yasui ask everybody, "Man said he like to have two to three boys. You like to go?" Yes, I go. I go! Everybody go. Better than do nothing and stay home. The main thing is I make more money.

First time I went to Mr. Porter's place in Pine Grove. They had forty kinds of apples—just same dark color. Pretty hard to remember, you know. Some pickers all mixed up other apples. Oh, Mr. Porter said he pretty mad. I had five years of English in high school, so Mr. Porter tell me I watch for pickers and tell them, "This kind different, same color but different apple." [There were] three, four kinds of yellow apples—pretty hard to tell. I like job. I paid three dollars for a ten-hour day. Boys who picked earned same amount of money—paid by the day, not the box.

Chiho Tomita (*at top of left ladder*) and other young Japanese worked as fruit laborers for Caucasian orchardists in 1911. The Issei men shared a single dwelling,
slept on straw strewn on the floor, and cooked Japanese meals together. (Courtesy
of Polly Timberman, *Hood River News*)

Everybody stay in one house. No bed—just straw on the floor
and then put on a blanket and sleep. Each other [everyone] cooked.
In the morning, *miso-shiru* [bean paste soup]. For lunch just *gohan*
[rice], *tsukemono* [pickled vegetables], and some vegetables with
chopped meat, like sukiyaki. Some don't know how to cook and
cook rice all black—strong fire. They tried to pay so much for a
friend to cook. They tried to get me to cook, but I just refused.

While apples and pears were common in the valley, a mile upstream of
Hood River along the waters of the Columbia, a twenty-acre truck farm
flourished. Since 1894, Koberg family peaches, asparagus, and tomatoes
had made a name for themselves in Portland. After a dike was built in
1907 to protect the farmland, the Kobergs extended their river frontage
to create a public recreation site. Koberg Beach, with its large stone and
concrete pavilion, became a popular place for dances, picnics, water
carnivals, baseball games, and other recreational events.[6] In 1917, Mr.
Miyozo Yumibe obtained his first job on the Koberg farm:

I worked for the Kobergs, weeding asparagus and tomatoes at their truck farm along the Columbia River. I was considered pretty small then, but I was able to do the work. I earned maybe twenty-five cents an hour. That was all right because hoeing was not difficult. I worked ten hours a day from 7:00 A.M. to 6:00 P.M., with a one-hour lunch break. We worked six days a week. (I don't remember what I did on Sunday—maybe I did some laundry.) It was enjoyable working with others. I lived in a cabin on the Koberg place and ate meals with the Norimatsus. Koberg Beach nearby had a fine swimming facility and a large dancing pavilion—but lots of mosquitoes.

Another Issei, welcomed in 1921 by a pair of hightop work shoes and a river flood, soon realized that money would always be the priority. On her first job in the valley, Mrs. Misuyo Nakamura cut asparagus and planted tomatoes on a Japanese truck farm close to the river:

Just to walk to work was a frightening experience! Papa and I walked on railroad ties, then crossed the river on a railroad bridge. If you looked through the ties, you could see the water below! My husband hung onto my arm, and we walked together on the tracks. I wore a pair of hightop shoes with slightly higher heels, which Papa purchased for me. I had to lace the holes, you know, and it was quite an effort to get them on each morning. (I cannot understand why my husband bought them for me, because everyone else wore short shoes. I was embarrassed to wear them, but I kept my feelings to myself.)

On June 6 a dike gave way, and the Hood River flooded.[7] That morning when we were cutting asparagus, Munemoto-san's (Mr. Munemoto's] father yelled to us that we should evacuate immediately. By then we had moved into a tent with lumber floor on Munemoto-san's land. We hurried into our tent to gather our belongings, but all we were able to get were some cooking utensils and food. The water rose too quickly! We ran up to the road, which was slightly higher than the farm, but it too flooded. Both the tent and Munemoto-san's house were located above water level, so we rowed a boat back and forth. That night we slept in the hay in Mr. Butler's barn, located on higher ground.

Working next for Oana-san, I helped to hoe the strawberry plants—a big operation, because there were nineteen acres! I worked ten hours a day, from 7:00 A.M. to 6:00 P.M. Of course, that was exhausting—by the end of the day, I was simply putting in my hours. About that time, I was also in my early pregnancy, so I occasionally had *tsuwari* [morning sickness]. I vomited, but since I could not eat, all that came up was water. When I rested, Papa admonished me, "At least work enough to provide food for yourself." Because he ordered me, I felt compelled to do so, although it became a strain. Today I would probably reply, "I won't do it." Men were paid twenty-five cents an hour and women were paid twenty cents. I do not know why there was a difference in pay, but that was considered normal. Even though we women hoed the rows at the same pace, we still received five cents less.

For Mrs. Hatsumi Nishimoto, who originally believed that farmwork was behind her when she left Japan, the unfamiliar field labor in Hood River seemed even more difficult:

Because I did not have children at that time, we helped other Japanese farmers. Our consuming interest was to work hard, earn a lot of money, and return to Japan as soon as possible. For three weeks, my husband and I picked tomatoes at the Nakamotos', and I cannot forget how tiring that work was! We had to stoop to pick the tomatoes and place them in a small basket. Once the basket was full, we were quickly given another one. Compared with rice harvest in Japan, this was more difficult, because it was new to me. When we hoed strawberries and my husband had finished his row, I would be only halfway down my own row. By the time I finished, I was so exhausted, I would wonder, "Does making a living on an American farm have to be this hard?" And even though I was working as hard as I could, my husband would often scold me for working so slowly.

After a full day's work, I could not relax in a washtub placed outside! So, every Saturday, I walked the mile and a half into town to use Morita-san's Japanese bath.[8] Since I did not think it appropriate to wear regular clothing, I wore high-heeled shoes laced six inches above my ankles! Taking a shortcut through the field, though, I frequently stumbled. When I finally reached the bathhouse, I cleansed myself outside the tub, as we did in Japan, then relaxed in the hot water. This cost maybe twenty cents.

Next we worked at the Tamiyasus' apple orchard in Oak Grove and lived in their house with about ten other workers. People slept everywhere—someone even slept in the bathroom! With only a wood stove in the downstairs living room, my husband and I were very cold in our small bedroom upstairs. I remember one couple resorted to sleeping *under* their mattress. Finding it too heavy, they solved their problem by hanging the four corners of the mattress from the ceiling. This was typical of how Issei coped with difficult times! One family also produced sake at a nearby farm. When the men drank, their moods become jovial, and they danced merrily with each other.

Over a period of seven years beginning in 1918, Mrs. Nishimoto and her husband labored on five separate farms and, for another five years, leased one hundred acres: "The distasteful part of this life was having to move from place to place. In Japan one almost never moved. But, while we disliked moving, it was really quite simple because we had no furniture. Our chairs were just wooden apple boxes. I remember one cabin had large cracks in the walls. By early morning, the fire in our wood stove had died, and we were so cold in bed that the vapor from our mouths froze on the blanket."

Gradually, as Issei gained experience with farming, they, like the Nishimotos, progressed from migrant labor to renting and leasing their own farms. As in other locales, including the Santa Clara Valley in California,[9] rents charged to Issei were often higher than those for Caucasians. Whereas Hood River rents had previously been $4 to $15 per acre, Issei paid $6 to $40. This was reportedly because of concern about their credit, but landowners were also aware that the anxious Issei would pay higher rents.[10]

Packing Fruit

Until the 1930s, growers commonly set up packing sheds on their property and packed their own fruit in storage boxes.[11] For Mr. Masaji Kusachi, his second day in Hood River introduced him to the delights of Hood River apples: "Those Spitzenbergs were certainly tasty! I had never seen an apple before, and I do remember eating lots of apples! My job was to stack boxes of cull fruit after the apples had come down the conveyer belt. I was so busy taking care of culls that I could only take a bite of my apple now and then! I really enjoyed working in the packing house."

After Mr. Miyozo Yumibe's father contracted to pack an orchardist's fruit, his family and friends cooperated with assembly-line teamwork:

Farmers had their own packing sheds and equipment, so all we had to do was furnish our own bodies. For about two months five of us sorted, graded, and packed Spitzenberg and Newtown apples. I dumped the apples onto the grader. The grader was a long slanted table with moving belts which divided the fruit by size into "fancy" or "extra fancy" grades. Then two people sorted out the culls. My father packed the fruit by wrapping each apple in tissue before placing it in a wooden box. He was the only packer; so when I had time, I helped him. I did what I thought was necessary. My job at the end of the line was to nail the covers on the wooden boxes and stamp them each with the grower number and the grade of fruit. Then Mr. Copperly loaded the fruit boxes on his wagon and delivered them to the Apple Growers' Association (AGA) distribution point in Dee. Pretty cheap pay—twenty-five cents an hour.

By 1915, many Hood River Issei received higher pay than those in other locations, reportedly $2.00 per day for ordinary work, compared with $1.10 to $1.50 per day paid to others.[12] This was probably lower, however, than wages in California, where the scarce prune harvesters in Santa Clara commanded $2.00 per day in 1910, wages higher than those paid to Caucasians.[13] By 1920, a Hood River newspaper reported average Issei wages of $3.60 to $5.00 per day for men and $2.00 to $2.75 per day for women.[14]

13

Issei Acquisition of Orchards

At first Issei were content simply to be employed, for, as one woman maintained, "We had no intention of buying. Our objective was to return to Japan." Gradually, however, they began to acquire property, and by 1905 more than one-third of the Issei in Oregon had become farmers.[1] In Japan many had gained farming experience, and so they were attracted by the greater independence it brought as well as the opportunity to reap the benefits of their own diligent work. Nevertheless, Mrs. Hatsumi Nishimoto did have mixed feelings after she and her husband finally purchased twenty acres of apple and pear orchards in 1930: "My worry was that if we bought property, our return to Japan would be postponed. My husband's position was that, whether we leased or bought property, the payments would be almost the same. So he looked forward to the time he could make the property his own."

Saving what they could from their meager earnings, most could afford only tracts that were marginal—logged-off acreage, brushland, or swamps. Those who were railroad employees were offered first rights to purchase stumpland. One to two thousand acres were usually sold at a time in the state of Washington, but shortage of labor after World War 1 prompted the Oregon Lumber Company to subdivide land in the Dee area into five- and ten-acre plats (subdivisions) to attract laborers.[2]

In Hood River County, the first recorded deed to a Japanese was dated August 3, 1908. Hiyakuichi Watanuki, from the prefecture of Hiroshima, purchased twenty acres from Troy and Annie L. Shelley for a thousand dollars.[3] Watanuki and co-owners Kichizo Noji (Asayo Noji's husband), Yoshiharu Yabitsu, and Tsunetaro Okita, all from Hiroshima, depended on two pairs of horses, dynamite, and their own muscle power to clear their property. While Yabitsu worked daily on the new property, the others were employed elsewhere to support themselves and then joined Yabitsu on Sundays. Eventually, to supplement their incomes, they cleared much of the Parkdale woods as well.[4]

By 1910, Issei operated seven farms in Hood River.[5] By 1920, about seventy Japanese farmers owned twelve hundred acres, part of it in uncleared land, or an average of slightly more than seventeen acres per farm. Those farms were apparently larger than those of Issei in other parts of the state. As an incentive for clearing their property, some local Caucasian landowners had offered plots of land to Hood River Issei in exchange for labor.[6] Developing their newly acquired property was intensive, however, both in time and money. While contracting to purchase their acreage, Issei were often forced to hold second jobs, lease property on a share basis, or work as tenant farmers. Whatever the circumstances, years of labor were required to clear and nurture the land before crops could be produced. Clearing the land alone cost approximately $100 to $150 per acre.[7]

To maximize their labor with a minimum of capital, Issei employed enterprising strategies. They shared farm equipment, engaged family members as their labor force, and used intensive farming techniques.[8] For quick cash crops, they planted strawberries, cane berries, and asparagus between their rows of fruit seedlings. Mrs. Itsu Akiyama described their strenuous work:

> If you had an acre in 1919, it would sell for one thousand dollars. That was a lot of money! We had ten to twenty acres, and a few more acres were cleared after that. But all we did was work! We spent almost ten hours a day hoeing strawberries between the young orchard trees. In Japan the only farm help I had done was to plant rice. This was the first time I had worked so hard! We went to work at seven o'clock in the morning to hoe and irrigate. During strawberry harvest, we women also packed strawberries in crates as they were carried in by the pickers. We delivered them to the Apple Growers' Association [AGA] and were paid about $1.25 a crate.

In 1917, the average strawberry price at the local Apple Growers' Association was $1.56 per crate. By 1919, the average price had increased to $3.00.[9] To cultivate their land and reap the greatest profits, husbands and wives worked equally long hours. What was it like to take on almost sole responsibility for a developing five-acre strawberry field? At the suggestion of her husband's employer, Mrs. Misuyo Nakamura took on the burdensome task:

Oana-san [Mr. Oana] suggested that Papa continue to work for him. He told us, "Your wife can take care of the five acres." Well, I thought maybe I could, but it turned out to be exhausting work. Five acres is a lot of strawberries for one person to tend! (On my husband's free days, we were able to work together.) I can tell you we had a terrible experience raising strawberries! When we planted our strawberries, we did not have money to clean the field too well, so many small roots from timber were left in the field. This made it most difficult to hoe or cultivate. In fact, this caused Papa to develop *rokumaku* [pleurisy]. He was not able to work for about a month, so the fieldwork became my job alone. Today I wonder how in the world I was able to do this!

Mr. Masaji Kusachi also became very knowledgeable about those fleshy, red berries. As a *yoshi*, he had been adopted into the Kusachi family in Dee when their son was killed in a hunting accident. After marrying the Kusachi daughter-in-law, he began work on the family farm in 1929. Much of his time was spent raising strawberries: "You know, in our orchard we had six acres of strawberries so that was 'all-year work'—cultivation, hoeing, big job! Each planting produced good berries for only two to three years. By the fifth year, berries were so small they were processed into jam instead at the AGA or the Washington cannery, and we planted a cover crop of clover or vetch for a year. Then we 'clean cultivated' the field, working the ground over with horse and plow all summer to get rid of as many weeds as possible. The next year we planted more strawberries."

Local Indians, who had maintained amicable relationships with Hood River residents, had been relocated by the government in 1856 to the Warm Springs Reservation south of Mt. Hood.[10] Yet, according to Mr. Kusachi, every year many families returned to Hood River to pick strawberries: "They put up three or four tents next to our strawberry field by wrapping canvas around spliced, twelve-foot poles. We probably had more than ten Indians. Yes, there were a lot of Indian children running around! My wife, being a Nisei [second generation Japanese], spoke English, so she was able to communicate adequately with them, for they spoke English, too."

Work on the strawberry field was tedious, as Mr. Kusachi related:

My primary work was to irrigate the strawberry field. Our water was supplied from the irrigation company's main ditch line and delivered to the high point (head) on our property. Wooden flumes then diverted the water alongside our strawberry rows, and we regulated the flow of water by adjusting the size of holes bored in the sides of the troughs. After that, we had to make rills in the ground to allow water to run down to the plants. But very frequently the water would disappear into a gopher hole! And in some rows the water might not flow all the way to the end. To monitor the flow, I placed a stick beside each row which had enough water, then came back up to the head to turn the water down. I had to walk back and forth, back and forth! What made irrigating even more difficult was that I had to wait until evening to irrigate the rows of strawberries we were going to pick that day. So it was a big job!

My wife's job was to watch [supervise] the picking and packing of our fruit. She had to be sure the Indians picked all the ripe fruit. If they overlooked some, the fruit would rot by the next picking. We raised two varieties of strawberries. Clark's Seedlings were easier to handle, although the "improved" variety had a tendency to ripen much faster and made picking more difficult. Our workers picked the fruit in carriers, which each contained six hallocks. They earned four and a half to five cents a carrier. A Caucasian family named Westover came from Oklahoma, and they were particularly fast pickers. Mr. Westover was a big, husky man who could haul six carriers at one time! Indians, by nature, were kind of slow; but they worked not just for the money but for permission to gather and dry leftover berries.

The strawberries picked in the carriers were dumped into a small tray. Then we "faced" them in hallocks, lining the top of each hallock with fruit of uniform size. Neighborhood Caucasian girls packed our fruit for eighteen cents a crate. (One crate contained twenty-four hallocks.) Our packinghouse was close to the field— gee, I wonder how much fruit we had. Anyway, our fruit was taken to the Dee Sawmill area where the AGA had a packing plant. Those who delivered fruit were also responsible for loading their crates onto the railroad car. During the depression, I recall we were paid $1.75 a crate. At that price, we did not have much money left after expenses."

In 1923, Oregon's Alien Land Law prohibited persons ineligible for citizenship from owning or leasing land. A common Issei practice, however, was to buy property through trusted Caucasian friends or in the names of their children, who were U.S. citizens.[11] After laboring twenty-seven years in the valley, Mr. Chiho Tomita finally purchased his first twelve-acre plot. Speaking in English, he described his experience:

I'm so poor, no money to pay down first payment, so I borrow money from three to four Japanese friends. Issei could not buy land, so we bought in my son Taylor's name. Orchard looked pretty good: mostly d'Anjou and Bartlett pear and some apple and cherry trees. Young trees about ten years old. I worked around all day long every day. Start by clearing more land, then set trees, then need irrigation for summertime. Get ditch company give about two-inch-square hole water for ten acre.[12] Make a river every two to three feet both side of tree and run all day, all night. When get ground all soaked, why quit, go to next row. That's pretty hard time. Have to watch for gopher hole, so have to start in morning and go up and down, up and down all day.

Then spray trees for disease with fifty-gallon tank. One man pump all day, and one man nozzle and hose—I think ten or fifteen feet long. Put fifty-gallon drum on sled and horse pull all day. Not like speed sprayer—pretty slow. I covered mouth with some cloth [to avoid spray]. When harvest, pick apple and take down into lug box. After fourteen to fifteen lug boxes, carry them from orchard in wagon pulled by two horses. Then truck owner from AGA help me load fruit to deliver.

The Apple Growers' Association, first established in 1913, became a growers' cooperative for packaging, storing, distributing, and marketing deciduous fruit crops. Since both Japanese and non-Japanese producers were members and served on the board of directors, this decreased the possibility of competitive pricing between farmers.[13]

The struggle to make a living was continuous, however, which had serious consequences for Mrs. Hisa Wakamatsu's family:

We had ten children, so my stomach never really had a rest. I would tell Papa, "We have a lot of children. These will be trying times." And he would reply, "Whenever I lie on your stomach, we have another child." So Papa decided to go away for awhile and found a job in a sawmill in Snohomish, Washington. But he developed *haien* [pneumonia] and could not work.

Then came a time in 1919 when *O-jiisan* [Grandfather] returned to Japan, and Papa and I went into the dairy business in Alderton, Washington, for five years. Although we had as many as twenty cows, we did not really make money. But we did raise ten acres of hops that paid our expenses. The market for hops then was sixty-five cents a pound. *O-jiisan*, a greedy person, had gone back to Japan with our money and told us, "When the price increases to one dollar a pound, sell, and send me the money." But the hop price, instead of going up, came down to about ten cents a pound.[14] *O-jiisan* still insisted that we send him money. And, even though he had taken our money, we complied. My husband, who was also a gambler, borrowed more money. We were always short of funds.

By 1910, with 468 Japanese residents, Hood River County had the largest population of Oregon Japanese outside Portland. In 1920, despite dwindling labor opportunities on the railroads, Hood River still had 351 Japanese, the third largest Japanese population in the state, after Multnomah and Clatsop counties.[15] Three-fourths of those Japanese scattered through the valley were involved in farming and had an average daily wage of $4 and an average yearly income of $1,200.[16] With nine-tenths of their land cultivated in vegetables and berries,[17] Hood River Issei produced 75 percent of the valley's strawberries. During the early 1920s, they had also ventured into asparagus production; and by 1928, through the Mid-Columbia Vegetable Growers' Association, they shipped fifty thousand crates of asparagus annually to eastern markets.[18] Later the Hood River Japanese diversified by planting pears as well.

14

Anti-Japanese Sentiments

WITH ALARMS of an impending "yellow peril" resounding, anti-Japanese hysteria began to escalate along the West Coast. California residents, roused by economic competition and the protests of organized labor, had been incited by newspaper crusades against the "little brown men."[1] In San Francisco, the school board's segregation of ninety-three Japanese students from its primary schools had prompted the Gentlemen's Agreement of 1907-8, which President Theodore Roosevelt negotiated with Japan to curb Japanese immigration.[2] By 1913, the movement to "keep California white" resulted in that state's Alien Land Law,[3] barring land purchases by aliens ineligible for citizenship and forbidding leases for more than three years.[4]

In Hood River, as Japanese farmers gained measured success in their farming ventures, fears began to mount among their Caucasian counterparts. With the price of strawberries increasing to four dollars a crate during World War I,[5] Japanese farmers began to profit, although their earnings did not necessarily augment their savings, as Mrs. Misuyo Nakamura pointed out: "We leased five acres for eighty dollars a year and raised four crops of berries. Fortunately we raised large berries and the price was excellent—$3.60 a crate in 1925. I remember that, because— even if I had worked all day—I would not have earned that much! One season we might have produced as many as eight hundred crates. With that money we were able to pay off our debt on forty acres of property (with a swampy area) that we had leased the year before for $1,200 a year."

Stories circulated, however, that, by working longer hours, residing in unsightly shacks, and maintaining lower standards of living, Japanese were able to offer a higher price per acre than their Caucasian neighbors.[6] Certainly there was a reaction when the Nishimotos purchased their twenty acres: "My husband was willing to pay cash, so he was able to buy a twenty-acre orchard for $1,000 instead of $2,000. One Caucasian was surprised that anyone could pay $1,000 in cash and was heard to remark, 'Maybe the Japanese have a lot of money on them!' "[7]

While fears of rapidly expanding Japanese land purchases were gaining momentum, the increasing Japanese population was also creating alarm. Japanese births were said to equal 10 to 20 percent of the county births, despite the married Japanese population's forming only 1.5 percent of the Hood River population.[8]

Local residents also voiced concerns about the plight of Japanese family members, who all shared the work load on the farm. "Often," Mrs. Miyoshi Noyori recalled, "our neighbor observed our young daughters hoeing in the field. He cautioned us not to work our children so hard, because they were only twelve and thirteen years old and their bones were not yet strong. But times were difficult, so we needed their help.[9]

The Japanese and "his family can and do work longer hours every day than his white neighbor thinks should be allotted out of the twenty-four," according to a local newspaper editorial. It further sympathized with the "drudgery" faced by newly arrived picture brides.[10] A farmer in the area proclaimed the Japanese "lousy orchardists" and "unfair competition," criticizing them for allowing pregnant women to spray trees and pick fruit."[11] Likewise, Mayor Joe Meyer, a leader of the local anti-Japanese organization, complained, "The farmers of this valley object to competing with Japanese farm labor—where all the family gets out and works on the land."[12]

Aware of this continuing antagonism, the Chiho Tomita family remained discreet in their working habits, as Mr. Tomita explained in English: "We work every day—no holiday, no Sunday. When we have first-time orchard, we don't mind to work on Sunday. But that time American people pretty particular go to church on Sunday. So if Sunday, we work way inside orchard, so nobody see from road."[13]

Racial tensions in the valley intensified as Hood River residents became increasingly threatened by encroaching Japanese farmland, the relative economic success of Japanese, and their purported high birthrates. The question addressed at a public debate, "Shall Hood River Valley be peopled by Americans or Asiatics?" began to fuel local anti-Japanese sentiments.[14]

Oregon's first bill to prevent Japanese purchases of land had, in fact, been introduced in 1917 by a Hood River senator. George R. Wilbur's bill, similar to California's law, was withdrawn, however, because of the State Department's concern for keeping Japanese on the Allies' side in World War I.[15]

Two years later, Hood River residents formed the Anti-Alien Association (AAA), with Wilbur serving as vice president and legal adviser.[16] The thirty-eight who attended the initial meeting[17] pledged that "America should be preserved and protected for Americans" and vowed to neither sell nor lease land to the purported eight hundred valley Japanese. Their signed oath advocated that children of aliens should be denied citizenship and the right to own or lease land. In addition, they opposed further immigration of "Asiatics."[18]

The Japanese community, led by Masuo Yasui, took issue with the AAA charges. It claimed that the Japanese population actually stood at 362, a decrease of one hundred in ten years, since a large number of laborers had since moved.[19] They did concede an increase in landowners to a total of sixty-three, although Japanese owned only 2 percent of the tillable land in the county. It was natural, they said, to seek to own land where one was familiar with soil and local conditions. The group also denied a previous charge that the Japanese government had subsidized their land purchases.[20]

A crucial issue for the AAA had been the low Japanese standard of living, in particular their poor and unsightly homes. Their profits had been reinvested into their farms, the Issei reasoned, because raw stumpland bought at $100 per acre had required $250 to $300 per acre to cultivate. They expected, though, that increased strawberry prices the preceding two years would allow them to improve their premises. The majority pledged support for a "better homes and better gardens" movement.[21]

Shortly afterward, the American Legion, with Kent Shoemaker as president and Wilbur on the executive committee,[22] voted unanimously to join forces with the AAA against Japanese immigration and Japanese possession of land.[23] At the November 1919 American Legion national convention, the Hood River post was instrumental in the adoption of anti-Japanese resolutions.[24]

Desiring to bridge the widening gulf between Japanese and Caucasian ranchers, Issei sought a compromise. Japanese leaders offered their cooperation to prevent further immigration of Japanese to the valley, to check future efforts of Japanese land purchases, and to strive to improve Japanese homes. When a conference was proposed, the prospects for valley harmony brightened.[25] Members of the AAA, however, unanimously declared a moral obligation to continue their move for state and federal legislation against the Japanese.[26]

Elsewhere in Oregon, anti-Japanese sentiments, propelled by fears of Japanese competition and settlement, were also heated. In central Oregon, a scheme to use Japanese labor in collaboration with an agricultural tycoon from California created a "wild furor" in Jefferson, Crook, and Deschutes counties.[27] The Portland-Deschutes Land Company, through its president, George L. Burtt, had purchased 13,800 acres near Redmond in 1919. Burtt's enterprise was an arrangement to raise seed potatoes for George Shima [Ushijima], a Japanese recognized as the "potato king" of California.[28] After he employed several Japanese as experts in potato planting, however, local farmers protested. Led by the Deschutes County Farm Bureau, they eventually came to an agreement that the company would employ only six expert Japanese to supervise the planting and harvesting. After two more Japanese "experts" were hired, protests continued and Burtt withdrew the agreement. The intensity of this public opposition, however, had a greater impact than did legal or economic factors in discouraging Japanese from settling in the area until after World War II.[29]

In Gresham, east of Portland, Issei had been accused of leasing "the very best farm land" to produce their berries and vegetables. Although residents expressed concern about competing with Japanese growers, some in fact endorsed this work, which Americans did not favor anyway and which did meet consumer needs.[30] In nonagricultural communities, Issei also tended to engage in work their American counterparts disliked.[31] There was little incentive, therefore, to take action against them. Merchants and business people especially recognized the impact of meeting consumer needs for these new residents. An Oregon report of the Bureau of Labor Statistics stated that, while food and goods purchased by Chinese were 60 percent foreign and 40 percent domestic, Japanese imported only 11 percent from Japan and bought 89 percent of their goods in the United States.[32] Sentiment among Oregonians was thus decidedly mixed.

Yet the tiny Hood River community was gaining a reputation for its actions. " 'The Japanese Question' is more acute in Hood River than in any other place in Oregon," reported Frank Davey, a state legislator, in his report on the Japanese situation to Governor Ben Olcott in August 1920.[33] Citing the leadership of the AAA with its membership of prominent citizens, Davey recounted their fear that the Japanese would drive Americans out of the valley by forcing property owners surrounded by Japanese to sell their land. He observed that Japanese landholdings in Hood River were actually larger than in the rest of the state, because many Japanese had been given tracts of land in exchange for clearing jobs. Their short stature made them particularly adept at the stooping posture required for vegetables and berries. Japanese orchards, acknowledged Davey, were "well kept and in very good condition, better, on an average, than those of the white owners."[34]

Davey did note that there were business people, bankers, and commissioners who did not share the fear of a Japanese menace. These citizens claimed that Japanese were bringing land into a high state of cultivation, were good customers, and were quiet and well-behaved residents. One upper valley storeowner expressed the view that, although he would not want Japanese as neighbors, they were good people; in ten years of trading, he had never lost a cent from them.[35]

Finally Davey recognized the high Japanese birthrate and charges of unsightly dwellings. Considering that thirty-nine years was the average age of Japanese men in Oregon and twenty-eight the average age of women, he predicted a decline in birthrate over the next ten years. He also cited a noticeable improvement in the condition of Japanese homes over the previous ten years.[36]

The anti-Japanese sentiment in Hood River remained intense, although actions were directed not against individual Japanese but "against the entire race." Valley residents consisted largely of retired business people, army and navy officers, and young college graduates drawn by the apple industry.[37] Newspaper editorials, while recognizing the need to check the Japanese population, discouraged abusive attacks. A Hood River News editorial described the Japanese as "law-abiding, thrifty, hardworking, up-to-date in methods. . . . These people are nice people so long as they are in a minority." It countered, though, with an admonition that if the Alien Land Bill became law, the Japanese who had already established themselves in the state should be protected, closing with the statement, "As we are strong; let us be just."[38] The Hood River Glacier noted that "they are here to stay and their qualities outweigh any faults" but that the valley just could not countenance more Japanese moving in.[39]

The "Japanese problem" in Oregon was temporarily diffused in the early twenties with the passage of two laws. The first, Oregon's Alien Land Law, finally passed in 1923, forbid owning or leasing land to aliens. Issei nonetheless bypassed the law by purchasing land under the names of their young but American-born children and then operating their farms as usual.[40] The second law, the federal Immigration Act of 1924, prohibited aliens ineligible for citizenship from entering the United States.[41]

During the next ten years, the population of Japanese in both Oregon and Hood River increased because of the high proportion of young married Japanese. By 1930, the Japanese population of 4,958 in Oregon and

514 in Hood River reached its prewar peak. By 1940, after twenty, not ten years as Davey had predicted, the birthrate and number of Japanese began to decline. Between 1910 and 1940, Japanese in Hood River accounted for between 4 and 6 percent of the county population.[42]

PART FIVE

Life in America

Hirugao no
Karamari noboru
Yuiboku kana

Wild flowers
Coil round and up
A prop of support.

Haiku written by Mrs. Hama Yamaki and
translated by Mr. Ben Kino

15

Issei Women

PERHAPS THE biggest surprise for Asian newcomers to the United States was the elevated status of women. As noted in chapter 3, *Onna Daigaku*, a Confucian-based treatise, prescribed duties of lifelong obedience for women. While all women were expected to observe strict rules of propriety, married women were to serve their husbands as lords, with absolutely no notion of disobeying. The "three obediences" had, in fact, specified that women were to obey their fathers when unmarried; their husbands when married; and their sons when widowed.[1] No priority at all was placed on their own needs or desires. For Issei women accustomed to these subservient roles in Japan, their treatment in the United States was eye-opening:

> What really surprised me was how well men treated women here. Unlike in Japan, women in America are really appreciated. I was very impressed when I saw men open car doors for ladies. Then, when the couple arrived, the men stepped outside again and opened the car doors. Of course, these were the Caucasian men, not the Japanese! My husband? Never! [Mrs. Hatsumi Nishimoto]

> I had a surprise one day when I was packing strawberries. A comb fell from my hair, and a Caucasian man picked it up for me. In Japan a man would never do that. I was so impressed! [Mrs. Itsu Akiyama]

> I was impressed at how women were treated in this country. In Japan women were placed at a lower level, but here women were considered *taisetsu* [precious] and even called Mrs. Men here are not necessarily addressed with honorifics, like *-san* attached to their

names, as they were in Japan. So I thought the difference was good.
[Mrs. Asayo Noji]

I was surprised that hakujin [Caucasian] women were daiji [cherished], which was not the case in Japan. I was treated well by my husband Namba. He even bought me good shoes to wear outside. I do not remember that he ever scolded me much. On the other hand, he expected me to work outside too. [Mrs. Miyoshi Noyori]

Other Issei women in Hood River also recalled being reproached by their husbands for their food preparation or pace of work, even while pregnant. Although the ideal role of women was to be "dutiful wives and intelligent mothers" (ryosai kenbo), the historian Yuji Ichioka affirmed that, with economic realities, women found it necessary to assume third roles, as unpaid farm laborers.[2] Indeed, among working Japanese women, one-third, the highest proportion, were employed in agriculture between 1920 and 1930.[3] While almost 26 percent of Japanese women were employed, only 18.5 percent of their Caucasian counterparts had jobs.[4] Women, like Mrs. Tei Endow, felt the burden not only of handling domestic chores but of providing economic support on the farm as well: "For a woman in those days, there was no Sunday! Days were short, because there was so much to do. I made breakfast, cleaned the house, washed by hand, and still had to weed strawberries in the field. It was probably best that I had to work so hard, though. I was able to remain healthy and put all my energy into my work—This may have been a good thing."

The success of Issei men was possible "because of the companionship and the working partnership of their wives," acknowledged the brief Issei Story, compiled by the Mid-Columbia Japanese American Citizens' League (JACL) in 1961.[5] Some scholars maintain that women, by contributing to the labor force and rearing families, were the prime factor in the development of permanent Issei communities.[6] Certainly Mr. Chiho Tomita, speaking in English, recognized the added demands placed on the shoulders of Issei women: "In Japan most women stay inside work—housecleaning, washing, cooking. Not work outside. In America wife cook, wash, besides picking apples. She said she like make money together—make rich. I told her how to clean—everything. Women work harder in the U.S. She don't say anything—just work."

As they became familiar with American ways, however, Issei women, like Mrs. Itsu Akiyama, became increasingly aware of the disparity between the roles of women and men:

My husband was probably a typical Japanese man, so he would never permit me to take a bath before he did. He was truly the boss of the family. Life in America probably did not involve the same

Tei Endow had no need for her tailor-made suits and silk blouses when she settled into her spartan life and ten-hour work days on her husband's farm. Strawberries planted between young apple trees provided quick, cash crops during the summer of 1918. (Courtesy of Tei Endow)

kind of sacrifices women made in Japan. We shared much of the work, but women had to come home from work early to prepare the meal. Then, after the meal, we had to clean up. While I was busy cleaning, my husband would retire to the other room to read and rest. There was one advantage for women here though. When men go out in this country, they dress by themselves. But in Japan, a woman was required to arrange the man's clothing before he dressed. So I thought that at least there were some good things about living in America.

Takie Sugiyama Lebra in her book *Japanese Women* affirmed the "ineptitude and total dependence" of Japanese husbands on their wives' cooking, laundering, housecleaning, and "around the body" services.[7] Japanese wives simply took for granted these daily routines:

Women were busy all the time. We came home from work a few minutes earlier than men so we could prepare meals. While men had the luxury of relaxing and reading the newspaper after meals, we women still had domestic chores like washing. So we spent a lot of time working in the field and in the house. Women who married into poor families in Japan had much work, but their physical work was nothing compared to what we went through! [Mrs. Miyoshi Noyori]

Women's work never ended. During the week, I labored in the fields. I drove the Ford tractor when we sprayed.[8] (That was better than driving a team of horses—"I scared!") Sometimes I even sprayed. Same as the men, I worked until 6:00 P.M. But when I came home, I had to cook too. After dinner during harvest, we boxed the fruit. Then when everyone went to bed, I cleaned the house. I heard of others who rose so early, they slept with their shoes on! Even on Sundays, I had laundry and housecleaning chores. My husband, who was more relaxed than many, would frequently go fishing with our two sons. [Mrs. Hatsumi Nishimoto]

Despite the division of labor, women tended to heed *Onna Daigaku's* principle that "however humble and needy may be her husband's position, she must find no fault with him, but consider the poverty of the household which it has pleased Heaven to give her."[9] Gradually, however, as they became more aware of the elevated status of American women, Issei women became more vocal. Yet, as Mrs. Misuyo Nakamura admitted, there were still feelings of remorse:

In Japan, the men's position was much higher and women followed men's desires. When we first came to America, we lived Japanese-style. But as time went on, we noticed that American women had their say. So, even within the Japanese community, women freely expressed disagreement with their husbands' desires if they felt the need to do so. All our feelings were not fully suppressed in America, and this probably surprised me the most. One example might be that, even in difficult times, a man might wish to buy a car. His wife, though, might find this purchase to be a little beyond their means and prefer to save the money. Yet the husband might still see the car as a good bargain and wish to buy. There were times I expressed my opinion, which may not have been the same as my husband's. Yet, if I differed with him—because of my upbringing in Japan—I would feel regret.

This disparity between the self-expression valued in American society and the collectivity and concensus-orientation of Japanese society did indeed create conflict within many Issei women.[10] Contrasting the decision-making styles in Japan and the United States, Mrs. Hama Yamaki tended to view life in Japan as more democratic, or, at least, in her opinion, involving some type of family discussion:

Here there are times when the husband probably makes his own decision without discussing it within the family. In Japan usually most decisions were discussed. It seems to me that it was more harmonious that way. For example, because of the hard work of silkworm culture, my mother would ask, "How would it be if we take time off and go to the hot springs?" My father would always say, "Please go." When they could not go together, my mother would sometimes go with a friend. If my father did not agree, though, we would not go. In America there are probably more head-of-the-family decisions, because these are mostly business. I did most of the decision making concerning the children, and I usually took care of family affairs myself.

Domestics

At the turn of the century, more than 50 percent of working Japanese women were employed in domestic service, generally performing housekeeping tasks for wealthy Caucasian families. By 1920, although second to agriculture, domestic service still employed more than one-fourth of the labor force of Japanese women. [11] While earning wages, Issei learned American customs—at least, the ways of more affluent Americans. Mrs. Masayo Yumibe, for one, was fascinated by the life-style of her employer:

Strangely to me, Mrs. Skin ate her morning meal in bed. For her comfort, I would build a fire in her bedroom, serve her breakfast, and bring her the newspaper. Then she took a bath and dressed up and went out in the garden. These were obviously wealthy people! I recall times when Mrs. Skin ordered material and hired a seamstress from Portland to make her dresses. The seamstress even stayed for a week or so. "Yeah, I cooked, too." The daughter looked up the recipe, and I wrote the instructions in *Nihongo* [Japanese] in my notebook. I remember thinking, "They certainly eat well." We ate a lot of roast meat. And even for cooking, they did not use animal fat or lard—they used butter. I also washed the clothes in a machine with rollers that squeezed the water out. I was paid forty dollars a month. That was considered good money, because I also received my room and food. The Skins also gave me two sets of work clothes and a maid's hat. I sent the money to my father in Dee. If I had saved it in the bank, I would not have known what to do with it. The Skins told me I could have the day off on Sunday, but there was no place for me to go and not much to do.

Encountering a water spigot, an iron, and a carpet sweeper for the first time, Mrs. Asayo Noji spent part of her first summer in America performing laundry and cleaning chores for the Barrow family:

> Since the Barrows had a water tank, all I had to do was turn on the water spigot to get water—unlike in Japan where we drew water in buckets from a well. This was pretty good! So when it came time to wash clothes, all I had to do was open the spigot, draw the water, heat it on the stove, pour it into a washtub, and then wash the clothes on the washboard. But I had never seen an iron in Japan! I had to heat two irons on the stove, for when one cooled, I used the other one. The two Barrow ladies were tall even for *hakujin,* and at that time they wore long dresses, so their garments were large and long! One of my most difficult jobs was cleaning the floor rugs. In Japan I had simply used a broom and dustcloth to clean the house. Here I pushed a carpet sweeper, but the very deep-tufted bedroom rug made it difficult to pick up the debris. There was so much lint left in the bedroom that I finally had to pick it all up by hand!

Children

In the Hood River area, the first child of an Issei couple, George Okamura, was reportedly born in 1911. Destined for fame, he would become the "Great Togo" in the professional wrestling circuit. [12] Not coincidentally, George had numerous namesakes in the valley. When local Issei were ready to deliver their babies, they often called Dr. Howard L. Dumble, a kind Hood River doctor. Dr. Dumble not only delivered the babies but also exercised the privilege of naming them. Boys were always "George," and girls were named "Mary." Among the Japanese children, then, there were numerous "Georges" and "Marys," thanks to the good doctor. [13]

Offspring of the Issei were Nisei, the second generation of Japanese in the United States. Because Issei arrived during the peak of their child-bearing years, the Japanese population increased rapidly. From 1900 to 1910, the number of Nisei children grew from 269 to 4,502. By 1920, six times as many Nisei, or 29,672, had been born. [14] By 1930, the 68,357 Nisei almost equaled the 70,477 Issei parents. [15] In Hood River, the Nisei population surpassed the number of Issei in 1928, with 265 Nisei and 208 Issei. [16]

As they became pregnant, Issei women often persisted in their farm duties, frequently without seeking prenatal care. Many, in fact, found it necessary to work until just a few days before their deliveries. Midwives—

or husbands—often substituted for doctors in cutting the umbilical cords.[17] For Mrs. Tei Endow, who gave birth at home, her prime concern was her inability to speak English:

I was healthy so I sorted at the Apple Growers' Association (AGA) packinghouse almost until the day of my son Sho's birth. The doctor's car broke down, so he did not arrive in time for my delivery. But in those days, hospital births were not common, so most Issei women learned birthing through friends. (A hospital birth would have been worrisome, anyway, because then I would have had to speak English. So I was relieved to deliver my son at home.) When Dr. Dutro [another local doctor] finally arrived, he told us how to care for the baby and how to place him in cotton batting. My husband could understand English well enough to write the doctor's instructions, and he used the dictionary when necessary.

My husband said he needed a son. (Sons in Japan are important, because they work hard and continue the family. Girls are expensive to raise, and then you give them away.) It was hard raising children in a foreign country. For our first two, we made diapers from the inner liner of empty rice sacks. Later we purchased what we needed—clothing or diapers—through stores or even through the catalogues.

Whereas in Japan, families relied on elderly grandparents to baby-sit young children, Issei couples in America lacked their extended families, or *ie*. Addressing the increased pressures they faced, several Issei women lamented the plight of working mothers:

All my babies grew up in a wooden baby box. The doctor told me, "You can't work for at least three weeks." After a month I had to go out to work, and we left the baby home. I would come home every two or three hours to feed her and would find her crying—and I cried with her. In Japan this may never have happened, but here it was necessary to work. [Mrs. Itsu Akiyama]

While we were working in the field, we saw a family confine their children by tying them to chairs. In Japan the elderly people had cared for children, but here there were no baby-sitters. I thought, "Is this the only way to make a living in America?" [Mrs. Hatsumi Nishimoto]

In the fall I sorted fruit at the AGA packing house. Sometimes my daughter Kane would come and tug on me, asking me to come home. It did please me that Kane could express such sentiments, but I was not always able to come home when she insisted. Somewhat saddened, I thought to myself, "Is it necessary to work this hard?" [Mrs. Tei Endow]

Perhaps I can best describe my feelings in this way. If I were trying to make my way through a brushy area, I would close my eyes and cover my head. Then I would work my way through the brush. This is the feeling I had about raising children and still having to work outside. . . .

"That time no help—no Grandma, no help—just myself, you know. Pretty busy." We women placed our babies in small apple boxes and worked alongside the men. When we changed diapers, we were so busy we did not even have time to wash them. We had to put that off until evening. And I had little time for housecleaning. At times when I cleaned smudge from the kerosene lamps, I could even see grains of rice on the floor—but I really had no time to clean it. [Mrs. Miyoshi Noyori]

As Mrs. Noyori further explained, her resourceful children found ways to amuse themselves. One day, however, this brought about near-tragic results:

I told my children to stay home and play, even though we had no toys. I gave them a bit of candy, but we did not have that much, so I hid the rest in the shelves. When I came home to check on them, they would be searching the house for the candy. Sometimes they played on the bed and tied corners of sheets to bedposts to form a tent. At other times they tied ropes to chairs and pulled them around the house for amusement. We simply did not have toys for them.

One morning I was sharpening my hoe to top the strawberry plants. I happened to look toward my children in the front yard. They were scurrying around in alarm and hollered to me, "Ditch! Ditch!" I dropped my hoe and dashed along the road. My neighbor, Mr. Edgar, saw me running in an urgent manner. I tried to explain the problem to him. We found Mark, only eighteen months old then, floating face down in a four-foot-wide ditch. The children had apparently been picking thimbleberries along the ditch, and Mark probably reached too far. He was unconscious, and I would say he was almost dead—at least 90 percent gone! Mr. Edgar pulled Mark out and carried him into his house. Then he covered him with a large towel and applied burning heat to his body. I was so stunned, I just watched—I thought he was dead! This happened at eight o'clock in the morning. Finally at around eleven o'clock, he called, "Mama." Ah! That was a happy moment! But my other children were nowhere in sight. I finally found them watching from the upper floor of the barn. They were frightened, because the baby had been in their charge.

Unfortunately, for another working mother, tragedy did result. Mrs. Misuyo Nakamura attributed the death of her infant daughter to the family's ongoing concern about finances:

> What I really cannot forget is that, because I was so involved in work, I lost my thirteen-month-old daughter. We needed money badly because we were in debt on our lease. And I was so involved in my work sorting strawberry plants that all I could think of was the money I would earn. When it was time to go home, I would look at my clock and tell myself, "I will work just five more minutes." Then, when five minutes passed, I would again prolong my return, thinking only of the money. I was working in a shed adjoining our house, which was only two or three rooms away from our baby's room. Momentarily I heard a child cry—I listened, but when I did not hear any more crying, I assumed the child had gone back to sleep. After I returned to the kitchen and fired up the kerosene stove for lunch, I checked on the baby and found her strangled. Her throat had become caught between the table and bed.

Language

Another major obstacle for Issei was their lack of proficiency in the English language. With their multiple roles as wives, homemakers, mothers, and farm laborers, women had little time to devote to leisure or to learn English. In efforts to avoid uncomfortable situations, some Issei women simply shunned Caucasians:

> Our biggest difficulty was not being able to converse in *Eigo* [English]. So, because of our apprehension, we avoided mingling with *hakujin*. I observed how my children were able to get along so well with their *hakujin* friends. And yet, I could not talk with them. We mostly kept to ourselves. Those were trying times. [Mrs. Tei Endow]

> Papa told me to go to school with my children and learn to speak *Eigo*. He told me to study with the children at home, but I fell far behind. Parents usually went to PTA [Parent Teacher Association] meetings, although I only went once. [Mrs. Itsu Akiyama]

Women were inclined to rely on their husbands, who, in their normal working days, more frequently encountered Caucasians and thus became more proficient in the language. Among rural Issei in the United States in 1920, 48.6 percent of the men learned to read and write English, while only 13.3 percent of the women mastered the language.[18] In Hood River several women admittedly avoided shopping altogether, which sometimes resulted in their spouses having to make embarrassing purchases, as Mrs. Misuyo Nakamura recounted: "I could not converse in *Eigo*, so Papa did all the shopping for us. I stayed home to work. Once Papa had to purchase panties for me. It was said that the clerk laughed to see a man buying women's intimate apparel."

For Mrs. Hama Yamaki, a desire for a frozen mouthful of ice cream helped her overcome feelings of awkwardness at the store: "On a hot day two to three months after coming to America, I wanted ice cream but was kind of embarrassed to buy it. That was probably the first time I used *Eigo*. I said, 'I-su ku-reem-u pu-reez.' Since I was a frequent customer, the store owners could guess what I wanted." Yet, when words seemed useless, Mrs. Yamaki employed a common sense solution: "I did have difficult moments when school children came to the house to sell small items, like pictures. Although I said, 'I don't want it,' they did not leave. I would finally have to close the door on them."

Mrs. Hatsumi Nishimoto developed an enterprising method for breaking the communication barrier during her shopping trips:

> What troubled me the most was my inability to talk to Americans. It was especially difficult for me to make purchases at the store, so my husband usually accompanied me. But it took me so long to decide what to buy that he would scold me. Being a woman, I usually like to shop a little bit, so the next time I went alone. My husband asked me, "How are you going to conduct yourself to make a purchase?" This is the way I did it: When I went to the store to buy fabric, the sales clerk would ask me what I was going to sew. Generally I had to show her the pattern. Then she would bring out a variety of fabric I could choose from. That is the way most women shopped. Men just hated to go with us, because it took so long! There were many times, though, when I could not get my ideas across, and I had to settle for a different item than I had in mind.

Issei women were awed as much by the deferential treatment accorded American women as they were by their more extravagant life-styles. Compelled to work from dawn to dusk for their families' survival, they found little time to socialize or to learn English. They were also burdened by the feeling that work prevented them from properly attending to the needs of their precious children. Added to those dilemmas were the inequities they began to recognize in male-female roles. Yet, in the manner of their traditional upbringing, they persisted—with fortitude and modesty.

16

Yoshi Marriages

To RETAIN THE family line when there were no male heirs, the *yoshi* tradition of adopting sons was followed in a limited way in the United States.[1] This adoption of often unrelated sons not only prevented the extinction of families but also ensured a head of the household for bereaved widows and their families after the death of a spouse and father.

Mr. Miyozo Yumibe, a *yoshi* who was born into the Tanabe family in Japan, had been called to join his adoptive family in the United States when he was sixteen. After living as a Yumibe son for eight years, he married one of their daughters:

> Because I came to America as a *yoshi* to the Yumibe family, it was probably understood that I was to marry a Yumibe daughter. In 1921 *o-jiisan* [Father Yumibe] advised me that he was calling his second daughter from Japan for marriage purposes. (The oldest daughter was already to marry someone else. She was the same age as me, whereas my wife-to-be was three years younger. In Japan it was common practice to marry a younger woman, maybe as much as four or five years younger.) Three years later, our wedding ceremony was held at the preacher's home in Hood River. I am sure that I was wearing a suit. We were married in the afternoon of July 2, 1925. Mr. [Masuo] Yasui was our witness—there were just three of us there. Where was my family? "I don't know. No honeymoon." After we married, I went right back to work at the sawmill. My wife and I did not live together for five months. I continued to live at the sawmill camp. My wife lived with her father. She worked on the farm and cleaned house for a *hakujin* [Caucasian] family. About December of that year, my wife was able to join me at the sawmill camp.

Miyozo Yumibe, a son adopted from Japan by the Yumibes to carry on the family name, married the Yumibes' daughter Masayo on July 2, 1925. After a simple wedding and automobile ride, both returned to work and their separate households. After five months, they were finally able to live together. (Courtesy of Miyozo and Masayo Yumibe)

The twenty-one-year-old bride, Mrs. Masayo Yumibe, also recalled the simple wedding preparations and the inopportune living arrangements:

> He used to come up to visit us on Saturday, his day off. What I remember is that my father suggested we two ought to get married. Because it was suggested, *shikata-ganai* [it is beyond control; it cannot be helped so accept it as it is]. I had to go through with it. I was living with the Skins at the time [where Mrs. Yumibe was housekeeper] so I asked them to buy a suit of clothes for me. The next time they went to Portland, they brought home two or three suits for me to pick from. I think I chose a suit of green wool with some stripes. We had a simple wedding at the preacher's home. Afterward Mr. Yasui gave us a ride around the area in his car. Then I returned to my work at the Skins' home, and my new husband returned to the sawmill. "Oh, not so good!" Because my father had become aged, I stayed on the farm to help him during the summer.

Yoshi marriages had occurred so frequently in Japan that Mr. Masaji Kusachi seemingly accepted his adoptive role as husband and father with little thought:

> When I was twenty-six, I was adopted into the Kusachi family. They were also from Okayama. Their son was killed in a rifle accident in Salem. The dog apparently unlocked the trigger, and, when son Hiroshi reached for the rifle, he was shot in the chest. Hiroshi already had a Nisei [second-generation Japanese] wife who was with child, and she lived with her father-in-law. But in Japan it was very important to keep the family line intact. Without the husband and father, the Kusachi family line would be discontinued. For that reason, I was asked to be *yoshi* and, in effect, to marry Hiroshi's twenty-six-year-old widow. Mr. Fukai, an insurance man in Portland, became an intermediary between our families, acting as a *baishakunin*. I agreed to the arrangements for marrying the Kusachi widow. After the *yoshi* deal was arranged, we had a family wedding at the Kusachi home in Dee in 1929. But I did not regard this as anything special, because *yoshi* were very common in Japan.

Four thousand miles from Japan, maintaining family ties was still essential, taking precedence over romance in marriage arrangements.

17

Japanese Families in America

ISSEI RAISED their children in the tradition of the close-knit, cohesive families they remembered in their own native land. In Japan, family status and harmony had been valued over the individual, and one's actions reflected heavily on the family's reputation. The "traditional Japanese family," observed the sociologist Harry Kitano, placed great emphasis on solidarity, a patriarchal system, and mutual support. Japanese observed clear roles and patterns of deference.[1] This duty and obligation of family members to each other was especially apparent on Issei family farms.

Mrs. Hama Yamaki recounted how her family worked together: "My husband had to work outside, so the responsibility of raising children was mostly mine. I was a little bit more strict. I wanted my children to come home straight from school. Then I insisted that they go through their piano lessons. I was strict about them attending church school too. All the children helped on the farm. We had twelve acres of asparagus. They got into a work pattern, cutting asparagus before school. Our children were very willing workers, and our older children would take care of the younger ones."

When their children were young, Issei fondly observed the Japanese customs reminiscent of their homeland. They ate the malodorous *tsukemono* (pickled vegetables) with cold rice, over which they poured hot tea. In preparation for the traditional Japanese New Year, they pounded hot rice into a glutinous mass and shaped it into small balls filled with sweet beans. At home they conversed freely in *Nihongo* (Japanese) with their children. But, as the Nisei attended public schools, these priorities began to change. Eager to be accepted by their Caucasian classmates, the children began to discard many of their Japanese ways, as observed by their mothers:

When Hama Yamaki and her husband first arrived in Hood River, they lived
with her brother and family on his leased farm. In this July 1917 photo, Hama
Yamaki (*center*) held nephew Hideo and was flanked by her brothers, Kunikichi
and Sanosuke Sato, and her two children, Eiko and Bill. (Courtesy of Hama
Yamaki)

At first we followed Japanese customs at home. We taught our
children to say, "*itadaki-masu*" [polite expression for "I am about to
take the food/drink"] before eating and "*gochiso-sama*" [polite expression for "The food/drink was very tasty"] following the meal.
We also asked them to say "*ohayoo gozai-masu*" [good morning] in
the morning. They paid attention to what we were saying when
they were young. But as they grew older, we got away from things
like that. Because our sons attended school and were living in
American society, we encouraged them to live American-style.
[Mrs. Hatsumi Nishimoto]

Hanbun [half], *hanbun*. It seemed that we strived for half-
Japanese and half-American ways of life. For breakfast and lunch we
ate typical Japanese meals: *chazuke* [cooked rice in tea] and *tsukemono*. In the evening I tried to prepare an American-style meal:
meat and vegetables from our garden. We raised Plymouth Rock
chickens and hogs for home use, so we served fried chicken and
pork quite often. [Mrs. Hama Yamaki]

Until 1924, Nisei, as offspring of Japanese citizens, received automatic citizenship in Japan. After 1924, however, Nisei children could not have dual citizenship unless their births were registered at a Japanese consulate within fourteen days of birth.[2] At this point, Mr. Masaji Kusachi, among others, realized that his children's roots were in the United States, not in his native land: "Our children were born in America, so their birthright was American citizenship. I did not make an effort to register them as Japanese citizens."

Others may have viewed the registration process as an inconvenience or, at least, a low priority, as Mrs. Tei Endow did: "The Japanese government proclaimed that dual citizenship was not required and that American citizenship should be sufficient. If necessary, we could apply at our pleasure. But, to register for Japanese citizenship, we would have had to travel to the consulate in Portland. So we neglected to register our children."

As their children attended local schools, Issei encouraged them to study diligently and to be obedient to their teachers, who were respected as authority figures.[3] Nearly all the Hood River Issei had gained more than the required six years of school in Japan. With strong influence from Confucian traditions valuing education, they viewed schooling and good citizenship not only as ways their children could get ahead in the competitive American society but also as a means of breaking through discrimination barriers:[4]

> I advised my children not to get into quarrels. Because I had no English education, I wanted my children to benefit. I asked them to listen to the instructors carefully, to get along, and to try not to get into any accidents. They had an exceptional teacher who understood the Japanese, so my children had no problems at all. [Mrs. Itsu Akiyama]

> I repeated to our sons that they must do whatever the teacher told them and—never, never—take anybody else's property. We did not want our children intimidated when they saw others had belongings they may have wanted. Even though it was difficult, we usually managed to buy these items for them. [Mrs. Hatsumi Nishimoto]

> I always told my children to study hard so they would not get behind. After school they almost always told me about their studies and the day's events. Then we would talk about what was right and what was wrong. I would ask the children questions and have them explain to me in *Eigo* [English]. It got to a point where I was learning *Eigo* from my children.

As they grew older, they experienced more discrimination in high school. I felt terrible about that! I tried to keep the children neatly attired so their clothing would not reflect badly on them. I remember Eiko saying that some looked down on Japanese, making *baka* [fools] of them. But when her teacher gave arithmetic problems to the class, Eiko was quick to answer. So students who had looked down on her seemed to change their attitudes. Once the teacher asked whether a student in class could play the piano. Most could not play but Eiko could! The other students were surprised, remarking "We did not know Eiko could play the piano so well!" [Mrs. Hama Yamaki]

Issei took immense pride in the accomplishments of their sons and daughters. Placing high priority on their children's welfare while minimizing their own individual needs, they often sacrificed their own small pleasures. This might have been expressed by giving choice portions of food to their children or by purchasing lower quality goods for themselves to benefit their young ones.[5] This filial piety or reciprocal obligation between parents and children was an enduring factor for Issei families:

Raising children is *tanoshii* [joyful] for parents. We looked forward to raising them! Issei parents have made many sacrifices raising children in this land. We did everything we could to give our children a good education. A good example I recall involved my oldest son. From the age of nine, it was his desire to become a doctor. Even at that young age, there were certain books he wanted to study which were not available in the local library. So he had to order books from the state library in Salem. Later I sought advice from Mr. [Masuo] Yasui, whose son had become a doctor. He did not give us any encouragement, because it would take so long and cost so much to attend medical school. And even in internship, you would receive minimal pay. So when my son was in the army, I wrote to him, asking if he could choose another career. But he wrote back and said, "Even at nine years old, it was my desire to become a doctor. I do not want to change." He knew that the GI Bill of Rights would give him about three years of schooling. So he asked us to help him out just for the first year. Of course, we wanted to encourage him, so we told him we would help. This perhaps expressed my confidence in him and our own personal feeling in sacrificing part of our life earnings so our children could get a good education.[6] [Mrs. Masayo Yumibe]

Probably because we gave the highest priority to achieving higher education for our children, we have made sacrifices, and we have devoted all our working force to saving as much money as we could. It was most satisfying to be able to send our children to school and know today that they are doing well. I probably spent more time worrying about our youngest. But we were able to send him to Oregon State, and he presently has a good business.[7] [Mrs. Tei Endow]

My biggest regret was being unable to send Mam to college. Papa had been worried when Mam was elected student body president at Parkdale High School, for he might be treated badly. But when Papa attended a school function, others congratulated him, and he was very happy. We had hopes that Mam could attend college a year or two later. Then he was drafted into the army. But after Mam helped, we were able to expand our farm. That is on my mind, even today.[8] [Mrs. Asayo Noji]

For Issei, strong family ties and opportunities for their children became priorities as they assumed parental roles. Their early lessons in Japan emphasizing dedication and filial piety became abiding principles in their endeavors to succeed in America.

18

The Hood River
Japanese Community

IN HOOD RIVER VALLEY, with its uneven terrain and poor roads, separate communities emerged: Parkdale and Dee at the higher elevations rising toward Mt. Hood at the south; Odell, Pine Grove, and Oak Grove in the rolling hills near the town of Hood River. Unlike many Issei who lived in concentrated areas, such as the Japanese colonies in northern California's San Joaquin Valley[1] or the Japanese towns in Pajaro Valley south of San Francisco[2] and Gardena Valley south of Los Angeles,[3] Hood River Issei farmed and resided in separate valley communities and patronized Caucasian businesses.

Though the daily work cycle and geographical distances isolated them, Hood River Issei developed cohesive community bonds and created a "tight-knit insulated racial-ethnic enclave."[4] In Japan, where Issei had been raised to place the welfare of their family and village over their own personal interests, they had relied on extended families for mutual support. They applied those same principles to life in America as Japanese neighbors began to function as extended families.[5] Drawn together by the security of common language and customs, Issei developed strong ties and support systems within the local Japanese community. For some, like Mrs. Asayo Noji, this extended to combining residences as well: "For four or five years, we shared a house with two other families. Papa owned property with those other men, so we all worked together and lived together. As children were born, our crowded house held eighteen of us altogether! Later our family moved into the top floor of a large, new barn Papa had planned and built. The main floor was used as a packinghouse, and a vacant area upstairs became a community center for judo classes and Japanese movies. I liked living there, because we were high above the ground and had a fine view." Continuing to emphasize duty and obligation to each other, the Japanese formed cohesive networks and highly organized associations that provided friendship and mutual assistance.

Japanese Associations

Most Issei belonged to *kyokai* (associations), composed of those with common interests who met periodically. Early organizations in the valley during the period from 1909 to 1918 included Boeki Kyokai, a trade association; Nogyo Kyokai, an agriculture association; and Kyorei Kyokai, a formal society.[6]

Japanese Farmers' Association of Hood River (Nogyo Kyokai)

Japanese farmers' associations in the United States resembled those in rural Japan. Through these associations, members shared not only information and methods but labor and equipment as well. The associations also offered a means of pooling capital to meet preseason expenses, effective marketing through group contracts, and cooperation between farmers and merchants.[7]

Recognizing that Japanese landowners and tenant farmers needed to be in closer contact, five local Japanese founded the Japanese Farmers' Association of Hood River on January 10, 1914.[8] Twenty members attended the first meeting and elected officers, with each district selecting its own councilors. Members gave contributions ranging from fifty cents to seven dollars, with most donating one to two dollars.[9]

The association also saw the need to "reconcile with" and "keep peace with" *hakujin* (Caucasians). Accordingly, it made plans to "invite influential *hakujin* for peace conferences."[10] A year later, it printed its first report on cultivation, farm equipment, fertilizers, marketing, agriculture laws, and spraying. Members also formed study groups to gain information on current farming practices. Over the next nine years, they organized information sessions on the following topics: fertilizers (with a report from Mr. Peterson from Swift Fertilizer), pruning and cultivation (with a lecture by Mr. Brown from the Hood River Agricultural Experiment Department), strawberry and asparagus cultivation, vermin control, market conditions, experiments in fertilizing apples and strawberries, and winter freezing of apple trees.

In 1915, after the group questioned the low price for strawberries given by "the Association" (Apple Growers' Association) in contrast to the prices offered by the Fruit Exchange, members invited Caucasian representatives from the AGA to meetings for two consecutive years. Speaking for three hours at the 1916 meeting, the AGA representatives detailed the problem created by market oversaturation driving the price down and emphasized their efforts to establish larger markets in the East. They also encouraged members to "Trust us. Work with us."[11]

The Japanese Farmers' Association also concerned itself with issues beyond agriculture. Faced in 1915 with the movement to prohibit Japanese from acquiring property, it called for unity, with one member quoting a Buddhist teaching that "justice will be done and the right will prevail."[12] By 1921, the anti-Japanese mood had heightened, and Japanese in Portland and The Dalles had been arrested for breaking prohibition laws. After a heated discussion, all members present agreed to control the amount of liquor they consumed, despite the part it played in their customs: "If it is not possible to completely ban drinking, at least we can control the amount that can be consumed. Never go out when drinking. Never offer drinks to visitors. No more making wine at home."[13] That month members pledged over a thousand dollars to the Oregon Japanese Association's drive to stop the anti-Japanese plan, a sum "never heard of in this area."[14]

The association also developed a mutual support plan for valley Japanese, specifying types of assistance to families in need.[15] Other business matters included reception plans for Japanese ambassadors visiting the valley; contributions for a cemetery plot and an appreciation fund for Caucasian efforts to stop Hood River Senator George Wilbur's bill to prohibit Japanese ownership of property;[16] decisions on cooks for meetings;[17] and the annual community picnic.

Formal Society (Kyorei Kyokai)

As a means to maintain ties between all valley Japanese, Issei organized Kyorei Kyokai around 1915. Male members regulated group functions, as Mrs. Misuyo Nakamura pointed out:

> There was a consensus that an organization was needed to hold the Japanese community together. I believe Mr. [Sagoro] Asai[18] suggested organizing a club named Ian [recreation]. Some, though, felt that the word *club* suggested it might be a gambling club, which was inappropriate. So it was renamed Kyorei Kyokai [Formal Society]. This was later centered at the Japanese Community Hall. I did not attend meetings, for they were male-dominated. In fact, if we did attend, women would just be hangers-on. Kyorei Kyokai—*kyorei* means *cooperative* or *together; rei* means *encouragement; kai* means *association*. I do not remember too many times when we got together except for pleasure.

Hiroshima Prefectural Society (Hiroshima Kenjinkai)

Outside of their own families and relatives, Issei felt a particular affinity with those from their own *ken* (prefecture) in Japan, where they identified with common dialect, rituals, and preparation of food.[19] In fact, a *kenjin*, someone from one's own *ken*, was regarded almost as a blood relative, despite being a stranger. Issei were inclined to trust, assist, and conduct business with fellow *kenjin*. They even attributed characteristics to people of different prefectures (e.g., those from Hiroshima were considered industrious and thrifty, while those from Okayama were shrewd and clever).[20]

To reinforce their native bonds, the eighteen or so Hood River Issei families from Hiroshima organized the Hiroshima Kenjinkai, a prefectural society. Later, when membership was extended to others, as many as thirty participated. Kenjinkai meetings were primarily social, but they also functioned as a mutual aid society, collecting dues to assist needy members:

> Yes, I do recall Hiroshima Kenjinkai. In essence, this *kenjinkai* appeared to be a savings and loan cooperative. We pooled our membership dues (about ten dollars a year), and members could request loans as long as they had at least two witnesses or cosigners. But if a person was unable to repay, the cosigner was responsible to make the payments. Naturally there was hesitancy to become a willing witness if the man was not reputable or had a poor record of repaying. Some were turned down. I recall a man, since moved to California, who was in dire straits supporting his large family. He really needed help but could not get anyone to witness his request. So Nishimoto-san [Mr. Nishimoto, husband of Mrs. Hatsumi Nishimoto] stated, "If there is no one here to become his witness, I will vouch for him and pay if he is unable to pay." When my husband related this story to me, I thought, "What an outstanding and wonderful man this Nishimoto-san is!" On the basis of Nishimotosan's offer, that man was able to borrow money. There was probably only one man who was unable to repay his loan completely. At that time there were many Hiroshima people in the valley. A lot of Okayama and Kyushu people joined too.[21] I did not attend any *kenjinkai* meetings—this was all handled by the menfolk. Some women attended but only to have wifely visits among themselves. [Mrs. Misuyo Nakamura]

> Most of the meetings were held at our home, because Papa was the "boss" [president] of the group. We also had a banquet after each meeting. At first the group was composed of just Hiroshima people, but toward the end there were Okayama people who wished to join. Probably there were around thirty or more members. Those who wished to borrow put their applications in early, saying "If I cannot get the loan, I will be unable to continue my farm." It

seemed that the *kenjinkai* matched those who needed a loan with those who could make a loan. [Mrs. Asayo Noji]

Women's Organization (Fujinkai)

Many of the women, like Mrs. Hatsumi Nishimoto, belonged to a *fujinkai* (women's society), partially social and partially civic in function: "We had a Japanese ladies' organization, headed by Mrs. Yasui. She often explained American ways of life to us and taught us to show good manners toward the *hakujin* so our behavior would not be an embarrassment to the Japanese. When meetings were held at our own home, women met inside and the men baby-sat outside."

Japanese Language School

While most of the Issei spoke Japanese, their children, who attended public schools in Hood River, were learning English and were easily adopting American ways. By 1925, after many Issei had determined they would become permanent valley residents, they expressed a desire for their children to learn Japanese. Concerned about attitudes of Caucasians, Mr. Masuo Yasui, Issei spokesman, met with the county school superintendent for two hours. He maintained that learning Japanese would help the children grow to "know and understand the two countries and work to bring two countries closer." Emphasizing that "it is parents' responsibility to raise our children to grow to be useful citizens of the United States," he sought the school system's help.[22]

Issei, too, recognized the need for their children to retain a sense of heritage while also bridging a widening gap in language and values between the two generations:

> All four of my children went to Japanese language school. We felt it was important that the children learn how to speak *Nihongo* [Japanese]. Japanese parents could not speak *Eigo* [English] and were so busy they did not have the time to teach their children the language. At Japanese language school, the children could learn *Nihongo*, and relations between the two generations could be improved. By the end of the classes, the children were learning very difficult *Nihongo!* This improved our conversation. When we lived in Oak Grove, we held Japanese school at the grade school. Eventually that became inconvenient, so school was held at our large home. Forty children came to my house every Saturday for one hour. They filled our house! [Mrs. Hama Yamaki]

My children Toshi and Kimiko attended a Japanese school at the Dee Japanese Community Hall. People in this area thought the Japanese ought to be able to speak *Nihongo*. Even though it was difficult, the children attended Japanese school every day after their regular school. The children at times went straight from regular school to Japanese school and stayed as late as six o'clock. When it got dark, I would go to meet them. I believe they attended Japanese school on Saturday too. It cost six dollars a month. [Mr. Miyozo Yumibe]

Issei recognized, however, that their Americanized children did not necessarily view classes in a positive light:

Most of the children did not really like it too well. *Nihongo* is very difficult. But because we are Japanese, we thought they should learn to speak *Nihongo*. [Mrs. Tei Endow]

In earlier days, we had ambitions to return to Japan, so we encouraged our children to learn *Nihongo*. (Of course, all that changed with the coming of war.) *Nihon-gakko* [abbreviated form for *Nihongo-gakko*, Japanese language school] was spent mostly reading and writing in *Nihongo*. Our children did not like to attend, but we insisted. [Mrs. Miyoshi Noyori]

Our children attended only because we asked them. And, although the cost may seem small today, it was quite expensive during the depression. [Mr. Masaji Kusachi]

In these times, when frugality became an accepted way of life, Japanese families were often unable to spare money for Japanese language school. Mrs. Misuyo Nakamura described how she and her husband took on the teaching duties themselves: "No, no money. These were financially difficult times so we could not send our children to Japanese school. Instead, we purchased books from Japan. My husband taught *Nihongo* to our oldest son Terushi, and I taught *Nihongo* to my second son Sumio. We did not study every night, but we may have studied two to three times a week."

Japanese Community Halls

During the 1920s, two community halls were erected by groups of Issei who lived in opposite ends of the valley. The halls, one in downtown Hood River and one in upper Dee, became popular meeting places as well as recreation and cultural centers for local Japanese.

Hood River Japanese Community Hall

On February 1, 1925, at the first meeting of the Zairyu Doho Taikai (Association of Japanese Living in the Area) held at the Barrett Grange Hall, Mr. Ikutaro Takagi gave the following speech: "We are proud that Japanese are building a community in this beautiful Hood River. The only regret is that this fine organization does not own a meeting place. The K.P. [Knights of Pythias] Hall, which had been our meeting hall for over a decade, was burned down in the summer of 1924. We now feel an urgent need for our meeting hall. We also would like to start a Japanese school as the next generation grows in large numbers."[23]

After considering the positive and negative factors in a centrally located school, members cast a secret ballot. Seven of the seventeen votes favored a meeting hall and separate school, which was the most popular of three options. Mr. Takagi estimated that with 150 to 160 children in the valley (50 to 60 of school age) and 180 to 200 adults, the building should have dimensions between forty-by-eighty feet and forty-by-a-hundred feet. The group elected seven committee members to study the matter further and gather ideas for a location. Members examined the situation carefully, for, as one Issei stated, "We cannot give those anti-Japanese activists any excuse to harass us."[24]

At a Zairyu Doho Taikai meeting of all Japanese in April, the committee recommended purchasing two acres on the north side of Columbia Lot North Road. The estimated cost was $5,700, including $1,200 for the property and $4,500 for the building contractor's price. With the vote thirty-six to seven in favor of the plan, a seven-member committee chaired by Mr. Masuyo Yasui was elected to collect contributions. Deciding to visit door-to-door as a group, members solicited on Sundays, generally beginning at 10 A.M. and concluding by 11:00 P.M. for dinner and discussion. On one particular Sunday, however, diligent committee members did not reach the Nakamura home until 1:00 A.M. Undaunted by the late hour, they woke him to ask for his contribution and finally left at 2:30 A.M. By mid-summer, they had received sixty-seven contributions, totaling over $7,200. That July at the third Zairyu Doho Taikai meeting, area Japanese unanimously decided to "construct out" (contract out), choosing the "lowest bid with good personality" from four or five professionals. The long-term project, they said, should meet not only recreational needs but spiritual and mental development ones as well. They concluded the hall should be large enough to hold all the Japanese in the area. Members elected an eleven-member construction committee to supervise the building,[25] and the Hood River hall was completed in 1926. Mr. Chiho Tomita recounted in English:

The Oak Grove Band, composed of young Nisei, performed at a church conference at the Japanese Community Hall in 1934. (Courtesy of Itsu Akiyama)

About 1918 our Japanese community have lots of people, lots of children—need own hall. Four or five times, maybe more, have discussion. At last we settled to build. Seven thousand dollars big money! At that time people not very rich. So some $50 donate, some $100, some $200, some $25 donate. Then make $7,000. Carpenter contract built quite a big two-story house on West Sherman Street downtown. It had a full basement and kitchen. Used for Japanese school and for Japanese picture show and parties. Some people dance *odori* [Japanese dance] and sing; everybody take food potluck. After war they give to Nisei Committee.[26]

Issei enthusiastically recalled a variety of memorable events at their hall, including plays and musical performances:

We had talent shows about twice a year. We all sang together. Even Parkdale people participated. Everybody came, even *hakujin!* I wore a kimono of silk crepe and performed *ocha* [tea ceremony] on the stage. We also displayed ikebana [flower arrangements] to show our *hakujin* friends. We even had plays where we charged admission to raise funds for the hall. In a play about General Nogi, I performed as a maid, dusting and cleaning the stage and welcoming

The Dee Japanese Community Hall, constructed completely through volunteer labor, was a social center for about thirty-five families in 1927. (Courtesy of Chiye Sakamoto)

visitors. I very much enjoyed it in those days! I remember that Mrs. Norimatsu impersonated a man—she played the part so well! We brought *byobu* [folding screens] and *shoji* [opaque rice paper screens]. Under Inouye-sensei's [the Reverend Isaac Inouye, minister of the Japanese Methodist Church] direction,[27] volunteers built a house on the stage. It is a wonder we worked so hard! [Mrs. Hama Yamaki]

Inouye-sensei organized programs at the Japanese Community Hall. We also had the Oak Grove Band. My son George played trombone; Nobi played alto (French horn); Chitose played saxophone. They performed for Christmas and New Year's parties at the Japanese Hall. They even played Japanese songs! [Mrs. Itsu Akiyama]

Dee Japanese Community Hall

During the mid-1920s, about thirty-five Japanese families resided in the tiny, hillside community of Dee. Their local hall, on land donated by Mr. Shiroye Sato, was a fifty-by-a-hundred-foot wood building with a half-basement, constructed completely through voluntary labor. A popular meeting place, the hall became the site for dances featuring Caucasian orchestras, kendo and judo lessons taught to local residents, and a platform for the Christian evangelist Dr. Smith, who was long remembered for his Japanese message, "*Yukai-deshita* [It was wonderful]!" Outside the north end of the hall, chicken wire extended ten feet high to surround modest dirt courts for local tennis tournaments.[28] Mr. Masaji Kusachi, a Dee resident, recalled the parties with fondness:

> I remember we used to have New Year's parties and weddings. In Japan the New Year was celebrated for three days. We brought this custom with us to the United States, but our party lasted just one day. Our gathering of fifty to sixty was *nigiyaka* [lively] with lots of children. We all dressed in our suits and fancy clothes and ate Japanese food potluck. School children taught by Tsuji-san, the Japanese schoolteacher, put on plays in Japanese.
>
> We also showed films from Japan—as many as four or five showings a year—and they always drew a big crowd. In those days people toured the country showing Japanese films in Japanese communities.

Buddhist Church

Many Issei retained their Buddhist faith while in America. By practicing the daily rite each morning in front of their family altar, they began their days with a sense of righteousness and order.[29] "In Japan," Mrs. Hatsumi Nishimoto recalled, "we had observed Buddhist rituals at our family altar, and Father chanted his rituals before breakfast and after supper. Brought up in this religious family background, I found I could remember those chants in the United States."

In 1898, ten years after the Christian church began mission work among Japanese, the Buddhist church finally organized in the United States. While Issei had been hesitant to establish an institution so closely rooted in Japanese fundamentals, Buddhist church leaders in Japan were also reluctant to commit missionaries and finances to America. Within ten years after the first Buddhist association organized in San Francisco, seventeen new churches formed, including one in Portland.[30]

Hood River Issei, who represented several Buddhist sects, including Shin and Nichiren, regularly traveled to Portland to attend services. In time, visiting priests from Portland reciprocated and conducted services locally. "Our Buddhist church services in Dee were held every Friday at members' homes," Mr. Masaji Kushachi recounted, "We took turns hosting the services. At our home we provided a meal for the *o-shonin* [priest] too—be it lunch or supper. His sermon was based on *Okkyo Bun*, the Buddhist book. It reflected common sense applied to our everyday lives. In the Nichiren Buddhist Church, we burned *senko* [incense] at every service, although I do not know why.[31] Also we each placed little grains into the incense burner at each service. Afterward we ate refreshments—some sweets or candy."

Buddhist practices extended beyond the spiritual to include health care as well. A number of valley Issei practiced *yaito*, a ninth-century health treatment said to be developed by a Buddhist priest. *Yaito* was based on the theory that applying heat to one of 657 vital spots on the body could cure illness by stimulating blood circulation and the nervous system.[32] Mr. Masaji Kusachi explained it more fully:

> *Yaito* is a Buddhist practice. Before war, I picked up three apple boxes at once and popped out my back. A lady in Portland applied *mogusa* [moxa; soft wool of wormwood leaves] in a circle of nines and, in two weeks, my back felt much better. *Yaito* is a treatment where *yamogi* [yellowish, dried and crushed wormwood leaves] was burned on the skin. An amount the size of a grain of rice was lit with *senko* until it felt good and the *mogusa* burned. But if you did not place the *mogusa* on the right spot, you might make the ailment worse. *Yaito* used to be passed on from father to son. During the war, when prisoners of war saw Japanese applying this treatment, they thought Japanese were setting themselves on fire.

Japanese Methodist Church

By 1914, about 4 or 5 percent of Issei in the United States had become Christians, either through missionary work in Japan or Christian missions on the West Coast.[33] In Hood River, the Christian message was first brought to Japanese laborers in 1920 by a Seattle Methodist minister, Rev. Murphy. Shortly afterward, Rev. Seiji Uemura traveled from his pastorate at the Portland Japanese Methodist Church to conduct monthly services.

In October 1926, with one minister, two full members, and a rented house, a Japanese Methodist church had its modest beginnings in the tiny community of Odell. The house reportedly also became a parsonage for Rev. Inosuke Taira, appointed by the Japanese Mission Conference to serve a congregation consisting of Mr. and Mrs. Kamegoro Iwatsuki and three preparatory members.[34] "Taira-sensei [Rev. Inosuke Taira] had a large family," Mrs. Tei Endow remembered, "and I think it was difficult for him to make a living here. He did not have a car, so he had to call on families by foot. Housing was not furnished for him, so the few church members had to contribute to the rental of a house."

Rev. Inosuke Taira remained about a year before the arrival of a new minister in 1927 initiated rapid growth in spiritual and communitywide programs among the Japanese. Rev. Isaac Inouye, trained at a Methodist seminary in Japan, was highly educated, having also received degrees from Emory, Boston, and Harvard universities in the United States.[35] Mrs. Hama Yamaki remembered him well: "Inouye-sensei [Rev. Isaac Inouye] began a church at the Japanese Community Hall. Inouye-sensei had graduated from Harvard. Since he was able to speak English as well as Japanese, he drew all the young people, including those in Taira-sensei's classes. We had as many as one hundred people at our services! After serving for less than a year, Taira-sensei departed, and the two groups united. Inouye-sensei had a very good reputation with the Japanese and stayed for about fifteen years.

Dynamic and outgoing, Rev. Isaac Inouye expanded his congregation of 10 or 11 families to a full membership of 84, with Sunday school attendance at 112 and a Youth Epworth League of 60. Spreading his ministry to White Salmon, Washington, and other surrounding areas, he also organized social and cultural gatherings.[36] "Inouye-sensei was probably somewhat disappointed to be assigned to this backward area," Mrs. Tei Endow commented. "Because he was single, Inouye-sensei was given living quarters in the basement of the Japanese Community Hall. He was responsible for some plays: the *Mikado* and seven or eight on the life of Jesus."

Mrs. Hama Yamaki vividly recalled the church's activities:

> Our church was strong and had many members, so we had a singing group. We even went to The Dalles and sang hymns in *hakujin* churches. My favorites were "Blessed Assurance" and "Sweet Bye and Bye!" We also had a ladies' auxiliary, and we went to conferences in Seattle, Spokane, and Tacoma. Six or seven of us practiced tea ceremony and flower arrangement. Other church members participated if they wanted to learn.
>
> Japanese Methodist churches in the Northwest held a conference every year. After Inouye-sensei came, we held a gathering of M. E. Kyokai [Methodist Episcopal Church Association] people at Tilly Jane [Mt. Hood camping area]. Delegates came from Seattle, Spokane, Yakima, Portland, and Tacoma. We prayed together and sang hymns and exchanged church experiences. We stayed two nights and set up tents for sleeping—we were worried about bears!

During the 1950s, Issei began a building fund for their own sanctuary. After realistically assessing the churchgoing habits of their children, however, they disbanded the project. Mr. Chiho Tomita reminisced in English about the church: "1926, I think, start church. Go every Sunday for service at Japanese hall. We tried to build a church building beside the

Rev. Isaac Inouye, a Harvard-educated minister who spoke both Japanese and English, was prominent in the development of the Japanese Methodist church and Japanese community life in Hood River. (Courtesy of Alice Ito)

hall, but the Hood River Nisei people go to all different church. Oak Grove people go to Oak Grove *hakujin* church. Pine Grove people—Pine Grove church. So we said, 'No use to build a Issei church.' We donate $3,000 in savings account to Asbury church in Hood River.) At that time Asbury remodel inside, need lots of money."[37]

Community Gatherings

During the early years, with farm needs so pressing, Issei had limited opportunities to meet socially. Their few get-togethers thus became joyous occasions and included observing Japanese traditions as well as learning American ways.

County Fourth of July Celebration

On the Fourth of July in 1914, Caucasian and Japanese communities both contributed to a novel interpretation of the traditionally all-American celebration. That year the Fourth of July parade featured twenty young Issei men who depicted different classes of Japanese society. The Japanese laborer, mechanic, Shinto priest, swordsman, knight of the higher class, and knight of the lower class each marched in ceremonial costumes before local parade viewers. That evening, at Hood River's Chautauqua, when George Wilbur made his entrance on stage as the mikado, he was accompanied by a chorus of Japanese men, including Masuo Yasui, M. Okido, U. Saiki, Chiyokichi Nakamura, Kozo Karasawa, T. Okada, Shohei Endo, and G. Sasaki. The eventful day culminated with fireworks provided by the Issei, who had raised three hundred dollars for the festivities. Their display was organized by Tadao Sato, who had learned to make fireworks in Japan.[38]

Japanese Opera

At the invitation of Rev. Isaac Inouye, a Japanese diva and her troupe performed *Madame Butterfly* for the local Japanese and Caucasian communities during the late 1920s,[39] which Mrs. Hama Yamaki remembered quite clearly: "Miura Tamaki, an opera singer, was also revered in Japan. She was on tour in Portland and performed for a very large gathering at the Hood River High School. She was very stately and had a beautiful voice. There were even *hakujin* in the audience. Everyone enjoyed it immensely."

Picnics

The 1921 minutes of the Japanese Farmers' Association of Hood River memorialized the annual *undokai* (picnic and sports contest day), an eagerly awaited Sunday outing: "Beautiful view. Lifted up our spirits. About 300 attended. Program started at noon. Many games were played. All went home when the sun set behind western mountains."[40]

For Mrs. Tei Endow, *undokai* was a welcome break from work, as she delightedly recounted in English: "Every year during summer vacation we had *undokai* at Parkdale school ground—all the Japanese in Hood River. We take sandwiches and buy ice cream. I like *nihon-shoku* [Japanese food] but son Sho no like. Ten families eat together. Everybody telephone, 'Do you want to go on picnic?' 'Yeah.' 'Good.' Children play and run around. They had three-legged race. Women and men had nice time: just talk, talk, talk. You know, all time stay home. Just one year—one time get together. So lots of stories."

Races were always the highlight for the energetic Mrs. Asayo Noji:

> We held *undokai* every year in the Parkdale area right behind McIsaac's store and at times in mountain clearings along the loop highway. In one contest, two baskets were raised high on poles. Each group of men and women tried to be first to fill their basket with colored balls. We also had races—three-legged races, running, and contests juggling three or four balls. I usually won first place in juggling but not in running. I remember one slim, tall lady from the Tsubota family in Bingen who was a very fast and young runner. I wanted to beat her at least one time. But, even though I tried hard, I was never able to do that. So I always came in second. One year first prize for that race was a *jubako* [lacquered tiered boxes]. How I wanted that! For second place I received a Chinese vase and silk stockings. The vase was donated by Kohara Store, an import shop in Portland. At that time Japanese businesses—Ban Shoten [store], Kohara-san, Teikoku—donated quality merchandise for our prizes. We all looked forward to *undokai*!

Adjusting to their new homeland, Hood River Issei used both formal and informal means to maintain strong ethnic bonds. Formally, Issei consciously organized systems to support their farming ventures, their finances, their cultural adjustment, the language development of their children, their religious faith, and their needs for socializing and maintaining their traditions. Informally, adopting practices used in their own families in Japan, they relied heavily on each other, particularly those from their own prefectures in Japan, for mutual assistance and social support. These support systems offered both solace and insulation as they made efforts to adjust.

19

Celebrations

ISSEI CONTINUED to observe, to different degrees, some of the festivals they had celebrated in Japan. On these occasions, solemn rituals were combined with joyous tributes.

New Year's Day

On New Year's Day, Japanese cast away evil influences and declared the birth of a new year with its fresh promise and good fortune. In preparation, they traditionally completed their unfinished business, paid the year's debts, scrupulously cleaned their homes, and visited shrines to pray for good health and happiness during the year ahead.[1] For Issei in Hood River, the most celebrated holiday of the year became a time for feasting and socializing with friends and relatives. Even then, distinctions between the roles of men and women were evident:

> We celebrated the New Year for a whole week by cooking for the menfolk who paid us their respects. We offered them o-sake [rice wine; o- is honorific], o-sashimi [sliced raw fish], and o-nishime [assorted boiled and seasoned vegetables]. Women did not go with the men, for they were busy cooking. [Mrs. Hatsumi Nishimoto]

> We ordered fresh fish from Portland to celebrate New Year's Day. Since our house was large, the Oak Grove gathering was usually at our home. Only the men came. (Women stayed home to care for the children.) Men arrived early in the morning to prepare the food. We served baked sakana [fish], sashimi, chicken, and rice curry. After the meal, the men drank sake. I remember singing with them too. Afterward the men took portions of leftovers home to

their families. We had so much to do, it was most exhausting. Later
we held potluck celebrations at the Japanese Community Hall, with
. over one hundred people attending. We bought huge steaks [roasts]
and prepared them there. [Mrs. Hama Yamaki]

During the slack winter work period, families in the Parkdale community took advantage of extra time to extend best wishes and celebrate
with their friends, causing one school-bound child to earnestly ask his
mother, "Whose house shall I come home to tonight?" Mrs. Asayo Noji
had fond memories of those days:

O-shogatsu, traditional Japanese New Year, was enjoyable. We
celebrated most of January by visiting, feasting, and staying over-
night with other families. We ate nishime and o-sushi. We were not
always able to get fish, for winter conditions sometimes made travel
to Hood River impossible for as long as a month. After the evening
meal, we ladies played cards—hana and hyakunin-isshu, where one
person began reading a saying on a card and the rest of us tried to
find that card and grab it. Then, in another room, the menfolk
played other card games, like poker or twenty-one. At night our
children slept on the floor just everywhere. It is amazing they did
not catch colds!

Girls' Day (March 3)

On the third day of the third month, families in Japan honored their
daughters by displaying prized, miniature models of the Japanese Court on
five- to seven-tiered shelves covered with bright red fabric. Customarily,
little girls dressed in fine kimonos and invited their friends to admire their
dolls and partake of cakes, candies, and tiny bowls of rice boiled with red
beans.[2] Mrs. Tei Endow, like many other Issei, celebrated Girls' Day in
the United States:

Even in those days, our children were small and our highest priority was making a living. So we did not have too much time for
other activities. But we did celebrate O-hina [Dolls' Festival, or
Girls' Day]. When I was growing up in Japan, we observed it regularly by displaying our dolls—no, you did not play with them. In
America about all we were able to do was to explain the story[3] to
our children and serve a special meal: mochi [rice cakes] shaped in
a triangle and decorated with candles. In Japan it is true that boys
were stationed higher in life. But, because we only had one son and
we had two daughters, we did not do much for Boys' Day.

Boys' Day (May 5)

Boys' Day, the fifth day of the fifth month, was a time for families to pay tribute to their sons. Japanese expressed hope that their sons, like the brave samurai warriors, would possess courage, perseverance, health, and fortitude as they overcame obstacles in their lives.[4] Mrs. Hatsumi Nishimoto described the celebration more fully: "On Boys' Day we displayed a huge *koi* [carp] kite outside so the wind would blow it high. We hoped our boys would grow to be strong like the *koi* that swam upstream.[5] For a special meal, I prepared *mochi* in *hasu* [lotus leaf]. We also gave these as gifts, but only to our closest friends."

Emperor's Birthday (April 29)

A holiday to honor the emperor's birthday began on the first year of the Meiji reign in 1868. Issei continued to celebrate this holiday, as Mr. Chiho Tomita recounted in English: "Most every year the emperor birthday party [was held] before [the] war. People come together and read some emperor's message on April 29."

Ancestors

After a family member's death in Japan, relatives held memorial services at designated intervals during the year. On particular yearly anniversaries of the death, services were held to honor the memory of the deceased and to ensure that person's place in paradise.[6] Some, like Mrs. Misuyo Nakamura, upheld this tradition, even if they abandoned all others: "As far as practices of Japan, I probably went no further than observing the anniversary of my parents' passings. On those days I would mention, 'This is Grandfather's day' or 'This is Grandmother's day.' I remember that my mother instilled this tradition in me when I was a child."

O-bon

On O-bon, Japan's Memorial Day, families feted their ancestors, whose spirits they believed had returned to their earthly homes on that day. Both a solemn and joyous occasion, O-bon was a time to memorialize and express gratitude to ancestors,[7] as Mrs. Misuyo Nakamura explained:

We used to come together for O-bon [All Souls' Day or the Feast of Lanterns] services at the cemetery. I will try to explain its mean-

ing so you can understand:[8] There was once a great teacher of the
Buddhist religion. In a moment of deep meditation, he saw that his
mother, who had been a greedy person during her lifetime, was suffering in Hell. His starving mother had become skin and bones.
When he saw her suffering so, this Buddhist teacher offered food to
his mother, but it burst into flames. Then Buddha told the teacher
to make an offering of food to his fellow teachers and pray for his
mother. When they saw that his offering saved all beings from Hell,
they clapped their hands in joy. This was the source of the O-bon
dance. Buddhists believe that on this occasion the spirits of our deceased family members return to join us in dance.

Traditionally, we offer special foods to their souls: *o-hagi* [sweet-
ened bean jam filled with mashed rice], *o-mochi* [rice cakes], and
various fruits and flowers. But, perhaps in respect to those who have
passed on, we do not offer meat or fish, which represent flesh. In
Hood River we observed O-bon on a day which fell between American Memorial Day and traditional O-bon day on August 15. We
did not observe O-bon by singing and dancing, as they did in larger
areas, like Portland. A minister conducted a service at our cemetery. The Hood River Japanese belonged to different religions, so
each year we rotated ministers from different churches—usually between the two sects of Buddhists and a Christian minister.

Fourth of July

Issei paid tribute to America's Independence Day in their own unique
ways:

My manner of recognizing American holidays, like Fourth of July
and Christmas, was to prepare a special dish for dinner. This was
naturally a Japanese dish, like chow mein[9] or *o-sushi*, for I did not
know how to prepare American dishes. But I did sometimes bake
pies and cakes. At that time, very few Issei women knew how to
bake. [Mrs. Misuyo Nakamura]

We did not celebrate any of those traditional Japanese holidays,
but we did have a Fourth of July celebration! Papa and Mr. Kawachi
displayed American flags on the front of their trucks, and we rode
to Odell. The children were delighted! We all ate fried chicken and
makizushi [rolled vinegar rice filled with vegetables and fish] and
made our own ice cream. The children ran around, and the adults
visited. [Mrs. Itsu Akiyama]

Spirited reunions with friends brought a necessary balance to Issei's daily challenges and labor intensive routines. Whether their celebrations were traditionally Japanese or newly adopted American, they became regular and eagerly anticipated observances for Japanese families in Hood River.

20

Trying Times

IN THE BIRTHLAND of their children, Issei were fervently attempting to bring both their young orchards and their young families to productivity and maturity. Yet awkward moments with neighbors, persistent financial problems, and doubts about their return to Japan continued to plague them.

Neighbors

Very often, Issei became self-conscious and uncomfortable in their encounters with Caucasians, even when bestowed with kindness. To avoid such situations, they frequently resorted to avoiding their Caucasian neighbors altogether. As Mrs. Hatsumi Nishimoto expressed, the problem stemmed from language: "Our neighbors brought produce from their garden and invited me to their house. Usually I did not go, because I was frustrated that I could not speak English." Others recognized blatant discrimination yet tried not to take offense:

> When I first come, young kids throw rocks at me. But I like living America. People are so nice. Neighbors sometimes make pies and cake for me. Just few American people *haiseki* [discrimination, used here as "discriminatory"] to Japanese. Some Americans *haiseki* outside but in private no *haiseki*. I work for doctor in Pine Grove. I help spray and prune, everything. He was a nice man, but he don't like the Japanese.[1] I don't know why. [Mr. Chiho Tomita, in English]

> In 1935, when we bought this property in Pine Grove, we were the only Japanese in the area. We bought the property in Eiko's

[daughter's] name, because Issei were not able to purchase land. A neighbor down the road did not appear to be very friendly and asked if we would sell our land to him. My husband said, "We just barely got here. Why would we want to sell this place?" The man had no other words for us and went home. Other people in this area were most kind. I do not recall that anyone treated us unfairly. I believe that they were all good people. [Mrs. Hama Yamaki]

For Mrs. Misuyo Nakamura, however, a humiliating experience would leave a lasting impression: "One time Papa had a flat tire on his old Ford car, so he was repairing it by the road. Some young people drove by and threw an apple toward Papa. This so infuriated him that he said, 'Some day I will have a better car.' And you may recall that Papa almost always had a large, good car. This is probably a result of the treatment he received from those people."

Financial Difficulties

Scrimping, saving, and sacrificing, by necessity, became second nature to the Issei:

We did have our most difficult times. But, because we were so isolated, we were not aware most of the time how poor we really were. Whenever we needed anything, though, my husband would provide money. [Mrs. Tei Endow]

We were a poor family, so we were seldom able to eat meat. Every day we ate fried potatoes. But my children ate their meals without complaining, because they realized we were very poor. As they grew older and required more food, my husband saw that it took a lot of rice to feed them. Life was difficult for him. Nevertheless, he insisted that these growing children should be fed well. Gradually we were able to eat more pork and chicken. [Mrs. Hisa Wakamatsu]

Our most trying time before [the] war was when we raised strawberries and we were not paid sufficiently. There were years when we were not able to eat *o-mochi* [rice cakes] for New Year's Day, which was traditional. We could only look forward to the next year's crop and hope we would be able to earn more money. [Mr. Chiho Tomita]

The Great Depression

The collapse of the stock market in 1929 signaled economic panic throughout the country. Banks closed, businesses failed, and employees were discharged. As credit tightened and hundreds of thousands found themselves without incomes or savings, most families struggled in their efforts to provide even the bare necessities:

It was a most difficult time. We seemed to have gotten by. Friends lost money at the bank, but we did not suffer that loss since we kept most of our money at home. We did not have too much to worry about, anyhow. I recall times during the depression when it was even hard to buy shoes for the children. My husband was resourceful, though, so he earned money by packing fruit and working for others. When I think about it now, it is surprising that we managed as well as we did. But all our friends shared the same problem. [Mrs. Tei Endow]

We postponed buying items we wanted badly, like clothing. "Stop everything!" [Mrs. Hatsumi Nishimoto]

In the early 1930s, we were banking with Butler Bank in Hood River. When it went bankrupt, we lost everything there. We were penniless! We had no money to buy bread, so at times we made pancakes for the children's lunch. [Mrs. Itsu Akiyama]

During the depression, we barely managed to eke out a living. At that time in the early 1930s, the Butler Bank went *gachan* [bang (bankrupt)]. This had a devastating effect on the valley. I did not keep a savings account there, but we lost all the money in our checking account. We survived only because I was able to find temporary work on the railroad and at the sawmill. A store in Odell gave us credit and made deliveries once a week. About once a month a Japanese store from Portland took our orders and delivered goods, like rice and *shoyu* [soy sauce], to the Dee depot. A Trout Creek dairyman also delivered milk to my home for eight cents a quart. Those were trying times, because there were always three or four children going to school. [Mr. Masaji Kusachi]

Many Hood River farmers, including Issei, were overinvested during this period and suffered greatly. Since Issei were just beginning to gain a foothold in the agricultural market, this was a particular hardship. Yet, through community support and monetary sacrifices, they survived. Very few Japanese families, in fact, sought or received government welfare during the depression.[2]

Decision to Stay in America

Most Issei had planned to remain in America for a mere three to five years. But, with growing families, a lack of funds, and declining relations between the United States and Japan, their situations changed:

I tried to go back to Japan. But I married and have babies: three, four, five children—too much expense for living. I said to my family in Japan, "I have no money. I can't go back." I send them twenty-five dollars every month while I working—fifty yen, big money in Japan. So I don't save any money. After my children grow, I ask them about go back to Japan. They said, "No, don't like." They like to stay this country, so I stay here. [Mr. Chiho Tomita, in English]

We had such a large family that there was no chance of going back to Japan. It took too much money to return, and we had no home in Japan—so we had no choice. We had to stay. [Mrs. Itsu Akiyama]

Before [the] war, it was always our desire to return to Japan. But at the beginning of the war, we seriously reconsidered the matter. We decided that—for our children's sake—it would not be fair to return to Japan. Our sons had little understanding of the Japanese language, and they would find it difficult to live in Japan. [Mrs. Hatsumi Nishimoto]

By 1940, 126,948 Japanese resided in the continental United States, constituting less than one-tenth of 1 percent of the population. Almost nine out of ten Japanese resided in the three West Coast states.[3] Approximately 45 percent of those employed were engaged in raising crops.[4] In Hood River, the number of Japanese had decreased to 462, less than 4 percent of the county's population and just 11 percent of the Japanese in Oregon.[5] After withstanding oppressive conditions in this country and finally deciding to make the valley their home, Issei were gradually increasing the productivity of their young orchards. Yet their perseverance was to be severely tested.

PART SIX

War Years

Tsune no hi wa
Ware ni shitashiki
Hito narishi
Kyo ikameshiku
Shimon toritari

Once close friends,
Today they are Americans.
They take our fingerprints
And are unmoved.

Tanka written by Mrs. Shizue Iwatsuki and
translated by Dr. Stephen W. Kohl

21

Pearl Harbor Sunday

AT DAWN on Sunday, December 7, 1941, Japan took American forces by surprise and bombed U.S. ships and planes at Pearl Harbor, Hawaii. More than 3,500 Americans were killed or wounded, and 2 American battleships and 149 planes were destroyed.[1] The next day the United States responded by declaring war on Japan, and Germany and Italy followed Japan into the war. For the Issei, a nightmare was to begin. Mrs. Hama Yamaki clearly recalled her alarm:

"I was most frightened by the bombing! I was surprised that Japan was able to bomb Pearl Harbor while the ships were lining the harbor. My husband, my daughter Mitsie, and I were in Los Angeles to see my first grandchild. I went to the third floor of the hotel and looked toward the ocean, although I could not see anything. We had to consult a lawyer to get a permit to return home. Two weeks passed before we were able to return. After we read newspaper articles about Nihonjin [Japanese] in Idaho being shot,[2] we were very frightened and drove right home. We only stopped once at a restaurant to have coffee. Even though the rooms were dark, we could see that others were staring at us. No one said anything to us, but we drank our coffee hurriedly and left. Then as we were driving home during a snowstorm, our car stalled in the middle of a mountain road. We were very frightened! But a car drive right up and a Caucasian man offered to help us. Without a word about Pearl Harbor, he brought out his tools and worked on our motor. The car ignition started smoothly! I wanted to clasp his hand in appreciation, but all I said was, "Thank you! Thank you!" We were really relieved to be able to continue on our way.

For Mrs. Tei Endow, the day had begun with wistful thoughts of her American-born son, who was serving his country in the armed forces. By the end of the day, however, she was consumed with fears for his safety: "December 7 happened to be my son Sho's birthday. He had earlier volunteered for the military, and I was thinking that we would be celebrating his birthday if he were home. I heard the news of Pearl Harbor directly from Japan on our shortwave radio. They were claiming all kinds of victory. I was seriously worried about what would become of my son."

How ironic that Mrs. Asayo Noji, who had taken such pride in her son's service to the United States, should now be forced to ponder her own fate:

> This news was a terrible shock! To think that the United States was at war with Japan was unbelievable! I worried a lot, because my oldest son Mamoru had already served in the U.S. Army one month. And the Pearl Harbor bombing happened about a month or two after a banquet at the Hood River Japanese Community Hall. We had honored three Nisei inductees (including my son) into the army. There were rumors that we might be forced to leave the country, and some thought it might be best to return to Japan. But we knew we could not go to Japan, because my son was already in the service. Others feared that our property would be taken. The area was rampant with rumors.

For others, such as Mrs. Miyoshi Noyori and her family, Japan's bombing would help to sort out ambivalent feelings about national loyalties:

> I was at home. Our children had been at the local community hall preparing for a Christmas program. They returned to tell me Japan had bombed Pearl Harbor. My personal thoughts were difficult to put into words—this was a crushing feeling. We assumed this was inevitable. This was a long war, so we had heard continuing war stories from the Orient. We talked quite frankly with our neighbors about the Japan war, but we did not discuss these events with our children. They were, after all, American citizens. But from that time on, I realized I would be more inclined to remain in this country.

The dramatic news was taken in stride by Mr. Miyozo Yumibe, whose trusting nature prevented any cause for alarm:

> This is the way I remember that Pearl Harbor Sunday: I was taking care of the boiler at the sawmill. Our electric man, my supervisor Harold Brower, approached me and said, "Japan has bombed Pearl Harbor." He asked if I had heard the news. That was the first

time I had heard, and I just said, "That's too bad." Work at the sawmill seemed no different the next day. I do not remember any reaction from the other workers. After all, we Issei had nothing to do with the bomb—this was an affair of the Japanese government. I continued working until two weeks before evacuation time, about the first of May.

When they learned the horrendous news, many of the lower valley Japanese were preparing for an evening talent show at the downtown Japanese Community Hall. The event was to be a fundraiser for a new flush toilet to replace the outhouse several hundred feet down the hill.[3] "That day," Mr. Chiho Tomita recounted in English, "we had last day of training [practice] for talent show next Sunday. Everybody—whole family—at Japanese Community Hall for training. Some dance, some sing. I was chairman. While we have training, policeman come over and said, 'We are at war. You Japanese shouldn't be together. Stay home.' So we quit the show. No more show. Everybody confused."

From the confusion rose disbelief, as Mrs. Itsu Akiyama vividly recalled:

> We went out in the orchard and saw a number of planes flying overhead—more than we had ever seen before. We wondered what was going on. Papa had been reading in the newspaper that war with Japan seemed imminent. That Sunday Papa was at a gathering at the Community Hall. He turned the radio on when he returned that afternoon, and there was some wild talk about war starting. A neighbor boy about ten years old told us, "War has started. Japan has started war." That made me shiver with fright! What I could not really understand—and what we questioned at the time—was why Japanese would attack in a surprise instead of having declared war first. *Bushido* [ethical code of the samurai] in Japan said that if two samurai were attacking each other and one had a broken sword, the man with the full sword would not attack until the other person held a new sword. Brought up in this tradition, I just could not believe that Japan would attack without declaring war.

Within a few hours of the bombing, Issei were branded "enemy aliens" by the government. Along the Pacific Coast, agents of the Federal Bureau of Investigation (FBI) began rounding up Issei community leaders, who were suspected of subversive acts against the government. By evening, hundreds of Issei in the Pacific Northwest had been taken into custody, and 2,192 Japanese nationals were arrested by February 16, 1942.[4]

Mrs. Itsu Akiyama relived the anguish of that evening—anguish that continued throughout the one and a half years she would be separated from her husband:

We had been very concerned, because Papa was head of the local Japanese society and had all the books. We were sure that authorities would come—and, if they found the books, we would be in real trouble. Finally we decided to burn them in the stove.

We were so worried about the war that we had a sleepless night. About three o'clock in the morning, headlights from a car flashed on our upstairs bedroom window. Then somebody knocked on our front door so forcefully that we were afraid the door might break down! That was when Papa went downstairs. The conversation was very loud and aggressive and was kind of scary to me. A young FBI man and a local policeman named Hollenbeck scooped everything from our desk, even advertising from Yasui's store. Upstairs they stared at our sleeping children and searched all our drawers and shelves. I had kept all the letters my mother had sent me from Japan. This disturbed the investigators so much, they asked, "Why do you save all your old letters?" I was unable to express my feelings in English. All I could do was cry! They took all my letters, saying, "Don't worry. We'll return them to you." But I did not receive them until after the war.[5] After the men had collected my letters, I accompanied them down the stairs. When they decided to take Papa, we had to change his clothes. I was really concerned about the children going to school the following day. As the men were leaving, I asked if it was all right for the children to attend school. They said that was all right. Papa had no parting words. He did exactly what he was told. At that time the FBI said that he would not be gone too long, so I was really not too worried.

The two officials left with Mr. Akiyama at 6:00 A.M., after spending three hours searching the family's home and barn.

After I got out of bed that morning, I still was not too much concerned, because I thought Papa was coming back. I just told the children that Papa had gone out for a while and would return soon. I did not mention that he had been taken by the FBI. Mr. Munemoto, a neighbor, came over and said that we Oak Grove people ought to have a meeting. When I described to him what had happened, he was astonished. We did not have the meeting, because everyone was so worried. I was hoping that other people would not be pulled in like Papa was. I waited for days and days, and he did not return.

Two to three weeks after he was taken, I met Papa in the Portland jail. He was called into a visitors' area, and we spoke through a screen. I neither asked nor did he tell me how he was treated. We

When her husband was imprisoned in a Justice Department internment center in Missoula, Montana, Mrs. Itsu Akiyama and her five children sent him a family photo. (*front, from left:* Saburo, George, Noboru; *rear:* Mrs. Akiyama, Henry, Kiyo) (Courtesy of Itsu Akiyama)

had bought a lot of fertilizer, and, if I had to farm, I was not sure how much to put around each tree. So Papa instructed me. Then he said, "Since I've been here, I have been baptized." He encouraged me to be baptized at home. I asked him, "When are you going to be released?" He could not tell me.

For the Issei, there were few explanations or answers. Unknowing victims, they were caught in the midst of a wartime frenzy between the only two countries they knew. How would others view them? What was the condition of their sons serving in the U.S. military? Would they ever see their relatives in Japan again? What would be their futures in this country? The emotional pain inflicted on them would be only a small part of the trauma they would face. In the coming months, the civil rights of Issei would be tested, and their lives and those of their families would be severely disrupted.

22

Precautions

"JAP BOAT Flashes Message Ashore"; "Caps on Japanese Tomato Plants Point to Air Base"; "Two Japanese With Maps and Alien Literature Seized"; "Banker Urges Check Caution"; "Officials Feel Japanese May Try Anything"; "Jap Strategy Map Told." Newspaper headlines such as these incited fear, distrust, and threats of sabotage among a generally nervous American public.[1] West Coast rumors ranged from charges that Japanese gardeners hid shortwave transmitters in garden hoses to accusations that a Japanese farmer had grown flowers that, when viewed from the air, formed an arrow toward the airport.[2] Repercussions against West Coast Japanese thus came quickly. In Hood River, all alien Japanese were advised to remain on their premises and leave only when accompanied by Caucasians. Mrs. Misuyo Nakamuro's reaction was typical: "I felt as if I had been personally crushed! I was so frightened I really wondered if the world was coming to an end for us. It was said that we should confine our bodies to our own property. At home Papa and I did not do anything. We were too agitated and worried, you see."

That order, issued jointly by County Judge C. D. Nickelsen and Sheriff John Sheldrake, was a "precautionary and protective measure to head off any untoward incident" by a community member. The two noted that Hood River normally bore a reputation for a high degree of tolerance.[3]

Over the next four months, other restrictions were imposed. Travel five miles beyond one's property was curtailed, and checkpoints were set up along the road. Japanese were forbidden to assemble in groups,[4] and a curfew was set from 8:00 P.M. to 6:00 A.M., with penalty of arrest. The Caucasian community was urged to report any violations.[5] Immediately after the bombing, Japanese assets had been frozen by the federal government, though they were lifted a week later to allow families to draw living expenses.[6]

many years ago. With Christmas
candles it was a beautiful setting.

The next fellowship supper will
be Thursday, January 1, in the
church social room, with Mesdames
Rouson, Wood, Gibbs, Walton,
Thomas and Welty as the hostesses
for the dinner. This is an occasion
to be enjoyed by friends of the
United church.

There were 52 registered and
fingerprinted by the Defense Council Friday evening in the high
school. A fingerprinting outfit will
be stationed in McIlsaac's store so
Violet Cooper can complete the registration.

We hope many of the community
will visit our library on Friday or
Tuesday afternoons to enjoy our
festive look, and read the little
Christmas books on display. New
books just added are: "Bambi" by
Walt Disney; "Nursery Rhymes Set
to Music," with gay illustrations;
"Prayers for Children," a lovely
book; "Seeds" gay and instructive;
also Bess Streeter Aldebck's Christmas story, "The Drum Goes Dead."
Those who met Mrs. Babson's
cousin, Miss Ethel Hague Rea four
year ago, will remember her singing
and acting when a member of the
cast of the Christmas play was ill
and will be interested in her work
this Christmas. As a member of the
national board of the American Red,

Young People's Societies at 7:30,
both junior and high school groups.
New Year's Eve program about
9:30 p.m. New Year's eve. See the
old year out and the new year in
with the young people. An enjoyable
time is assured.

Fellowship supper Thursday evening, January 1.

What then remains? Courage, and
patience, and simplicity, and kindness, and, last of all, ideas remain;
these are the things to lay hold of
and live with.—N. C. Benson.

Medical officers in the U. S. Navy
conduct daily inspections of the
ship's galleys where the food is
prepared.

WARNING

To Japanese Nationals

You are hereby re-
quested to remain on
your own premises
and not leave the
same unless accompa-
nied by an Ameri-
can Citizen.

Signed:

C. D. Nickelsen
County Judge

J. H. Sheldrake
Sheriff

Two and a half weeks after Pearl Harbor was bombed, Issei were warned to remain on their property unless accompanied by an American citizen. (*Hood River
News*, December 26, 1941)

"Enemy aliens" were prohibited from possessing firearms, weapons,
ammunition, explosives, signal devices, shortwave radios, and cameras,
among other items. All such belongings were to be immediately turned in
to the sheriff's office.[7] "I took a few sticks of dynamite, a shortwave radio,
and a big 30/30 rifle to the courthouse," Mr. Masaji Kusachi recalled. "I
did not own the gun and I did not use it. (In earlier days, people would
hunt for deer in this area, so I am guessing that whoever came to hunt left

TO ALL ENEMY ALIENS

Italians, Germans, Japanese

At 11:00 p. m. Monday, December 29, the time for turning in to the Sheriff's office various banned articles, expired. If you have in your possession Cameras, Short-wave Radios, Firearms of any kind and ammunition, the same should be turned in to this office immediately.

By complying with this order you may avoid confiscation of the articles and serious trouble for yourself—for the law provides for prosecution of any person evading this order.

JOHN SHELDRAKE,
Sheriff of Hood River County.

Issei were given less than twenty-four hours to turn in banned items to the sheriff's office. (*Hood River News*, January 2, 1942)

the gun.) We had no ammunition for it. I turned everything over to authorities and received a receipt."

Although the federal ban did not constitutionally apply to the second-generation citizens, many Nisei observed the ruling too, in hopes that their efforts would improve treatment of their Issei parents. Since the order was given on Sunday and released locally with a Monday 11:00 A.M. deadline, however, it was physically impossible for all to comply.[8]

In its editorial, the *Hood River County Sun* warned against idle rumors, malicious gossip, and thoughtless acts during those trying days. The December 12 issue included an anonymous letter from an Issei fruit grower, who declared:

> Doubtless, all of us so-called Alien Japanese in this country sincerely prayed, hoped and expected that there would be some way to iron out the difficulty between the United States and Japan peacefully. It was so sudden and unexpected, I could hardly believe the news that war was declared and almost lost my mind about what to do, but time gradually gave me my senses back and now I know very distinctly what to do if possible directly or indirectly. I will fight against any enemy including Japan, to protect my children and wife all of them who are American citizens, and defend the community where they live. . . . I solemly [sic] pledge my loyalty to this Community and sincerely hope that America is big enough to give me the opportunity to to [sic] prove it.[9]

Publicly professing their devotion to the United States, members of the Mid-Columbia chapter of the Japanese American Citizens' League (JACL), through their president, Mark Sato of Parkdale, announced that they would "confine loyalty exclusively to the United States" and pledged "service useful to the country."[10]

Likewise, the Hood River Issei collectively expressed their appreciation and support for the United States in a pledge submitted to Oregon's Governor Charles A. Sprague, with a copy given to the local newspaper. The letter contained 148 Issei signatures:

> "WE, the permanent Japanese resident nationals in this county of Hood River, do express to you and through you to the federal, state and local officials, and to the American people at large, our heartfelt and sincere gratitude for the generous treatment accorded us by our courteous American friends. We are grateful for the many kindnesses and sympathies expressed to us.
>
> Most of the alien Japanese residents are devoted to this great Democratic America though we are not eligible for citizenship. We love this country so much that we wish to live here permanently, obeying American laws, policies, and administration always and especially during the present

situation; and to cooperate whole-heartedly, endeavoring to prove our destinies common with that of the American public.

The local Japanese natives have signed with the local civilian defense committee to volunteer for whatever purposes called upon. Fourteen of our American born boys of Japanese ancestry have answered the call to duty with the United States army.[11] We hope there will be further opportunities to prove our mettle as good, law abiding nationals, maintaining the good will of our American neighbors.

May we pledge our loyalty to the Stars and Stripes just as do our children who are patriotic American citizens, with our prayer for a more peaceful kingdom on earth, which is the divine bequest of the American people for future generations.[12]

"We are all of alien origin," an editorial in the *Hood River News* reminded its residents on January 9, 1942. "No lengthy period has elapsed since all white Americans were either alien born or children of foreign-born parents."

Yet, tales of Japanese sabotage were widespread, as related by Mrs. Arline Moore, a local businesswoman, in answer to questions from the editor of a New Hampshire newspaper:

> Stories of sabotage were on every hand. Some one [sic] was supposed to have first hand knowledge of a threat to poison the water supply, a group of Nisei were supposed to have been picked up tearing at a dangerous speed over the highways who stated that they "were celebrating Pearl Harbor." Some one else was supposed to have listened in upon the Japanese Language Shcool [sic] and knew that the children were being taught that Japan would some day own these United States and that they must learn and carefully keep the traditions of Japan. Some one knew that the meetings in the Japanese Community Halls were training places for fifth column work to be put into practice as soon as invasion troups landed. They were reported to have had full information on the plans for the Pearl Harbor attack as early as the August previous. Perfectly innocent games of sport were tabbed, "military training." Some other person had been told that if Japan and United States went to war all Japanese people living in this country would have to kill their best Caucasian friends, by some Japanese neighbor whom he had befriended. And so the propoganda stories grew and enlarged with each telling.
>
> The populace were literally scared "pink" and actually seemed to think the few thousands of Japanese people living among our one hundred thirty or more millions were some sort of supermen endowed with the ability to travel unseen to any point and there commit unlimited sabotage without being caught in the act.[13]

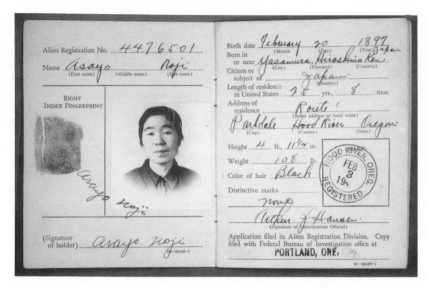

Issei were required to be fingerprinted and to carry identification certificates.
(Courtesy of Asayo Noji)

After a small group of citizens demanded further restrictions on local
Japanese, patrols were set up for "protection." Temporarily paid from
county emergency funds, guards monitored transportation arteries, water
supply headquarters, power plants, and other public services.[14]

By the beginning of February, "all unnaturalized aliens . . . 14 years of
age and over" were required to carry identification certificates. Issei were
instructed to apply at their local post offices by providing photos and answering questions about their current activities. After careful checks, ap-
plicants received identification certificates bearing their photos, index
fingerprints, and signatures. Those failing to comply were "liable to severe penalties and internment as enemy aliens for the duration of the
war."[15] Yet travel restrictions almost prevented Mr. Chiho Tomita from
following those instructions, as he recalled in English years later: "One
day we had fingerprint at courthouse. I try to go to town on fingerprint
date, but policeman stop me and say, 'You have to stay home.' I said I
have to go to fingerprint today. 'That's all right. You go home.' So I come
to home and stay, and I couldn't fingerprint that day. Go back next day."

When the Justice Department authorized the reregistration of enemy
aliens, it again weighed the question of civil rights versus national security. Pressured by the Western Defense Command, it finally consented to

multiple spot searches of Issei property without warrants, conceding that merely being an enemy alien would be sufficient cause for a search.[16] In Hood River, the FBI conducted a two-day "dragnet for aliens," assisted by county and city law enforcement officials.[17] By that time, Issei had taken precautions to destroy any Japanese possessions that might have been cause for suspicion:

> We used apple wood to build a fire outside and burn our diaries and the picture of the emperor. I apologized *gomen-nasai* [excuse me] to the emperor's picture for destroying it. [Mrs. Hama Yamaki]

> We were so scared that we burned some treasured records of Japanese music and destroyed a large, square Japanese flag my mother had sent us to show our children. [Mrs. Misuyo Nakamura]

Although regretful, Mrs. Nakamura was later to consider that decision a timely one, for the subsequent search of her home was extremely thorough:

> My husband loved sake and we had at least twenty bottles lined up in our basement. I was really scared about that! But since sake was not contraband, it did not cause us a problem. The two FBI men instructed us to remain in our living room during their search. (Earlier I had seen these two characters. They were wearing raincoats and boots and were walking back and forth down our road. I wondered what they were doing, because they did not look familiar.) The FBI men took two hours to search our small home, lifting the mattresses, opening suitcases, looking through closets and bookcases. I did not understand why they were so thorough. They certainly could not have missed very much! They pulled all our dresser drawers out too—and if we had kept our Japanese flag, I am sure my husband would have been taken away. The FBI conducted their search very diligently and discreetly. They were not abusive, and they returned everything to its original state. I distinctly remember that when they left, they said thank you. I was impressed by their manners.

Mr. Miyozo Yumibe and his family, certain of their innocence, were most accommodating to the FBI:

> I gave my permission when the FBI searched our home, saying, "Look anyplace, go ahead, and sit down." Before they came, we had taken the precaution of removing the emperor's framed photo from our wall. But an FBI man pulled one drawer out which held that photo and asked, "Where did you get this?" I replied, "My sister in

Japan sent it a long time ago." It was just a picture. They did not take it. And they did not take a photo of my brother, who was serving in the Japanese army in Manchuria—they simply glanced at it. The three FBI representatives were very thorough in their search but very pleasant. For one-half hour, two men searched the drawers and closets in our house, and one searched outside. They did not take anything.

The FBI actually did make a seizure at the Nishimoto home. Mrs. Hatsumi Nishimoto was understandably distraught when the FBI arrested her husband for what seemed an insignificant find:

About three days after Pearl Harbor, four FBI men came to our farm and spent three hours searching for contraband. We had been required to take to the courthouse our dynamite, guns, bullets—anything considered dangerous. While we thought we had turned in everything, the authorities found one small bullet in the woodshed. This caused them to take my husband even though he had been pruning outside and was still wearing his boots. They took him in this condition straight from the orchard! When I attempted to speak to my husband, the head of the search group told me no and even kept us bodily apart. At that time, I was more than disappointed at the treatment we received from these people, because they acted so pompous about the whole affair! After my son Koe returned from school, he attempted to see his father at the courthouse in Hood River. But my husband had already been taken to Portland. What worried me the most was that this left me with two children and I had to assume full responsibility for the farm. We were not able to hire anyone at the time, so I had to prune the trees myself. Now I was head of the household, and I wondered how we could manage without my husband. . . . [18]

Search regulations were apparently observed haphazardly, for, according to Mrs. Tei Endow, her family did not suffer consequences for their bullets:

Two FBI men searched everywhere—the beds, drawers, closets, even shining a flashlight under our piano. In a drawer in our son Sho's room, there were some small bullets, but the men did not make a big fuss about them. If the bullets had been on my husband's body, there is no question that he would have been taken away. The men told us they had orders to confiscate radios. We were in no position to object, because this was a federal regulation. Our shortwave radio [a four-foot, wooden RCA Victor radio] was so big that both men had to carry it. We also had a six-tube, small table radio, but we were allowed to take this to camp. The men stayed about fifteen minutes. I had an extremely lonely feeling—a desperate sadness. There was nothing we could do. I recall that our five-year-old son innocently followed one of the men as he searched our house.

At the Noji home, since Mr. Noji was acquainted with one of the searchers, the investigation seemed to be handled with much less scrutiny. Mrs. Asayo Noji recounted:

> Our two teenaged children were living on our lower eighty acres, and the rest of us lived on the upper property. Hideo Suzuki telephoned to ask if we knew the FBI had been to our lower place. Of course, this was news to me! He told us the FBI had thoroughly searched his home and barn. They turned everything upside down, so I was really frightened for Chiz and Toru. I immediately telephoned Chiz to see how they had fared. My daughter calmly assured me, "No, there was nothing to be alarmed about. One FBI agent told us he knew Papa well." They had opened a few dresser drawers, but they simply felt the contents at the top. So it was not frightening for them.

According to the local newspaper, the methodical search of 151 homes and property resulted in a "negligible catch of 'enemy' aliens" who had violated recent federal laws and "not one case of illegal possession of arms." The newspaper reported that the Japanese readily submitted to questioning and did not attempt to hinder a search of their homes. At the conclusion of the search, four Issei were confined to the county jail and later transferred out of the county for allegedly storing stumping powder and, in one case, failing to turn in a shortwave radio.[19] After scouring the valley, the FBI reportedly confiscated some photo developing and printing devices, two pairs of cheap field glasses, several feet of fuse for detonating dynamite sticks for clearing stumps, and several commercial maps of the valley.[20]

Hugh Ball, editor of the *Hood River News* attributed the scarcity of contraband to " 'enemy' aliens anxious to observe the regulations" and urged that the "complete absence of any 'incidents' in this area to date should be accepted as proof that the policy . . . has produced the results desired."[21]

By May 1942, the FBI had taken possession of 2,592 guns, 199,000 rounds of ammunition, 1,652 dynamite sticks, 1,458 radio receivers, 2,015 cameras, and other items on the West Coast. Some items had been voluntarily surrendered by Japanese; others had been taken not only from home searches but also from a sporting goods store and a store warehouse. All in all, the Justice Department concluded that there was no evidence of any subterfuge from the searches.[22] Yet the army's fear of sabotage and espionage—as well as the public's stormy reaction—heavily influenced the Justice Department's policies for treatment of West Coast Japanese.

23

Executive Order 9066

"THE JAPANESE RACE is an enemy race and . . . the racial strains are undiluted. . . . The very fact that no sabotage has taken place to date is a disturbing and confirming indication that such action will be taken." With this justification, Lieutenant General John L. De Witt, commander general of the Western Defense Command and responsible for West Coast security, recommended to Secretary of War Henry L. Stimson that Japanese be excluded from the West Coast.[1]

Sensational and inaccurate reports had circulated about the work of a Japanese fifth column of foreign agents and sympathizers in Hawaii. Eight days after the bombing of Pearl Harbor, Secretary of the Navy Frank Knox spoke to the press of "treachery" in Hawaii and credited this to "the most effective fifth column work that's come out of this war, except in Norway."[2] Actually, the real cause of the disaster, according to the historian Roger Daniels, was the unpreparedness and incompetence of the local military commanders. Nevertheless, Knox's unfounded statement carried considerable weight, for the government took no measures to refute his words or affirm the loyalty of Japanese, according to the report of the Commission on Wartime Relocation and Internment of Civilians.[3]

Yet mainland intelligence sources and government officials did not all suspect Issei and Nisei of espionage. Lieutenant Commander K. D. Ringle of the Office of Naval Intelligence in southern California vowed that there was no need for mass action against those of Japanese ancestry, estimating that 3 percent (3,500) of the citizens and aliens could be identified as saboteurs but that many Nisei leaders had voluntarily contributed valued antisubversive information to government agencies. In a 1941 report read, in summary, by the president, Curtis B. Munson, a businessman who assisted a makeshift intelligence agency for the White House, wrote that "there will be no armed uprising of Japanese. . . . For the most part the local Japanese are loyal to the United States. . . . Japs here are in more danger from us than we are from them." FBI Director J. Edgar Hoover shared the opinion that mass evacuation for security reasons was unjustified since suspected enemy aliens had already been apprehended, including 2,192 Japanese, 1,393 Germans, and 264 Italians. Attorney General Francis Biddle continued to oppose evacuation on the grounds that there was no evidence of planned attack or sabotage.[4]

On the West Coast, Governor Charles A. Sprague of Oregon became the first state official to urge constituents "not to discriminate against either the Japanese citizen or alien [for] in no wise was there to be any persecution of Orientals."[5] While setting aside two proposals for protecting Japanese in the state,[6] he maintained that local communities should work out their own solutions to Japanese problems.[7] A month later, however, he sent a telegram to Attorney General Francis Biddle stating, "I do not believe measures now being taken are adequate and urge further and prompt measures to remove this menace and recommend internment." He requested "positive protection for Americans, with decent treatment of Japanese."[8] When residents in Hood River sought to move more quickly to control the local Japanese nationals, Sprague was obliged to notify them that the removal of Issei was a matter to be handled by the U.S. Attorney General and Department of Justice.[9] According to Marvin Gavin Pursinger, "Oregon's governor did not in any way involve himself with the federal military authorities for effecting a humane solution for Oregon's Japanese."[10] In fact, his announcement that it was each local community's responsibility to solve the Japanese problem became an invitation in the state for economic reaction and race baiting. At the end of February, Sprague was the only West Coast governor to deliberately boycott Congress's Tolan Committee, which held hearings in Portland, among other West Coast cities, to examine the problems of evacuation.[11]

West Coast politicans began to take up the anti-Japanese cry. By the end of January, congressmen from the Pacific Coast were urging the president to give the War Department control over alien enemies and U.S. citizens who held dual citizenship in enemy countries. They further encouraged him to authorize "evacuation, resettlement or internment."[12]

Even before any effective orders, Japanese were ousted from Terminal Island, a fishing community near San Pedro, California, which was adjacent to naval facilities. Most of the men had already been taken into custody, and in February the navy expelled two hundred families, who ultimately received two days' notice to pack, store, and sell their belongings.[13]

Meanwhile, in Hood River, a local news editorial cited the disgust of some Hood River merchants when two Japanese "who profess no interest in Japan" conversed in their native language while considering a purchase.[14] American Legion and Grange members began to stage speeches by out-of-towners who supposedly had knowledge of disloyal Japanese activities. These appeals before civic and fraternal groups were intended, according to one local resident, "to arouse feeling to the point whereby the laws of this country could be changed and the Japanese people, citizens and aliens alike, could be arbitrarily removed to Japan. . . . The fears and antagonisms of the general public were fanned to a white hot heat."[15]

In the swell of increasing demands for evacuation and on the recommendation of his secretary of war, President Franklin D. Roosevelt signed Executive Order 9066 on February 19, 1942. Ten weeks after the attack on Pearl Harbor, the order authorized the secretary of war and his military commanders to "prescribe military areas . . . from which any or all persons may be excluded. . . . "[16] The order was directed at not only the Issei but also their Nisei children, who were U.S. citizens. It did not include the 150,000 Japanese who made up more than a third of Hawaii's population, for their labor was critical to the main island's economic welfare. Nor did it include German and Italian aliens, whose impact at the polls was significant and for whom prominent figures testified.[17]

A month later, on March 2, General De Witt issued Public Proclamation No. 1, which established military areas on the West Coast. Military Area No. 1 included the western portions of Oregon, Washington, and California, plus the southern third of Arizona. In Oregon, Zone A-1 (the prohibited zone), from which all Japanese and Japanese Americans were to be evacuated,[18] extended from the coastline to U.S. Highway 99-W, plus Portland, Hermiston, La Grande, and Pendleton. Zone B (the restricted zone) included Hood River and the area between U.S. Highway 99-W and U.S. Highway 97, running south midway through Oregon.[19] At this point, Japanese were encouraged to move voluntarily out of the prohibited and restricted areas but were otherwise free to go where they chose.[20]

In the meantime, the Tolan Committee, headed by Representative John Tolan of California, held its West Coast hearings in four cities. On February 26 in Portland, a delegation from Hood River was vociferous in testifying for the removal of valley Japanese during the war. Representing the local American Legion, Chamber of Commerce, and Civil Defense Council, the group expressed concern that as much as 16 percent of the county's orchard land (2,898 of 36,800 acres) was owned by seventy-seven Japanese nationals and their offspring. They maintained that five to six hundred first- and second-generation Japanese engaged in fruit or vegetable harvest. Although removal of Japanese would affect the growth of crops, local orchardists voiced a commitment to take over those properties, stating that "national defense comes first."[21]

That day Judge C. D. Nickelsen, on behalf of the newly created local Japanese Evacuation Committee, sent letters to Attorney General Biddle and General De Witt requesting that Japanese be removed from the county: "Hood River County is a very small county and we have approximately five hundred Japanese located here who produce approximately a third of the fruit tonnage grown in this valley. The situation at present is becoming very tense and the opposition against the return of the Japanese population in this valley is becoming very pronounced."[22] Other groups, including the Dee lumber and sawmill workers[23] and the local Elks lodge,[24] petitioned the governor to urge evacuation of Japanese.

By this time, the proposed "voluntary resettlement of Japanese" was clearly unsuccessful. Only two thousand had migrated from Military Area No. 1 during the three weeks following March 2.[25] Fearful and uninformed residents of interior western states asked: If Japanese were dangerous enough to be excluded from the coastal zone, why should they be forced upon inland residents? And who could guarantee that sabotage would not occur there too?

Consequently, voluntary evacuation ended on March 27, 1942, with the army's Public Proclamation No. 4, which barred those of Japanese ancestry from moving out of Military Area No. 1. A plan for compulsory evacuation thus gained momentum.[26]

24

Disposal of Property and Belongings

WITH THE LIKELIHOOD of their evacuation increasing daily, Issei farmers had been forced to consider arrangements for the care of their orchards and property. At one point the frightened Parkdale area Japanese had even considered leasing an orchard together in Idaho, out of the demilitarized zone. Confused and uncertain whether they would be allowed to return, many made the painful decision to sell out completely. Consumed by panic and goaded by the rumor mill, distraught residents became victims of opportunists who purchased or leased their property at a fraction of its value:

> Caucasians came to buy our cow and calf. They told me, "This is forty dollars. This is fifty dollars." I would just reply, "All right." We had a Fergie [Ferguson] tractor. We sold it, because we did not know whether we would return. [Mrs. Itsu Akiyama]

> Our neighbor wanted to buy our 1934 Chevrolet, so we sold it for four hundred dollars. We did not get full value for it. But as long as we had a buyer, we wanted to sell it. [Mr. Miyozo Yumibe]

Most Issei were forced to make heavy sacrifices, selling farm vehicles with less than one year's wear for amounts lower than three hundred dollars, knowing that replacing them would cost several thousand dollars.[1]

The value of West Coast Japanese property was considerable. Their 6,118 farms were worth almost $73 million and their equipment was valued at $6 million. While the average value per acre of all West Coast farms in 1940 was $37.94, the worth of Japanese farms, which averaged forty-two acres, was $279.96 per acre.[2] In Hood River, 68 farms were operated by Japanese: 51 (three-quarters) were fully owned, 4 were partly owned, and 11 were tenant-operated.[3] Of the 154 employed Issei and Nisei over fourteen years old, 125 were involved in agriculture. Among others, 12 were employed in logging and milling, 3 in wholesale and retail trade, 3 in personal service, and 11 in other occupations.[4]

Eventually, the government designated federal and community agencies to assist Japanese property owners. The Federal Reserve Bank of San Francisco assumed dual and seemingly contradictory roles: to prevent Japanese from being exploited as they leased and disposed of their property and to facilitate as rapidly as possible the transfer of property.[5] Bank representatives urged Japanese residents to "avoid hysteria" and "be patient for a few days" before entering property agreements.[6] Calling this a "Big Brother Program," S. A. MacEachron of the Federal Reserve Bank warned white American growers at Hood River's Apple Blossom Cafe: "Any individuals who are toying with the idea that they can turn a dishonest penny by exploiting the Japanese of Hood River Valley . . . might as well abandon their plans to get rich quick, for they are destined to find the going plenty tough." He also warned that Japanese should be treated favorably to prevent any reprisals against American prisoners in Japan.[7]

The Wartime Civil Control Administration (WCCA), responsible for the actual evacuation of Japanese, assigned relocation responsibilities to four federal agencies. It delegated to the Farm Security Administration the task of overseeing the transfer of farms to Caucasians to ensure the continuing care of crops.[8] As an arm of this agency, the Wartime Farm Adjustment Program not only supervised property arrangements between Japanese and Caucasians but also helped Caucasians gain credit or loans.[9] In April the WCCA opened one of its sixty-four service centers in Hood River. Its expressed purpose was to carry out the evacuation and "prevent Japanese from liquidating property foolishly or from becoming the dupes of unscrupulous persons." Staff members included a social worker and representatives from the U.S. Employment Service, Farm Security Administration, and the Federal Reserve Bank.[10] The local Apple Growers' Association (AGA) also set up a department where Japanese could secure advice for leasing property.[11]

This intervention by the government was comforting to Mr. Masaji Kusachi: "I do not feel that the government mistreated the Japanese in the valley. Even when we were evacuated, county authorities (who may have been acting under federal direction) assisted us in leasing our property. If we desired, they would help us in selling too. In matters of lease papers, unless they were approved by government officials, we were not permitted to affix our signatures. This in essence protected the interests of the Japanese. The AGA would also turn down leases that were not appropriate."

Yet, even among government agencies, confusion existed about policies, and the process was so slow that most Japanese relied primarily on their own resources:

I leased property to neighbor. Very simple agreement: He keep
my 40 percent in the bank in my account. He spend rest for spray,
labor, expense. We had written agreement. He was a real good man.
[Mr. Chiho Tomita, in English]

A man from Pine Grove leased our property. I did not know him.
He approached my neighbors, the Satos, first. After they had made
an agreement, he asked us to lease our place to him, too. My father
said he did not want to sell, so the only alternative was to lease.
Although we were innocent victims of this tragedy, we thought we
would eventually be able to return. This probably had a lot to do
with the idea of keeping the property instead of selling out. I have
forgotten the percentage of profits we were to receive, but our lease-
holder paid us cash for the work we had done up to the time of evacuation. He also bought our equipment and was to have paid all the
operating expenses. Mr. Sato noticed that when this man wrote
him a three thousand dollar check for equipment, his hand was
shaking! [Mr. Masaji Kusachi]

After seven years of toil that were finally bringing forty acres to production, the Noji family was primarily concerned about care of their precious trees, as Mrs. Asayo Noji explained: "Papa felt it was very likely we
would be returning, so he did not request large sums of money from our
caretakers. Instead, he asked that they 'just take good care of our orchard.' He left all our equipment and fertilizer and other materials necessary to keep up a good orchard. Because of that, we did not fare too well
money-wise."

For the Yamakis, too, the arrangement for their belongings and property was not intended to bring monetary gain:

Mr. Earl Moore, a *kainjin* [state representative] and a most
friendly and sincere person, said, "If there are any items you would
like to sell before you evacuate, I will purchase them from you." He
walked through our house and basement and even bought all our
fruit jars. We had planned to leave the beds and cots in our cabins,
but he even bought those. We told our neighbors, the Walter
Vanniers, that they could use our piano, small tables, doilies, and
pictures. Then we left most of our affairs in Mr. Moore's hands. We
made no formal request for payment. I believe my husband probably
had a written agreement.[12] [Mrs. Hama Yamaki]

In a unique situation, the Nakamuras were able to retain ownership of
their farm while leaving it in the care of a foreman:

We had forty-three acres of full-bearing apple, pear, and cherry trees. We had no intention of selling, because we had bought the place to pass on to our children. A nearby family was related to Billy Sunday, a Christian evangelist whom we all respected. This man had only a small orchard, and we believed him to be proper. So we approached him about running our orchard. Our written agreement was not a standard lease, for we hired this man to be foreman of our farm. He was to receive $150 a month and was entitled to 10 percent of the net income. All accounting was placed in the hands of Mr. Harold Hershner, an insurance agent, who mailed the statements and returns to us at camp. [Mrs. Misuyo Nakamura]

In the midst of this bewildering and increasingly hostile marketplace, a local newspaper editorial lauded Japanese for "swallowing their pride and . . . cooperating to the fullest extent." At the same time, it recognized that they were enduring neighbors' suspicions about their loyalty and the exploits of those white people who "take advantage of [an] unfortunate situation."[13]

25

Evacuation

Hood River Issei were given six official days' notice before their departure from the valley. At noon on May 7, Civil Exclusion Order No. 49 was posted, bringing the chilling news. Not only Japanese nationals but also Japanese Americans in Hood River, Wasco, and part of Sherman County would be evacuated by train to Pinedale, California. This came approximately six weeks after West Coast evacuations, which began on March 31 from Bainbridge Island, Washington, and extended to San Pedro, Long Beach, San Diego, and San Francisco, California.[1]

In Hood River, sixty soldiers camped at the Legion Hall in preparation for the evacuation, and army doctors began giving physical examinations. Following government instructions, all Japanese packed and carried their own bedding, toilet articles, extra clothing, eating utensils, and personal effects:[2]

> There was a shortage of suitcases in Hood River, so we had to order them by mail. We put some of our personal belongings into a suitcase. The rest we left upstairs, and we stored some of our kitchenware in the basement. [Mrs. Itsu Akiyama]

> We were told we could take no more than seventy pounds of luggage to camp. I had chinaware that I prized dearly, but I was not able to take it. We also chose not to sell our belongings. Instead, we loaned them to our Caucasian friends. We packed mostly clothing in our two *kori* [bamboo footlockers] and filled a small suitcase with toys for our little boy. [Mrs. Tei Endow]

Wednesday morning, May 13, 1942, was the day of departure. Leaving was wrenching, yet it underscored the sense of community among the Hood River Japanese. Mrs. Tei Endow captured the moment: "No one wanted to go, because we had lived here many years and our orchards were beginning to produce. A neighbor lady embraced the door of her home, crying 'I do not want to leave!' What finally eased the pain was that we were all leaving together."

Somehow, even their pets seemed affected by the deep-seated emotions of that morning. "Probably what I remember most about that morning," Mrs. Misuyo Nakamura lamented, "was that Lassie, our long-haired Scottie, followed our old pickup all the way down to Highway 35 [approximately a mile away]. I remember this very well for he had never followed us before. At our emotional parting, we had patted Lassie and said goodbye in the manner one might talk to a child. I thought this was our final parting, and I can only guess Lassie sensed this too."

Weighted down with duffle bags, *kori*, and suitcases, 431 Japanese arrived at the local Union Pacific train depot before their 10:00 A.M. departure.[3] Family members were readily recognized by tags dangling from their clothing and imprinted with appropriate family numbers. While military troops and local and state law officials stood by, several hundred Caucasians gathered to witness the event. Mrs. Tei Endow remembered that neighbors offered kind words and gestures at their departure: "Many friendly people came to see us off, and the caretaker of our property brought us a box of chocolates. The AGA [Apple Growers' Association] also delivered a few boxes of Newtowns [a variety of apples] for us to eat on our trip."

In the backs of their minds, however, some Issei, like Mrs. Itsu Akiyama, questioned the well-wishers' motives: "There were many Caucasian people to see us off. We had to wonder whether they were sincere in our leaving or maybe they were wishing we would never come back."

One local newspaper observed that "there was not the least evidence of any hostility towards any of the evacuees" and noticed instead "a most friendly spirit . . . of compassion."[4] Another newspaper described an attitude of willing cooperation and "an evident atmosphere of a holiday spirit."[5] Issei, however, remembered their departure differently:

> Our departure was somewhat quiet and reserved. Everyone seemed willing to express good feelings rather than bitter ones. Naturally we did not like what was happening, but we tried to suppress our feelings and leave quietly and with goodwill. If there were any unpleasant conversations, it appeared they were private.
>
> The train we boarded was so old-fashioned that we thought it might have come from a museum! Once inside, we all talked and talked, curious about where we were going. My five-year-old son thought it was great to ride on a train! But my husband and I

commiserated with Mr. and Mrs. Tamura, crying together about our fate. All we knew was that we were traveling to Pinedale, and it was three hundred to four hundred miles away.[6] [Mrs. Tei Endow]

We were herded onto the train just like cattle and swine. I do not recall much conversation between the Japanese. But I do remember sitting next to Etsuko Abe from Parkdale, who offered to share a lunch she had made. My thinking was, "My goodness, how well this person prepared!" [Mrs. Misuyo Nakamura]

Moments after we had left the Hood River station, we received a telegram from Bill [their son serving in U.S. Army], asking, "Where are you going?" We ourselves did not know where we were going. [Mrs. Hama Yamaki]

Why, in fact, were the Japanese being uprooted from their homes? Issei speculated:

This was extremely difficult for us. Because Japanese as a whole were good farmers, I cannot help but feel that many others felt some envy toward us, which was expressed as discrimination. Americans may also have thought there were incidents of sabotage or other unfriendly acts committed by Japanese. They probably believed this was for security reasons. [Mrs. Hatsumi Nishimoto]

I believe that, even among the Japanese, there may have been some who would sabotage the government. Probably that was the reason we were evacuated. [Mrs. Tei Endow]

Quick to affirm the allegiance of the Issei, Mr. Masaji Kusachi added, "If there was ever any question of Japanese loyalty, people could go down to the courthouse and look up our records. They would not find any Issei who had been indicted for anything! So it is easy to conclude that the Japanese had a good record of loyalty to this country."

In spite of strong feelings about the illegality of their evacuation, the Japanese chose to comply. Years later, the injustice remained an issue for Mr. Chiho Tomita: "While there has been no evidence of sabotage, we do not believe there was legal standing to haul the Japanese in, because the Nisei were citizens of this country. There was even the instance of Mr. Min Yasui who dared to test the case by staying out after curfew in Portland. He was imprisoned and prosecuted. We do not believe that this was legal. Although we had strong feelings, we did not express them to people other than Japanese. And we went because we were ordered to go. At that time we did not know the reasons, so we left quietly."

Minoru Yasui, son of Hood River merchant Masuo Yasui and a member of the Oregon Bar, had intentionally defied the curfew in Portland. His

challenge was based on grounds that the curfew, evacuation, and internment orders violated his constitutional rights as an American citizen. Arrested on March 28 only after he turned himself in at the police station,
he was stripped of his citizenship, fined five thousand dollars, and sen-
tenced to nine months in solitary confinement in the Multnomah County
Jail.[7]

While Issei were aware of Yasui's resolute stand, they yielded to their
fate:

> I felt terrible about our evacuation, because this was leaving ev-
> erything we had! It was very difficult to see that we could be treated
> so miserably even when our son Billy was in the service. But we did
> not consider disobeying the orders. It was *meirei* [order], so we
> obeyed. [Mrs. Hama Yamaki]

> It was wartime, so we had to do what we were told. Inouye-sensei
> [Rev. Isaac Inouye] had our complete trust, and we did everything
> he told us. He said, "This is the will of God, so we should do ex-
> actly what we are told." We wondered whether we would ever be
> able to return to Hood River. But we had absolutely no thought of
> not complying. [Mrs. Itsu Akiyama]

The final issue of the *Mid-Columbia JACL Bulletin* on May 8, 1942,
gave an altruistic rationale in these words: "Individuals and groups are
not important when the life of the nation is at stake; therefore, we are
cooperating with the military measures which the Army believes is necessary to strengthen our national defense."

Yet leaving was heartrending:

> Because we had lived here a long time, we felt very lonesome.
> But we were all leaving together, and it was *shikata-ganai* [it is be-
> yond control; it cannot be helped so accept it as it is]. [Mrs. Masayo
> Yumibe]

> I cannot speak for others, but I myself felt resigned to do what-
> ever we were told. I think the Japanese left in a very quiet mood, for
> we were powerless. We had to do what the government ordered. In
> my own mind, I thought, "Surely we will be unable to return." I was
> so worried about what the future held for my children! We had
> struggled for many years, but we could lose everything. I was so
> frightened I actually did not think we would come home alive.
> There we so many outside people we did not know or trust that we
> feared someone at any time might take a shot at us. We took just
> one day at a time. [Mrs. Misuyo Nakamura]

We worried about whether we would be able to return. I remember that tears rolled down my face. [Mrs. Miyoshi Noyori]

Two days after their departure from Hood River, the following advertisement appeared in the *Hood River County Sun*:

To the People of the Mid-Columbia and to the People of the Northwest:

As we go forth from this majestic area in the midst of the Cascade Range, we leave with long years of love for this friendly community.

We take this humble privilege to thank all our friends who have befriended us through these years of association. We thank those friends who especially gave us their time and guidance during our preparation for evacuation.

While we are temporarily exiled, these memories of friendship and the love for our homes will be the invaluable source of comfort and consolation to us. To us, these same sentiments will always inspire us to be better Americans.

Mid-Columbia Japanese American Citizens League[8]

PART SEVEN

Relocation

Ibusekaru
Koko no seikatsu no
Aru mono ni
Imijiku furete
Kokorosabishi mo

Deeply moved
By wretched scenes
Of camp life,
My heart mourns.

Tanka written by Mrs. Shizue Iwatsuki and
translated by Dr. Stephen W. Kohl

26

Assembly Centers

Just wild place. No station. Just stop train.
Just hay fields. Just wild—nothing—no houses.
Nothing.
—Mr. Chiho Tomita

FIRST IMPRESSIONS of their new habitat almost defied words, though Mr.
Chiho Tomita, as he conveyed in English, would long remember the
sight. After boarding a rustic train headed toward an unknown destination, the fearful Hood River Japanese had finally arrived at Pinedale Assembly Center in California, a thousand miles from their beloved valley.
With Japanese from neighboring Wasco County, they would be the only
Oregon evacuees to be sent out of the state.[1]

Mrs. Tei Endow showed her dismay at their arrival: "Since we were on
a train which did not have priority, we were constantly sidetracked to allow other trains to pass. Finally, at ten o'clock at night, the train stopped
at an open field. We had to wade through the tall grass to reach Pinedale,
and I cannot forget how the burrs snagged our stockings."

Constructed quickly by the War Department as temporary quarters for
Japanese, Pinedale was one of sixteen such centers on the West Coast. A
former mill site in the desert near Fresno, California, midway down the
state, it was to become the residence of 4,792 Japanese.[2] For anxious
newcomers, however, the first glimpse of their new homes was foreboding.
Barbed wire encircled them, and search lights scoured the darkness from
towers manned by armed guards:

> I remember seeing a large cactus when our train stopped at a field
> near Pinedale, so I guessed that we had arrived at a hot place. We

were completely fenced in, and there were watchtowers with soldiers bearing rifles. We felt like prisoners! [Mrs. Itsu Akiyama]

I saw a soldier with a rifle who was stationed on one of those high towers outside the fence. I was very frightened! I was sure he had designs on shooting us! [Mrs. Misuyo Nakamura]

After they arrived that evening, Japanese were herded through lines, issued blankets, and assigned to hastily constructed, incomplete tar-paper barracks. Overcrowding and lack of privacy became immediate problems as families (or, frequently, pairs of unacquainted couples) were assigned tiny one-room compartments. Four-person families were housed in eight-by-twenty-foot rooms, six persons in twelve-by-twenty-foot rooms, and eight in twenty-by-twenty-foot rooms.[3]

Despite the primitive setting, Japanese were cautioned not to use the term *camp*. Officials apparently considered the facility an assembly center rather than a concentration camp.[4] *Camp*, however, became the commonly used term for this new domicile:

The camp was incomplete, so construction was ongoing. Our room had a concrete floor and a lightbulb with a drop cord. Our only furnishings were beds with bare springs, thin mattresses, and blankets. We were helpless to be confined here. *Shikata-ganai* [It is beyond control; it cannot be helped so accept it as it is]. But because it was wartime, there was nothing we could do. [Mrs. Itsu Akiyama]

Our beds were army cots. We slept on mattresses filled with a bit of straw. They were so lumpy and uncomfortable that I could not sleep. A Nisei camp volunteer who inquired about our comfort gave me a permit to see the doctor. After we registered our complaint, I received a new mattress, which helped a little bit. In that way, the government was considerate. Four of us—my husband and I, Kane, and my little boy—shared one room. We hung sheets for privacy. It was quite noisy, for you could hear everything the neighbors said—and our neighbors had a large family. But we were able to adjust. [Mrs. Tei Endow]

Living quarters at Pinedale were grouped as "blocks," with each block composed of eighteen to twenty barracks aligned in two rows and housing six to eight hundred people. The monotonous rows of units with their identical doors and paned windows caused some consternation for Mrs. Masayo Yumibe: "In camp it was confusing that all the rooms in the barracks looked alike and were numbered the same. If you did not take the trouble to remember where your assigned room was, you would get all mixed-up. Many people accidentally strolled into the wrong rooms. Once when I walked into someone else's room, I felt kind of funny. But I just laughed and apologized, 'Oh, excuse me!' Later I made a curtain to mark our room so there would be no more mistakes."

Each block had centralized facilities: showers, laundry rooms, and—most distasteful of all—open toilets:

> Probably most trying was that the camp was incomplete. The toilet facilities were barren, set in a row with partitions but no doors. We could see everyone who came in! That was the one thing I hated the most! There were so many complaints that doors were finally added. [Mrs. Hama Yamaki]

> Not very complete camp . . . not quite finished. Toilet pretty bad shape. No flush—just two-by-twelve-foot board on top of big hole. Every time sit down, four to five people sit down together. Too bad. [Mr. Chiho Tomita, in English]

Meals were served in large mess halls, notable for their long lines and distasteful food, dished up at an average cost of thirty-nine cents per person each day:[5]

> What really sticks in my mind was the inconvenience of the mess hall. Once, while we were in line to eat, my five-year-old son was cut off right at the entrance, because the mess hall had already filled. He cried and fussed, so I traded places with someone behind me and waited with him for the next shift in ten to fifteen minutes. It was so terribly hot that most of us dampened towels to cover our heads while we waited.
> A government regulation required that we bring our own forks and spoons. Since we did not like all the food, we were often still hungry after eating. I did not care for the sardines, yet they served them time and time again. *Matta* [not again] sardine! The cereal and milk we ate in the morning were okay. Those people unhappy with the food generally cooked on hot plates in their rooms. Sometimes I asked the cook for leftover rice to make sushi [*makizushi,* rolled vinegar rice typically filled with meat and vegetables] and seasoned it with fresh lemon. [Mrs. Tei Endow]

> Frequently our meal was a plateful of white beans, four or five fresh spinach leaves, a piece of bread, and sometimes a couple of weinies. That was all we were served, so we had to eat it. [Mrs. Miyoshi Noyori]

> Our food in camp was not very agreeable. When we were served raw spinach, we wondered whether to eat it! (I still do not like raw

spinach!) Outside the mess hall, it was so hot in line that we felt we might faint! By the time we were served, we were so hungry that we ate the food even if we disliked it. Shig and Mitsie [Mrs. Yamaki's son and daughter] complained that our bodies probably could not tolerate this kind of food, so they volunteered to cook in the kitchen. Gradually the food improved. [Mrs. Hama Yamaki]

The climate, unfortunately, did not. Dubbed "Hell's Acre" by more than one, Pinedale boasted sagebrush, wind-whipped swirls of dust, and temperatures soaring to 120 degrees in the shade.[6] Only one word seemed adequate to describe those formidable conditions:

Atsui [hot]! It was a terribly hot place to live. It was so hot that when we put our hands on the bedstead, the paint would come off! To relieve the pressure of the heat, some people soaked sheets in water and hung them overhead. [Mrs. Hatsumi Nishimoto]

The heat was so unbearable! Quite often we threw water on the concrete floor. Then, as it dried, we lay down to rest. When we hung our laundry, we could actually see the clothes drying. I have never experienced hot weather like that! [Mrs. Hama Yamaki]

With their sixteen dollar monthly allowances, family members placed catalog orders for umbrellas and hats in efforts to withstand the sun's rays.[7] To ease their discomfort, several times authorities gave each family a block of ice, which they set in the middle of their concrete floors, chipping off pieces to suck.[8]

Faced with such intolerable living conditions, adults made valiant efforts to repress their emotions. Youngsters, on the other hand, were uninhibited, openly expressing their revulsion:

I have a lasting impression of Pinedale. When we entered our assigned barrack, my eleven-year-old son, George, was overcome with frustration by the dismal conditions. He became so disgusted that he threw himself on the concrete floor, screaming and pounding his feet! I can still picture George going through this motion. Our feelings were very similar to George's—but we did not express them. We had a difficult time facing prospects for the future. We were actually living from day to day, not knowing what tomorrow might bring. [Mrs. Misuyo Nakamura]

While stay in Pinedale, my second son, Louie, was just nine or ten. He said, "Pa, go home, go home. I like to go home." I can't say nothing—maybe someday go home. [Mr. Chiho Tomita, in English]

Portland Assembly Center

For twelve Hood River Japanese, odors of animal manure would prevail in their crude, new lodgings.[9] Nine members of the Kusachi family,
detained because of Mrs. Kusachi's illness, and a soon-to-be married
Nisei girl traveled to the Portland Assembly Center rather than to
Pinedale. Actually the site of the converted Pacific International Livestock Exposition, the Portland center consisted of eleven acres of an
animal pavilion housed under one roof. Mr. Masaji Kusachi expressed
his shock:

> What really surprised me was to enter the Portland center
> which, you know, was a former stockyard. My family of ten was as-
> signed a small room that had no doors—just curtains hung over the
> doorway.[10] The plywood walls extended eight feet high, but we had
> no ceilings so you could hear everything the next-door occupants
> were saying. Wire fences surrounded us, and there were guards at
> every corner. We were distraught to think we would be confined to
> an area like this when we had not committed any wrong.
>
> The odor was so bad! One-foot-by six-foot planks had been laid
> over the stable floor, but there were plenty of smells left and lots of
> flies. After all, this was where the horses had lived! If they had
> dumped the animal refuse far away from the assembly center, that
> would have been all right. But they disposed of it just outside the
> fence! Naturally it drew the flies. We complained, but all the offi-
> cials did was to furnish us with flypaper! We strung a line and hung
> maybe a dozen pieces of flypaper in our tiny room. If this facility had
> been subject to a Red Cross inspection, it surely would have been
> condemned!

Because the offensive manure was actually dumped by the nearby packinghouse on its private property, government officials were unable to
prevent it.[11] Meanwhile, other sanitation and safety problems persisted.
Flies were so prevalent that spiral, yellow flypaper became familiar ceiling
decorations, and the dubious winner of a fly-catching contest displayed a
gallon jug of 2,462 dead flies.[12] One section became so infested with lice
carried by rats and flies that it required fumigation. Without ceilings or
doors, chilling winds from the Columbia Gorge swept into the spare units
and created health problems, particularly for the elderly. Despite the inadequate electrical circuits and gas mains, the center did not permit
wood-burning stoves because of the threat of fire hazards.[13]

Meals served in one-hour shifts were mass produced, quickly served,
and just as mechanically consumed. Seventeen hundred people could be

seated and eating in four and a half minutes. Quality was understandably sacrificed, however, since the average weekly cost of rations per person in Portland was 12.8 cents per meal through July. Yet in an audit by a government inspector, Portland's mess hall was praised as the "most successfully operated . . . rating 99% up to ideal standards!"[14] Mr. Masaji Kasachi provided a different picture of the mess hall:

> The meals were all right. Of course, it helped that I worked in the kitchen! We cooked rice in a big pot that tofu-making people in Portland had used. In the camp cooking area, I worked under many professional cooks from Portland restaurants so I learned quite a bit.[15] My K.P. duties included peeling potatoes and onions and cleaning pots and pans. We had mostly Japanese meals, and we ate meat quite often. Every morning we made coffee, bacon, and scrambled eggs. We were real busy making scrambled eggs—we got eggs by the case. The mess hall had very poor eating conditions—it was crowded and there were flies all over the place.

For Issei and their families, their first lodgings away from home were generally dismal, confining, and often unsanitary quarters. Yet around 92,000 Japanese resided at these assembly centers, some for as long as a hundred days.[16]

27

Camp Tule Lake

"LIKE CATTLE, we were herded through the gates onto an army truck," Mrs. Itsu Akiyama reminisced. By summer's end, the Hood River Japanese were transferred to Tule Lake, one of ten government concentration camps, or, as the government called them, relocation centers. These were located in seven states: Arizona, Arkansas, California, Colorado, Idaho, Utah, and Wyoming. Each of the sites was on federal property, which the historian Roger Daniels termed "godforsaken" places where "nobody had lived before and no one has lived since."[1] This change brought Japanese from the custody of the Army's Wartime Civil Control Administration (WCCA) to the civilian custody of the War Relocation Authority (WRA) and directed their futures toward confinement rather than resettlement.[2] Altogether, 120,313 of Japanese ancestry would come under the WRA's custody,[3] 73 percent of whom were American citizens.[4]

In north-central California and just a few miles south of the Oregon border, Tule Lake was situated in a dry, isolated lake bed. Shaggy willow trees, sagebrush, and a stubble of desert grass were all that survived the arid climate and annual rainfall of but ten inches a year.[5] To the west, Castle Rock provided the only relief to the barren desert surroundings. With little vegetation to secure the dust and sand, the dust storms were all-too-familiar, as Mrs. Asayo Noji remembered well: "Dust storms were so intense I could hardly see! The wind blew so fiercely I could not walk straight ahead—it whipped me aside. And dust always seemed to find its way inside! It settled everywhere! Every morning I had to shake the dust off our bed covers."

The ever-present dust became such a problem that a frustrated block manager appealed to residents through the *Daily Tulean Dispatch*, the

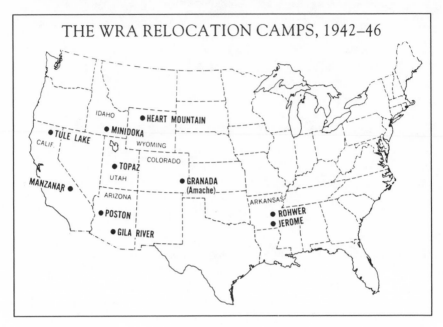

THE WRA RELOCATION CAMPS, 1942–46

West Coast Japanese were relocated from the temporary assembly centers to one of ten government relocation centers. (Map reprinted from Roger Daniels's *Concentration Camps* [1981] with kind permission of the author)

camp newsletter. Because dust raised between the barracks "hampers all efforts to keep apartments and washings clean, he urged them to walk only on main roads."[6]

Security at Tule Lake, as at Pinedale, was heavily enforced. Barbed-wire fences encircled the one-and-a-quarter-square-mile area,[7] and armed guards remained vigilant from watchtowers along the fence. At the entrance to the gateway, all incoming and outgoing traffic was registered by the provost marshal's office. Immediately inside were the fenced-off quarters of the military police as well as the administration buildings. Beyond these were the warehouse and factory buildings, the base hospital, and the schools. Separated by a wide firebreak was the "colony," living quarters for approximately sixteen thousand Issei and Nisei.[8]

The basic community units in the colony were "blocks." Each of the sixty-four blocks was composed of fourteen barracks, with nine blocks forming a ward. Communal facilities were again the order of the day, with block residents sharing centralized mess halls, recreation halls, toilet facilities, men's and women's shower rooms, an ironing room, and laundry rooms[9] (where clothes were often bleached with grapefruit halves saved

Camps were organized into blocks of identical barracks, where residents shared dining, toilet, and laundry facilities, as they did here at Minidoka. (Courtesy of the late Katsusaburo Tamura)

from breakfast). The familiar barracks were built of shiplap covered with tar paper, although evacuee construction crews later added firboard ceilings and sheetrock walls as part of a winterization project.[10] Rooms, furnished with coal-burning stoves, were a bit larger than those at Pinedale, ranging here from twenty-by-sixteen feet to twenty-by-twenty-five feet.[11]

For Mrs. Hama Yamaki, "Camp life in Tule Lake was improved over Pinedale. Tule Lake was larger, the facilities were better, our rooms were better, and the food was much better." Conditions did improve, although they still seemed incredibly crude.

Again Issei, like Mrs. Tei Endow, were resigned to their fate: "Oh, Tule Lake was ten times better than Pinedale! The barrack construction was superior to Pinedale, probably because our stay was longer and the area was cold in the winter. Wallboard covered the inside walls and ceiling of our room. 'One thing, everybody don't like toilets.' The toilets were all in a line and not partitioned. Even my son would hesitate to go inside. But we all became resigned to camp life. *Shikata-ganai!* [It is beyond our control; it cannot be helped so accept it as it is]! At least we had roofs over our heads and were served food, so we accepted the situation."

Admittedly, in such close, poorly insulated quarters, it was difficult to conduct one's private life without drawing the attention of next-door neighbors. Ever able to see the positive side, Mrs. Itsu Akiyama did learn more than she expected: "Our room was not insulated, so we heard noises from our neighbors. The Tanakas were very conscientious teaching their grandchild 'Jesus Loves Me, This I Know. . . . ' I could hear that very clearly!"

Intent on improving their stark living conditions, residents were prone to scavenge and even steal lumber, plasterboard, and fiberboard to construct their own furniture, closets, and room partitions. Bewildered by this curious change in behavior, Mr. Masaji Kusachi speculated:

> Our biggest surprise at Tule Lake came when we late arrivals found our buildings stripped. Even the pressboard partitions in the room and the six-by-six-foot coal box were gone. Our room had only a coal stove and ten beds. We believe that those who had arrived earlier had taken the wood to improve their own living quarters. So we were forced to scrounge around for other building materials, for example, from a load of new lumber at a construction site. It was such a strange period in our lives to be confined in those centers that our attitudes made a complete turnaround. At home we would never, never have given a thought to taking property from another person! But, confined as we were, circumstances had so changed that we had no qualms about taking those pieces of board. This was a strange personal phenomena! I do not recall that anybody was ever caught taking those items, because there was no policing and no Japanese would turn you in. There was kind of a mutual feeling that we were trying to improve our own living conditions. It was a different life.

So it was. The WRA anticipated a change in life-style when it issued advice in a ten-page booklet, *Questions and Answers for Evacuees:* "Be prepared for the relocation center, which is a pioneer community. So bring clothes suited to pioneer life and in keeping with the climate or climates likely to be involved. . . . Temperatures may range from freezing in winter to 115 degrees during some periods of the summer."[12]

Since many evacuees found themselves unprepared for cold winter temperatures (which occasionally dipped to 30 degrees below zero), those employed at the camp received monthly clothing allowances in the form of redeemable scrip for themselves and their dependents. By September the clothing schedule was adjusted to the following rates: sixteen years of age and older, $3.75 per month; eight to sixteen, $3.25 per month; under eight, $2.25 per month.[13] The government also supplied GI pea jackets, sizes thirty-eight to forty-four, appreciated for their warmth if one could ignore the style and fit.[14] Some, like Mr. Miyozo Yumibe, did not seem to mind: "I was furnished food and board, and each of us also received an allowance of $3.75 a month for clothing. I thought that was pretty good."

Meals, served at mess halls, continued to be institutional fare at fifty cents per day, a limit equaling the cost of army rations. Actual cost, however, was approximately forty-five cents per person per day, sometimes falling as low as thirty-one cents.[15] Each week two meatless meals were served, and on other days third-grade beef was supplied.[16] Because mess halls served two to three times the three hundred people they were equipped to handle, long lines and crowded conditions were customary.[17] Mrs. Itsu Akiyama described the institutional conditions:

A bell rang at mealtime, and people drifted into the mess hall. We picked up our food at a counter and sat at the long tables in the order we stood in line. There were no times when families could sit together. Everything was *shikata-ganai* [recognition that the situation was beyond our control so accept it] in camp. At breakfast we had toast and apple butter. For lunch we were served bread and a lot of canned food, like beans. We ate it even if we did not like it. I remember being served an odd looking fish that had triangular bones protruding. Some of us thought it was snake—so I did not eat it. Nobody ate any of it! The cooks served it now and then, and we wondered where it came from.

Within the colony, a dry-goods canteen, shoe repair shop, barber shop, beauty parlor, newspaper stand, and bank were available. Canteens in other sections sold food and general merchandise to evacuees,[18] as Mrs. Itsu Akiyama recalled: "We bought foodstuff, candy, and daily needs at the canteen and used coupons from our $2.50 book of tickets. I do not remember what I bought with the one-cent coupon!"[19]

Employment

By July 30, one-third of the 5,500 resident Tuleans were employed. Five months later, the number of workers had increased to 6,800.[20] "I got job," Mr. Chiho Tomita recounted in English. "Everybody have job in camp. I got to make hot water for the bathroom—keep fire going on the stove (coal boiler) so hot water all time. People need washing water and take bath. I make sixteen dollars month."

Compensation was minimal, with the pay scale set at $12 a month for unskilled labor, $16 for skilled labor, and $19 for professional employment. As low as they were, these rates still amounted to an increase over the original scale of $8, $12, and $16.[21] Rather than consider these sums as wages, the government apparently viewed them as spending money offered in addition to the room and board provided the Japanese.[22] This pay scale was also a concession to public pressure on the WRA that

evacuee pay should not exceed $21, the base pay for the U.S. military.[23]
To earn these low wages, however, evacuees worked forty-four hour
weeks, on weekdays from 8:00 to 12:00 A.M. and 1:15 to 5:15 P.M. and on
Saturdays from 8:00 to 12:00 A.M. Employed in all areas of camp operation, 6,800 evacuees, including Issei from Hood River, labored in food
production, home winterizing, health and sanitation, security, or
maintenance:[24]

> I was doing janitor-type work in camp, mostly cleaning the toi-
> lets and laundry facilities in my block. There were four of us from
> Hood River working together: Mr. Nishimoto, Mr. Takagi, Mr.
> Yasutome, and me. So I thought it was a pretty good job. I was paid
> sixteen dollars a month. [Mr. Miyozo Yumibe]

> The mess hall requested help from those of us who did not have
> small children. Men did most of the cooking. (Since the mess hall
> served food in large quantities, many of the skillets and pans were
> too heavy for women to carry.) Other jobs—like dishwashing, serv-
> ing food, and preparing salads—were mostly women's work. But
> when the men washed the salad vegetables, they simply wet them
> down and did not clean them. (I would not eat their salads—some-
> times there were worms!) But I did enjoy having the men cook.
> Even then, it is very difficult to cook rice properly. When it came
> out too soft or too hard, we women would complain to the men!
> They usually replied, "Well, if you don't like it, you do it!" Yeah. I
> probably worked from seven o'clock in the morning to about six
> o'clock at night. With breaks, I am guessing that we worked about
> five hours a day, six days a week. I earned sixteen dollars a month
> and could buy fruit and candy at the canteen. [Mrs. Hatsumi
> Nishimoto]

Considering that she might be unable to return to the family orchard,
Mrs. Miyoshi Noyori equipped herself with new job skills. With genuine
zeal and good intentions, she conscientiously began her new job:

> In the backs of our minds, we tried to develop other skills to
> make a living. I had on-the-job training cutting hair. But whenever
> a client came, I became flustered and made mistakes—I might have
> cut one side too long and the other side too short! I even left little
> marks on someone's head. While using the shears, I once tried to
> cut the hair so close that I cut my own fingers! Blood oozed, so my
> boss had to tape my fingers and then correct my mistakes. That was
> very embarrassing! For close to one year, I earned nineteen dollars
> a month while most other jobs earned sixteen dollars. Yeah, it did

become useful, for I was able to cut my husband's hair. At no time since did he have to go to the barber.

In August, twenty-five hundred acres of vegetables were planted on the Tule Lake farm site seven miles away. The September harvest included five hundred pounds of beans, a thousand dozen bunches each of green onions and radishes, two hundred sacks of daikon, and a hundred sacks of potatoes.[25] By the end of 1943, residents of Tule Lake and other centers produced 85 percent of their own vegetables as well as selling 2.5 million pounds locally.[26]

"The government required that we raise as much food as possible in camp," Mrs. Tei Endow explained. "Large plots of ground were assigned outside the camp. (I heard there were ten thousand acres.) In a cooperative system, produce from Tule Lake was exchanged with other camps. They grew cabbage, *napa* [Chinese cabbage], daikon, carrots, *gobo* [burdock root], potato. I did not go out to work. In fact, I did not even see the field, for it was quite a distance from camp. This was cheap labor, for the workers earned only about eight or nine dollars a month. The government had provided our food and shelter, so I had everything that was necessary."

Later, a poultry farm, hog farm, and pickling plant for processing *napa* and daikon contributed to dietary needs of the colony.[27]

Camp Life

Within the artificial community of camp life, Issei and their families adjusted as best they could to their cramped and barren quarters, the lack of privacy in their daily rituals, and the endless practice of waiting in lines. Yet, for the first time in their lives, they did find themselves free from the daily rigors of orchard labor and the regular household chores. Now in the position of relying on the government for food, shelter, medical care, and schooling, they did have more opportunities to broaden their own interests and spend their days in more leisurely ways. Many enrolled in classes:

There were all kinds of classes at camp: flower arranging, haiku [Japanese lyric poem of seventeen syllables], tea ceremony, sewing. I wanted to learn *Eigo* [English] and I had the time. So, carrying my pencil and pad, I earnestly attended classes. We met two to three times a week, and our Nisei instructor taught us to spell. During the test, I remember I could not write the words she gave us. It was so difficult! We were instructed in writing as well as conversation, but we spoke *Eigo* only during the class—as soon as we left, we spoke

Japanese. It would have been wonderful if we Issei had been able to talk to each other in *Eigo*. Once we were taught to sing "Should Auld Acquaintance Be Forgot." I really tried, but it was awkward for me to get the words out. [Mrs. Itsu Akiyama]

Nearly every day Hamada-san, Sato-san, and I walked to the wooded area just outside camp to find materials for ikebana. We were allowed in the surrounding area without special permits, and we always returned with armloads of sagebrush and willow to share with others. Creating tranquil ikebana gave me much pleasure! When my arrangement did not look quite the way I wanted, sometimes I worked until midnight to find a suitable branch or flower to give the right effect. And, when there was not enough room to display them in our apartment, I placed two or three arrangements on one table. [Mrs. Asayo Noji]

I went to classes in sewing and *shishu* [embroidery]. Our instructor was an eighty-five-year-old man who did not even have to wear glasses! I used to make embroidered cranes which could be framed in glass. [Mrs. Hatsumi Nishimoto]

Many created crafts using objects found within the camp site or materials purchased from the canteen:

In our spare time we dug shells from a ditch inside the camp. They were all over in the sand—you could dig them with a stick. Then we bleached them and made pins and jewelry. [Mrs. Asayo Noji]

We collected tiny shells inside the camp fence and cemented them to twisted cotton balls to form flowers. After coloring them with paint, we made leaves from paper. I did not worry that this took a lot of time. At camp I did not cook or wash. We had a lot of time and a lot of sea shells! My friends and I made flowers together and enjoyed ourselves immensely. I remember selling one outside [the camp] for five dollars.

I also crocheted, using an *Eigo* instruction book. Since I could only read simple characters like A, B, C, my daughter read it to me. I crocheted a big bedspread and a small tablecloth. Suma's [a niece's] husband would marvel, saying, "*Mainichi, mainichi* [every day] you spend time making this!" We had a lot of time to crochet. But I did not use the bedspread. I just put it in the trunk, because I had nowhere to display it. [Mrs. Itsu Akiyama]

Some of the men foraged for scrap lumber and plyboard or purchased low-grade, plywood two-by-fours at the canteen to improve their stark living quarters:

Sometime government give free material, so I made desk. Pretty fancy desk—six drawers and big top. Then yellow wax stain on plywood. I made big plywood furniture: table, sofa, chairs. [Mr. Chiho Tomita, in English]

Papa spent most of his time in carpentry. Sometimes he got lumber from the maintenance crew; other times he used wood supplied for our stove. He built a lot of furniture for our apartment, including a double-decker bed to save space, a heavy dresser with drawers, a lamp, and a folding screen decorated with carvings and a Japanese scene (handpainted by a friend). He worked on the large objects in front of our apartment, and people passing by would stop to watch him. Papa gave away little tables and a lot of wooden vases—all shapes and sizes. He felt so much joy giving away his handcrafted goods! We used to say, "If you wanted it, it was yours." It was funny how much he enjoyed giving after all that work. But, if it made him happy, it made me happy. [Mrs. Asayo Noji]

Eventually visitors to the Noji barrack could enter through a covered porch. In an attempt to beautify the stark, monotonous grounds, they also created a scenic rock garden with bonsai (dwarf ornamental trees) and flowers planted from seed catalogs.

Religious services conducted throughout the camp offered Issei spiritual comfort and time to renew their religious faith. "Every Sunday," Mrs. Itsu Akiyama related, "I attended Inouye-sensei's [Rev. Isaac Inouye's] 'church,' actually a barrack filled with benches. I remember the minister telling us that although we were suffering greatly in such an undesirable place, this was wartime so we should not have ill feelings. It was probably the will of God."

One newfound opportunity at camp was the chance to develop friendships with a broader range of Japanese from Washington, California, Arizona, and other parts of Oregon—and even to renew acquaintances with former neighbors from Japan:

Tule Lake was a very large camp, and I almost had the feeling that I was in Japan. There were a lot of Japanese—many from Oregon and Washington—so we were able to visit and watch other people. Many from Los Angeles were actors and actresses, so I recall they even had plays. [Mrs. Hatsumi Nishimoto]

One of our most pleasant memories was visiting friends who were originally from Fukushima, our hometown. We had many good times, but we did miss Hood River. And we longed for matsutake [mushrooms]. Since we had left two boxes of canned, fried matsutake at home, I asked our neighbor to send us two quarts. We shared them with all our neighbors, who treated them like treasure! [Mrs. Hama Yamaki]

Matsutake, or pine mushrooms, were highly prized, brown mushrooms with thick, meaty stems. Wild growths in undisturbed stands of pine trees, their growing season extended only a few weeks during autumn. During normal times, Japanese families cherished annual fall treks to search for these delicacies.

Return from Imprisonment

For Mrs. Itsu Akiyama, the transition to life in camp was particularly troubling, for she faced each new and difficult situation alone. Her husband, a leader in the local Japanese community, had been imprisoned in Justice Department internment centers after being taken from his home early the morning of December 8, 1941. After a separation of almost thirteen months, reassuring news finally came to her at Tule Lake:

Papa sent me a letter that he was coming home. I was so relieved! He was the first to be released from the Louisiana internment camp.[28] I thought it only proper that he be permitted to return. There had been rumors that those interned in the federal prison camp might be sent to Japan. I knew, though, that in other wars in the past, many in internment camps had been killed—and I had been greatly concerned that he might never return. So, before we had left Hood River, I sent everything I could to Papa in Livingston—suits, shirts, everything! People at the internment camp wondered why he was the only one receiving all those goods from home. But in the past, prisoners had not returned. That was always on my mind—.

It appeared that Papa's treatment had been satisfactory. In Missoula, Montana, the Japanese lived in a group and cooked for themselves. A group of Italians lived there too. Papa was then transferred to Oklahoma and finally to Camp Livingston, Louisiana. His letters were censored. Papa had written that a man had been shot while trying to escape over a fence. (That part of the letter was blackened out, but I was still able to read it.) George visited Papa there and exclaimed in his letter that "my father's living like a king, he's being treated so well!"[29]

After over a year, we met in the barracks. Papa had arrived on an army truck. The family made no special preparations, because we had nothing to prepare—well, we probably got one extra bed. My worry for my husband and my children was greatly relieved. Yes, I had suffered so much. When Papa came back, I thanked the Lord for his return.

Their disjointed lives evoked an odd flashback to the early days of their arrival in the United States. In both periods of their lives, they had faced dismal living conditions, unexpected circumstances, and inequity in their pay and treatment. There were some differences, however. In the camps, they lived in intemperate climates in segregated Japanese communities. And this time there were armed guards and barbed wire enclosures—they had no choice.

28

The Loyalty Questionnaire

CONFUSION, TENSION, and controversy came to a head in February 1943 when "loyalty questionnaires" were administered in all the camps. After announcing plans to form a special Nisei combat team, the War Department had designed a questionnaire to reveal "tendencies of loyalty or disloyalty to the United States" of all draft-age Nisei males. The War Relocation Authority (WRA), however, resolved to give the questionnaire to all Japanese men and women over seventeen years old. According to the WRA's logic, the move was intended to determine the loyalty of all internees and, in a statement drafted for the president, to ensure that "no loyal citizen of the United States should be denied the democratic right to exercise the responsibilities of citizenship, regardless of his ancestry. . . . "[1] The loyalty questionnaire thus became a mass screening, not only for military induction but for work permits and clearance to resettle outside the camps.[2]

Among the forty questions, there were two that created the most controversy. Question twenty-seven asked, "Are you willing to serve in the armed forces of the United States on combat duty, wherever ordered?" This was later amended for women to read, "If the opportunity presents itself and you are found qualified, would you be willing to volunteer for the Army Nurse Corps or the WAAC [Women's Army Auxiliary Corps]?" Question twenty-eight asked, "Will you swear unqualified allegiance to the United States of America and faithfully defend the United States from any or all attack by foreign or domestic forces, and forswear any form of allegiance or obedience to the Japanese emperor, or any other foreign government, power, or organization?"

Issei's reactions differed:

I believe *chusei* [loyalty questionnaire] implies security or safety. The questionnaires were distributed by Japanese at an assembly. A speaker faced the people and explained the papers. There were many who did not understand *chusei*, and there were differences of opinion. Those who had no children may have tended to be more pro-Japan, but those who had children and could see they would be living in this country were pro-America. This strained relations between those who had opposing viewpoints, for your friend may have been on the other side. [Mrs. Hatsumi Nishimoto]

Our block manager gave us forms to complete. I do not remember whether they were in English or Japanese. My husband and I discussed the matter in our room and then filled in our forms. [Mrs. Itsu Akiyama]

About all I remember is that we were mailed a questionnaire. It was printed in English, so we had to ask others the questions. We signed it at the block office. [Mrs. Miyoshi Noyori]

Although administrators consulted Issei leaders and lead informative group discussions at some camps, they were considerably less diligent at Tule Lake. When camp officials gave a cursory overview and then announced that registration was compulsory, many evacuees refused to complete the questionnaires. Gangs of resisters, in fact, prevented some from registering.[3]

With little notice and few explanations about the questionnaires and their purpose, interpretations varied. "Government ask me one question," Mr. Chiho Tomita recounted in English. " 'You shoot emperor with gun?'[4] No, I can't. Most everybody same question. After while they change question: just loyalty to this country. I said if I have citizen[ship] this country, I go to war mostly any place. I be good citizen. I don't think anything about Japan."

Since Issei were ineligible for American citizenship, forswearing loyalty to the emperor could have placed them in the untenable positions of becoming "stateless persons." Question twenty-eight was thus revised: "Will you swear to abide by the laws of the United States and to take no action which would in any way interfere with the war effort of the United States?"[5]

Debates in the camps became intense. How could the United States, while confining its Nisei citizens, ask them to volunteer to defend American principles of justice? Might an all-Nisei outfit be sacrificed as cannon fodder? Might question twenty-eight be a trick question that could be interpreted as an admission of prior allegiance? Should Japanese affirm loyalty to a country that imprisoned them in such a manner? If Japan became a victor in the war, would evacuees be punished for disloyalty? Might families be separated if their responses differed? After two moves in eight months, would a "yes" answer mean Japanese would be forced to move again? Adding to the confusion, the form completed by all Japanese was entitled "War Relocation Authority Application for Leave Clearance."[6]

For some Issei, the decision to complete the questionnaire came fairly easily, despite these unanswered questions:

> On the surface, it appeared to be a difficult decision, but actually it was quite simple for us. We were originally from Japan and naturally our feelings had some connection with the land of our birth. But our outer feelings were "pro-," because this was for the benefit of our children. So the decision was not that wrenching. [Mrs. Hatsumi Nishimoto]

> Since our children were American citizens and we had a son in the army, we were naturally loyal to America. Almost everyone in our area expressed loyalty to America. [Mrs. Itsu Akiyama]

> I did not give it too much thought, because my mind was already set. I had already made the decision to say yes. If I had been a single person, I would have had the freedom to choose yes or no. But with a big family of seven children, it became almost impossible to say no. [Mr. Masaji Kusachi]

> We chose to say yes because we had no intention of returning to Japan. We were going to spend our life in America. Those who probably wished to return to Japan replied no, and those who wished to remain said yes. [Mrs. Masayo Yumibe]

Discussions among evacuees became heated. Suspected informers were labeled *inu* (dogs). Rumors and propaganda were rife:

> Some brought shortwave radio into room. We stuck our heads under blanket to hear radio. News said many American ships sunk and Japan winning all time. We had many arguments—how could American ships be the only ones sunk? [Mr. Chiho Tomita, in English]

> A pro-Japan group claimed that each time the mess hall bell rang, that meant Japan had won another battle. They spread rumors that Japan was winning the war. But Takagi-san, who could read *The Oregonian*, said, "According to *The Oregonian*, Japan is losing!" [Mrs. Itsu Akiyama]

Tensions heightened as pressure was applied by those with deep-rooted resentment and disillusionment:

> I did hear that this became a problem in many families when relatives went different directions [gave different answers]. After the segregation issue came up, there were conflicts of interest and things became a little bit rowdy. [Mr. Masaji Kusachi]

> Our most difficult time came when the "No-Yes" questionnaire arrived. My son Shige had said, "It would be much better to be on the outside than to go through this." If my children were going outside [work release program], I wanted to go too. People from California were most vociferous. I do not know too much about what people were saying, but the situation was getting out of hand. So we wanted to leave camp to avoid this. [Mrs. Hama Yamaki]

In Block 42 at Tule Lake, after two-thirds of the residents had failed to register, a delegation of thirty-four youth demanded the right of expatriation. WRA officials and military police, armed with machine guns and bayonets, refused their request and instead transported the resisters to jail. These actions, while panicking some, strengthened the resolve of others. In Ward V, most residents agreed that they would not cooperate with the administration, and groups circulated petitions resolving not to register. One defiant group threatened to beat *inu*, and some who openly favored registration were ostracized and threatened.[7]

Again, confusion reigned, and Issei reactions varied:

> I believe that those with strong feelings at Tule Lake were mostly *Kibei* [Nisei who spent their early years in Japan and returned to the United States]. There were also Issei who felt strongly that they had been mistreated by being sent to concentration camps. [Mrs. Miyoshi Noyori]

> In our block, we had no violence—it was very quiet. We heard that in other blocks there were verbal confrontations. People would ask, "In view of what happened are you still 'pro-?' " [Mrs. Hatsumi Nishimoto]

There were distinct areas of "loyalty" and "disloyalty" among blocks. Blocks near and adjacent to Block 42 could be most clearly distinguished as the "zone of disloyalty." Sixteen of the sixty-three blocks had 50.0 to 74.4 percent "disloyals," thirty-six had 20.0 to 49.9 percent "disloyals," and eleven had 1.0 to 19.9 percent "disloyals."[8]

At Tule Lake, 3,218, or almost a third, of the residents ultimately refused to register for the questionnaires. In contrast, at five of the ten camps, everyone registered; at four others, a total of only thirty-six refused.[9] The government therefore designated Tule Lake as the segregation center for Issei who had applied for repatriation, Nisei who had applied for expatriation, those who had answered no to the loyalty question or had refused to register, and family members of segregants. Approximately thirteen Hood River families remained at Tule Lake. (None of them chose to return to Hood River.) Eventually 5,766 Japanese Americans filed papers to renunciate their citizenship, and 95 percent were Tule Lake residents.[10] So-called loyals were to be transferred to other camps.

More than 18,000 Japanese and Japanese Americans were segregated at Tule Lake. A third responded no to question thirty-eight; a third were their family members; and a third were "Old Tuleans" who simply chose not to leave.[11] Of the 75,000 Japanese who completed the loyalty questionnaires, approximately 6,700 responded no to question twenty-eight. Almost 2,000 qualified their answers in some way but were still listed as "disloyal." A few hundred simply left the space blank. The vast majority—more than 65,000—answered yes.[12]

Years later, Issei from Hood River recalled:

I think most of the people from Hood River answered yes. In the Dee area, I only recall one family who said no—and they probably wanted to return to Japan. [Mr. Masaji Kusachi]

People had different opinions for different reasons. You cannot help that—you just have to do what you believe. Even when we were leaving, Papa was distressed that some on the negative side had bitter thoughts or fears about our leaving. [Mrs. Asayo Noji]

Humorously, there were some who returned to Japan and told us, "If you ever return to Japan, we won't let you land." Oddly enough, one of these people chose to return to live in America. [Mrs. Miyoshi Noyori]

Departing from Tule Lake was most painful for us, because we would be separated from longtime friends. Our pro-Japan friends warned us, "Just as soon as we can repatriate to Japan, we are going. Our future will be much more secure. If you leave Tule Lake, you may never be able to return to your former home." Those were some of their parting thoughts. [Mrs. Hatsumi Nishimoto]

Once again, indecision and anxiety wrenched the lives of the Hood River Issei. Within sixteen months, this would be the third time they would be forcibly removed from their homes and plunged into new and daunting situations. In this case, however, there was a sadder consequence for them, because the tensions of their uprooting created physical and emotional fallout between some Japanese friends and neighbors.

29

Moving to Other Camps

For seventeen days, beginning on September 13, 1943, approximately 6,250 "loyal" Tuleans were transferred to other relocation centers.[1] Moving for the third time in sixteen months, Issei and Nisei were again subject to long, hot train rides in cars where blinds were drawn and armed guards observed them constantly.

Mrs. Itsu Akiyama kept a diary of her trip from Tule Lake to Minidoka, located in south-central Idaho. Here she relives that journey—her itinerary, her thoughts, and the breadth of her emotions:

> We left Tule Lake at around two o'clock in the afternoon on September 25, 1943. We could only leave with our suitcases; our other belongings were sent later. We packed our belongings on a truck and left our barracks through the front gate. At the gate, we were given a farewell song and some Japanese friends came to say "Bye, bye." (I am trying to remember whether that song was in English or Japanese!) Our departure was quite emotional, because we were leaving our friends. Many were dabbing their eyes with handkerchiefs, so it was probably as difficult for them as it was for us. We thought, "Surely we will not return to this place again." Then we boarded a train at a nearby station.

After traveling through the mountains and entering Oregon, she yearned for a glimpse of Hood River:

> When we stopped at the Klamath Falls train depot, I noticed that all the workers were women in overalls. I realized then that we were truly at war. I remember viewing the ducks on Klamath Lake, thinking that they were not concerned about war or evacuation.

Armed guards monitored traffic at the entrance to camps, as they did here at Minidoka. (Courtesy of Asayo Noji)

They seemed to have a pretty happy life. The train stopped momentarily, and we were told this was Eugene. It was time to eat; so, while the guards watched us, we moved to another car which had tables arranged with food. As we proceeded on our journey, I looked forward to seeing Hood River again! At times, I peeked around the window blinds. Then we saw a lot of lights outside. We knew we were in a BIG city, so this must be Portland! Yes, we had stopped at the Union Depot. As we came up the valley, we could again see lights, probably the Bonneville Dam area. I really was homesick for Hood River! I was hoping to see it—but it was night-time, and I was to be disappointed. As dawn arrived, though, we saw Indians netting salmon at Celilo Falls near The Dalles. When our train stopped in Pendleton, passengers saw another train there and exclaimed, "*Ara!* [Oh] There are Japanese!" We were told that these Japanese were headed for Tule Lake. Moving on, we traveled through many small towns; and our locomotive needed two helper units to climb the mountain. As we descended on the east side, we rode through many more small towns.

After two cramped days of travel, they arrived at their destination to find surprises—both pleasant and unpleasant:

Again we stopped in a field of sagebrush. Army camp trucks arrived, and three Japanese welcomed us. This was the morning of

September 27, 1943. Two families loaded onto our army truck, and we drove in a cloud of dust through miles and miles of sagebrush. I stretched my neck trying to glimpse the sights, but I could not even see any mountains. Eventually I was able to see a white water tower. And then the hospital chimney and barracks came into view. *Yare, yare!* [Oh, dear, oh, dear! How glad I was!] At the gate was a big welcome sign, and people we did not know gave us cups of soda water and cookies. It made me so happy to be welcomed in this way! Our luggage was then searched by the military police, and we reloaded onto another truck that drove us to our assigned barrack. Our room was very similar to [the one at] Pinedale, with four beds and two blankets each. But the blankets were covered with sand, so I hung them outside. There was a bathtub in our washroom, so Kiyo and I were able to take baths. This seemed to relieve our exhaustion from the journey. Our baggage, which held our clothes and sheets, did not arrive for ten days. We had no change of clothes, so we probably bundled up in blankets. *Shikata-ganai.* "Can't help!"

Hood River "loyals" spent the rest of their camp days at Minidoka, in south-central Idaho near Twin Falls; Heart Mountain, in northwest Wyoming; or Jerome, in southeast Arkansas. For the evacuees, their daily routines continued, as Mr. Masaji Kusachi described:

I got a job operating a large road grader at Minidoka. During summertime I ran the road grader to repair the road and clear the sagebrush outside the camp. Once we even cleared enough land for an airplane landing strip used occasionally by the director of our camp! Another time I dug an irrigation ditch to bring water into the camp. Also the camp had an obligation to clear three thousand acres of land to raise produce, mostly potatoes and cucumbers, for camp residents. We were to exchange any surplus produce with other camps. So, to clear this three thousand acres, two large tractors dragged a rail between them to loosen the sagebrush. My job was to run the grader and push the sagebrush into a pile. Then twelve men set these sagebrush piles afire. At times I also leveled coal for the kitchen crew. They used large chunks of coal in the kitchen, leaving small stuff piled outside. When I leveled this coal off for them, the kitchen staff appreciated it so much that they brought me hot coffee. Of course, during wintertime I drove the snowplow. I was paid nineteen dollars a month for my work.

Heart Mountain, Wyoming, the northernmost of the ten centers, was located in an area known for its harsh winters and severe dust storms.

Like Minidoka, it was the former site of an undeveloped government rec-
lamation project. Years later, Mrs. Hatsumi Nishimoto recalled:

> Heart Mountain [was a] nice place. It was much cleaner and it
> had a much larger area—but they still had fences and guard stations
> with towers. When we arrived, the mess hall served sashimi be-
> cause we were newcomers. People told us this had not happened be-
> fore, and they were delighted.
>
> In the past the Heart Mountain area must have been under wa-
> ter, because there were a lot of small seashells. We dug them, then
> polished and painted them to make artificial flowers. Since our bar-
> rack was near the canteen, my dear friend from Seattle asked me to
> sell her corsages and pins. Word got around, and people from all
> over camp came to buy them for about $1.50. I received a small
> commission. At Heart Mountain, I also attended sewing classes and
> made my own dresses. At that time, dressmaking patterns were very
> difficult.
>
> My husband had a job unloading coal from the railroad car at
> both camps. He was paid twenty dollars a month, more than the
> usual camp wages, because this was dirty, strenuous work. Most of
> the Heart Mountain residents were former city dwellers, so they
> were not used to heavy, physical work. Both of our children at-
> tended school and played baseball all the time.

The most painful memory of camp days for Mr. Masaji Kusachi was the
extended illness and eventual death of his wife, which would leave him a
single father of seven young children:

> My wife was in and out of the hospital. After Dr. Togasaki, a
> woman doctor, diagnosed her illness as cancer of the bones, my wife
> was sent by train to a Portland hospital for radium treatments. (She
> was in no condition to travel by herself, so someone from camp per-
> sonnel accompanied her. I would not have been permitted to go.)
> She returned in a week; and I brought meals to her in our room, a
> common camp practice for those who were ill. She spent most of
> her time in bed and was quite often in pain. Learning that she had
> cancer, for which there was no cure, was one of our most difficult
> times in camp. I was devastated, and I did not know what to do.
> Our children, who were quite young, were probably not yet able to
> understand the problem. For me, though, it was tragic to realize I
> might have to rear the family by myself. At Minidoka my wife's con-
> dition was very poor, and our doctor told us to do all we could for
> her. I think what was unsaid was that she did not have much longer

to live. So I was able to take her to Lava Hot Springs, Idaho, a hot spring resort area. We returned in a month and sent her to Salt Lake Hospital, where a Japanese doctor specialized in cancer. After a week we received a call that my wife did not have much longer to live, and her sister brought her home. Two days later, at the age of thirty-seven, my wife died at the camp hospital. She was able to see her family, and then she passed away. She had become comatose.

Cremation was not permitted in Idaho, so we had to send my wife's body to Salt Lake City. At Minidoka, funeral services were conducted outside because the recreation hall was too small. Many people attended, especially those of the Nichiren Buddhist faith from Sacramento, Seattle, and Portland. It is difficult for me to express it in words, but I cannot forget that service. My son Fred, who may still have been in grade school, carried my wife's urn for us.

As in prewar times, some life and death routines were inevitable. But tragedy seemed to weigh even more heavily inside the barbed-wire enclosures.

30

The Work Release Program

WITH THE SHORTAGE of seasonal farm labor and the potential of losing their crops, anxious farmers petitioned the White House for assistance. By mid-May, the War Relocation Authority (WRA) responded with an agricultural leave program for evacuees. During the spring and summer of 1942, more than fifteen hundred Japanese worked in the fields of eastern Oregon and the intermountain states.[1] By mid-October, ten thousand evacuees were on seasonal leave in Idaho, Utah, Montana, Colorado, and eastern Oregon.[2]

The leave program promoted the WRA's plan of permanently reset-tling Japanese in different parts of the country, for they could also apply for indefinite leaves for education or employment outside the relocation area.[3] For the indefinite leaves, Japanese were expected to show that they could support themselves and that their presence was likely to be accept-able in the community. Furthermore, there was to be no evidence that they were security threats, and they were to agree to notify the WRA if their addresses changed.[4]

Work releases for Japanese also required that they receive prevailing wages, transportation to and from the job, and suitable housing at no cost. In addition, employers were to attest that Japanese laborers would not displace local workers.[5] The process was lengthy, however, sometimes involving three months to clear a request through the FBI and other intelligence agencies.[6]

The WRA nonetheless encouraged Japanese to apply for these ex-tended leaves. The Yamakis complied. "We eventually leased a house and about eleven acres," Mrs. Hama Yamaki recalled. "We raised lettuce and onions. That was really hard work! On my hands and knees, I used a hand tool with claws to rake the vegetable shoots. After half a day in the heat, I was very exhausted. We were able to hire a large crew, so the work was quickly finished; and we had more time to ourselves. But I cannot quite say whether we made a lot of money or not! We lived in Idaho for three years."

Mrs. Misuyo Nakamura's family also left camp to work in Idaho:

> To get a permit to leave camp, we had to have a job as well as a place to stay. We had become acquainted with Matsuura-san [Mr. Matsuura] of Sherwood, who had moved to Emmett, Idaho,[7] instead of entering camp. We had asked his opinion about leaving camp, and he encouraged us. So Papa had scouted the Emmett area. The area seemed attractive to us, because there was not much discrimination toward Japanese.
>
> We left camp for the sake of our children. I hesitate to be too critical, because I do believe the government may have done the best it could. But there were a lot of people, and there was certainly no way to supervise our children. This was a deep concern to me so we chose to leave.

To the chagrin of many, including Mrs. Yamaki, provisions at the work sites appeared to be only minimal, despite WRA regulations:

> Our employer said, "We don't have any housing, but we have an old barn where you can stay." Mitsie asked me, "Are you willing to put up with this?" I, in turn, asked my daughter, "Are YOU willing to sleep in this place?" She did not reply, so I questioned the owner about other housing in the area. The owner was a very good man and served us a large chicken dinner that evening. He told us that as soon as housing was available, he wished to employ us. But we could not sleep in a barn that housed cattle! So we telephoned the family of Billy's [son's] fiancée. They told us, "Oh, my goodness! Don't stay in a place like that! Come to our home." The Yamamotos had about a hundred acres of farmland, and they employed many people from camp. But I cannot forget a man from Scotland who lent us his home, saying, "You can have my house, because I can sleep outside on the wagon." His house was surrounded by cows and was in much disarray, but he cleaned it for us. In those days, housing was limited, so we were able to live in his house for over half a year. He stayed in a hut nearby.

Like Mrs. Yamaki, Mrs. Nakamura found their accommodations appalling: "Our two-room house had no beds, so we all slept on blankets on the floor. Five of us were lined up like a bunch of fish! The irony was that I could neither laugh nor cry. All we had inside was a stove. The privy was outside, and we had no sink or tap water. We got our water from an irrigation ditch. I could see trash and debris floating in the water, so I scooped what I thought was the cleanest water at the top. I let it set for awhile so the debris would settle to the bottom. Then we boiled it for drinking or cooking. To take a bath, we heated the water and poured it into the washtub."

Despite substandard conditions at their work sites, Japanese worked diligently throughout the duration of the war. In several western states, they were credited with saving the sugar beet crops.[8] Among those employed in Montana, the Endow family received standard wages, set for beet operations by the 1937 Sugar Act: 55 cents per hour for blocking and thinning, 50 cents an hour for the first hoeing, and 65 cents per hour for harvesting.[9]

Mrs. Tei Endow described their experience:

> From about September, during sugar beet topping season, men came to camp to recruit workers for their fields. The government had a policy that people should be helpful in the nature of war programs. So, although we did not even know what a sugar beet looked like, we agreed.
>
> Four of us left camp for the Garryowen, Montana, sugar beet fields in September 1943. My husband, with fifteen other workers, topped sugar beets. I did not go out to the fields but stayed to do housework, cooking, and sewing at our little house. During winter my husband worked on a railroad gang.
>
> There were many times when the temperature went down to thirty degrees below zero! My youngest son went to school on an Indian reservation, and we had to walk a considerable distance to catch the bus. It was so cold that ice would form on his pant legs. When he got off the bus, he would run toward me, saying, "It's so cold! It's so cold!" To see my son suffering so much in the cold was more than I could stand.

For others, family considerations overruled any prospects of outside employment. "We were approached in camp by Caucasian orchardists from back east who wanted our help on their apple farms," Mr. Masaji Kusachi explained. "I was promised housing if I would go to a 180-acre orchard in Michigan. Even though I was asked several times, I turned the offer down. I had no desire to drag my family of nine way back there. And besides, I told them I had a home and farm in Dee." Having heavily invested their time, effort, and money in their valley orchards and everhopeful of returning to Hood River, many Issei, like Mr. Kusachi, whose wife had died at the Minidoka camp, were loathe to relocate. Yet, while life outside the camps was uncertain, the lure of the valley orchards was constant.

31

Camp Reflections

THE PERIOD of internment, as long as three years for some, had a significant effect on the Japanese, affecting relationships with their families,
the roles of family members, and their own personal habits and attitudes.
Reflecting on their camp experiences, Hood River Issei expressed a range
of emotions—tension, frustration, acceptance, and even pleasure. But
underneath it all, explained Mrs. Hama Yamaki, there lingered a hollow
sense of loss: "The biggest difference in camp was that we lost our freedom—we were not free to do what we wanted. It was kind of a lonesome
feeling when we had to leave home for camp. The lonesome feeling is
something I find difficult to express in words. *Shikata-ganai* [It is beyond
control; it cannot be helped so accept it as it is]. We had the feeling that
we all had to work together."

Resigned to their fate when the situation seemed hopeless, Issei were
fortified by a sense of community, knowing they were enduring the same
difficult conditions that their Japanese friends and neighbors were. The
patterns of communal living, however, began to replace normal family
functions, as family members spent less and less time together. Characteristic of many of the Issei, Mrs. Hatsumi Nishimoto was still able to
make concessions as she recounted her unhappiness with family life
in camp:

> I do not recall any pleasant experiences in camp—not even one.
> What bothered me most was that there was virtually no family din-
> ing. Young people ate with their friends, men dined together, and
> women ate in their own groups. Perhaps one positive thing about
> camp was that life was scheduled—without question, everything
> occurred on time. But then, if you did not go to the bathroom early,

Naoichi and Maki Hamada and friend Mrs. Morioka *(center)* reflected the sense of loss and frustration with their new life-styles at Minidoka, December 27, 1944. (Courtesy of Asayo Noji)

all the hot water would be gone. And early in the morning, there were many people. "All the time run out of hot water!" On the other hand, life in camp could be described as happy, because we had time on our hands and could attend classes for free.

Others, too, held disparate views. Mrs. Tei Endow's overriding concern, however, remained the poor atmosphere camp afforded for raising children: "I did not go outside to work, and I really just baby-sat my children, so I thought camp was a good vacation. But my five-year-old child was so active and got into so much mischief, I had to 'all the time watch' him.[1] Once when Mr. Fujimoto was walking to 'Alaska,'[2] he reported that he had seen our son throwing rocks at another boy. 'Your boy's fighting again,' he told me. Because it was kind of troublesome watching my son in camp, I just hated camp life."

Under conditions where they were neither free nor self-reliant, Japanese were primed to change their behavior patterns. In *Japanese Americans: Evolution of a Subculture,* the sociologist Harry Kitano maintained that "dominated groups have historically adapted to their status through a variety of adaptations including ritualism and superpatriotism, internalization of stress, work slowdowns, inefficiency, strikes and tardiness, aggression, displacement, ethnic humor, withdrawal, and intoxication. All of these adaptations were part of camp life."[3] Mr. Masaji Kusachi, too, analyzed those actions in camp that he found so uncharacteristic of Japanese:

In camp we were restricted and guards would not allow us to go outside without a permit. It is not as if we were guilty of a crime— we had done no wrong. Yet, we were placed in a prisonlike atmosphere. As I observed the guards at the station, it really upset me to think that we innocent people could be confined like that. Under those distressing conditions, strange thoughts would go through our minds, and we may have had antigovernmental sentiments. By human nature, when things are imposed upon you, you kind of feel rebellious. Small incidents like relieving [releasing] gas from camp equipment or going fishing made up somewhat for those feelings. I recall that even when there was unused bread from the meals, we made no attempts to save it. Instead we fed it to the seagulls. This action can probably only be explained by the fact that we were defying the government for confining us. On other occasions, I would enter a warehouse and come out with overcoats—not just one, but coats piled on coats. I did not really feel that I was stealing them—I felt that this was a consequence of the government's mistreatment.

And I did not take these clothes selfishly, because I gave them to people who needed extra clothing. Anyway, I would have to say that our feelings and emotions in camp were not those of normal people, because we were confined against our will. Our minds were quite confused and mixed-up. In retrospect, it is even difficult for me to understand how our minds and our thinking could have been so warped. I suppose that—because of the treatment we were receiving—by human nature, we were rebelling and doing things we certainly would not have done under normal conditions.

As family life deteriorated and children became less dependent on parents for their livelihood, the authority of the Issei abruptly changed. Traditionally, the providers and decision makers, fathers now had little authority, responsibility, or opportunity to improve their futures—or those of their families. Daisuke Kitagawa, Christian minister and author, maintained that Issei men "were the most badly affected of all" for they "could not hope for a future of [their] own in America."[4]

On the other hand, many women, freed from traditional housekeeping tasks, found it easier to accept camp life. Kitagawa acknowledged that life for women in the relocation centers "was really and truly a well-earned and highly deserved holiday. It meant liberation from lives of continuous drudgery. For the first time in their lives, they had something akin to free time. . . . *Issei* women thus unwittingly became the happiest people in the relocation center."[5] With newfound leisure hours, they attended classes, created handicrafts, and enjoyed more social contacts than would have been possible during their intensive workdays on their farms:

> At first it was very trying, for we were naturally worried about our future. But after two or three years, as we got accustomed to camp life, we had classes to attend and all kinds of shows for entertainment. They fed us well, and we did not even have to clean up. It was like a good vacation! (At home in Hood River, we were always at work and had very little time to ourselves.) And we became acquainted with a lot of Los Angeles people at camp. I think camp life was probably more liveable and happy and certainly more leisurely than life in Dee. [Mrs. Miyoshi Noyori]

> Probably the greatest change was that we had virtually no responsibilities, so our lives were relaxed and enjoyable. I had no assigned work, you see, except helping in the camp kitchen, which really did not take much time. I was able to take classes in ikebana [flower arrangement] and *ocha* [tea ceremony] from teachers with

high degrees. Afterward Iwasa-sensei [the teacher, Mr. Iwasa] forwarded a recommendation to Japan, and I received *menjo* [certificate] in both classes. It would have been impossible to gain these skills in Hood River. In the first place, there were no classes; and at home I would have had to work. [Mrs. Asayo Noji]

Everybody was the same—no rich men, no poor men. We did not cook; we did not wash [dishes]. I do not recall too many difficult moments, because we were all Japanese, and we were all in the same camp. I would not describe our camp life as happy, but neither was it *tsurai* [cruel]. We had our moments—even some of the children were given treats from the mess hall. [Mrs. Tei Endow]

Amid their fears, some wondered, in fact, whether they might have been fortunate to be held in detention by the government:

Privately we wondered how life might be elsewhere. I really do not have many bad memories of camp, though, because our food and everything was provided. I remember our neighbor Mori, who lived outside [the camp], would tell us when he visited, "Don't ever leave camp. If you live on the outside, meat and sugar are rationed. If you live in camp, you have everything furnished." I wondered if that were so. Also, in Hood River, I had not gone out very often, so my acquaintances were mostly my neighbors. But in camp, I made many friends.

Probably it was better for us that we were evacuated, because we heard about Japanese being mistreated and shot. Some people can be very wild! Since we did not have citizenship and were easily identified as Japanese, I considered camp life a better life. After my husband returned from prison camp, he told me, "If this had happened in another country, we might have been killed." [Mrs. Itsu Akiyama]

Certainly there were mixed emotions as Issei reexamined their camp experiences. The sociologist Amy Iwasaki Mass recognized that the shame and humiliation of their incarceration were typically expressed through unconscious defense mechanisms. Repressing or denying their feelings, rationalizing their internment, or identifying with the government helped Japanese deal with their sense of betrayal and injustice and adjust to their new situations.[6] Inevitably, the abrupt changes in Issei roles, their relationships with family and friends, and their living conditions affected their own senses of self-worth and self-determination. Beset with new anxieties, fears, and hopes, they would again be forced to contemplate their futures.

32

Sons in the Military Service

DURING WORLD WAR II, while Issei and their families were confined, thirty-three thousand Nisei served their country in the military in Europe and around the Pacific Ocean.[1] Immediately after the bombing of Pearl Harbor, many enlisted Nisei servicemen had been reclassified "4-F" (physically, mentally, or morally unfit) and then "4-C" (unacceptable because of nationality or ancestry).[2] While some were promptly discharged, others were simply transferred from combat units to lower security positions in kitchen or hospital duty, where they were often guarded by military personnel. Later, in part through the urging of Mike Masaoka, the national secretary of the Japanese American Citizens' League (JACL), and the War Relocation Authority, the War Department readmitted Nisei to the army. This action enabled Nisei to demonstrate their loyalty to the country of their birth.[3]

The first Nisei enlistee from Hood River was Bill Yamaki, son of Mrs. Hama Yamaki. With her son in the army and her family behind barbed wire, Mrs. Yamaki recalled the pain of separation:

I do not remember too many good things about Pinedale. The one bad feature about Pinedale was that I was not able to meet with my son. Bill was stationed in Minneapolis and could not secure a permit from the army to enter Tule Lake. This was most distressing to me, because I had to wonder when we would meet again. On March 19, 1941, Bill had been the first Japanese to be inducted from Hood River. He was found to be in good physical condition— they could find nothing wrong with him! Since he knew he would not be declared unfit, he volunteered for three years.[4] *Shikata-ganai* [It is beyond control; it cannot be helped so accept it]. It was the draft, he was a man, and he had to go. So I told him to do well. (At that time the war had not begun.) In a letter, he expressed the thought, "It might be a long time before we see each other again." So I replied, "Do your best while on duty."[5]

Reliving the joy of a short reunion when her son was on leave, Mrs. Itsu Akiyama also exposed her agony in the knowledge he was off to war—perhaps never to return:

> It was April 8, 1944, at Tule Lake. My husband and I had just reminded each other that George would be arriving soon, when there was a knock on our barrack door. I answered, "Come in," and there was George, on leave before going overseas. Five days later, when we saw him off at the camp gate, I broke down crying. I did not know whether I would see him again. Even after I came home, all I could do was cry. And the next day too! My neighbors sympathized with me. I suppose I was weak from crying so much. (Of course, my husband was a man, so he did not cry.) What troubled me most was that I did not really know how to pray for George's safety. In Japan my parents had been Buddhist and prayed to a local shrine. Here in America, I was not yet a Christian so I had no one to pray to. Yet I felt a desperate desire to pray. Then I recalled Seiji Kibi Mabi, a man from my *mura* [village] in Japan who lived at the Imperial Palace in Nara and had become quite famous.[6] So I prayed to him.

Mrs. Akiyama's son would enter the bloody campaign in Italy, where he served in the all-Nisei 100th Battalion. An assistant squad leader who earned both a silver and bronze star, George almost lost his life in a simultaneous exchange of fire with a German soldier. After thirty-two minutes of fierce fighting, the Nisei unit secured northern Italy's Georgia Hill from the Germans.[7]

In a bloody campaign that slowly moved the Allies up the Italian peninsula, the 100th Battalion suffered heavy casualties, earning nine hundred Purple Hearts and the nickname "Purple Heart Battalion."[8] In June 1944, the 100th became a part of the 442nd Regimental Combat Team, a newly formed Nisei unit. Its motto, "Go for Broke," a Hawaiian crapshooter's term for "shoot the works," was clearly illustrated in their rescue of the "Lost Battalion." In thirty-five minutes, the unit broke a Nazi stronghold and rescued three hundred Texans who had been surrounded for a week. The 442nd suffered 60 percent casualties in the bloody battle, which later earned them honorary citizenship among Texans.[9] By the end of the war, the 442nd became one of the war's most decorated combat teams. In seven campaigns, the regiment suffered 9,486 casualties, including 600 deaths. Casualties actually numbered over 300 percent of its original strength, since soldiers were often wounded in more than one battle.[10] Among the wounded was the son of Mrs. Tei Endow:

> Sho had originally served in Alaska, and then he was wounded while serving in the 442nd in Italy. Shrapnel missed his spinal column by a fraction of an inch.
>
> When we first heard that Sho had been injured, I was very worried that he would not come home alive. I received a very nice letter from the War Department that we were welcome to visit him. My feelings then were so unsettled—while I wanted to see Sho desperately, I was also burdened with a young boy of only five, so there would have been three of us to go. We thought the matter over and decided it might be best not to see him at that time. So we met Sho while we were working in Payette, Idaho. I cannot help but think that perhaps we were treated more fairly during war because we had a son serving in the army. I felt very proud of that fact. Sho received the Purple Heart.

During the spring of 1941, the army had begun training Japanese language translators. More than six thousand men eventually graduated from what became the Military Intelligence Service Language School in Minnesota. Many served in the Pacific translating battle plans, defense maps, tactical orders, intercepted messages, and diaries. Their contribution to the war effort enabled U.S. commanders to anticipate actions of the enemy, evaluate strengths and weaknesses, avoid surprises, and strike unexpectedly.[11] In the opinion of General Charles Willoughby, chief of staff for intelligence to General Douglas MacArthur, the invaluable intelligence work of these Nisei shortened the Pacific war by at least two years and prevented hundreds of thousands of American casualties.[12] Mrs. Asayo Noji's son Mamoru served as interpreter for Japanese prisoners on New Caledonia, New Guinea, and the Philippines: "At first I was really worried, because Japan was our enemy. But there was nothing I could do. We heard of others who were killed. I just hoped Mam would come home safely."

Among those who served in the U.S. military during World War II, approximately half were from the mainland and half represented Hawaii.[13] Nisei supported the war effort not only through infantry and translation work but also through service as medics, mechanics, language instructors, and clerks in government offices.[14] Among the thirteen families represented by Issei interviewed for this book, twenty-one sons served in the U.S. military. Whatever the role, their contributions unquestionably demonstrated loyalty and patriotism to the United States—proof that for six hundred meant the ultimate sacrifice of life.[15]

PART EIGHT

The Hood River Situation

Sono mae wa
Shitashi kari ni shi
Kono aruji
Monouri kobamu
Ozuozu to shite

He was kind to us before.
But now—the shopkeeper
Nervously refuses to serve us.

Tanka written by Mrs. Shizue Iwatsuki and
translated by Dr. Stephen W. Kohl

33

The Anti-Japanese Campaign

"So SORRY! Japs Are Not Wanted in Hood River," declared hundreds of valley residents who signed one of five full-length newspaper ads during the first three months in 1945.[1] In the two and a half years since the evacuation of the Japanese, a group of community members not only had sponsored an embittered, outspoken campaign against the return of Japanese but, in doing so, had brought nationwide attention to the tiny valley.

Just six months after the Japanese had left Hood River, "our Japanese problem" had been debated in a local newspaper. Even in peaceful times, the editorial conceded that "hatred of Japanese" was more intense than for other foreigners for "they have remained very definitely Japanese and unassimilable." If the government should justify such action, there was "no great problem in deporting Issei to Japan," but the newspaper acknowledged that Nisei citizens presented a constitutional "headache for our lawmakers." It concluded with a plea against exacerbating the racial problem.[2]

At the forefront of an anti-Japanese campaign, the American Legion Post in Hood River unanimously adopted resolutions on January 4, 1943, to amend the U.S. Constitution. Not only would the post attempt to prevent the return of persons of Japanese ancestry to the county but it wished to limit citizenship to children whose parents were citizens and to deport all those of Japanese descent to Japan.[3]

Other community organizations publicly supported those views. A member of the Parkdale Grange affirmed that group's stand: "There isn't room enough in the Parkdale area for the Japs and us too; and we don't aim to leave."[4] Likewise, the Hood River Lions Club[5] and the Hood River City Council endorsed the American Legion plan.[6]

"Shall the Japanese return here after the war?" asked the *Hood River County Sun*. According to the newspaper, local residents favored excluding the Japanese. From a poll of 352 residents who reportedly represented a cross section of the county, the newspaper printed the following statistics in January of 1943: 84 percent did not wish Japanese to return at the end of the war; 9 percent would allow only the return of citizens; 5 percent favored their return; and 2 percent were undecided. Results from the Hood River poll revealed more strident viewpoints than did Gallup polls, which asked the same questions of residents in California, Washington, Nevada, Arizona, and other parts of Oregon. Gallup data in the other five states showed that only 31 percent would not permit Japanese to return, 24 percent would allow only citizens, 29 percent would allow all, and 16 percent were undecided.[7] Three months later, the *Sun's* editorial declared, "They must never return . . . [for] if they do return we must expect bitterness and violence the like of which we have never had before."[8]

Taking a more moderate position, the *Hood River News* publisher Hugh Ball noted that Japanese who, thirty or more years earlier, had been "welcomed with open arms" during the labor shortage were now branded as undesirables.[9]

Further action by the American Legion, however, brought the valley into the midst of controversy not only in the state but throughout the nation. During the fall of 1943, Legionnaires had unveiled a war memorial on the east wall of the courthouse, which displayed names of every county resident serving in the armed forces.[10] Fourteen months later, on November 29, 1944, the names of sixteen Nisei soldiers were removed: George Akiyama, Shoichi Endow, Sumio Fukui, Isao Namba, Mamoru Noji, and Billy Yamaki, the sons of interviewed Issei, as well as Masaaki Asai, Taro Asai, Frank Hachiya, George Kinoshita, Seiji Nishioka, Harry Norimatsu, Setsu Shitara, Harry Takagi, Noboru Takasumi, and Harry Tamura.[11]

In a ten-page pamphlet providing a rationale for its actions, the American Legion voiced its concern for the dual citizenship of Nisei[12] and stated that names would not be reinstated on the memorial until Nisei had completed their tours of service or until a decision had been rendered on their dual citizenship. The American Legion also cautioned against a Japanese scheme to "control the coveted Pacific slope," bolstered by "the old sure game of infiltration by reproduction" and through decreased values (and forced sales) of land adjoining Japanese property. Accusing them of racial segregation and of depositing earnings in Japanese banks, the American Legion maintained that heads of families had met almost nightly before the bombing of Pearl Harbor and that "every adult Jap in this valley knew what was brewing." The overriding concern, however, seemed to be that "through the years we have seen, not the Americanization of the Japanese here, but the rapid and sure Japanization of our little valley."[13]

A backlash of protest began with a number of local residents. Margaret Herod wondered if American Legion members who removed Japanese American names would not "be sorry they can't associate with some of these same boys in heaven."[14] Hazel V. Smith implored, "Let us first win this horrible war, then fairly and calmly settle our internal differences."[15] Former resident Bliss Clark chided, "Put them back, Hood River. . . . Put them back, or be ashamed!"[16] Declaring that the problem had economic roots, Jack Hanser wrote, "The ones doing the most yelping are getting rich—and I do mean rich—off these same Japanese places. . . . Selfish greed is at the bottom of it. . . . "[17]

"Every person in Hood River is disgraced," agonized Sherman Burgoyne, the minister of the local Asbury Methodist Church. He proposed that the post "take their names up on the hill to their own building there and scratch off all the names they wish."[18] The congregation of the Odell Methodist Church unanimously adopted a resolution requesting that the American Legion restore honor roll names. If names were not restored, it proposed that the county replace the roll.[19]

Religious and civil rights organizations came to the defense of those "law-abiding citizens whose character and conduct had not been called in question," according to the Portland Council of Churches. The American Civil Liberties Union voiced regret that "race prejudice of any sort takes precedence over patriotism."[20] The Methodist church, claiming that "this Post is a disgrace to the state of Oregon," offered cooperation and hope for "victory in Europe, the Orient and Hood River."[21] Nine ministers in the County Ministerial Association issued a supportive statement that any serviceman willing to suffer and die for the United States was "worthy of . . . unhindered freedom to live among us."[22]

Robert D. Cozzens, the War Relocation Authority's assistant director who was himself a Legionnaire, protested to the Hood River post: "You have betrayed the Legion by a deliberate insult to our army, its uniform, and the brave men who wear it. . . . You desecrate the grave of the unknown soldier."[23] In response to "regrettable reports" of discrimination on the West Coast, Secretary of War Henry Stimson stated it was "wholly incongruous" that Japanese servicemen would be subjected to "unworthy discrimination."[24]

To counter the "black eye" given the American Legion by the Hood River action, the sixteen U.S. soldiers were invited to join the Captain Belvedere Brooks Post in New York City after the war.[25]

Accusations from other newspapers were printed in the local newspaper: "Not So American" was the title of the *Chicago Sun's* editorial suggesting that the American Legion serve democracy by restoring the names.[26] "Is This Americanism?" asked the nearby *The Dalles Optimist,* adding, "The American Legion . . . may next choose to outlaw the Jews in this country, or the Negroes, or the Italians, or Russians."[27]

In the one-and-one-half-month period following the American Legion action, the *Hood River News* printed five editorials from other newspapers and twenty-five letters, with only one letter favoring the move. Sixteen of the letters were postmarked outside Hood River. The *Hood River County Sun* printed two letters in support and two letters critical of the action.

Editors and columnists throughout the nation admonished the valley:

> Un-American: The Iron Cross for the most spectacularly un-American act of the war should go to the American Legion post of Hood River, Oregon. . . . [It] should be given an elementary course in the principles of common decency and basic Americanism. [*Argus Leader,* Sioux Falls, South Dakota[28]]

> Dirty Work at Hood River: That is tops in blind hatred, a record of some kind for ingratitude, possibly an all-American low in intolerance and bigotry. [*Collier's Magazine*[29]]

> The Roots, as Usual, Are Economic: . . . Offhand, we'd say it is a pretty ugly business. [*Register,* Des Moines, Iowa[30]]

> The American Legion should hammer some American history into the Oregon post. . . . Those Legionnaires . . . aren't fit to carry the tommy guns of those American Japs! [Ed Sullivan, *New York News*[31]]

> A Nomination for the Award for Most Contemptible Deed. [Frank Sullivan, *PM,* New York[32]]

Servicemen assailed the action as well:

> We cannot forgive them, because they indeed know what they do. . . . [*The Defender* (U.S. Army Newspaper)[33]]

> Legion Post Arouses Ire of 7th's GIs: If the Hood River, Oregon American Legion Post hasn't been getting much mail lately, it can stop worrying. All along the 7th Army front today, American combat troops were bitching loud and long about a recent announcement by the Hood River American Legion Post: "People back home ought to know that if it wasn't for the Nisei, a lot of their sons would be dead now. . . . " "Our boys don't say these Nisei are as good as we are. We say they're a helluva lot better. . . . " "Those Legion people ought to sell their property and give it to these Nisei. They deserve it more. If these Japanese-Americans are good enough to die for their country, they ought to be good enough to live in it." [*The Stars and Stripes* (U.S. Army newspaper)[34]]

More than three hundred servicemen in the Pacific mailed letters to the *Hood River News*. According to editor Hugh Ball, only one of those letters expressed approval of the American Legion's removal of names.[35]

The commander of the 2nd Battalion of the 442nd Combat Team in Europe, Lieutenant Colonel James M. Hanley, was also sufficiently incensed to reply. In a letter reprinted from his hometown newspaper in Mandan, North Dakota, Hanley countered with acts of Japanese courage, wondering "just what we are fighting for. I hope it isn't racial prejudice."[36]

Adding to the furor, two and a half weeks after the American Legion's action, Public Proclamation No. 21 rescinded the mass exclusion order of the Japanese on December 17, 1944. During the spring of 1943, the government had concluded from the loyalty review that there was no longer military justification for excluding loyal U.S. citizens. Yet a recommendation was not presented to the president until May 1944, and the president waited until after the 1944 election to act.[37]

The American Legion immediately launched a vigorous campaign to discourage the return of Japanese to the valley, printing a "Statement to Returning Japanese" in the following week's newspaper. It warned, "Under the War Department's recent ruling, you will soon be permitted to return to this county. FOR YOUR OWN BEST INTERESTS, WE URGE YOU NOT TO RETURN. . . ."[38]

The January 3 death of Hood River resident and serviceman Frank Hachiya brought even more untimely notoriety to the valley. Sergeant Hachiya, a former political science major at the University of Oregon, had graduated from the Military Intelligence Service Language School and served as an interrogator in the Pacific.[39] During the invasion of Leyte Island in the Philippines, he had volunteered to gain critical information from a Japanese prisoner of war. According to one account, he was mistaken for the enemy and mortally wounded while crawling toward U.S. troops.[40] The *New York Times* reported that he managed to give his report while his mortal wounds were bound.[41] Lieutenant Howard M. Moss of Sergeant Hachiya's military team recounted that the twenty-five-year-old Hachiya was hit at close range by a Japanese sniper after outrunning his bodyguards.[42] Hachiya's Silver Star citation credited him with attempting to pursue three Japanese soldiers through a wooded gorge. Fatally wounded in the abdomen by a twelve-man enemy patrol, Hachiya died four days later.[43]

"Who is un-American now?" berated *The Oregonian*.[44] In a nationally syndicated daily column, Washington, D.C., correspondent Thomas L. Stokes condemned "racist activities" of the American Legion, asking, "Will his name go back on the honor roll?"[45]

Statement to Returning

JAPANESE

Under the War Department's recent ruling you will soon be permitted to return to this county.

FOR YOUR OWN BEST INTERESTS, WE URGE YOU NOT TO RETURN.

Certain incidents have already occurred that indicate the temper of the citizens of this county.

Public records show that there are about 25 or 30 families, out of some 600 Japanese, who have not already sold their property in Hood River County. We strongly urge these to dispose of their holdings.

If you desire assistance from this Post in disposing of your land, we pledge ourselves to see that you get a square deal.

If you do return, we also pledge that, to the best of our ability, we will uphold law and order, and will countenance no violence.

In this program we ask the support of the citizens of this County.

> HOOD RIVER POST NO. 22.
> American Legion,
> Department of Oregon.

The American Legion warned Issei and their families not to return to the Hood River Valley after the U.S. government repealed the orders excluding them from the West Coast. (*Hood River News,* December 22, 1914)

Undaunted, the American Legion continued its campaign to rid the valley of Japanese and proposed a special election to determine public opinion. County Judge C. D. Nickelsen ruled, however, that results would be unofficial and would have no bearing, since the federal government would decide the issue.[46]

To avert "misguided or ill-advised action" that reflected poorly on the other twelve thousand posts, the American Legion's national office applied its own pressure on the Hood River Legionnaires. In January 1945, Edward N. Scheiberling, national commander in Chicago, recommended the immediate restoration of Nisei names on the civic plaque. Although he conceded that the American Legion opposed the return of Japanese until the war's end, he also countered that "there is no room in the American Legion for racial hatreds or animosities."[47]

In April, two and a half months after receiving its notice, the Hood River American Legion Post restored the names of fifteen of the Nisei[48] to stand along the names of the more than thirteen hundred local residents who served in the armed forces. Although Post 22 had voted originally to table this request, its change of heart came on the heels of a pending investigation that could have resulted in the loss of its charter. Despite the reversal, Jess Eddington, Post commander, made it clear that the action was simply a token gesture and did not alter the Post's attitude about the return of Japanese to the valley.[49]

Public sentiment did appear to be largely against the former valley residents:

> Hood River, Golden Valley in the hills,
> Who is to possess its acres and its rills?
> A horde of aliens from across the sea
> Or shall it be a paradise for you and me?

This verse expressed the opinions of several hundred who had signed the second of a series of full-page ads warning Japanese that they were not welcome to return and urging them to dispose of their property.[50]

The following week, an ad listed Japanese who either owned or controlled property in the county. The avowed goal was to check each name off to show that the total 3,000.4 acres had been sold.[51] "We should never be satisfied," a subsequent ad vowed, "until every last Jap has been run out of these United State [sic] and our Constitution changed so they can never get back!"[52] Another penetrating ad, in support of the statement "once a Jap, always a Jap,"[53] concluded that "the Jap is just an 'educated,' unbridled, sadistic, modernized barbarian."[54] All the advertisements, signed by community residents and printed in both the local newspapers, were organized by Kent Shoemaker, a resident who had served not only as former manager of the Chamber of Commerce but also as former commander of the local American Legion Post. His first letter, signed "Yours for a Hood River without a Jap," left no doubt whatsoever about his stand.[55]

Despite the vigilance of the American Legion, supporters of the evacuees apparently believed that backers of the anti-Japanese campaign were

Another newspaper ad by the American Legion encouraged Hood River residents to purchase all land owned by Issei. (*Hood River News*, February 9, 1945) not "old Hood River families" but a few "loud speakers" motivated by Japanese competition. Many petition signers, they felt, complied to avoid argument. Mrs. Arline Moore, Hood River merchant and advocate for local Japanese, speculated, "I feel safe in stating that two out of every three persons didn't care to refuse a neighbor and further most of them felt the problem would be solved without any direct effort on the part of the local people. It is most likely that no one of those people ever expected their names would be published as they later were. Many of the people were recent new comers [sic] to this valley. Very few of them had ever had any direct dealings with the Japanese people. A check of the names showed that [either] many had signed several times or there had been reprints of names." She further stated that petition names had actually been secured by Grange members in 1943 and were simply appended to the weekly American Legion ads.[56] The War Relocation Authority also noted that "several" American Legion members resigned to protest the anti-Japanese campaign and joined the Veterans of Foreign War (VFW).[57]

That same month, however, the *Hood River County Sun* editorialized, "We sincerely hope that those who wish to return will think twice before returning at this time or any time in the near future."[58]

Adding fuel to the blazing fire of discrimination, the Oregon legislature unanimously passed a bill to tighten the state's landownership restrictions. The Alien Land Law of Oregon, enacted at the end of March 1945, forbade aliens not only from owning land but also from operating or controlling land or farm equipment and from deeding land to relatives. Specifically, the law prevented agreements to "acquire, possess, enjoy, use, cultivate, occupy, and transfer real property for farming or agricultural purposes." Those who violated the law were subject to a maximum fine of five thousand dollars and imprisonment of up to two years.[59] Such was the atmosphere when the Issei pondered their return to the valley.

34

Returning Home

IN BRAWLEY, California, thirty-five hundred citizens congregated on the high school athletic field for an anti-Japanese meeting. After an orator bellowed, "Do you want these yellow-bellied sneaks to return to Brawley?" the crowd clamored, "No!"[1] In San Jose, California, a Japanese farmer woke to discover his home had been doused with gasoline and set afire. After he put out the flames, someone fired a shot at him.[2] In Livingston, California, shots were fired at Japanese homes in seven separate incidents. Feeling vulnerable, local Japanese lined their bedrooms with mattresses, rice sacks, and sheet metal.[3] Las Vegas, Nevada, pronounced itself 100 percent anti-Japanese, a sentiment shared by the highest state officials.[4]

In Seattle, Washington, promoter Arthur J. Ritchie speculated, "Why not band the nation's Japanese-haters together and put the whole business on a paying basis?" After offering a bust of "America's Number One Jap Hater" (a likeness of General Douglas MacArthur), he harangued a crowd in outlying Bellevue. When Gresham, Oregon, citizens founded their "Oregon Property Owners' Protective League, Inc.," Ritchie assisted their transition to the "Japanese Exclusion League," a dues-paying organization.[5]

In Portland, Oregon, a Japanese farmer was boycotted at the Portland Farmers' Market when he delivered a truckload of vegetables.[6] In Orting, Washington, and Gardena, California, townspeople removed names of Nisei servicemen from honor rolls. Half a dozen other American Legion posts also followed Hood River's lead.[7]

In Hood River, Oregon, Mayor Joe Meyer maintained, "Ninety percent are against the Japs! . . . We must let the Japanese know they're not welcome here."[8] Issei understandably had mixed emotions about return-

ing to their valley. They were fully aware of the valley's embittered anti-
Japanese campaign. Their fears had turned to horror when the American
Legion removed the names of their sons from the county's war memorial
board:

> I quit taking the *Hood River News* at camp after Nisei names were
> removed from the honor roll. When I saw that article in the paper,
> I was very disturbed. America and Japan were at war, but we had no
> control over that. This was a very barbaric act, and we Hood River
> Japanese were incensed about it. [Mr. Masaji Kusachi]

> When the Nisei were in the army risking their lives, I thought
> this was cruel. My thinking was, "Is this what war brings?" But in
> war, there was nothing that could be done. That gave me a lonely
> feeling. [Mrs. Asayo Noji]

There was agony in recognizing names of so-called friends on anti-
Japanese ads. "The *Hood River News*," Mr. Chiho Tomita related, "had
signed petitions warning Japanese not to return. When we saw these
names, we recognized some that we thought were friendly. We were very
worried."

There were fears of hostile receptions at home. A news account in the
local paper told of a planned "reception" committee at the train depot to
meet any Japanese returning to Hood River. The avowed purpose was to
discourage them from resettling.[9] If "Japs" returned, an American Legion
spokesman was said to have predicted attacks and bloodshed by the
" 'common man' or 'the people in the pool halls.' "[10] A survey of prominent citizens conducted by the Oregon State Police indicated, however,
that eight of the nine interviewees did not believe there would be mob
violence. Two did anticipate fires or acts of assault, the superintendent of
the irrigation district foresaw mob violence, and the newspaper editor reported rumors that several residents carried firearms and threatened to
"shoot the first Jap on sight."[11]

Issei corresponded with friends and property lessees to test out attitudes about their return. "We kept in constant contact with our property
caretaker in Hood River," Mrs. Tei Endow revealed. "At one time, we
expressed our desire to come home. I remember that he replied, 'It's probably best not to come home too soon. Things don't look that good. It
might even be dangerous.' We were also warned that another neighbor
coveted our farm and wished to buy it cheaply."

Others, like Mrs. Miyoshi Noyori, felt the burden of returning to life-
styles that had been so physically demanding: "I wished we could have
stayed at camp longer! I had become accustomed to life there, although

I did want to come home. Before camp we worked so hard in Hood River that I wondered if life would be that difficult when we returned. So we had mixed feelings."

In fact, only 40.3 percent (186 out of 462) of the prewar Hood River Japanese did return to the valley. This contrasted with like figures of 68.9 percent in the state, 51.9 percent in California, and 40.2 percent in Washington.[12] The total Japanese population had, it should be noted, increased with the births of almost six thousand Nisei, countering the deaths of more than eighteen hundred. Many Issei had sold their property either before or after evacuation. Some remained near the communities where they had been confined in the Rocky Mountains, northern California, and Idaho or resettled in other parts of California, eastern Oregon, and the midwestern and eastern states. More than forty-seven hundred returned to Japan.[13]

"Those people who did not own their land chose not to return. Those who did own their land wished to return," Mrs. Tei Endow explained. The homeward draw was strong for many, though. "When we made up our minds to return, this made me happy because I was going home," Mrs. Miyoshi Noyori remarked. "Even though my own birthplace seemed insignificant," Mrs. Misuyo Nakamura said, "I wanted my children to return to their birthplace."

In early January 1945, the first three to return to the valley were young Nisei friends who had been temporarily employed as mechanics in the Midwest. Ray Sato, formerly with the Yellow Cab Company in Cleveland, Ohio, reunited with recent Chicagoans Minoru Asai and Satoru Noji, the twenty-four-year-old son of Mrs. Asayo Noji. Braced for the hostile "welcoming party" that had been threatened, the three were relieved to be met by just a single person on the cold, snowy day of their return. Clyde Linville, the large, soft-spoken War Relocation Authority (WRA) agent, drove them to Sato's home and commuted daily from his Portland office to check on their well-being. Confronted with jeers from children, glassy-eyed stares from merchants who denied them service, and widespread accusations of Japanese infiltration, the trio faced agonizing days in the beginning. Yet Linville's gestures of support enabled the trio to "stick it out," when their impulses, acknowledged Sato, might easily have led to quick returns to the Midwest.[14]

Apprehensive about their son's return, the Noji family decided to join him as soon as possible on their 120 acres of farmland. In doing so, they became a " 'test case' to determine the attitude of the Hood River American Legion post toward the parents of Nisei fighting with American forces against Japan."[15]

Mrs. Asayo Noji remembered anxious moments when they returned:

In spite of rumors of intense discrimination, Papa was determined to return no matter what, because our son Sat was there. Almost everyone we knew discouraged Papa, warning that strong anti-Japanese feelings made our return much too dangerous. But Papa was determined to return, so my daughter and I had no choice but to accompany him. We were one of the first to leave, so our friends warned us to be careful.[16]

We were so frightened! I jumped at every sound! Even at night, I did not sleep well. We were not afraid of anyone in particular—it was just a general feeling of insecurity. Whenever we saw a stranger, we were unduly alarmed for we did not know what to expect. What eased us the most was that WRA representative Linville came daily to see how we were doing. It was such a relief to see him! He looked out for our welfare. (There were so many gophers that Papa asked him to get us gopher traps.) Also McIsaac [Mr. R. J. McIsaac, the Nojis' property caretaker and the owner of McIsaac's Store in Parkdale] stopped by occasionally. These two men made our first few months more tolerable. When they visited, I had the feeling they were like parents to us. As it turned out, nothing really happened, and we were grateful.

After two and a half years of confinement, Issei were indeed frightened at the prospect of venturing beyond the pseudosecurity of an all-Japanese community to reintegrate with potentially hostile neighbors. By January 1945, when only one out of six Issei had left, camp officials began to persuade evacuees to leave.[17] Their plan was to move sixty thousand Japanese from the camps by the end of December 1945.[18] Those who left received transportation assistance and financial aid (twenty-five dollars for individuals and fifty dollars for families) and were required to pass security checks and ensure their employment.[19]

For Mr. Masaji Kusachi, now widowed with seven young children, this change was both opportune and troublesome:

Around February, camp administrators asked me, "Would you like to return to Hood River to see what the situation is like?" It was obvious then that they were anxious to close the camp. Our orchard lease arrangement specified that if we returned before March 15, we would be allowed to harvest the crop for that year. But if we came home after March 15, our leaseholders would get the crop. So I purchased a sugar beet hauling truck from Mr. Nakamura. We packed our family goods in the truck and hurried on home. Leaving camp, though, meant I would have to bring my seven small children home, not an easy situation.[20] So I did not look upon my return as a happy occasion. (After we returned to the farm, Mrs. Hori and her two daughters lived with us and helped raise the children. At one time, there were seventeen of us living in this house—my family, my father, the Horis, and the Iwatsukis, who helped on our farm. Every morning I made a stack of hotcakes this high [about eight inches high]!)

The first glimpse of his home and property was unsettling, to say the least:

When I returned, I found that my home had been ravaged. All that was left of our furnishings was the kitchen stove. We had also left many belongings in a locked room, but the locks had been broken. When we opened the door, there was nothing left. Even our *ohina-sama* [an expensive, tiered doll stand for the Girls' Day Festival] was gone. I remember, too, that there was no sign of our many Christmas decorations. Everything was stolen! And the condition of our orchard was deplorable! Our trees resembled willows, because they had not been pruned.[21] Limbs were hanging down so low that you could pick the fruit sitting down—you could! If trees are not properly pruned, you cannot raise a good crop. But by that time, it was too late in the season to prune, and there were no laborers available during this war time.[22]

It was bad enough to discover that our home and orchard were in terrible condition. But when our caretaker presented us with a bill for $1,700, that was a terrible blow! Naturally I was infuriated! Mr. Clyde Linville, the local head of the WRA, was also enraged and developed a case permitting us to countersue. Mr. Avon Sutton of Parkdale acted as our witness, and attorney [Gus] Solomon[23] from Portland represented us. We itemized our damages and loss of house goods and made a successful countersuit in excess of what our caretaker had requested. No, we did not have to go to court. It was apparent that our caretaker was going to lose, so our attorneys designed [negotiated] an agreement and mailed us a check. I did not have anything further to do with our caretaker. I could see that he had even set our mailbox on his own property. Besides that, he bought a lot of fertilizer on my account, stored it at my neighbor's, and then sold it to others. All that time he was pocketing the cash. He was not an upright citizen. This man had leased several Japanese properties in the valley; he shortchanged practically everyone! Although he had owned very little money before war, he became a rich man.

By May, twenty-one Japanese families had returned to the valley, and among them were the Akiyamas. Enchanted with the Mid-Columbia's lavish greenery and breathtaking fruit blossoms, Mrs. Itsu Akiyama reminisced about her travels home:

> After hours of traveling through sagebrush country, dawn arrived just as we approached The Dalles. When we came to Hood River at 4:30 in the morning, it was almost light. (At the train station, two WRA men greeted us. One was Mr. Clyde Linville.) I saw such beautiful sights riding home! In contrast to the drab sagebrush and open fields in Idaho, everything here was green, with flowers and apple trees in bloom. That was such an impressive sight to me! I remember seeing blossoms on the Newtown trees behind our house—they were so beautiful! But in the front yard, I noticed our own belongings scattered everywhere. The place was in such disarray that I thought wearily, "Well, I'm home at last." Papa, Kiyo, and Nobi were already home. I had remained at camp until May so Henry could graduate from camp high school. So when I entered the house, Kiyo offered me coffee. This was so delicious! (The Idaho coffee had been tasteless, probably due to the poor water.) It made me happy simply to return home alive. In Japan there is a poem about soldiers returning to their country. This struck me, because this was just the way I felt. We had thought our lives were at stake when we left, so we returned with much the same feeling as those soldiers:

> "To have life and return to my birthplace
> As we approach the station
> The colors of dawn appear."

Her joy in returning was short-lived, however:

> All our belongings were gone except for six plates with Japanese motifs. Even the ropes on the windows had been cut and taken. And it appeared that our property caretakers did not put anything in but took everything out. We had four to five acres of asparagus which had become just a field of weeds one-and-a-half-feet tall. In fact, there were so many weeds that we had to haul them away on a truck.

> These people took what they could without taking care of the orchard. And we did not receive any money for our produce. Our written agreement had been that, if these people would take care of our place and pay the property taxes, we would not ask for money in return. But we did not make a big issue with our caretakers. The

man claimed he had become somewhat disabled falling from a cherry tree, and his wife was very heavyset and probably could not do much work. Obviously, their children were not brought up like ours and did not do too much work. We were not citizens, so we did not speak up. That was our weakness.

According to a WRA report, fair and equitable property agreements were an exception. It was a common practice for the lessee to pay water costs, taxes, and fire insurance (with the operator taking all the income in excess of fixed charges). Only rarely did Japanese landowners receive even half the return income. In many cases, operators earned annual average profits of five to twenty thousand dollars. "There could be no question that the tenant . . . was in a much better position than had he owned the land," the WRA reported.[24]

Despite returning to a neglected farm, Mrs. Akiyama and her family had determination and hope that they could restore it:

We rose early in the morning to cut asparagus and devoted the rest of the day toward recovery of our orchard. In the evening after dinner, we packed our asparagus for shipment. I do not ever recall going to bed any earlier than midnight in those days. What I remember most was that, although we were faced with hard work, we found inspiration in our efforts to restore our orchard. I am still amazed that we had such ambition! Our children became so involved that they did not even complain about the hard work. One day our pickup simply quit running. At that time, no one would help us repair it. So Nobi and Henry got a repair manual from Montgomery Ward and tried to repair it themselves. By 2:00 A.M., I finally asked them to come home and rest. "No," they said, "we're determined to repair this." Finally they returned, but only because the light had gone out.

A few of the Issei were satisfied with the condition of their property:

I walked around my orchard and saw that it was in pretty good shape. [Mr. Chiho Tomita]

My husband said our orchard had received good care. And we found that minor repairs had been made on the house and that the woodshed was already filled. Of course, this was all charged to farm expenses. Our house was in liveable condition, ready to accept us. [Mrs. Tei Endow]

Others, like Mrs. Misuyo Nakamura, simply accepted the deteriorated conditions as more in a long line of wartime sacrifices: "Our orchard had deteriorated quite a bit and showed very little growth. It is my belief that the foreman may have been so shorthanded that he could not get around to doing the work. Our house itself was still intact, but it was unkempt."

Some, like the Yamakis, suffered expensive equipment losses. "Before we were evacuated," Mrs. Hama Yamaki recalled, "we had turned our packinghouse machinery over to another man. We asked him to take care of it, and that is the last we heard of it. But I did not want to make a lot of noise about this. I thought this was *shikata-ganai* [beyond our control, so accept it]. My husband said we were resigned to the loss."

Most became victims of property neglect:

> Our children were the ones most excited, but I looked upon our return with both pleasure and worry. Our caretaker had frequently written to us in camp that he did not have much time to care for our property. He really had the desire to buy it, so, in effect, he was trying to discourage our return. When he sent us checks at camp, he would complain of small returns or damage to our crop. We assume he wanted to keep as much money as he could. When we arrived—in February or March 1945—we were distressed to see that our orchard had been neglected and our dwelling was filthy. We had been promised that our house would remain vacant, but another neighbor told us in confidence that the orchard foreman had lived in our home. As soon as we returned, we sprayed the inside of the house with germ killer and mopped the floors.
>
> The first thing we noticed about our orchard was that our trees had not been properly pruned. In that condition, you cannot produce good fruit. Most other orchards had been disked,[25] but we saw no evidence of that on our place. When I saw the condition of our orchard, I was quite downhearted. What was most cumbersome was that the two of us had to do all the work. There were plenty of workers around, but we were unable to hire anyone. I imagine people had unfriendly feelings toward us. During harvest, though, we were able to hire many transient laborers. There was a general feeling among Japanese that we would cooperate among ourselves. But before harvest, we all had to work on our own farms, so we were not able to help each other as much. Our work was so exhausting that I lost six pounds that first week! It took us about three years to return our orchard to its normal condition. [Mrs. Hatsumi Nishimoto]
>
> When we returned, our biggest difficulty was that we had no income while we were gone and we had sold most of our equipment. Our concern was great, because our orchard was not kept up. It had

certainly not been sprayed or pruned. The undersides of the tree
bark were yellow with insect eggs. When we harvested the fruit,
they had large scab markings and worms. The market was so good,
though, that we were able to sell all of it. But it took us three years
to return our orchard to its former condition. We were determined,
so we worked very hard in the orchard. We did not immediately
take on responsibility for running the farm, because we were not
certain the AGA [Apple Growers' Association] would accept our
fruit. So our foreman operated the farm for another year, and we
worked under him. We had an agreement prior to our leaving—it
might have been 60 or 40 percent. We got that share from the crop,
and we also received wages for working. Our concern was based on
rumors and the unfriendly attitudes of some people. [Mrs. Miyoshi
Noyori]

Workers at one AGA packing plant had reportedly threatened to strike
if Japanese farmers brought their apples and pears to the plant.[26] The crucial question, then, after strenuous efforts to harvest, became whether
packinghouses would process the fruit of Japanese farmers, as Mr. Masaji
Kusachi pointed out:

During harvest time I faced another uncertain situation: Would
the AGA accept and handle our fruit? This was the big question. A
government man, whose name I do not recall, acted on our behalf
and attended public gatherings to monitor attitudes about the Japanese. He told me, "Deliver your fruit to the National Warehouse
(AGA's cold-storage plant). They will make provisions to accept
the Japanese fruit there." (At that time the National Warehouse
provided living quarters for four or five Negroes who were working
for the AGA but were unable to get housing in town.) "Failing
that," he said, "if the AGA does not abide by their contract to accept your fruit, you have the right to sue." The field man advised
me to leave my picked fruit in the orchard if I was not able to deliver it. I was told this could be the basis for a legal suit. As it turned
out, the AGA handled my fruit in the proper manner. No trouble.
This was surprising to me, but I believe they may have been pressured by the government.

Administrators at the Apple Growers' Association were evidently obligated to accept produce from Japanese farmers and were more benevolent than many of their employees, who initially refused to crate apples
from Japanese orchards.[27] Once the fruit was delivered, however, Mr.
Kusachi had additional doubts: "Our apples were almost black with scabs,

because our caretaker had not applied dormant spray to prevent disease.[28]
I asked, in fact, if I had saleable merchandise and they told me yes. Surprisingly, we even made money that year. In the past, such scabby fruit would not have been packed, but our fruit fit a grade called 'unclassified.' Earlier unclassified fruit had meant just 'cut skin on the fruit,' but now 'unclassified' included scabby fruit too. In this war economy, as long as you shipped something out, you were able to sell it."

Ironically, the war that had uprooted the Japanese and prevented them from caring for their farms would also enable them to sell their low-grade fruit on the market. Victims of property neglect and loss, they faced exhausting physical labor to restore their farms and homes. Again, each new day seemed to bring new and unforeseen obstacles.

35

The Hood River Community

WARY OF REACTIONS by valley residents, most Issei avoided venturing into the community and mingling with Caucasians:

Our neighbors did not call on us, and we did not call on them. We did not make too many remarks on the telephone about our *hakujin* [Caucasian] neighbors, because we had a party line—and who might be listening in? [Mrs. Hatsumi Nishimoto]

When I greeted others, their replies were not always friendly. We could sense their true feelings in their motions and their faces. If people made obvious unfriendly gestures, we simply had nothing more to do with them. Not everyone was unfriendly, though. When others expressed their friendliness, this pleased us. [Mrs. Miyoshi Noyori]

At first, when I said hello to our neighbors, they would say hello but little else. As time went by, our relationships improved. We had so much work to do, anyway, that I did not make any special efforts to communicate. [Mrs. Tei Endow]

Some Issei became victims of harassment and discrimination:

Although there was much "anti" feeling, we had already returned, so we decided to make the best of it. Someone shot holes through our spray machines and killed our chickens. We were not allowed to deliver our asparagus to the Apple Growers' Association (AGA), so Mr. Linville, our WRA [War Relocation Authority] representative, found a Seventh Day Adventist church member to deliver our produce.

I did not personally face discrimination, because I stayed at home. But I recall that Papa did. He was still on parole, so he was required to mail papers to the government regularly.[1] One day Papa approached the owner of a fruit company to cosign his parole papers. This man refused, saying, "You Japanese people came home much too soon!" My husband was so dejected. Finally a man named Captain McCann consented to sign his form.

Another time my son George was still in his army uniform when he entered a barbershop downtown. He was refused a haircut. He heard that the barber commented, "I should have cut that Jap's throat." Another patron, Captain Sheldon Laurence of Parkdale, paid us a visit later and apologized for George's treatment in the barbershop. [Mrs. Itsu Akiyama]

George Akiyama, too, remembered the incident. Returning from Fort Lewis, Washington, he stopped downtown to get a haircut before meeting his family. Confident his army uniform would permit him entry, he took a seat in a barbershop. To his shock, the barber approached him, waving a razor threateningly while admonishing him. With a quick retort, George left just as Sheldon Laurence, an air force captain, entered. Later that day, although it was "snowing like heck," Laurence walked up the Akiyama's steep hillside to express his regret over the incident. Later Captain Laurence wrote a letter to the editor of *The Oregonian* newspaper in Portland, renouncing "such unjustified prejudice and insults to a small group of some of the nation's best fighting men."[2]

Other local businesses refused to serve Japanese:

Once, when we were shopping, our son really wanted a canned peach. Yet, the salesclerk made no move to help us. When we were refused service, I felt that this was a stab in our backs. At the worst times, Nisei friends traveled as far as The Dalles, thirty miles away, to buy us a loaf of bread. (Most Issei were afraid of being refused, so Nisei bought groceries for many families.) The Safeway store did sell to us. As I recall, the manager of the Hood River Safeway called the head office to ask if Safeway could sell to Japanese. The reply was, "If anyone comes in with American money, sell to them." [Mrs. Tei Endow]

We could not even buy food at most stores, because they displayed signs that they would not welcome Japanese trade. One day after my husband had entered a store, he was reprimanded: "Didn't you read the sign?" Mr. Linville [the WRA representative] asked us to call on him whenever we had problems shopping. A ten-year-old neighbor boy, Glen Cody, also offered to buy us goods when he went to the store. [Mrs. Itsu Akiyama]

One time I went to meat market on heights. I tried buy meat. The boss said, "No, I don't trade with 'Jap.'" Okay, so I go. So Mr.

Burgoyne [Rev. Sherman Burgoyne] I asked to buy. After war Odell stores don't trade with Japanese anymore so we don't go there. Then change mind and welcome Japanese but Japanese never go. [Mr. Chiho Tomita, in English]

Once I went to purchase an article in a Hood River store. I do not remember now what it was, but I do know that I saw it on the shelf. Yet the store owner told me, "We don't have any." I didn't say anything. It was apparent that they had very strong anti-feelings toward Japanese, so I just walked out. I was not too upset, because I know there are unfriendly people in this world. [Mrs. Masayo Yumibe]

Store owners who entertained thoughts of serving Japanese were fearful of being labeled "Jap Lovers" or were threatened at mass meetings with boycott by other business owners or community members. Mrs. Arline Moore, a local businesswoman, explained that "the idea was to force [Japanese] to leave again by cutting off their sources of supply. Six stores, operated by Legion members, led out in this program and refused to sell to the Japanese. A few others joined with them because of fears of being forced out of business. Others, however, stood out for the American Way and seemed to suffer no ill effects."[3]

A number of local businesses did succumb to community pressure, however, and changed their sentiments toward Japanese. In her family history, Mitzi Asai Loftus recounted the family's surprise at a store owner's change of mind. When the family had left Hood River in 1942, the proprietor of the Westside Store expressed warm sentiments, shedding tears and giving them a farewell gift. Yet, upon their return, they saw a "No Jap Trade" sign hung at his store.[4] Issei related other similar encounters with merchants:

Mr. Watanabe telephoned to tell us that the owner of a store in Odell would deliver foodstuff to us in the evening but not during the day. Many *hakujin* did not look kindly on those who favored Japanese, so the man did not want others to see him. Some stores explained to us, "We would really like to sell to you, but we're afraid of the reaction of the 'anti-'[Japanese] people." [Mrs. Hatsumi Nishimoto]

Since our belongings had been stolen, I went downtown to buy furniture—but the store refused to sell to me. In front of the store, I had noticed four or five *hakujin* people. When I walked inside, the owner asked me to step to the back room, because he had a few words for me. "I honestly would like to sell to you," he told me, "but those men will disturb my store if I do." This was a very common threat from businessmen. It became common knowledge that Hood River businesses would not sell to Japanese. I recall that the grocery store in Rockford had a "No Japs" sign posted. I do remember buying gas in a fifty-gallon drum from the Shell gas people; and Sheppard's Farm Equipment Store also sold to the Japanese. Most of our food was purchased at McIsaac's Store in Parkdale, because he even stocked rice for us. Still, our feelings were hurt; and we made many purchases at The Dalles, where stores welcomed us. [Mr. Masaji Kusachi]

Fear and discrimination also left their mark on the young, as Mrs. Tei Endow regretfully conceded:

After we returned, my youngest son Billy was in his second year at Centralvale School, where there were only ten students and two teachers. He reported that he was not welcome at school and cried, saying that he did not want to go. I felt so sorry for him! He came up with excuses like, "Oh, I don't feel good," "I have a headache," or "I'm sick." At the time we were evacuated, Billy had been only five years old. He probably was not very conscious of the war and of being Japanese. But after we were evacuated and he went to different schools, he learned a little bit more about worldly affairs and about the consequences of war. Many times I heard him say that war was a very hateful thing.

Once gas rationing was eliminated, Japanese were quick to patronize the more hospitable stores in neighboring communities. For Hood River merchants, this amounted to losses of many thousands of dollars worth of business.[5] The wartime campaign waged against Japanese thus had economic effects on the Caucasian community as well.

League for Liberty and Justice

Amid the much publicized anti-Japanese furor, a group of Hood River citizens, with little fanfare, joined forces to demonstrate to the country "that there was tolerance as well as intolerance in Hood River, that many Hood River people believed in fair play."[6] Naming their organization after words in the "Pledge of Allegiance" to the American flag, they formed the League for Liberty and Justice. Their purpose was to counteract propaganda with facts and to present a program of education in intercultural relations, including speakers and the WRA film *Challenge to Democracy*, which showed life at the Heart Mountain relocation center. The League

also urged that intercultural programs be included once a month in ser-
mons from local pulpits.[7] Meetings, held twice a month in members'
homes and churches during the height of the crisis, were reportedly well-
attended.[8]

Another League effort was an ad reprinting the supportive letter about
Japanese American soldiers, which was written by a commander of the
442nd Infantry.[9] Avon Sutton, corresponding secretary for the organization, wrote letters to J. C. Penny, Safeway, and other chain stores, en-
couraging them to sell to Japanese. At his own expense, he also printed
in the local newspaper a full-page letter entitled "Witch Burning." In it
he criticized the "witch-burning spirit" of prejudice that was causing the
country to denounce Hood River residents and that could reduce them to
bankruptcy. "Shall we write into the Bill of Rights, 'For Citizens
Only' . . . ? . . . Let us not burn any witches in Hood River!"[10]

The League also mailed letters offering help to area Japanese:

> We want you folks to know that there is a group of fair minded people
> in the city and valley who have watched with growing resentment and con-
> cern, the injustices to which you have been subjected the past few months.
>
> We were probably shocked as much as you were by unreasonable prej-
> udice and vicious actions of certain individuals, and we feel a sense of
> shame that anything like this could happen in America.
>
> We have organized a group specifically for the purpose of assisting you
> people, and our numbers are steadily growing. We call ourselves the "Hood
> River League for Liberty and Justice." Already our influence is being felt,
> and when ordinarily fair minded people recover a bit from this war hyste-
> ria, they will reconsider their present decisions, and return to the good
> American principle of "live and let live."
>
> Please accept our deepest sympathy and understanding in your present
> trouble. It is a shameful, unjust and unnecessary ordeal, but we firmly be-
> lieve that out of it (a trial by fire, as it were) will emerge a better under-
> standing and deeper friendship than we have ever experienced before.
>
> If you should need any help, don't hesitate to call on us. This is the
> purpose of our organization. We would like to do something, even if it is all
> too little, to offset some of the wrongs you have endured. . . .
> Very sincerely,
> Hood River County League for Liberty and Justice.
> Hazel V. Smith, sec.[11]

League members provided service to some Japanese by meeting them
at trains, driving them to their homes, making purchases for them when
they were refused by merchants, and driving produce trucks to ware-
houses when workers threatened not to accept their fruit. In appreciation, Hood River Japanese raised $170 in donations for the League.[12]

The Reverend Sherman Burgoyne

The most outspoken advocate for Japanese who emerged during these trauma-ridden months was Rev. Sherman Burgoyne of the Asbury Methodist Church. After the American Legion's removal of Nisei names from the county memorial board, Rev. Burgoyne boldly voiced his opinion that "the Hood River courthouse belongs to all the people of the county. No incomplete honor roll can stay there; an honor roll is incomplete so long as it makes distinction because of race, creed or color."[13] In a public letter to the *Hood River News*, Rev. Burgoyne reiterated, "The people of Hood River deplore the fact that about thirty misguided men should create the impression that Hood River County is so shamefully un-American and race-prejudiced. Hundreds of our county deplore the nazi principles of this Legion post."[14]

Because of his forceful stand, Rev. Burgoyne "had a lot of people on his neck," according to a friend of Burgoyne's, a retired Methodist minister in Oregon. Yet, at the congregation's annual business meeting in 1945, members unanimously voted to request that the bishop return Burgoyne for a fourth term as pastor.[15] Following that announcement, the editor of the *Hood River News*, Hugh Ball, paid tribute to Rev. Burgoyne for his "type of Christianity which is entitled to recognition from his neighbors" and asserted that he was "too valuable a man for this community to lose."[16]

Both Rev. Burgoyne and his wife suffered repercussions for their courageous stands, though. Ray Sato, one of the first three Japanese to return to the valley, remembered that Mrs. Burgoyne offered a highly appreciated gesture of goodwill. Upon his first visit to a downtown Hood River bank, he was astonished when Mrs. Burgoyne, with tears in her eyes, dashed out of her teller booth to shake his hand. The bank lobby became instantly quiet as others stared and sneered at the duo. Apparently, after her open and exuberant greeting, Mrs. Burgoyne was shunned by her coworkers.[17]

Mr. Chiho Tomita, too, was fully appreciative of Rev. Burgoyne's valiant efforts on behalf of Japanese, knowing that with courage of convictions came persecution as well. He recounted in English:

> While I been in camp, most of my nice friend all sign petition: "No more Japanese boys come back." And at that time Mr. Burgoyne [was] minister of Asbury Church in Hood River. While Hood River people [said] Japanese boys can't come back to own place, he said, "That's not right." He fight all the Hood River people, so Hood River people pretty mad he help "Jap." They said to him, "I don't want you. Go." So he quit minister job, and Mrs.

Rev. Sherman Burgoyne, minister of the Asbury Methodist Church in Hood River, became an outspoken advocate for Japanese rights. (Courtesy of Glada Kays)

Burgoyne quit her teller job at First National Bank. He tried to find some job to get money to eat, so he had to [be a] schoolbus driver and Mrs. Burgoyne just stay home. Pretty hard he lost his job.[18] The Bible said, "I LOVE!" Most important is love—love each other. That's way I catch point. Mr. Burgoyne lost his job but for Japanese come home safely.

Rev. Burgoyne's cause for the advancement of democracy did not go unrecognized, for in 1947 he was one of sixteen recipients of the national Thomas Jefferson Award given by the Council Against Intolerance in America. Selection was based on a poll taken among fifteen hundred civic, religious, and education organizations and five hundred newspaper editors throughout the country.[19] The Hood River Japanese American Citizens' League (JACL) showed their appreciation by presenting the couple with a set of luggage and financing their trip to New York City to accept the award at the Waldorf Astoria's "Hundred-Dollar Banquet." Among other recipients that year were Albert Einstein, Eleanor Roosevelt, and Frank Sinatra.[20]

Mrs. Arline (Max) Moore

The proud and moving spirit of the League for Liberty and Justice was a stout and jovial grandmother who jointly operated a local business with her husband. With Mrs. Arline Moore's reassuring presence, Moore Electric Shop became a haven where Japanese could congregate without fear. When they were refused service elsewhere, Mrs. Moore was always willing to oblige them—despite her limping gait and frequent need for a cane:

Mrs. Moore ran an electric shop with her husband. She was very helpful to the Japanese. In spite of the fact that they charged more, we shopped there. We used to ask them to help us buy different items. [Mr. Chiho Tomita]

We asked Mr. or Mrs. Moore to make purchases for us, and we waited for them in their store. The Moores were most friendly toward the Japanese, and we had great feelings for them. [Mrs. Hatsumi Nishimoto]

Unger Machine Shop refused to do business with us. So, whenever we required their services, we simply took our equipment across the street to the Moores, and they delivered it for us. [Mr. Masaji Kusachi]

Aroused into action, Mrs. Moore was said to have boldly marched into stores that displayed anti-Japanese signs, rebuking owners, "Naturally, since you do not want the business of people whose parents came from one enemy country, you must mean all such people from all such countries. My people originated in Germany. Naturally, you do not want my business, and you certainly are not going to get it." A number of store owners were apparently shamed into removing their signs.[21] Mrs. Moore's correspondence with noted author Pearl Buck was apparently instrumental in the removal of an anti-Japanese sign in a Hood River Chinese restaurant.[22] The beleaguered Issei fully appreciated Mrs. Moore's stand on their behalf, and they maintained their devotion to this forthright and sensitive woman.

Mr. R. J. McIsaac

Despite "Jap Lovers" signs painted on his store windows, kindly Mr. R. J. McIsaac continued selling goods to Japanese at his Parkdale community store. "The Japanese enjoyed a good relationship with Mr. McIsaac even before war," Mrs. Asayo Noji recalled. "When all other stores in the valley refused to sell to Japanese, we all made our purchases at McIsaac's Store in Parkdale. He even stocked Japanese food for us. In the meantime, he was the object of criticism from others in the community who threatened not to buy from him if he continued serving Japanese. He answered them, 'At no time have I ever lost money from the Japanese. They always paid their bills and have always been sincere. So if you don't come to my store, I don't really care.' "

Mr. McIsaac also served as caretaker for one of the Noji orchards, and the family was gratified to find their orchard in fairly good condition and, in addition, to receive honest financial returns. A respected community figure, Mr. McIsaac served nearly fifteen years on the board of directors of the Apple Growers' Association as well as presiding for six years as president of the board.[23]

Other Congenial Gestures

"Any Japanese-American soldier home on furlough will find friendship, good food, warm bed and peaceful atmosphere in comfortable home of Joe Haviland and June Eaton Haviland, one and a half miles west Columbia River highway. No phoning necessary. Welcome at any hour."[24] Issei who returned in January 1945 were comforted by this offer placed in the *Hood River News*. They were especially grateful for any gestures of friendship from their neighbors:

I went to visit our neighbor, Mrs. Vannier. She showed me all kinds of odds and ends in her attic and asked if I wanted to send them to Japan. She gave me a whole closetful of clothes, even including her wedding dress. Most everyone was sending care packages to Japan; and, because of Mrs. Vannier's kindness, we were able to mail about ten boxes of clothes. [Mrs. Hama Yamaki]

People in camp told us to be careful, because others might be hostile. I cannot describe my happiness when neighbors were kind to us! The Suttons lived way up the highway, but they brought us canned raspberries. Other people offered to lend us beds and said to let them know if we needed help. If it had not been for neighbors like them, we would not have been able to stay. [Mrs. Asayo Noji]

Returning servicemen, too, took issue with the strong-willed stands of their parents. Ed Shoemaker, son of the local American Legion leader, wrote to the local news editor to recount pride in his Nisei friends and disagreement with his father. A marine captain who had Nisei in his Pacific regiment similarly condemned his father's window sign by retorting, "What the hell is this, Dad?"[25]

"Certainly," offered Mrs. Arline Moore, "a man cannot serve side by side with another man day after day, sharing the same risks and the same rations, often owing his life to that individual and continue to think of him as unfit for peacetime association."[26]

Japanese Society

After their return, Issei organized the Japanese Society as a mutual interest association for all Japanese nationals in the valley. Local officers, older respected residents, became communication links with the Japanese consulate. When, for example, a prominent visitor from Japan came to the United States, Japanese Society officers extended hospitality.[27] As president for almost twenty years, Mr. Masaji Kusachi explained the group's functions:

In postwar years, many citizens of Japan still lived in Hood River. A Japanese society was necessary to conduct affairs with the Japanese consul. For that reason, we organized the Nihonjinkai, Japanese Society. (This organization united smaller community societies that were formed before the war: Doshikai for the Dee Japanese society and Kyorei Kyokai for the Hood River Japanese society.) We held one general meeting a year, a family potluck affair on New Year's Day. At that time, four representatives were elected, one from each of the districts: Parkdale, Dee, Odell, Oak Grove. From the four, officers were selected by written ballots. We elected a president, vice president, treasurer, and secretary. Everybody voted. Women were also members, but they did not want to be officers. We collected annual dues of $2.50 per member, spent mostly for the people's enjoyment. We frequently rented Japanese movies. I was president for almost twenty years, including the period in the 1950s, when we held citizenship classes. That was our largest project. I also represented our organization at special functions in Portland, for example, when the Japanese training ship and navy ships came in and on April 29, the observance of the emperor's birthday. In 1967 our Japanese Society donated five or six blossoming cherry trees to be planted at the Hood River courthouse and at the high school.[28]

Issei faced cautious gestures and outright animosity as well as offers of kindness and advocacy, reminiscent of their initial encounters in the valley near the turn of the century. Having experienced dislocation and racism, they continued to make efforts to be accepted.

PART NINE

Issei Today

Toshiyori te
America shimin tari
Oshogatsu

After I was older
I achieved American citizenship
And greeted a new year.

Haiku written by Mrs. Hama Yamaki

36

Compensation, Citizenship, and Redress

WITHIN SEVEN YEARS after the end of the war, Congress passed two acts that granted further rights and opportunities to Japanese and Japanese Americans: the Japanese-American Evacuation Claims Act of 1948 and the McCarran-Walter Immigration and Naturalization Act of 1952. Then, forty-three years after their return, with the signing of the Civil Liberties Act of 1988, the U.S. government acknowledged that the internment of Japanese Americans had been a mistake.

Evacuation Claims

Designed to compensate Issei and Nisei for losses suffered from their evacuation, the Japanese-American Evacuation Claims Act of 1948 allowed Japanese to claim "damage to or loss of real or personal property." Claims were limited to material losses,[1] and compensation, as Mr. Miyozo Yumibe pointed out, was only minimal: "We probably received in the area of two hundred dollars for evacuation costs. Most farmers received a lot more. The government did not pay us for loss of wages—this only paid for things like suitcases necessary for evacuation. That was just a very small part of our losses."

A 1980 Presidential Commission concurred, noting that "there were many kinds of injury the Evacuation Claims Act made no attempt to compensate." These included the stigma and psychological impact of evacuation and relocation, the deprivation of liberty, the loss of earnings and profits, physical injury or death during detention, and losses from resettlement outside the camps.[2]

The process of filing claims was particularly frustrating for Issei. As proof of losses, the law required written records and documents. Yet, in the process of their hasty evacuation, many papers had been lost or were simply not available to families after their return. Many finally gave up, as Mrs. Miyoshi Noyori related:

> We did not receive one cent! We filed many, many times. We originally asked for $25,000, but our attorney insisted we claim more. I remember we made many trips to his office—yet we received nothing! We did not fully understand the reason. But we had not understood the instructions on the claim form, and we had doubts about the honesty of our attorney. (One had to wonder whether he did not pocket the money himself! Perhaps he was not friendly to Japanese either.) The lawyer continually asked for documents. He requested an inventory of equipment and tools plus documents supporting our previous income. Some we had difficulty supplying. And every time we gave him materials, he asked for more! It was so frustrating that we decided to quit! Because of the complications, we asked him to request just $2,500, but the attorney insisted this was not enough and suggested at least $6,000. We suppose this confusion made it more difficult too. So we gave up! This became a burden, because we had to buy tools and equipment to replace those we had sold.

With the entanglement of paperwork and the lengthy review process, only 232 of more than 26,000 filed claims had been settled by 1950.[3] Those claimants had requested an average of $1,030 each but received instead an average of $450. Ironically, the government spent about $1,400 per case to determine the $450 compensation.[4]

To expedite the claims process, Congress authorized a program for compromise settlements in 1951: $2,500 or 75 percent of the claim, whichever was less. As a result, 22,000 claims were settled by the end of 1955.[5] Minoru Yasui, a lawyer for compromise claims in Oregon who was raised in Hood River, stated that, for the first 130 of 160 claims he handled, a total of $500,000 was claimed and approximately $130,000 was received under the compromise formula.[6]

Because of the combined difficulty of producing records, the rigid procedures of the Justice Department, and the incentive to compromise for badly needed cash, settlements were, in the words of the government's commission, "well below the actual value of losses."[7] Issei concurred with this assessment:

> I did not believe that our compensation was adequate. If we had remained at home, we would have worked from dawn to dusk; and our financial return would have been much better. Our compensa-

tion was subject to a lot of deductions, so the net was inadequate. I do not know too much about the financial matters in those days, but I do recall that we were given compensation for a loss of props [ten- to twelve-foot wood beams used to support fruit-laden tree branches before harvest] and a loss of trees because of inadequate care. [Mrs. Tei Endow]

As I remember, our attorney Kenneth Abraham suggested we file a claim for $20,000. But we received only $6,000. I believe that most of the payment was based on our lease as well as the crop we would have received. [Mr. Masaji Kusachi]

We had our upper place held in the names of my two oldest sons, Terushi and Sumio. We had planted three acres of asparagus which were a total loss. I do remember making a claim for about $1,000. With the $200 we received, Terushi made a down payment on a house. We could not file claims on our present place, because it was operated for us rather than being leased. [Mr. Misuyo Nakamura]

We probably received something. If it had been a large figure, I would remember. So it was probably a small amount. [Mrs. Itsu Akiyama]

Of the 3,531 Oregon Japanese who were evacuated,[8] only 699 claims were filed.[9] Nationwide, 26,568 claims were filed, totaling $148 million. The total amount returned by the government was approximately $37 million.[10] Among nine interviewed Issei whose records were accessible, their claims totaled $207,710.98, for an average of $23,078.99. They were awarded a total of $19,078.31, or an average of $2,119.81 per family, just 9 percent of their requests.[11] For the Japanese in Hood River and elsewhere in the United States, restoration resulted in only a few cents on the 1942 dollar.[12]

In an analysis of the Federal Reserve Bank's role in protecting the economic interests of Japanese, Sandra C. Taylor concluded that the bureaucracy's emphasis was on speed rather than equity.[13] A War Relocation Authority report determined that the wartime handling of evacuee property was "a sorry part of the war record."[14]

Citizenship

The passage of the McCarran-Walter Act of 1952 effectively eliminated race as a barrier to immigration and naturalization. No longer would immigrants be forced to categorize themselves as "aliens ineligible for citizenship." Now, twenty-eight years after the Immigration Act of

Armed with Japanese dictionaries at classes to prepare for their citizenship tests, Issei studied the history and political system of the United States. Here teachers (*left to right*) Katsusaburo Tamura and Rev. Arthur Collins named city commissioners for Shizue Iwatsuki, Tomoyoshi Imai, and Shinjiro Sumoge. (Courtesy of Alice Ito)

1924 prohibited Issei entry into the United States, 185 Japanese, a token number, were permitted to immigrate. This was in addition to thousands who entered legally as nonquota immigrants through status as relatives of citizens, war brides, fiancees, or refugees.[15] But, most important for the Issei, this legislation also allowed them to apply for U.S. citizenship. Eager to become citizens, many, like Mrs. Hama Yamaki, enrolled in classes and studied diligently:

> We had a citizenship class in the Hood River heights, and Mr. Tamura and Mr. Hasegawa helped. Our books were in *Eigo* [English] so we had to study with dictionaries. Most of the book was concerned with the history of the United States. Rev. [Arthur] Collins would praise us for our answers and say, "You must have studied hard.' "[16] During our course of study, he gave us a questionnaire and told us, "You should be able to answer these questions on the test." I studied the questions and then practiced writing out the answers. My husband and I quizzed each other too. I even learned the "Pledge of Allegiance" in case they asked me to recite it. I studied so hard I felt that I just had to pass! The test was given on the second floor of a Hood River bank, and there were many questions.

The forty citizenship questions included "Who is our President? How many years does the President serve? What kind of government does the

U.S. have? How many senators represent Oregon and how long are their terms?"

By the end of the examination, Mrs. Yamaki's intensive study habits were rewarded:

> After studying so faithfully, I was able to give my oral answers to Dr. Collins and the immigration officer. When it was over, I was very relieved; and I wrote a haiku about my feelings:
> After I was older
> I achieved American citizenship
> And greeted a new year.

This haiku appeared twenty years ago in a Seattle newspaper.

Mrs. Itsu Akiyama had similar incentives for mastering the extensive information: "We took our citizenship tests in 1955. You know, alphabetically 'Akiyama' is first! So I got in the mood of my younger days and studied very hard."

Little could match the euphoric feeling of finally becoming a citizen of the United States. For Mr. Chiho Tomita, that special day came on July 6, 1953. He recounted in English what it meant to him:

> If Japanese have citizen[ship], very proud. I'm very proud. I could vote at election for president, mayor. Minister Collins was teacher of our citizen school. He had been in Japan fifteen years, so he talk pretty good Japanese. I remember Minister Collins translate into Japanese most important points. Then man come from Portland to ask question. One question: Senator—how many years? I forget now. Test ten minutes. Then have to wait eight to nine days. They send card. Card said, "Okay." I was so happy! Oh, yes, vote in next election. This country democracy. Everybody have equal chance.

For Mrs. Tei Endow, the privilege of voting also brought special pride: "I was most happy to receive this honor. I was able to vote, but I am trying to remember which president that was. . . . Before we voted, we studied sample ballots; and we asked our friends to make suggestions. I felt privileged to be able to cast my vote. I finally felt that my one vote may have mattered."

Mr. Masaji Kusachi took the privileges and responsibilities of citizenship most seriously:

> When I lived in Japan, I was still a young person and could not vote. So when I attained citizenship in this country and voted for the first time, I felt GREAT! Afterward I realized that with citizenship and voting privileges also came certain responsibilities, like

paying taxes. I had not given it that much thought in the past. Now, though, as a citizen, I could finally own land! (As aliens, we had been denied the right to own homes and property. That had been hard to take, although we had been able to evade that law by deeding land to our children. Japanese societies in Oregon spent a lot of money hiring an attorney to repeal that law.)[17]

Redress

In 1983 the government's Commission on Wartime Relocation and Internment of Civilians concluded that Executive Order 9066 was not justified by military necessity. It reported to Congress that "a grave personal injustice was done to the American citizens and resident aliens of Japanese ancestry."[18] The commission also recognized that "no amount of money can fully compensate the excluded people for their losses and sufferings."[19] To remedy the violations, however, it recommended that the nation apologize for the acts of exclusion, removal, and detention and that redress money be appropriated for those who were excluded.[20]

For the Japanese, the announcement was a welcome affirmation of their loss of liberty based solely on their ethnicity. Yet Issei also expressed a selfless concern for the government that had caused them this injustice:

> It was illegal to keep the Japanese in camp, but that was a time of war. The government is not that wealthy. So we should leave well enough alone. We will get by. [Mrs. Itsu Akiyama]

> I suppose I could say if we received redress money, I would be thankful. On the other hand, I also realize that this country has other bigger problems. [Mrs. Asayo Noji]

> While I certainly would not mind having the money, with the present financial condition of this country, it may be inappropriate. [Mrs. Miyoshi Noyori]

Some not only rationalized their exclusion but also vowed to give the money to others:

> Even though we suffered greatly, we became wards of the government. They took care of us when times were difficult and even when there was physical danger to us. So I have mixed feelings about this. Even if I did receive money, I have no desire to spend it on myself. I would certainly donate to churches. And when I see street people struggling for their lives, I wish I had money to help them. [Mrs. Misuyo Nakamura]

If I were awarded money for being confined in camp, I would donate it to church. If we were to have remained at home under those wartime conditions, we may have lived in constant anxiety about our freedom. Myself, I do not believe it is proper to receive this kind of money from the government. [Mrs. Hatsumi Nishimoto]

Beneath the concerns, there was genuine skepticism: would the government program actually be achieved? "Well, I don't think we will get it," Mr. Masaji Kusachi remarked. "Reagan and the Republicans will not take money from the treasury for that, although the Democrats might. For the Nisei citizens in camp, no matter what they receive, the money would be too little. I received money for my crop losses, so I do not think any more will be coming."

On August 10, 1988, the U.S. government did in fact make an effort to "right a grave wrong." President Ronald Reagan signed the Civil Liberties Act of 1988, which effectively apologized for the World War II removal of 120,000 people of Japanese ancestry. Through the redress law, affected individuals or their survivors would receive apologies and $20,000 tax-free payments for what Reagan termed was the government's "mistake."[21]

On September 27, 1992, the government authorized an additional $400 million to complete payments to an estimated 60,000 eligible Japanese Americans and to fund historical research and education programs. President George Bush's signing of the Civil Liberties Act amendments compensated for a funding shortfall in the redress program. An estimated 25,000 eligible individuals would receive their $20,000 payments during the fall of 1992 and the rest during the following year.[22]

Issei, while feeling the money was justified, had mixed reactions:

They should not do it. Once we receive our money, everyone will start disliking the Japanese again. [Mrs. Shigeko Fukui]

I appreciate it but it brought back memories. I do not really know how to express my feelings. I am happy but I am not overly happy. We lost so much more. [Mrs. Asayo Noji]

37

Issei Reflect on Their Experiences

How WOULD the Hood River Issei characterize their experiences? As they reminisced, the difficulties were most easily recounted:

Issei have gone through extremely difficult times. Everything in this country was different—from language to food to manners. In the middle of the depression there were always financial problems. On top of that, most Issei had big families. Surviving that and having raised our children, those difficult times are now in the backs of our minds.

There are those who were able to withstand the rigors of difficult times; and, of course, there were those who were not. I would say that when we immigrated here, Issei were determined to work hard and succeed. They were probably driven by a desire not to tarnish the Japanese image. We had come from so far away that we wanted to give our best efforts. [Mrs. Asayo Noji]

Despite the hardships faced, though, Mrs. Miyoshi Noyori pointed out that their predecessors suffered even more:

All the Issei were hardworking and honest. They spent much time in the valley improving the ground, so they have materially contributed to this country's welfare. I believe *iji* [strong will] or stubbornness to succeed probably made Issei overcome difficulties. While I had a very trying period, those men who preceded us had many more troubles. They were full of ambition, yet their inability to converse with *hakujin* [Caucasians] made their lives much more difficult than ours. The story is that when they made purchases,

Miyoshi Noyori felt particularly pleased that she had shared numerous stories in her interviews "without saying anything bad about anyone." (Courtesy of Mamoru Noji)

they could not be understood. So when they bought eggs, they went through the motions of cackling hens who were dropping their eggs! When they needed matches, they tried to describe the diamond brand on the matchbox.

In the face of financial hardships and discrimination in a foreign land, Issei persevered. To what would they attribute their will to endure hardships in America?

It is my belief that *shushin* [moral training] helped us to make life in America more bearable. *Shushin* was part of our study in school in Japan. At home, too, we learned to *gaman* [endure]. "Even though it is hard work, you must finish whatever you begin." After I immigrated to America, these thoughts were foremost in my mind. [Mr. Masaji Kusachi]

Hatsumi Nishimoto (*right*) and Misuyo Nakamura, pictured in 1986, enjoyed a friendship strengthened by their shared Hiroshima roots and strong Buddhist faith. (Courtesy of Mamoru Noji)

A lot of Issei planned to make their fortunes here and return to Japan. But it was not that easy. We worked and worked. We took whatever came. We did not want to fail here. [Mrs. Hatsumi Nishimoto]

No matter how difficult the situation, you should not depend on others to help you or do your work for you. So, whatever our ambition as Issei, we had to depend on ourselves. This feeling probably helped us to persevere. In my day in Japan, we had strict upbringing in *shushin*. *Shushin* taught us to be upright, honest, and not to harm others. You have to respect and take care of your parents, your siblings, and others as well. [Mrs. Misuyo Nakamura]

We persevered in our work and in our endeavor primarily, I believe, to ensure that our children were able to get the best education. [Mrs. Masayo Yumibe]

In the workplace and at home, the needs of their children were all-consuming, as Mrs. Tei Endow made clear:

The education of our children was our foremost goal. Even though we had a small orchard, we tried to do a lot of the work ourselves in order to save money for our children's higher education. *Hakujin* may have felt that we spent our lifetimes working and denying ourselves fashionable clothes and conveniences. But we felt education was so important that nothing else mattered. It was most satisfying to be able to send our children to school and know today that they are doing well. We also felt that we did not want to become a burden on society—we wanted to be self-supporting. But from now, we can relax and enjoy our lives.

Mrs. Miyoshi Noyori underscored the need for Issei to feel self-reliant:

Within my family—a very nice family—I have the feeling I do not want to become a burden. This feeling of *futan* [burden] is probably due to a long history of family obligations in Japan. One does not freely do things without concern for others. Probably older people would rather do things on their own—if they are able—rather than ask others for help. For example, I do not want to burden my son Mark with every little concern I have. I try to solve the problems myself. This strong feeling is very obvious among Issei in Hood River. (I often wonder about my own future and what would be best for everyone. I am, after all, eighty-five years old. If my health should break down, should I stay here and become a burden to Mark? After all, he must carry on his family holdings. Or, should I go to [the Japanese rest home in] Seattle or in Sacramento? After I pass on, I wish to be buried here in Hood River—even if I die in Sacramento. My children say it is a matter I should decide for myself. I spend so much time worrying about what I should do.)

Ninety-two-year-old Mr. Chiho Tomita, speaking in English, compared the heavily encumbered early days with the Issei life of today: "Issei getting too old, do nothing, just stay home. Pretty lonesome. I think better going to picture shows. Get together once or twice year at Issei Dinner and picnic.[1] Too hard work makes short life. Too easy now."

Mrs. Itsu Akiyama summed up how she felt Hood River Issei should be remembered: "Issei were born in Japan and are now American citizens, so now, although we cannot speak English, we are American citizens. That is the way I wish to be remembered. Besides working, there is not much left to tell. Despite facing discrimination, our goal was that our children would become good American citizens. We did not care about what we wore—we sacrificed greatly for our children."

38

Messages

Based on what they had learned from their own long lives, what messages would Issei give Nisei, Sansei (third-generation Japanese), and Yonsei (fourth-generation Japanese)?

While remembering their own Japanese cultural roots, succeeding generations of Japanese Americans should, in the view of Mr. Chiho Tomita, also work toward peaceful coexistence with Caucasians: "I would want the Nisei and Sansei to retain the proper uses of Japanese language and culture, because I believe we are losing them. We should also promote friendship between Caucasians and the Japanese in the valley. Our relationship is very good now, but I want to encourage us to continue in that direction."

Most of all, Issei advised that their descendants live highly moral lives:

I would like to ask that, as Japanese, our actions never embarrass other Japanese and that we live honorable lives. [Mrs Masayo Yumibe]

I would like to leave a feeling of righteous and straightforward living. Within that, whatever you want to do ought to be considered in how it will affect your fellow man. Place yourself in the other person's shoes before you do anything. Although we may make mistakes, we should always consider the effect on the other person. This is my thinking even though my head is not very intelligent. [Mrs. Misuyo Nakamura]

I would suggest saying, "Do no harm to other people. Do not take belongings of others, no matter how small." [Mrs. Hatsumi Nishimoto]

Eighty-two-year-old Masaji Kusachi had just returned from pruning trees before his first interview in 1986. (Courtesy of Mamoru
Noji)

As I view them from my own eyes, I would ask them to continue
what they are doing—continue their education and the way they
are approaching life. I think they are doing an excellent job. I
would request that young people lead a life which is *shojiki* [upright
and honest] and live by the virtues of democracy. [Mr. Masaji
Kusachi]

Religious faith was an important foundation in Mrs. Itsu Akiyama's
message: "I would like to leave to Nisei and Sansei the message of I
Corinthians 13 [I Corinthians 13:2] in the Bible: love to humanity. The
verse says that, even if you have enough faith to move mountains, if you

have no love, then it is of little value. We are all human, and there are many things we are unable to do. I regard this as the will of God, and I am able to accept that."

Mrs. Tei Endow thought that others would do well to learn from Issei mistakes: "I would like to tell Nisei and Sansei: do not make the same mistakes that the Issei did, but do those things which made us successful. If we tried to keep up with the Joneses, so to speak, and wore modern clothes and satisfied our children's pretentious desires, that is where our efforts may have been misspent."

The foremost thought was articulated by Mrs. Asayo Noji: "My hope is that Nisei and Sansei [and Yonsei] live an honest life in harmony with Caucasian neighbors and make a significant contribution to American life."

39

Issei Self-portraits

WHAT IMAGES did Issei have of themselves? How did they spend their later years? How would they describe themselves to others? Did they consider themselves more *Americajin* (American) or *Nihonjin* (Japanese)? Here are the portraits they drew of themselves:

> Well, I am a worthless person. If I could, I would like to be more *shinko* [devoted to faith]. This I find most difficult. *Americajin* or *Nihonjin?* I am an American citizen, but everything I do is still *Nihonjin*. I eat *gohan* [steamed rice], I speak *Nihongo*, and I think *Nihonjin*.
>
> When I am confined to the house in the winter, it becomes a bit of a problem. My eyesight does not allow me to do too much sewing or crocheting. So I read Christian books by Rev. Kagawa. If this were summer, I would be working in my garden. I grow tomatoes, green beans, green peppers, peas, spinach, cucumbers. I plant just about everything. [Mrs. Itsu Akiyama]

> I consider myself *Americajin*. I have voted, and my ties with Japan are more remote than ever. I believe my healthful condition is what probably helped me as much as anything else. All my life I have worked hard, and I have suffered very little illness.
>
> Now I like to rest, read newspapers and haiku, and listen to radio and TV. I talk to my children on the telephone too. In the summertime I go outside and garden. How would I describe myself? That is very difficult. Because this is my inborn trait, I do not have too much to say. My grandchildren might say, "Grandma sends me money on special occasions like birthdays, Easter, and Christmas." I have a bad back now and cannot lift heavy objects. One of my

pleasures is that my great-grandchildren often come to help me in my garden. American-style, I pay them. This makes me happy. [Mrs. Tei Endow (Mrs. Endow died in April 1992.)]

During the day I like to embroider cushions and knit pillows and afghans for my grandchildren. I enjoy reading books—mostly religious ones—and newspapers. I watch TV even though I cannot understand English. This is how I spend my day. (Nowadays my daughter-in-law takes care of the cooking and washing.) I want to keep my mind occupied, otherwise you can get *tobokeru* [absent minded]. I had a cataract operation; otherwise, I am *genki* [healthy] and have no physical ailments. How would I describe myself? *So-na* [I wonder]. I do not know what to say. I consider myself a Japanese rather than an American. [Mrs. Shigeko Fukui]

I returned to Okayama, Japan, in 1966 and married my present wife, who returned to Dee with me. In 1965, when I was ill, I gave my twelve acres of land, including six acres of orchard, to my son. Now I help him. This year my wife and I pruned one hundred of the full-grown trees, working four or five hours a day and pruning maybe two or three trees a day. If you sit at home, you grow old too easily! But, as long as you can move, if you work a little each day, you feel much better. I find interest in garden work, too, working in my one-acre garden to the point my health permits. My wife and I raise *gobo* [burdock root], which we sell to two Japanese stores in Portland. My operation in 1979 sapped my strength, so that winter I latch-hooked rugs for entertainment and to kill time. I also cooked quite a bit. When the Dee Fire Department was looking for ways to raise money, I was asked to be in charge of a chow mein dinner. But I have lost interest in cooking now—it is so difficult to prepare a meal. One fault of Japanese is that, even though they have the recipe, they do not religiously follow it. I think that Japanese cooks guess their ingredients whereas Americans meticulously follow their recipes. I understand that, presently in Japan, they do follow measurements. This is reflected in the superior construction of Japanese cars, computers, cameras, and other technological equipment.

Today, even though I now have citizenship, I realize there is a difference in Japanese and American education. I received my education and was brought up in Japan, so I suppose I would consider myself more Japanese. In Japan the sense of family was very strong. We were raised as one family group, in contrast to life in America, where the emphasis is more on individuals. Since the principles of life in two different countries are not alike, perhaps it is unfair to

Shigeko Fukui, pictured in 1986, showed her latest article of handiwork, a latch-hooked barnyard scene. (Courtesy of Mamoru Noji)

compare them. But, to me, it is difficult to accept the individualism found in this country. I have considerably more respect for the tradition of family in Japan. For example, the family line in Japan extended from grandfather to father to son. And, when the grandfather passed on, we deified him. Although we brought Buddhism to the United States, those Buddhist principles and Japanese traditions cannot be fully translated into English. [Mr. Masaji Kusachi (Mr. Kusachi died in September 1986.)]

I love to read! I subscribe to Japanese magazines and two Japanese newspapers. I also reread my old books, which are religious in nature. Every night I eat early so I can watch the news on television. One of my favorite programs is "The Price is Right." Every night I watch it! I like to see the people win.

Probably it is best said that I am part *Nihonjin* and part *Americajin*. Because of my strict upbringing in Japan, I still retain the teachings of my parents. I tell myself, because I am a Japanese, I do not want to do anything to embarrass the Japanese. I believe that because we live in this country, it is very important that Japanese live an honest life.

I get angry at myself, because I have lived in this country sixty-five years and I still cannot speak English. I often wonder, "What did I do wrong?" I hold no other person responsible. When there are words I do not understand, I look them up in the dictionary. My eyesight is bad so I have to bring out my magnifying glass. When I see how the words are used in certain situations, I write them down. But after I look them up, I soon forget. I try to get along the best I can, for I do not want to burden others with my problems. So I kind of "push" my explanation on others, using gestures. Frequently the other person is able to sort of guess and then nods yes, yes. [Mrs. Misuyo Nakamura]

In my own mind, I feel that I am more American than Japanese because I live in America. It could not be the other way around. My face may look different, but living here most of my life and now being an American citizen, I feel more *Americajin*. It is truly agonizing for me that I cannot show more friendship and talk more with my Caucasian friends. This has been a real handicap to me. When my son Koe was involved with the VFW (Veterans of Foreign Wars), many people called at our house and greeted me, "Hi, Grandma." I would try to express my thanks and say, "Thank you." That made me happy.

I would probably say I am not a very good person. Maybe my grandchildren would say, "Nice Grandma." Because of my physical condition, I am unable to do very much now, but I do like to raise vegetables and beautiful flowers. I also work inside doing housework and helping to cook. I enjoy watching TV, but, since I cannot understand English, I have to guess what the people are saying [Mrs. Hatsumi Nishimoto]

"Happy, happy *mainichi* [every day]!" I am grateful, grateful all the time! I have carefree moments so I watch TV and look forward to taking care of the garden and flowers. With my son Mam, I have traveled throughout the United States—almost all the states from Hawaii to Texas to Florida. And lots of trips to Japan and even once to Brazil. I have been fortunate to see all this, and I say, "Thank you, thank you." I have lived in America almost seventy years, so I consider myself an American. I have nearly forgotten the life in Japan—I spent only nineteen years there. The rest of my life I have spent in the United States; therefore, my feelings are very strong for America. I would probably describe myself as an almost worthless and unknowing person. Living here so long and yet being unable to converse in English is my greatest liability. I regret being unable to talk in English to my neighbors. [Mrs. Asayo Noji]

I was brought up in Japan, and I learned all the teachings and customs of living there. This I do not forget. Yet I have spent a much longer period in America and have obtained citizenship here. I feel I have considerable responsibility in this country also. In that sense, I guess I give thanks that I am still in this country.

Giri [moral obligation toward others], *ninjo* [humanity], and *on* [obligation, kindness, favor] are essential to life, and these precepts were indoctrinated in me. These have been very influential in my life and probably should be in the lives of everyone. *On* is bestowed upon you in terms of kindness. *Giri* may be expressed as an obligation—if you are obligated to someone, you have to repay that kindness or favor. If you owe anything, you must repay the person. *Ninjo* is our feeling toward others. These three precepts are indoctrinated into Japanese families. An example would be: if I had a financial problem, I might impose on you by asking for a loan. Then the party who gave the loan would have *on* which I must be certain to repay. And this becomes *giri*, an obligation to return that favor. If I were to ignore the person who loaned me the money or if I made no honest effort to make a repayment, then this would be ignoring *giri*. A real good example of *on* is when Mark was saved by an American neighbor.[1] An example of *giri* is that Mark expressed his appreciation by giving Mr. Edgar a dish set.

I spend much of my time reading religious books. I find much pleasure in reading these books. One book contains health and food matters. An article tells where eating flesh does not contribute to good health and perhaps to good feeling. When an animal is sacrificed, it is *okoru* [angered]. And therefore the anger would be transferred in the blood and flesh—this cannot be good for your soul.

To what do I attribute my mental alertness? One point is that, when I help Naomi [daughter], I am physically active. "Another one point" is that I have religious faith. I believe these two points have probably contributed to my good health. One more point—all my children are healthy and are doing very well. That pleases me, so that must also contribute to my health. [Mrs. Miyoshi Noyori]

I would say I am neither a poison nor a real good man. I do not do anything now. Most of the time I read newspapers and church bulletins and watch baseball games on TV. In 1974 I received the Emperor's Imperial Award for promoting relations between America and Japan. I was head of the Japanese Society in Hood River for four years following the war. We had meetings to serve the Japanese people of the valley. [Mr. Chiho Tomita (Mr. Tomita died in April 1988.)]

I spend most of my time thanking God "*Arigato gozai-masu*" for my long life. I used to watch television a lot, but now, with my poor eyesight, I seldom watch. And I do not understand the English anyway. It has been a long time since I left Japan, so my memories of Japan are vague. Because I have lived in this country so long, I suppose I would have to say my attachment for America is probably greater than [to] Japan. It is my trait that I find pleasure in giving things to people. On the other hand, when I receive gifts, I feel very much *kinodoku* [regretful]. [Mrs. Hisa Wakamatsu (Mrs. Wakamatsu died in February 1989.)]

When I see other people, I wish I could be more like them. I find much pleasure in giving my handwork as gifts. I have given several hundred knitted creations away. All my children and grandchildren have many of my crafts. When they see a new one, they admire it and say, "*Chodai* [please give me]." They seem to really appreciate my knitting.

In this valley the air is clear, the water is pure, and I have lived a long life. Since the age of sixty, I have not been able to do physical work, so on nice days I weeded my flower gardens. In that way, too, I found material for writing my haiku [seventeen-syllable form of Japanese poetry]. Aspiring to long life, I grew flowers, arranged ikebana and bonsai, and wrote haiku. I urge people over seventy years old to take up activities for relaxation and to keep busy in

Hisa Wakamatsu was surrounded by photos of grandchildren and great-grandchildren in her home. (Courtesy of Mamoru Noji)

order that they may lead a fuller, longer life. [Mrs. Hama Yamaki (Mrs. Yamaki died in August 1988.)]

We have lived here a long time, and we really do not have any intentions of returning to Japan. And life in America is certainly easier. When you put these together, it probably means I consider myself more American than Japanese. Life in Japan was so much more formal and ceremonial. If we met an older person, we would have had to bow low and, if it was morning, say "*Ohayoo gozaimasu.*" (For an ordinary person, you could bow slightly; for the emperor, you would bow much more deeply.) We also had to use honorifics, like *o-* in our speech when we referred to father, mother, etc. When I came to America, you just said hello, hello, and that was accepted. Just saying hello in Japan would have been considered crude. Japan had a very formal society.

Now I spend the day the same as my husband—not much to do. I do like garden work—peas, cucumbers, tomatoes, cabbage, daikon, broccoli. This year we will move to California to be near our children. [Mrs. Masayo Yumibe]

"Nothing to do now." I watch TV and read Japanese newspapers and magazines. "That's all." Although I have the *Hood River News* here, I do not fully understand it—but I do look at the headlines. For the past twenty to thirty years, I have driven my car without an accident, so I receive rebates from my insurance company. I drive to Portland to visit my relatives and to make purchases at Anzen Japanese Store. I also succeeded Mr. [Hitoshi] Nakamura as organizer of our local Buddhist church group, because there were no other men. I am not fully competent, but I am doing the best I can. We have nine members at the present time, but only half of them are active. My position is to communicate with the reverend in Portland and to set up local church meetings within the valley. I also act as the treasurer, collect the dues, and pay the minister about twenty dollars for his visit. We meet four times a year at the homes of members.

After working for forty-one years at the sawmill, I now receive a pension every month all my life, as well as social security. So living is easy. I now feel I am an American person. Since receiving my citizenship, I have exercised my voting privilege, I feel I am American. [Mr. Miyozo Yumibe (Mr. Yumibe died in October 1990.)]

PART TEN

Concluding Comments

Tatakaite
Yo no utsuri kamo
Hanaregataki
Kokoku wo ware wa
Ima hanaremu to su

War and change,
My native land
Once so hard to leave,
Is behind me now forever.

Tanka written by Mrs. Shizue Iwatsuki and
translated by Dr. Stephen W. Kohl

40

Perspectives on the Hood River Issei

ROGER DANIELS likened intergenerational views by Japanese in the United States to a generalization offered by Marcus Lee Hansen, considered the father of immigration history. Hansen had observed that the second generation, wanting to become as fully Americanized as possible, tended to reject their parents' heritage. Likewise, the third generation seemed to reject their own parents' values, but they also attempted to recapture some of their cultural roots.[1]

While Hansen's insights may provide parallels to the transitions between the first three generations of Japanese in the United States, they also underscore incentives of the third generation Sansei. To better understand the Japanese side of our identities, many of us Sansei have become particularly eager to examine our ethnic heritage. This quest involves not only investigating events of our grandparents' generation but also unlocking doors to reveal their reactions and the meanings they attached to those events. It has become an effort to come to terms with the world of the Issei as they encountered American life.

Although many of the characterististics of these Issei may be common to those elsewhere, special aspects of Hood River lend singular qualities to the Hood River Issei experience. Hood River Valley, nestled at the base of Mt. Hood, is bordered on the north by the mighty Columbia River and flanked by the columnar cliffs of the Columbia River gorge. In addition to these geographic obstacles, limited transportation and communication links contributed initially to the isolation of this conservative, rural community. Later, some Hood River residents brought national attention to this small town during their wartime campaign against the rights of Japanese. Reflecting on their experiences, this chapter outlines common threads interwoven into the thought processes and responses of the Hood River Issei.

For the most part, Hood River Issei were raised in the conservative farming communities of Meiji Japan, where they were schooled in the moral teachings sanctioned by the 1890 Imperial Rescript of Education. Their outlooks on life were thus founded in nationalistic pride and ethical standards of behavior. Within the Japanese hierarchical system, where each individual held a specific position in the social structure, Issei lives reflected clearly prescribed roles, subordination of their own needs and well-being to those of the group, reverence for authority, and a conformity to rules for proper behavior. In short, they mirrored typical values of Japanese farmers in Japan itself.

When they immigrated to the United States, bringing these customs and values as "cultural baggage," Issei found that their traditions were contrary to the independent life-styles of Americans. For social and economic survival in a country where language was unfamiliar, Issei developed mutual support systems and clung to their Japanese heritage. At the same time, they clearly recognized that their American-born children were citizens of this new country and preferred the American way of life. As a "transitional generation,"[2] Issei were a link between Japan and the United States, meshing two distinct cultures while facing obligations to family members in each country. Their behavior and values were firmly anchored in their traditional Japanese upbringing, in particular, shushin, their early ethical schooling.

Shushin classes at schools in Japan, based on Confucian ethics, had emphasized moral principles and nationalism. Upholding the Imperial Rescript on Education, teachers extolled the virtues of duty, obedience, filial piety, harmony, industry, and self-dedication.[3] Acknowledging strict lessons in shushin, Mrs. Misuyo Nakamura admonished, "Your behavior toward others must never be harmful. Shushin taught us to be upright, honest, and not to harm others. You have to respect and take care of your parents, your siblings, and others as well."

The code of behavior in Japanese family interaction included filial piety, or reciprocal obligations between parent and child. This sense of devotion to their children also, in one sense, was a way to return the indebtedness Issei felt toward their own parents.[4] Issei worked long hours and denied themselves fashionable clothes and household conveniences to buy items for their children and save for their education. Education in itself was a priority, not only as a traditional value in Issei cultural baggage but also as a means to help their children compete in this new society. Issei dreams and aspirations were embedded in the success of their children in America—and they viewed education as the key to success.

As Mrs. Tei Endow avowed, "The education of our children was our foremost goal. We tried to do a lot of the [orchard] work ourselves to save for our children's higher education. *Hakujin* [Caucasians] may have felt that we spent our lifetimes working and denying ourselves conveniences. But we felt education was so important that nothing else mattered. It was most satisfying to be able to send our children to school and know today that they are doing well." Offspring of these interviewed Issei included physicians, engineers, orchardists, a Pentagon administrator, an optometrist, a teacher, a nurse, an artist, a realtor, a postal worker, and a state fruit inspector.

Issei also recognized that their individual actions reflected not only on themselves but on their families and the entire Japanese population in Hood River as well. In Japan, where great importance was placed on one's reputation, society imposed strong negative sanctions on undutiful persons.[5] In Hood River, where Issei were easily distinguished by physical features, their actions were unwittingly generalized to all Japanese. This became a factor in their 1921 decision to control their liquor consumption. The prohibition law was in effect, and many Issei believed their actions could feed growing anti-Japanese feelings in the valley. Driven by the desire never to embarrass other Japanese or tarnish their image, Issei openly endorsed life-styles that were *shojiki* (upright and honest).

While *shushin* provided a foundation, Issei consistently evinced principles of humility (*hikaeme*), perseverence (*shinbo*), and an acceptance of situations over which they believed they had no control (*shikata-ganai*). These emerging threads, manifested in Issei actions and words, are examined here in greater detail.

One of the most common threads among Hood River Issei was *hikaeme* (humility). Issei tended to show respect for others by humbling themselves. An old Japanese saying typified Issei embarrassment at being singled out: "The nail that stands up will be hammered down."[6]

In Meiji Japan, Issei had also been conscious of their specific positions in the Japanese social order: young deferred to elders, females deferred to males, and subordinates deferred to those with greater status. Issei learned that the well-being of the group took precedence over their own needs and that cohesion and harmony were valued above individual achievement. As Mrs. Misuyo Nakamura said, "Although we may make mistakes, we should always consider the effect on the other person. This is my thinking even though my head is not very intelligent."

This self-effacing concern was the basis for the *enryo* syndrome of Japanese behavior, which refers to one's inner self-control, modesty, and deference to superiors. Issei commonly emphasized their more negative rather than positive aspects and had difficulty accepting praise. When asked to describe themselves, typical descriptions included: "not a very good person," "neither a poison nor a real good man," "almost worthless and unknowing," and "not fully competent." None of the Issei used complimentary terms when referring to themselves.

This reserve and tendency toward obscurity even affected the willingness of some Issei to have their life events recorded for this project. One woman expressed surprise that her past would interest others, for she was "just a poor old woman," whose life should remain private. Another requested that the tape recorder be turned off. The realization that others would be sharing their stories became the turning point, for there would be many "protruding nails." They would not be alone—their stories would be part of a group history. Once Issei had committed themselves and had begun to participate, there was an unmistakable eagerness to help as much as possible, by checking diaries, writing notes, and bringing artifacts. The interview process did seem to serve as a catharsis, providing a format for bringing to consciousness those joys and sorrows that had been buried deep within them. Several admitted that through this project they would be sharing many of their stories with family members for the very first time.

A second shared principle among Hood River Issei was *shinbo* (perseverence). In the face of adversity, Hood River Issei demonstrated *shinbo*, the capacity to withstand difficulties that, as one Issei exclaimed, were "worse than I possibly could have imagined." Deluded by grand and exaggerated visions of America, Issei faced oppressive physical labor, miserable living conditions, and lonely existences without the support and benefit of close family or friends. Whether it meant living destitute and malnourished on a railroad gang, singlehandedly raising five acres of strawberries, or laboring ten-hour days while suffering morning sickness, Issei strove for success in the face of heavy obstacles. For several Issei, *shinbo* was a desirable quality in deciding on a spouse. One woman admitted that, though she had expressed a desire to return to Japan, her mother had requested that she *shinbo* in America.

As Issei gained relative economic success in Hood River and as racial tensions increased, their greatest test came in the form of discrimination. Uprooted from their homes for three years, they returned to communitywide campaigns fueled by a desire that all Japanese be deported. Some found that their orchards had received such poor care that it took them as long as three years to restore them. Mrs. Itsu Akiyama reminisced, "What I remember most was that although we were faced with hard work, we found inspiration in our efforts to restore our orchard. I am still amazed that we had such ambition!" Admittedly, "stubbornness to succeed" helped Issei overcome difficulties, and they continually reminded themselves that "you must finish whatever you begin."

Issei also embraced the traditional value of self-reliance, which helped them persevere. As Mrs. Misuyo Nakamura affirmed, "No matter how difficult the situation, you should not depend on others. . . . So whatever our ambition as Issei, we had to depend on ourselves." It was of great concern to them that they be "self-supporting," for they did not want to become *futan* (a burden) on their families or society.

Even today, as much as they are able, Issei manifest the diligence, endurance, and self-reliance of their younger years. In their eighties and nineties, most continued to work daily in their gardens, orchards, or homes for as long as four or five hours a day. Recognizing the value of hard work in maintaining good health and longevity, Mr. Masaji Kusachi explained shortly before his death, "If you sit at home, you grow old too easily! But, as long as you can move, if you work a little each day, you feel much better."

Among the Hood River Issei, a third underlying thread was *shikata-ganai*, a feeling that "it is beyond our control; it cannot be helped so accept it as it is." When difficulties occurred, one of the most frequent responses among Hood River Issei was "*shikata-ganai,*" resignation or acceptance of a situation. Issei have been likened to a willow tree that swayed with the storms and resisted uprooting.[7] *Shikata-ganai* may have rendered the Issei cautious about "rocking the boat," but it enabled them to accept untenable situations—whether those situations were provoked by themselves or by others.

Issei women exemplified this as they accepted traditional, subservient roles while becoming aware of the more liberated status of their American counterparts. Japanese women were often scolded by their husbands for working slowly in the fields, and one remembered being ordered to "at least work enough to provide food for yourself." Issei women were impressed by the manner in which American women were treated. They also recognized that, after a full day's labor alongside their husbands, men rested while women were saddled with domestic chores. After they noticed that American women were more outspoken, Japanese women became more prone to disagree with their husbands, one Issei woman observed. Yet she was quick to add that, when she differed with her husband, she felt remorse because of her traditional Japanese upbringing.

Restraint was especially evident as Issei faced oppressive conditions during World War II. Forced to abandon their homes and farms, Issei admitted suppressing their feelings and trying to show "goodwill" as they left their valley. When they settled into the squalid camp life, however, their children freely expressed the distaste that Issei were reluctant to convey. One frustrated eleven-year-old showed no inhibitions when he threw himself on the floor, screaming and pounding his feet. Still, recognizing that at least they had food and shelter, Issei accepted their situation, for "everything was *shikata-ganai* in camp." Upon their return to Hood River three years later, many were distressed to find their homes filthy, their orchards neglected, and their personal belongings stolen. Though they suffered heavy losses, they did not "make a lot of noise about it," according to Mrs. Hama Yamaki. "We were not citizens, so we did not speak up," Mrs. Itsu Akiyama explained, adding, "That was our weakness."

With their early schooling in *shushin*, Issei had a general disposition to accept authority. As they had deferred to the emperor in Japan, so too they complied with government orders in their new homeland. When FBI officials searched their homes during the war, Issei politely accommodated their uninvited visitors. One invited the FBI to "look any place, go ahead, and sit down," and another asked for permission for her children to attend school the next day. After Executive Order 9066 mandated the removal of all West Coast Japanese to relocation camps, Issei had no notion of disobeying, because it was meirei (an order). "We were powerless," explained one. "We had to do what the government ordered."

While they were resigned to submitting to government mandates, they also tended to rationalize the role of the government in their ill fate. Because federal officials had assisted them in leasing and selling property before their removal, one Issei believed the government had not mistreated them. Another was impressed by FBI officials' manners when they conducted a thorough search of her home in an unthreatening manner and thanked her before leaving. When her uncomfortable, straw mattress was replaced at camp, one woman characterized the government as considerate. Still another expressed reluctance to be critical of the government's management of camps, since it "may have done the best it could." When citizenship was in hand, an Issei would exult, "This country democracy. Everybody have equal chance." The sociologist Amy Iwasaki Mass has recognized that this coping mechanism "fit well with the propaganda of the government," but it exacted a high expense in individuals' self-worth.[8] The sociologist Wendy Ng termed this rationalization as an "internalized form of racism."[9] Tetsuden Kashima, a specialist in Asian American studies, referred to this "social amnesia" as an attempt to "suppress feelings and memories of particular moments or extended time periods . . . a conscious effort . . . to cover up less than pleasant memories.[10] Through their acceptance, submission, and rationalization, they were indeed resigned to their fate.

The lives of Hood River Issei were thus influenced by their moral training in Japan (*shushin*) as well as by their humility (*hikaeme*), perseverance (*shinbo*), and resignation to difficult situations (*shikata-ganai*). Concerned that they bring honor to the Japanese community, Issei scrutinized their own behavior as well as that of their families. Balancing their Japanese

Hood River Issei posed after an annual Issei Appreciation Dinner sponsored by the local Japanese community. *Row 1: fifth (left to right)*, Mrs. Hama Yamaki; *Row 2: third*, Mrs. Hatsumi Nishimoto; *fifth*, Mrs. Misuyo Nakamura; *sixth*, Mrs. Masayo Yumibe; *Row 3: First*, Mr. Chiho Tomita; *sixth*, Mrs. Itsu Akiyama; *ninth*, Mrs. Tei Endow; *Row 4: tenth*, Mr. Miyozo Yumibe. (Courtesy of Chiz Tamura)

heritage with newly acquired American customs, they sacrificed for their children's benefit and demonstrated quiet fortitude in the face of racial hostilities. At the same time, they converted tree-studded property to profitable orchards and proudly raised their children as U.S. citizens.

In more recent years, there has been evidence of the Hood River community's growing acceptance of Japanese and Japanese Americans. An Issei woman was selected Woman of the Year in Hood River. Among the Nisei, four have been honored as Outstanding Orchardist of the Year, one was appointed to the Oregon State Board of Higher Education, and another was installed as state commander of the Veterans of Foreign Wars. Sansei have been elected as leaders in their schools and are now successful in their careers, some choosing to return to their family orchards. A downtown Japanese restaurant is now patronized by both Japanese and Caucasians, and the town of Hood River maintains a sister-city relationship with Tsuruta, Japan.

The ultimate hope of Hood River Issei seems aptly expressed by the vision of Mrs. Asayo Noji: "My hope is that Nisei and Sansei [and Yonsei] live an honest life in harmony with Caucasian neighbors and make a significant contribution to American life."

Hood River Issei persisted in the face of financial hardships and racial persecution in their new homeland. In their pioneering efforts, Issei leave a legacy of courage, dedication, sacrifice, and honor. Their story is one that exemplifies the most basic values and dreams of our country's founders. Because of their contributions and the example they set, our country's heritage is richer. As succeeding generations of all ethnic backgrounds, we can indeed be proud of—and must do our utmost to safeguard—this promise for our future.

Tomo Ni Tomo Ni
Yasoji O Mukae
Oi No Maru

Together we have
Lived a long life
And reached our eighties.
A beautiful spring day;
How happy we are.

Haiku written by Mrs. Hama Yamaki and printed
on the program for Issei Appreciation Week,
September 1973, in Portland, Oregon

APPENDIX A

Japanese Population in the United States, Oregon, and Hood River County

Year	United States			Oregon				Hood River County[a]			
	Total	Japanese	Percent Japanese	Total	Japanese	Percent Japanese	Percent of U.S. Japanese in Oregon	Total	Japanese	Percent Japanese	Percent of Oregon Japanese in Hood River Co.
1860	31,443,321	0	.0000	52,465	0	.000	0	—	—	—	—
1870	38,558,371	55	.0001	90,923	0	.000	0	—	—	—	—
1880	50,155,783	148	.0003	174,768	2	.001	1.35	—	—	—	—
1890	62,947,714	2,039	.0032	317,704	25	.008	1.23	—	—	—	—
1900	75,994,575	24,326	.0320	413,536	2,501	.605	10.28	—	—	—	—
1910	91,972,266	72,157	.0785	672,765	3,418	.508	4.74	8,016	468	5.84	13.69
1920	105,710,620	111,010	1.0501	783,389	4,151	.530	3.74	8,315	351	4.22	8.46
1930	122,775,046	138,834	1.1307	953,768	4,958	.520	3.57	8,938	514	5.75	10.37
1940	131,669,275	126,947	.9641	1,089,684	4,071	.374	3.20	11,580	462	3.99	11.35
1950	151,325,798	141,365	.9342	1,521,341	3,660	.241	2.59	12,740	233	1.83	6.37
1960	179,323,175	464,332	2.5893	1,768,687	5,016	.284	1.10	13,395	329	2.45	6.56
1970	203,211,926	588,324	2.8951	2,091,385	6,213	.297	1.10	13,187	347	2.63	5.59
1980	226,545,805	716,331	3.1619	2,633,105	8,580	.326	1.20	15,835	230	1.45	2.68

Sources: U.S. Census Office, Tenth–Twentieth Census of the United States, 1880, 1890, 1900, 1910, 1920, 1930, 1940, 1950, 1960, 1970, 1980; Census of the Population: 1950, vol. 2, Characteristics of the Population, part 37, Oregon; County and City Data Book, 1952.
[a]Hood River County was established in 1908.

Japanese Society Minutes: Construction of the Hood River Japanese Community Hall

The following summaries and excerpts from meetings of Zairyu Doho Tai-kai (Association of Japanese Living in the Area), Hood River, Oregon, chronicle the events and decision-making processes that led to the construction of the Japanese Community Hall in 1926. Translated by Mrs. Yoko Gulde.

February 1, 1925, Barrett Grange Hall (pages 131–47)

After a fire destroyed the Zairyu Doho Taikai's regular meeting place at the Knights of Pythias Hall, an ardent Issei summoned support for constructing a Japanese community hall: "We are proud that Japanese are building a community in this beautiful Hood River. . . . We now feel an urgent need for our own meeting hall. We also would like to start a Japanese school as the next generation grows in large numbers."

Following extensive discussion and a secret ballot, the association voted to build a meeting hall and Japanese school. After surveying members to gain feelings about an accessible location, discussion turned to finances. Mr. Ikutaro Takagi suggested that the group accommodate the size of the building to the number of expected students. He estimated that Japanese children numbered 150 to 160, including 50 to 60 of school age. With an additional 180 to 200 adults, a building with dimensions between forty-by-eighty feet to forty-by-a-hundred feet was necessary. "Using our own labor," he cautioned, "we still have to have around $3,000 to buy materials. For the property and furniture, we need another $1,000. That is a $4,000 expense. Can we afford it?"

Others recognized the need for a "safe, solid building" and a fund drive allowing "two or three separate installments." Each member pledged an amount in an unsigned statement. As a result, among 44 pledges, the anticipated sum was $2,354. Seven committee members were elected to study the matter further.

March 22, 1925, Japanese Community Hall Construction Committee meeting, Mr. Masuo Yasui's home (pages 148–55)

Ever mindful that Caucasians might be suspicious of their venture, committee members were cautious when they selected the location of their proposed community hall. Because Caucasians did not wish to sell the old Barrett school building to Japanese, Issei regretfully gave up on that idea. Other members, fearful of stimulating anti-Japanese activitists, were careful when they inquired about other locations.

Mr. Masuo Yasui was also concerned about how Caucasians would view the teaching of Japanese to their children: "*Hakujin* [Caucasians] may take it wrong. They may become suspicious. What is important is that we explain to them what we want to do here. Their understanding is important. I went to see the county's school superintendent.[1] We exchanged our opinions for two hours. I told him that, because of the kind of work we do, most parents do not have an opportunity to learn English. If we do not teach our children Japanese now, in the near future there will be a gap of communication between the two generations. Our children must grow up to know and understand two countries and to work to bring two countries closer. Knowing both languages is very important to our children. The superintendent understood and agreed with me. I asked him if he could help us to use each community's schoolrooms to teach children in winter. He agreed to talk to each school district. It is the parents' responsibility to raise our children to grow up to be useful citizens of the United States. And they need the school system's help. The superintendent could not agree with me more. The discussion brought a good result.[2]

Through their discussion, members affirmed the value of a meeting hall:

Mr. Kyu Kinoshita: "Some people are worried that after ten years or so, many people will leave this country. Then we will be left with the bills. But I do not think that will happen. I believe most people will stay here for a long time. We can make ten and twenty year plans."

Mr. Ogura:[3] "If we meet only two or three times a year like we have been doing, do we really have to have a building that costs us $4,000 to $5,000?"

Mr. Ikutaro Takagi: "Two to three times a year is not enough. That is why we need a meeting hall. Our children are growing up. We have to do more for them. We should regularly gather to exchange our ideas of children's education. We could also bring all families together to console and entertain each other. We can keep our heritage alive. We could keep learning Buddhism ideals. Japanese school is, of course, important."

Mr. Yasui: "Because we did not have a meeting hall of our own, we must have missed many opportunities. By having our own place, we will gain more than we can count with monetary terms. It can be utilized in many ways to benefit all of us."

Mr. Tadao Sato: "We may not be able to build what is ideal for all of us right away. But we can start with a simple building and add to it as we grow. Let us study it carefully."

April 26, 1925, Zairyu Doho Taikai meeting, Barrett Grange Hall (pages 156–64)

The construction committee for the Japanese Community Hall recommended the purchase of two acres on the north side of Columbia Lot, North Road in Hood River. The proposed thirty-four-by-seventy-six-foot building, which would also serve as the school, was to include a meeting hall, stage, and two waiting rooms. The total cost was estimated at $5,700, including $1,200 for property and $4,500 for building, with the contractor's price included.

Chairman: "Our plan will cost us almost $6,000. Do you really think we can come up with that much money?"

Mr. Katsusaburo Tamura: "Our wish is to build a meeting hall and Japanese school for our next generation. We will give them education and a place to socialize. It will be a long-term operation. It should hold the present population. We ought to plan a complete building."

Mr. Yoshizaymon Mori: "It will be very difficult to come up with $6,000 all at once. We should consider about two years of planning and saving, then start building."

Mr. Gunichi Tamiyasu: "If we give everybody two years to pay up his pledged contribution, it should not be that difficult."

Mr. Akiyama: "It was a $3,000 to $4,000 estimate at last meeting. It is $6,000 today. Should we not ask all of us first if it is acceptable?"

Mr. Sagoro Asai: "In last year's estimate, we figured all of us would come out to take part in the actual construction. So that cost was for the purchase of property and material only. We also wish to build a better building that can hold all of the present Japanese population as Mr. Tamura said. It is not impossible if we make a long-term plan. Even if it costs $10,000, we can do it."

Mr. Jukichi Okamura: "Ten thousand dollars? I cannot allow that kind of extravagance."

Mr. Asai: "No, I did not mean to say we can spend that much. I just wanted to tell you that we can handle a large cost by planning well for many years to come. We have to think of the next generation, our future."

Mr. Tomeji Katayama: "Let us ask everyone."

Mr. Kyu Kinoshita: "How about everybody writing down how much he is willing to contribute. Then we can plan the building within that budget."

Mr. Yasui: "Six thousand dollars may sound a lot of money at first, but think of it this way: We are building the hall for advancement of our society and for education of the generation. We must do our best. If we put all of our efforts in, it is not impossible. If all of us can save twenty-five cents a day, we can reach our goal in less than a year."

Mr. Ogura: "I do not agree with the Japanese school idea. But if most of you agree to do it, then I will give a contribution too. We have been hearing from all of us. We know the committee's recommendation. Now it is time to decide. Do we agree to go with the recommendation?"

Mr. Takagi: "I agree. We exchanged our ideas. Let us see if the majority of us want to build the hall. If we have the majority, then we will form a committee to start collecting contributions. If we do not have the majority for the plan, then we have to come up with another plan."

Mr. Karasawa: "Enough talk. Let us vote."

Chairman asks everyone to raise a hand if the committee recommendation is agreeable. Thirty-six raised a hand. Only seven disagreed.

May 3, 1925, Japanese Community Hall Fundraising Committee meeting, Mr. Yasui's home (pages 166–70)

The fundraising committee of seven, chaired by Mr. Yasui, decided to visit members door to door to ask for contributions. By visiting as a group, they agreed they would be more successful. The group also made the decision to ask for cash contributions or, if inconvenient, a promissory note, with the first payment due by August 15 of that year and the second due by the same date the following year. During their visits, members planned to give their opinions about the operation of the school as well as ask for input from their hosts. That day the committee visited more than sixteen members, concluding at 11:00 P.M., adjourning to Mr. Takagi's for dinner and discussion, and finally leaving at 1:00 A.M. Four additional days were spent meeting with members, concluding anywhere between 1:00 A.M. and 2:30 A.M.

July 27, 1925, Third Zairyu Doho Taikai meeting (pages 172–81)

The third meeting included a report on the fundraising committee's progress, setting a construction date, and determining whether to sub-contract or to hire carpenters themselves. Members also decided the size of property to purchase, chose construction committee members, and invited residents of Dee to participate. At that point, sixty-seven people had contributed over $7,200.

Issei voted unanimously to "construct out" [contract out] the building to "the lowest bid from one with a good personality." In addition, they agreed to begin the project immediately.

Chairman: "How about the size of property to purchase? Please state your opinion."

Mr. Tamura: "We should build a large enough building to hold all the Japanese living in the area. There will be more needs for families to get together, not just for recreation but for development spiritually and mentally for the community."

Mr. Matsutaro Kajikawa: "I propose a building around $5,000, as we planned originally."

Mr. Hirata: "I agree. I also think we should leave some for chairs, etc. Building a house requires a lot more funds than we each think. We should choose a committee and leave the matter to them."

Chairman: "As the study committee proposed, we will construct a building with a budget around $5,000. Let us have a construction committee to oversee the construction. Since this is a building, we should give some leeway, say $500 over or under, to the committee. If you agree, please raise your hand."

All agree . . . .

Construction committee members elected: Yasui, chairman; Tamura, treasurer; vice chairman, Katayama; Sato, Ogura, Asai, Takagi, Kuga, Kajikawa, Takasumi, Hirasawa.

The construction committee voted to form a corporation which would own and operate the meeting hall. The corporation would be composed of three friendly *hakujin* who would retain 55 percent ownership and two elected Japanese who would own 45 percent of the corporation. Mr. Yasui and Mr. Sato were elected to represent the Japanese. Upon submission of a design from Mr. Price, an architect from The Dalles, estimates were to be requested from four Hood River contractors. The Hood River Japanese Community Hall was finally completed in 1926.

Notes

Preface

1. Yamato Ichihashi, *Japanese in the United States* (Stanford, Calif.: Stanford University Press, 1932), 13.

2. U.S. Bureau of the Census, *Eleventh Census of the United States; Twelfth Census of the United States* (Washington, D.C.: Government Printing Office, 1890, 1900).

3. U.S. Department of Commerce, Bureau of the Census, *Fourteenth Census of the United States*, vol. 3 (Washington, D.C.: Government Printing Office, 1920).

4. U.S. Bureau of the Census, *Fifteenth Census of the United States* (Washington, D.C.: Government Printing Office, 1930).

5. State of Oregon, *Report on the Japanese Situation in Oregon* (Salem: State Printing Department, 1920), 7.

6. Ruth M. Guppy, "Japanese Hood River Story Echoes History," *Hood River News*, April 20, 1978, 4.

Issei Profiles

1. Issei names are given in Western form, as opposed to the traditional Japanese method of listing the surname first.

2. Ages of Issei are recorded as of the interview period, between 1985 and 1986.

Prologue

1. Edwin O. Reischauer, *The Japanese* (Cambridge, Mass.: Belknap Press, 1981), 68.

2. The four relatively rigid social classes in feudal Japan were samurai, peasants (considered the primary producers of wealth), craftsmen (secondary producers), and the merchants (considered more parasitic than productive). See Reischauer, *The Japanese*, 71.

3. Ibid., 70; Robert A. Wilson and Bill Hosokawa, *East to America* (New York: William Morrow, 1980), 6.

4. Hugh Borton, *Japan's Modern Century* (New York: Ronald Press, 1955), 27–43.

5. Ichihashi, *Japanese in the United States*, 3.

6. Reischauer, *The Japanese*, 79–96.

Chapter 1. Early Life

1. Reischauer, *The Japanese*, 16–17; Basil Hall Chamberlain, *Things Japanese* (Tokyo: Kelly and Walsh, 1898; Rutland, Vt.: Charles E. Tuttle, 1971), 20.

2. Water from nearby streams or ditches was guided gradually from field to field.

3. Charles J. Dunn, *Everyday Life in Traditional Japan* (Tokyo: Charles E. Tuttle, 1969), 53.

4. Japanese custom dictated one's choice of dress according to sex, age, social position, and season of the year. See Richard K. Beardsley, John W. Hall, and Robert E. Ward, *Village Japan* (Chicago: University of Chicago Press, 1959), 102.

5. Dunn, *Everyday Life in Traditional Japan*, 59.

6. Winter planting of mat rush in December or January complemented the summer growth cycle of rice, allowing double cropping in the fields.

7. Straw stalks were dipped into a liquid clay solution to control the drying and preserve the color.

8. The first railway line between Tokyo and Yokohama was completed in 1872.

9. Siblings usually referred to each other in terms of their relative age, for example, younger brother, older sister.

10. Earlier Mrs. Nakamura's mother had moved into her parents' home, which was too crowded for her daughter to join her. Later the mother moved into her own home about two and a half miles away.

11. H. A. Millis, *The Japanese Problem in the United States* (New York: Macmillan, 1915), 6.

Chapter 2. School

1. Merry White, *The Japanese Educational Challenge* (Tokyo: Kodansha International, 1987), 50.

2. Ibid., 59.

3. Margaret E. Burton, *The Education of Women in Japan* (New York: Fleming H. Revell, 1914), 112.

4. This refers to six years by American standards, because a difference of one year exists in figuring American and Japanese birthdays. Mrs. Noji noted that in Japan she was considered one year old at birth, "maybe because we were in our mothers' stomachs for almost one year." January 1 was also considered a universal birthday. Rather than waiting until one's actual birthdate, some families added a year to their ages at the New Year. For example, a child born in December, who was already considered one year old, became two on January 1. See Chamberlain, *Things Japanese*, 502–4.

5. Thomas P. Rohlen, *Japan's High Schools* (Berkeley: University of California Press, 1983), 54.

6. Beardsley, Hall, and Ward, *Village Japan*, 301.

7. Only 10 percent of Japanese boys were able to pass the rigorous exams and enter government middle schools. From that group, about 19 percent went on to high school. John Whitney Hall and Richard K. Beardsley, *Twelve Doors to Japan* (New York: McGraw-Hill, 1965), 403.

8. Ibid., 404.

9. Takie Sugiyama Lebra, *Japanese Women: Constraint and Fulfillment* (Honolulu: University of Hawaii Press, 1984), 59.

Chapter 3. Japanese Women

1. This is a reference to the more independent behavior of Americans.

2. Chamberlain, *Things Japanese*, 502–4.

3. Ibid., 504.

4. H. V. Straelen, *The Japanese Woman Looking Forward* (Tokyo: Kyo Bun Kwan, 1940), 65, 69.

5. Ibid., 106.

6. Beardsley, Hall, and Ward, *Village Japan*, 222, 229.

7. Chamberlain, *Things Japanese*, 507.

Chapter 4. Thoughts of America

1. Millis, *The Japanese Problem*, 8.

2. Kazuo Ito, *Issei: A History of Japanese Immigrants in North America*, trans. Shinichiro Nakamura and Jean S. Gerard (Seattle: Executive Committee for Publication of Issei, 1973), 5; Yosaburo Yoshida, "Sources and Causes of Japanese Emigration," *Annals of the American Academy of Political and Social Science* 34 (September 1909): 384.

3. Wilson and Hosokawa, *East to America*, 46–48; John Modell, "Tradition and Opportunity: The Japanese Immigrants in America," *Pacific Historical Review* 40 (May 1971): 165.

4. Ichihashi, *Japanese in the United States*, 9.

5. Roger Daniels, *Concentration Camps North America: Japanese in the United States and Canada during World War II* (Malabar, Fla.: Robert E. Krieger, 1981), 6; Hilary Conroy, *The Japanese Frontier in Hawaii, 1869–1898* (Berkeley: University of California Press, 1953), 82–83.

6. Yoshida, "Sources and Causes of Japanese Emigration," 379.

7. Ibid., 380.

8. Japanese American Citizens' League [hereafter JACL], Mid-Columbia Chapter, Issei Story Committee (Mamoru Noji, chairman), "Japanese-Issei Story," Spring 1961, 1, Hood River County Museum, Hood River, Oreg.

9. Ichihashi, *Japanese in the United States*, 13.

10. Millis, *The Japanese Problem*, 6.

11. Wilson and Hosokawa, *East to America*, 54; Roger Daniels, *Politics of Prejudice* (Berkeley: University of California Press, 1962), 32–45.

12. Daniels, *Concentration Camps*, 21.

13. An 1889 amendment to a Japanese conscription law made all males eligible for military service. For many Japanese, this was an incentive to leave Japan, particularly as student laborers.

Chapter 5. Marriage

1. K. K. Kawakami, *The Real Japanese Question* (New York: Macmillan, 1921), 72.

2. Straelen, *The Japanese Woman Looking Forward*, 129.

3. Chamberlain, *Things Japanese*, 503.

4. Mr. Yamaki had lived in his future wife's home for ten years while learning about the family's silkworm business.

5. Mrs. Nakamura was paying homage to spirits of her ancestors.

6. Japanese spouses typically addressed each other according to their relationships to their children, for example, Papa, Grandma. The *o-* is honorific.

7. Since Mrs. Nakamura's father and eldest brother had both died, her second brother had become head of the household.

8. See Chamberlain, *Things Japanese*, 311.

9. White was the color of mourning, symbolizing the wife's death in her own family when she entered the household of her husband.

10. *Shin Sekai*, July 8, 1915, cited in Yuji Ichioka, "Amerika Nadeshiko: Japanese Immigrant Women in the United States, 1900–1924," *Pacific Historical Review* 49 (May 1980): 344.

11. Ichioka, "Japanese Immigrant Women," 344.

12. In the 1880s, a movement was begun to relieve women of the burden of heavily greased, ancient hairstyles. According to the Ladies' Society for Foreign Hair Styles, formed in 1885, these styles "are unhealthy because they often cause dizzy spells and the rushing of blood to the head." See Keizo Shibusawa, ed., *Japanese Life and Culture in the Meiji Era*, trans. Charles S. Terry (Tokyo: Toyo Bunko, 1969), 38.

13. Women's standards of beauty, fashionable from the Edo Period (1600–1868), included "a small mouth, eyebrows like a crescent moon rising in the mist over a distant mountain, hair like the wing of a wet crow, and a 'Mt. Fuji forehead.'" Japanese at that time admired "rice cake skin," with white powder popular for also concealing facial defects. Traditionally, Japanese women's sensual appeal was most prominently revealed in the napes of their necks. See Kittredge Cherry, *Womansword: What Japanese Words Say about Women* (Tokyo: Kodansha International, 1989), 20–21.

14. The Gentlemen's Agreement of 1907–8 allowed family members of those already residing in the United States to enter the country.

Chapter 6. Leaving Japan

1. Yoshida, "Sources and Causes of Japanese Emigration," 384.

2. Ichihashi, *Japanese in the United States,* 74, 77.

3. Ito, *Issei*, 12.

4. Dunn, *Everyday Life in Traditional Japan*, 59.

5. Mrs. Akiyama's family wanted her to return in ten years for her father's sixty-first birthday, celebrated in Japan. Japanese considered youth to extend from birth to the age of twenty, middle age from twenty to forty, and old age from forty to sixty. Reaching the age of sixty-one and beginning another cycle was thus con-

sidered an extraordinary event. See Chamberlain, *Things Japanese*, 62–63. Mrs. Akiyama was not able to return to Japan until 1971, after fifty-six years in the United States.

Chapter 7. Sailing to America

1. Wilson and Hosokawa, *East to America*, 54.

2. Ito, *Issei*, 12, 88. Between 1930 and 1937, the Canadian government's illegal Japanese Entry Investigation Committee reported that 145 Japanese smugglers were deported. This is very likely a small number compared with those who eluded the government. Ito's book includes a chapter of personal accounts by Issei who entered the United States through secret passage and ship jumping. Linda Tamura, "*Grandma Noji*" (unpublished manuscript, August 1984), relates how a Hood River Issei provided residence for a former stowaway in Hood River.

3. Daniels, *Politics of Prejudice*, 7.

4. *Maru*, meaning *round*, was attached to the names of all merchant vessels. The word was most likely confused at one time with *maro*, an archaic term of endearment. See Chamberlain, *Things Japanese*, 314.

5. Most Buddhist families did not eat meat from laboring animals and were also unfamiliar with dairy products.

6. Japanese spouses commonly addressed each other by parental terms used by their children.

Chapter 8. First Impressions

1. Many Japanese preferred sugar to the unfamiliar butter, which smelled repugnant to them.

2. Personal statements in Ito, *Issei*, 46 and 50, expressed similar views about the physical examinations, asserting that the budget at the immigration center was dependent on a specified number of residents. Other anecdotes reported that two people submitted specimens from the same bowel movement, with one passing and the other being detained.

3. Ichioka, "Japanese Immigrant Women," 346–47.

4. Ibid., 347. Among the four picture brides interviewed for this project, age differences with spouses were 7, 10, 11, and 13 years, with an average of 10 years' difference. For the other ten interviewees, involving nine couples, differences in spouses' ages ranged from 4 to 14 years, with an average of 7.8 years.

5. Susan McCoin Kataoka, "Issei Women: A Study in Subordinate Status" (Ph.D. diss., University of California, Los Angeles, 1977), 163. The eleven interviewed women had an average of seven and a half years of school, ranging from one to ten years.

6. Eileen Sunada Sarasohn, *The Issei: Portrait of a Pioneer, an Oral History* (Palo Alto, Calif.: Pacific Books, 1983), 27.

7. Ichioka, "Japanese Immigrant Women," 346.

8. This is a greeting extended when meeting someone for the first time. The *o-* is honorific.

9. Ichioka, "Japanese Immigrant Women," 347.

10. U.S. Bureau of the Census, *Thirteenth Census; Fourteenth Census.*

11. Ichioka, "Japanese Immigrant Women," 343.

12. *Beikoku Nikei-jin Hyakunen-shi [One Hundred Years of Japanese Americans]* (San Francisco: Shin Nichibei Shimbun-sha, 1961), in a section orally translated by Consul Shigenobu Suzuki, Japanese consulate in Portland, Oregon.

13. Roger Daniels, *Asian America: Chinese and Japanese in the United States since 1850* (Seattle: University of Washington Press, 1988), 147–54.

Chapter 9. The Japanese Methodist Church

1. Harry H. L. Kitano, *Japanese Americans: The Evolution of a Subculture* (Englewood Cliffs, N.J.: Prentice-Hall, 1976), 59.

2. Bill Hosokawa, *Nisei: The Quiet Americans* (New York: William Morrow, 1969), 129.

3. Ibid., 126.

4. *History of Epworth United Methodist Church, Portland, Oregon*, trans. Yoshimi Kamano; additions by Rev. Shinya Maruya. (Portland, Oreg.: Epworth Methodist Church, 1982).

5. Stories circulated about Issei designating boxes for their savings. One thousand dollars at one time was considered the amount that would allow them to return to Japan and live comfortably.

6. Kitano, *Japanese Americans*, 59; Ichihashi, *Japanese in the United States*, 110–14.

7. Mr. Tomita was referring to the name given to the Portland Methodist Church in 1968. By that time, it had moved to its present location at 133 S.E. Twenty-eighth in Portland.

8. Gerry Frank, "Surprise! It's Friday Already and Time for Page in History," *The Oregonian*, July 26, 1991, 26.

Chapter 10. Adjustments to American Life

1. *Hood River News*, 1921 issues.

Chapter 11. Railroads, Stumps, and Sawmills

1. Daniels, *Politics of Prejudice*, 8, 19.

2. Wilson and Hosokawa, *East to America*, 116.

3. U.S. Bureau of the Census, *Twelfth Census*. Millis, *The Japanese Problem*, 25–26, credits Washington with one-sixth of the Japanese population; actual calculations amount to one-fifth.

4. Millis, *The Japanese Problem*, 38–39. These undated figures were considerably lower than the wages reported for mission boys in chapter 9, herein. See Ichihashi, *Japanese in the United States*, 110–14.

5. Ito, *Issei*, 33.

6. Wilson and Hosokawa, *East to America*, 72.

7. Barbara Yasui, "The Nikkei in Oregon, 1834–1940," *Oregon Historical Quarterly* 76 (September 1975): 229.

8. Wilson and Hosokawa, *East to America*, 73.

9. Ito, *Issei*, 790–92.

10. Marvin Gavin Pursinger, "The Japanese Settle in Oregon: 1880–1920," *Journal of the West* 5 (April 1966): 252.

11. Yasui, "The Nikkei in Oregon," 230.

12. Statement by Mr. Otoichi Nishimoto in Ito, *Issei,* 318. Mr. Nishimoto, who died in 1982, was the husband of Mrs. Hatsumi Nishimoto.

13. Jack Cramer, "We, Too, Please, Are 100 Percent Americans," interview with Minoru Yasui, *Sunday Oregonian,* February 4, 1940, 5. At the time of the 1940 interview, Minoru Yasui, son of a Hood River merchant, had become the first Japanese admitted to the Oregon bar. He was national chairperson for the Legislative Education Committee of the Japanese American Citizens' League until his death in December 1986.

14. Ray T. Yasui, unabridged and unedited transcript of taped statement to Barbara Yasui, 1971, Ethnology Collection, MSS 1521, 3, Oregon Historical Society, Portland, Oreg.

15. Wilson and Hosokawa, *East to America,* 75.

16. Yasui, "The Nikkei in Oregon," 230.

17. Wilson and Hosokawa, *East to America,* 75, 116.

18. U.S. Immigration Commission, *Immigrants in Industries,* vol. 25 of *Reports of the Immigration Commission* (Washington, D.C.: Government Printing Office, 1911), 21, cited in S. Frank Miyamoto, "The Japanese Minority in the Pacific Northwest," *Pacific Northwest Quarterly* 54 (October 1963): 144.

19. State of Oregon, "First Biennial Report of the Bureau of Labor Statistics for Oregon," 1905, 74, cited in Marvin Gavin Pursinger, "Oregon's Japanese in World War II: A History of Compulsory Relocation" (Ph.D. diss., University of Southern California, 1961), 5.

20. Millis, *The Japanese Problem,* 32.

21. Hood River County Historical Society, *History of Hood River County* (Dallas: Taylor Publishing, 1982), 11–14, 38.

22. Yasui, transcript, 2; JACL, Mid-Columbia, "Japanese-Issei Story," 1; Hood River County Historical Society, *History,* 13.

23. Yasui, transcript, 1.

24. Ito, *Issei,* 485.

25. Guppy, "Japanese Hood River Story," 2.

26. JACL, Mid-Columbia, "Japanese-Issei Story," 3.

27. Because the plentiful timber had little economic value, it was burned in piles with little thought.

28. Wilson and Hosokawa, *East to America,* 75–76.

29. Miyamoto, "Japanese Minority in the Pacific Northwest," 145.

30. Millis, *The Japanese Problem,* 38.

31. Hood River County Historical Society, *History,* 22.

32. The Oregon Lumber Company, which built the Dee Sawmill and Mt. Hood Railroad, was owned by the David Eccles family, Mormons from Ogden, Utah.

33. Tom Inukai, interview, August 3, 1986, Odell, Oreg.

34. U.S. Bureau of the Census, *Thirteenth Census.* See also Appendix A herein.

Chapter 12. Early Farm Labor

1. Kitano, *Japanese Americans*, 17; Millis, *The Japanese Problem*, 80.

2. Yasui, "Nikkei in Oregon," 241. The second of the Yasui sons, Fujimoto, had became a *yoshi*, adopted son of his aunt, and thus had taken a new family name.

3. Maija Yasui, "Brothers' Store Rich Cultural Center," in *Panorama '91* (Hood River, Oreg.: Hood River News, April 17, 1991), 17–18.

4. Robert S. Yasui, *The Yasui Family of Hood River, Oregon* (n.p.: Holly Yasui Desktop Publishing, 1987), 4–5.

5. Yasui arranged labor contracts between Caucasians and Japanese laborers and lent Issei money for down payments on property, in exchange for a share of their land. He eventually held an interest in one of ten boxes of apples and pears produced in the valley. Yasui, "The Nikkei in Oregon," 241; Yasui, *The Yasui Family of Hood River, Oregon*, 11. Min Yasui stated that his father and uncle had "a half or a third, or some shares in probably about a thousand acres of farm and orchard lands in the valley, besides owning outright several hundreds of acres of farms." John Tateishi, *And Justice for All: An Oral History of the Japanese American Detention Camps* (New York: Random House, 1984), 64.

6. Hood River County Historical Society, *History*, 60–61.

7. The dike had been built in 1910 to protect low riverfront farmland from the high waters of the Columbia.

8. The Morita family owned a Japanese restaurant and bathhouse near the railroad station in the town of Hood River.

9. Timothy J. Lukes and Gary Y. Okihiro, *Japanese Legacy: Farming and Community Life in California's Santa Clara Valley* (Cupertino, Calif.: California History Center, 1985).

10. Millis, *The Japanese Problem*, 98–99.

11. Hood River County Historical Society, *History*, 42.

12. Millis, *The Japanese Problem*, 100–101.

13. Lukes and Okihiro, *Japanese Legacy*, 56.

14. *Hood River Glacier* [hereafter *Glacier*], October 7, 1920.

Chapter 13. Issei Acquisition of Orchards

1. By 1905, 35 percent of Issei had become farmers, 26 percent worked on the railroad, 10 percent were employed as cooks and house servants, and the rest worked as woodchoppers, students, merchants, and housewives. Pursinger, "The Japanese Settle in Oregon," 253.

2. Interview with Clem Pope, Hood River resident and later president of the Hood River Historical Society, July 2, 1986.

3. *Index to Deeds—Indirect, Hood River County, Oregon*, Book 1, 126, Hood River County Courthouse, Hood River, Oreg.

4. Tamura, "Grandma Noji," 25.

5. Wendy Lee Ng, "Collective Memory, Social Networks, and Generations: The Japanese American Community in Hood River, Oregon" (Ph.D. diss., University of Oregon, 1989), 21.

6. State of Oregon, *Report on the Japanese Situation in Oregon,* 14.

7. Millis, *The Japanese Problem,* 98.

8. Lukes and Okihiro, *Japanese Legacy,* 5, 31.

9. Letter from Lindsay Buckner, President–General Manager, Diamond Fruit Growers, July 23, 1986.

10. Hood River County Historical Society, *History,* 38.

11. Yasui, "Nikkei in Oregon," 247.

12. Water flowing in a wooden flume was directed into smaller flumes that supplied private property. By lifting a wooden weir (measuring device), owners regulated the amount of water flowing into their property. They were entitled to one-half inch of water per acre.

13. Ng, "Collective Memory, Social Networks, and Generations," 27–28.

14. Daughter Hana Kinoshita noted that because of Prohibition, effective in 1920, the hops price "dropped to nothing, so Dad was left holding the bag." Mr. Wakamatsu gave his share to his father, enabling him to return to Japan.

15. U.S. Bureau of the Census, *Fourteenth Census.* Statistics from the Bureau of Labor differ, giving the 1920 Japanese population in Hood River as 383.

16. Oregon Bureau of Labor, *Japanese Population in Oregon* (Salem: State Printing Office, 1920), Table I.

17. Report of T. Abe, president of the Japanese Association of Oregon, cited in *Glacier,* October 5, 1920.

18. Cramer, "We, Too, Please," 5; *Glacier,* August 5, 1920.

Chapter 14. Anti-Japanese Sentiments

1. Daniels, *Politics of Prejudice,* 21–27.

2. Ibid., 39–44.

3. Ibid., 46.

4. Commission on Wartime Relocation and Internment of Civilians [hereafter CWRIC], *Personal Justice Denied* (Washington, D.C.: Government Printing Office, 1982), 34.

5. Marjorie R. Stearns, "The History of the Japanese People in Oregon" (Master's thesis, University of Oregon, 1937), 11; U.S. War Relocation Authority, *Prejudice in Hood River Valley: A Case Study in Race Relations,* Community Analysis Report No. 13 (Washington, D.C.: June 6, 1945), 3. Confirming figures were unavailable at Diamond Fruit Growers, previously the Apple Growers' Association.

6. Editorial, *Hood River News* [hereafter *News*], September 10, 1919, 4.

7. Although this comment was made about a purchase made in 1930, it indicates a persistent concern.

8. *News,* October 8, 1919, 1. Confirming figures were unavailable at the Oregon Vital Records Office. Among the thirteen couples represented by interviewees in this project, the number of children ranged from two to ten, with six of the couples having five children.

9. This incident also occurred in the 1930s, reflecting a continuing concern for Japanese family labor.

10. Editorial, *News,* September 10, 1919, 4.

11. Richard L. Neuberger, "Their Brothers' Keepers," *Saturday Review of Literature* 29 (August 10, 1946): 28.

12. Beatrice Stevens, "Free and Equal? The Japanese-Americans in Oregon," a unit of work for secondary schools prepared for the Workshop on Intercultural Education, Portland, Summer 1945, appendix, 35, Oregon Historical Society, Portland, Oreg.

13. Mr. Tomita actually purchased his property in 1938. He and his wife became Methodists but not until 1947.

14. *News*, September 10, 1919, 4.

15. Ibid., January 17, 1917, 1, 7; February 17, 1917.

16. Ibid., September 24, 1919, 1.

17. *Glacier*, September 11, 1919.

18. *News*, September 10, 1919, 1.

19. State of Oregon, *Report on the Japanese Situation*, 9.

20. *News*, September 19, 1919, 1; October 8, 1919, 1.

21. Ibid., September 17, 1919, 1; *Glacier*, September 18, 1919, 1.

22. *Glacier*, October 9, 1919, 1.

23. Ibid., November 6, 1919, 1.

24. *News*, November 14, 1919, 1.

25. Ibid., June 16, 1920, 1; January 23, 1920, 1.

26. *Glacier*, February 5, 1920, 1.

27. State of Oregon, *Report on the Japanese Situation*, 10.

28. Ibid.; Wilson and Hosokawa, *East to America*, 62–63.

29. Pursinger, "The Japanese Settle in Oregon," 258–60.

30. State of Oregon, *Report on the Japanese Situation*, 6.

31. Stearns, "The History of the Japanese People in Oregon," 17.

32. Oregon Bureau of Labor Statistics, *Second Biennial Report*, 1907, cited in Stearns, "The History of the Japanese People in Oregon," 17.

33. State of Oregon, *Report on the Japanese Situation*, 7.

34. Ibid., 9.

35. Ibid., 8, 9.

36. Ibid., 15.

37. U.S. War Relocation Authority, *Prejudice in Hood River Valley*, 4.

38. Editorial, *News*, February 2, 1923, 4.

39. Editorial, *Glacier*, November 6, 1919, 2.

40. Pursinger, "Oregon's Japanese in World War II," 37–38.

41. Ichihashi, *Japanese in the United States*, 16.

42. U.S. Bureau of the Census, *Thirteenth, Fourteenth, Fifteenth, Sixteenth Census of the United States*. See also Appendix A herein.

Chapter 15. Issei Women

1. Chamberlain, *Things Japanese*, 500–504.

2. Yuji Ichioka, *The Issei: The World of the First Generation Japanese Immigrants, 1885–1924* (New York: Free Press, 1988), 168–69.

3. Evelyn Nakano Glenn, *Issei, Nisei, Warbride: Three Generations of Japanese American Women in Domestic Service* (Philadelphia: Temple University Press, 1986), 72–74.

4. Daniels, *Asian America*, 157.

5. JACL, Mid-Columbia Chapter, "Japanese-Issei Story," 3.

6. Lukes and Okihiro, *Japanese Legacy*, 55–56.

7. Lebra, *Japanese Women*, 131.

8. Trees were sprayed using a pump sprayer with two hoses and spray guns attached.

9. Chamberlain, *Things Japanese*, 503.

10. Glenn, *Issei, Nisei, Warbride*, 52.

11. Ibid., 72–74.

12. JACL, Mid-Columbia Chapter, "Japanese-Issei Story," 2.

13. Statement by Mr. Henry H. Nakamura in Ito, *Issei*, 500. Mr. Nakamura was the husband of Mrs. Misuyo Nakamura.

14. Ichioka, *The Issei*, 172.

15. Daniels, *Asian America*, 155–56.

16. According to a tabulation of residents of Dee, Hood River, Mt. Hood, and Parkdale, the Issei population consisted of the following: 180 married, 22 single, 5 widowed, and 1 divorced, for a total of 208 Issei and 265 Nisei. Oregon Bureau of Labor, *Census: Population in Oregon* (Salem: State Printing Department, 1929).

17. Emma Gee, "Issei: The First Women," In *Asian Women* (Berkeley: University of California Press, 1971), 14.

18. Millis, *The Japanese Problem*, 261.

Chapter 16. Yoshi Marriages

1. See the section on adopted sons in chapter 5.

Chapter 17. Japanese Families in America

1. Kitano, *Japanese Americans*, 33–34.

2. Wilson and Hosokawa, *East to America*, 168.

3. S. Frank Miyamoto, "An Immigrant Community in America," in *East across the Pacific: Historical and Sociological Studies of Japanese Immigration and Assimilation*, ed. Hilary Conroy and T. Scott Miyakawa (Santa Barbara, Calif.: American Biographical Center Clio Press, 1972), 235.

4. Wilson and Hosokawa, *East to America*, 163–65.

5. Kitano, *Japanese Americans*, 43.

6. The Yumibes' eldest son did indeed become a physician.

7. The Endows' youngest son, Bill, became a mechanical engineer for CGE in Las Vegas.

8. The Nojis' eldest son, Mamoru, served as a Japanese language translator in the Pacific during World War II. He became a successful orchardist and was named Hood River Orchardist of the Year in 1969.

Chapter 18. The Hood River Japanese Community

1. Kesa Noda, *Yamato Colony: 1906–1960* (Livingston, Calif.: JACL, Livingston-Merced Chapter, 1979), xiii.

2. Kazuko Nakane, *Nothing Left in My Hands: An Early Japanese American Community in Pajaro Valley* (Seattle: Young Pine Press, 1985), 48.

3. Lane Ryo Hirabayashi and George Tanaka, "The Issei Community in Moneta and the Gardena Valley, 1900–1920," *Southern California Quarterly* 70, no. 2 (1988): 127.

4. Ng, "Collective Memory, Social Networks, and Generations," 5.

5. Kitano, *Japanese Americans*, 53.

6. JACL, Mid-Columbia Chapter, "Japanese-Issei Story," 3.

7. Hirabayashi and Tanaka, "The Issei Community," 145–46.

8. The English name was changed from Hood River Japanese Farmers' Association to Japanese Farmers' Association of Hood River at the January 26, 1915, meeting.

9. The cofounders were Suekichi Ishikawa, Asaji Itami, Kyu Kinoshita, Goro (Sagoro) Asai, and Jinzaemon Tateishi. The first officers were Suekichi Ishikawa, president; Kyu Kinoshita, vice president; and Tadao Sato, treasurer. Minutes of the Japanese Farmers' Association of Hood River and Zairyu Doho Taikai, 1914–24, trans. Yoko Gulde, 1–3, Kusaji Family Collection.

10. Japanese Farmers' Association, Minutes, March 1, 1914, 6–7.

11. According to the association minutes on March 6, 1916, 38, Wilmer Sieg gave the following crate prices for strawberries: the average price in 1913 was $3.61, with competition driving the price to $2.06 in 1914 and to $1.12 in 1915. Wilmer Sieg was sales manager of the AGA from 1912 to 1916; and A. W. Stone was general manager from 1914 to 1922, as noted in a July 23, 1986 letter from Lindsay Buckner, president–general manager of Diamond Fruit Growers (previously the Apple Growers' Association).

12. Japanese Farmers' Association, Minutes, December 26, 1915, 23.

13. Ibid., February 18, 1921, 61.

14. Ibid., 64. Oregon's Alien Land Law, prohibiting Japanese from owning or leasing land, passed in 1923.

15. In 1916, the association approved the following plan of assistance: death or permanent disability, send five dollars with a letter; severe injury or illness requiring hospitalization, send three dollars and a letter; illness treated at home, send a letter; and in the case of a family member, same as members. For a *hakujin* who had been helpful to them, they endorsed the following plan: death, send flowers; illness or injury, send a letter. The system was revised in 1925: if member or family was hospitalized over two weeks, send a letter; death, send five dollars worth of flowers with an association leader expressing sympathy at the funeral; fire, send a letter. Japanese Farmers' Association, Minutes, December 9, 1916, 55–56; January 18, 1925, 107.

16. In 1917, $159 was collected from 112 members, with $61.85 designated for the cemetary fund and $62.50 for the appreciation fund. Japanese Farmers' Association, Minutes, February 4, 1917, 113–17.

17. At the February 4, 1922, meeting, it was decided that five women would cook for each meeting. Japanese Farmers' Association, Minutes, February 4, 1922, 74.

18. Mr. Sagoro Asai, also a cofounder of the Japanese Farmers' Association of Hood River, farmed in Oak Grove with his wife and eight children. In 1969, he would posthumously receive the Sixth Class Order of the Sacred Treasure of the

Emperor of Japan for sixty-five years of promoting Japanese-American relationships in the valley. Hood River County Historical Society, *History*, 104.

19. Miyamoto, "Immigrant Community," 231.

20. Bill Hosokawa, *Nisei: The Quiet Americans* (New York: William Morrow, 1969), 155.

21. Okayama is a prefecture in southwestern Honshu, the main island of Japan; Kyushu is the southernmost of Japan's four main islands.

22. Zairyu Doho Taikai, Minutes, January 18, 1925, 104–5. After Mr. Yasui's two-hour meeting, the school superintendent had agreed to investigate the use of schoolrooms for Japanese language classes during the winter. No reference was made to the results, but subsequent classes apparently met in Issei homes. Zairyu Doho Taikai, Minutes, March 22, 1925, 150–51. See Appendix B herein.

23. Ibid., February 1, 1925, 13. The Zairyu Doho Taikai of Hood River had held its meetings at the town's Knights of Pythias hall for over a decade. The original proposal to acquire a meeting hall and Japanese school was made at the association's January 18, 1925, meeting by the president on behalf of Mr. Tokuzo Takasumi, absent due to an eye illness. The plan called for a permanent, live-in Japanese teacher and students' boarding section, at an estimated cost of ten thousand dollars. Zairyu Doho Taikai, Minutes, January 18, 1925, 103. See Appendix B herein.

24. Ibid., February 1, 1925, 144.

25. Ibid., July 27, 1925, 172–81. The committee elected the following leaders: Mr. Masuo Yasui, chair; Mr. Katsusaburo Tamura, treasurer; and Mr. Tomeji Katayama, vice chair. Mr. Tamura, my grandfather, arrived in Portland in 1907, where he learned to speak and read English at the YMCA and was converted to Christianity, serving as piano and organ accompanist at the church. After returning to Japan in 1913 to marry the daughter of an officer in the Japanese Imperial Army, he and my grandmother settled in Portland, where he continued to work as a lens grinder for a jeweler. In 1918, the Tamura family moved to Hood River where they raised apples, pears, and strawberries. Grandpa was active in the Japanese Methodist church and assisted Issei in their citizenship classes after the war.

26. By the end of World War II, the old building had reportedly become a burden to the community. The Japanese American Citizens' League sold it for approximately eight thousand dollars.

27. *Sensei* is a respectful term of address for teachers and ministers, among others.

28. Conversation with the late Mrs. Chiye Sakamoto, former Dee resident whose family had donated property for the Dee Community Hall, August 3, 1986, January 2, 1987.

29. John F. Embree, *Suye Mura: A Japanese Village* (Chicago: University of Chicago Press, 1939), 238.

30. Mei Nakano, *Japanese American Women: Three Generations, 1890–1900* (Berkeley, Calif.: Mina Press, 1990), 52.

31. Incense was burned to purify the mind and body.

32. Mock Joya, *Quaint Customs and Manners of Japan* (Tokyo: Tokyo News Service, 1951), 50.

33. Millis, *The Japanese Problem,* 267.

34. *Fiftieth Anniversary Program* (Hood River, Oreg.: Japanese Methodist Church, May 1976). Mr. Kamegoro Iwatsuki immigrated to Hood River in 1906 and, four years later, purchased and cleared ten acres of timberland in Odell, where he planted apples and strawberries. His wife, Shizue, arrived in 1916 and became a leading Issei citizen. In 1923, Mrs. Iwatsuki organized the Japanese Women's Society to teach American customs to newly arrived Japanese brides; after the war, she began the Japanese Christian Women's Society. To perpetuate Japanese arts, she also taught Japanese flower arrangement classes to both Caucasian and Japanese women in the valley. In 1974, she was one of ten citizens invited to recite their prize-winning tanka poems at the Japanese Emperor's Palace. That year Hood River County chose her to be Woman of the Year. Hood River County Historical Society, *History,* 244.

35. Rev. Isaac Inouye received his education at a Methodist seminary in Kobe, Japan, and served on the island of Shikoku before coming to the United States. He earned his A.B. and M.A. degrees at Emory University, his M.R.E. at Boston University, and his M.A. in education at Harvard University. He would serve fifty-seven years in the Methodist church before his retirement in 1960. *The United Methodist Church Journal and Yearbook,* 133rd Session, California-Nevada Annual Conference (Dallas: TM/UMR Productions, June 1981), 298.

36. *Fiftieth Anniversary Program.*

37. Local Japanese Methodists donated $3,500 to the downtown Asbury Methodist Church's remodeling project. In return, the church made facilities available to the Japanese congregation, and a prayer chapel room was named *Izumi,* or "living water." *Fiftieth Anniversary Program.*

38. In 1917, George Wilbur, the "Mikado," would submit the first Oregon bill to prevent Japanese ownership of land. *News,* June 25, 1914, 1; July 2, 1914, 2; July 9, 1914, 1.

39. Guppy, "Japanese Hood River Story," 3.

40. Japanese Farmers' Association, Minutes, July 31, 1921, 67.

Chapter 19. Celebrations

1. Helen Bauer and Sherwin Carlquist, *Japanese Festivals* (Tokyo: Charles E. Tuttle, 1985), 81–89.

2. Ibid., 73–74.

3. Originally, dolls were considered images of gods or human beings and were used to protect against sickness and evil. On country outings, families would cast paper dolls into the rivers to rid themselves of sickness and ill fortune. Ibid., 72.

4. Ibid., 69.

5. *Koi* were considered courageous fish that could swim up waterfalls and, even on the carving board, accept the knife without flinching.

6. Embree, *Suye Mura,* 219.

7. Bauer and Carlquist, *Japanese Festivals,* 59.

8. Soon after Mrs. Nakamura related this fable, she requested time to check its accuracy. Her original words are thus edited slightly, based on written text supplied by her minister.

9. Japanese in America adopted chow mein as their own dish, combining fried noodles with thin strips of assorted vegetables and meats and serving the popular dish on special occasions.

Chapter 20. Trying Times

1. Mr. Tomita's employer was an officer in the local Anti-Alien Association.
2. Yasui, "Nikkei in Oregon," 248.
3. U.S. Bureau of the Census, *Sixteenth Census;* Daniels, *Concentration Camps,* 1.
4. CWRIC, *Personal Justice Denied,* 122.
5. U.S. Bureau of the Census, *Sixteenth Census.*

Chapter 21. Pearl Harbor Sunday

1. CWRIC, *Personal Justice Denied,* 47.
2. At least five deaths resulted from retaliation against Japanese after Pearl Harbor. Cases of shootings and stabbings were recorded in California as well as Illinois and Utah. Jacobus tenBroek, Edward N. Barnhart, and Floyd W. Matson, *Prejudice, War and the Constitution* (Berkeley: University of California Press, 1954), 72.
3. Mitzi Asai Loftus, *Made in Japan and Settled in Oregon* (Coos Bay, Oreg.: Pigeon Point Press, 1990), 88–89.
4. Dorothy Swaine Thomas and Richard S. Nishimoto, *The Spoilage: Japanese American Evacuation* (Berkeley: University of California Press, 1946), 5, 20.
5. After the war, Mrs. Akiyama's letters were returned to the head of the local JACL chapter, Kumeo Yoshinari.

Chapter 22. Precautions

1. Daniels, *Concentration Camps,* 33; *The Oregonian,* December 12, 1941, 19; *Hillsboro Argus,* December 25, 1941, cited in Timothy Olmstead, "Nikkei Internment: The Perspective of Two Oregon Weekly Newspapers," *Oregon Historical Quarterly* 85 (Spring 1984): 9.
2. tenBroek, Barnhart, and Matson, *Prejudice, War and the Constitution,* 70.
3. *News,* December 12, 1941, 1.
4. Ibid., December 17, 1941, 1.
5. Ibid., March 27, 1942, 1.
6. Ibid., December 12, 1941, 1; December 19, 1941, 1.
7. Ibid., January 2, 1942, 1. According to Mitzi Asai Loftus, contraband items were returned after the war, with the exception of guns, explosives, and swords. Some Japanese later recognized their own guns or rifles in the collections of private auction customers or friends of the sheriff. Loftus, *Made in Japan,* 95.
8. *News,* January 2, 1942, 1.
9. *Hood River County Sun* [hereafter *Sun*], December 12, 1941, 3.

10. *News*, December 12, 1941, 2.

11. In a cover letter enclosed with the pledge, Rev. Isaac Inouye, minister of the Hood River Japanese Methodist Church, added a handwritten postscript that two additional Nisei were to be inducted into the army, bringing the total to sixteen.

12. Governor Sprague letters, Sprague Manuscripts, Oregon Historical Society, Portland, Oreg.

13. Mrs. Max L. [Arline Winchell] Moore, Letter to Howard D. Samuel, Editor-in-chief, *The Dartmouth* (Hanover, N.H.), April 15, 1947, 1. In preparing a series on the American Legion, Mr. Samuel had requested information about discriminatory actions of the American Legion in Hood River in a letter written to Mr. Mamoru Noji on March 7, 1947. Since Noji had been serving in the Pacific at the time, he forwarded the letter to Mrs. Moore.

14. Ibid., 1.

15. *News*, January 30, 1942, 1.

16. CWRIC, *Personal Justice Denied*, 62.

17. *News*, February 13, 1942, 1.

18. Mr. Nishimoto and three other Japanese men were transported from the Hood River courthouse to the Portland jail and then apparently to Montana. Meals were subpar, with beans served frequently, but the men were treated decently. Since Mr. Nishimoto was, according to his wife, a man of few words, he related little about his experiences. On May 9, 1942, three days before the evacuation of the Hood River Japanese, Mr. Nishimoto returned.

19. This was reported in the *Hood River News*, February 13, 1942, 1. As noted earlier, however, Mrs. Hatsumi Nishimoto recalled that her husband was actually jailed because the FBI located one small bullet, not stumping powder, on the couple's property.

20. Ibid., 1.

21. Ibid., 10.

22. CWRIC, *Personal Justice Denied*, 88.

Chapter 23. Executive Order 9066

1. CWRIC, *Personal Justice Denied*, 82.

2. Daniels, *Concentration Camps*, 35.

3. Ibid., 35; CWRIC, *Personal Justice Denied*, 55–56.

4. CWRIC, *Personal Justice Denied*, 52–55, 83; Daniels, *Asian America*, 211–12.

5. Pursinger, "Oregon's Japanese in World War II," 104.

6. The Oliver Plan, submitted by Clarence Oliver, a Portland high school teacher, proposed that the governor appoint a committee of prominent citizens to serve as guardians of Oregon Japanese and work in cooperation with the Japanese American Citizens' League (JACL). C. B. Lewis, a Portland nurseryman, requested that the government select a statewide advisory committee to devise a plan wherein Japanese would volunteer to relocate east of the Cascade Mountains and be employed in federal work projects. Pursinger, "Oregon's Japanese in World War II," 71–75.

7. Ibid., 76; Governor Sprague, letter to Clarence E. Oliver, January 8, 1942, Sprague Manuscripts, Oregon Historical Society, Portland, Oreg.

8. Governor Sprague, telegram to U.S. Attorney General Francis Biddle, February 8, 1942, Sprague Manuscripts, Oregon Historical Society, Portland, Oreg.

9. *News*, February 27, 1942, 1.

10. Pursinger, "Oregon's Japanese in World War II," 134.

11. Pursinger noted that, in a 1957 interview, Sprague confessed that "his silent inactivity which became de facto silent concurrence in the movement and relocation of the Japanese was the single public act of his administration as governor he most regretted." Pursinger, "Oregon's Japanese in World War II," 104; see also 103–4, 134, 155.

12. CWRIC, *Personal Justice Denied*, 70.

13. Wilson and Hosokawa, *East to America*, 203–4.

14. *Sun*, February 13, 1942, 6.

15. Moore, Letter to Howard D. Samuel, 2.

16. Daniels, *Concentration Camps*, 208.

17. Ibid., 72–73, 81–82. San Francisco mayor Angelo J. Rossi insisted that German and Italian aliens "should be considered separately from . . . Japanese." Attorney Chauncey Tramutolo pled that evacuating [people like the] DiMaggios, parents of three famous baseball players, would "present a serious situation." Ibid., 75.

18. *Sun*, March 6, 1942, 1.

19. Map of Pacific coast defense area, *News*, March 13, 1942, 1.

20. CWRIC, *Personal Justice Denied*, 93.

21. *News*, March 13, 1942, 1.

22. C. D. Nickelsen, letter to U.S. Attorney General Francis Biddle, February 26, 1942, World War II, Japanese Manuscripts, Oregon Historical Society, Portland, Oreg.

23. Dee Lumber and Sawmill Workers' Local Union, letter to Governor Sprague, February 24, 1942, Sprague Manuscripts, Oregon Historical Society, Portland, Oreg.

24. Hood River B.P.O.E. No. 1507, Resolution to Governor Sprague, March 6, 1942, Sprague Manuscripts, Oregon Historical Society, Portland, Oreg.

25. CWRIC, *Personal Justice Denied*, 103.

26. Ibid.

Chapter 24. Disposal of Property and Belongings

1. Arline Winchell Moore, "Hood River Redeems Itself," *Asia and the Americas* 6 (July 1946): 316.

2. CWRIC, *Personal Justice Denied*, 122.

3. U.S. War Relocation Authority, *Prejudice in Hood River Valley*, 8. Hood River Japanese appeared to have fared better than other Japanese regarding property ownership. In Sacramento, the majority of Japanese were tenant farmers who could not afford to purchase their land. In fact, only 20 percent of the Japanese owned urban or rural property. In one county, less than half owned the farms they operated. See Sandra C. Taylor, "The Federal Reserve

Bank and the Relocation of the Japanese in 1942," *Public Historian* 5 (Winter 1983): 20.

4. U.S. War Relocation Authority, *Prejudice in Hood River Valley*, 8.

5. Taylor, "Federal Reserve Bank," 13.

6. *News*, March 13, 1942, 1.

7. Ibid., March 20, 1942, 2.

8. Taylor, "Federal Reserve Bank," 12.

9. Pursinger, "Oregon's Japanese in World War II," 141.

10. *News*, April 3, 1942, 1.

11. Ibid., March 27, 1942, 1.

12. Shig Yamaki, Mrs. Yamaki's son, noted that Mr. Moore paid on the principal and made interest payments on the property loan.

13. *Sun*, April 10, 1942, 6.

Chapter 25. Evacuation

1. Wilson and Hosokawa, *East to America*, 208.

2. *Sun*, April 8, 1942, 1.

3. U.S. Department of the Interior, *The Evacuated People: A Quantitative Description* (Washington, D.C.: Government Printing Office, 1946), 64.

4. *News*, May 15, 1942, 1.

5. *Sun*, May 15, 1942, 1.

6. Pinedale was actually a thousand miles from Hood River.

7. Minoru Yasui had resigned his position at the consulate general of Japan in Chicago after the bombing of Pearl Harbor. The U.S. Supreme Court, after hearing his appeal, ruled against him, deciding that the curfew order was justified by "military necessity." In 1983, Yasui filed a petition of *coram nobis* to reopen his case, based on newly discovered documents revealing that the Justice Department did not regard Japanese Americans as security threats during the war. After Judge Robert C. Belloni of Portland declined to consider the petition, Yasui appealed his petition's dismissal to the Ninth Circuit Court of Appeals. The case was again referred to Belloni, who returned the case to the Ninth Circuit judges. On November 12, 1986, before the case was decided, Yasui died of cancer. Despite his family's move for a Supreme Court review, the Court refused to consider the petition in 1987; with Yasui's death, the case, too, expired. Yasui, *The Yasui Family of Hood River, Oregon*, 58–61; Tateishi, *And Justice for All*, 71–82; Peter Irons, *Justice Delayed: The Record of the Japanese American Internment Cases* (Middletown, Conn.: Wesleyan University Press, 1989), 29–30.

8. *Sun*, May 15, 1942, 5.

Chapter 26. Assembly Centers

1. Ng, "Collective Memory, Social Networks, and Generations," 40.

2. CWRIC, *Personal Justice Denied*, 106, 138.

3. Ibid., 140.

4. Daisuke Kitagawa, *Issei and Nisei: The Internment Years* (New York: Seabury Press, 1967), 64.

5. CWRIC, *Personal Justice Denied*, 142.

6. Toru Noji, letter to Linda Tamura, July 12, 1983.

7. Tamura, "Grandma Noji," 74.

8. Loftus, *Made in Japan,* 108.

9. *Sun,* May 15, 1942, 1.

10. Mrs. Kusachi later joined the family, increasing its number to ten.

11. Pursinger, "Oregon's Japanese in World War II," 167.

12. Minoru Yasui in Tateishi, *And Justice For All,* 73.

13. Pursinger, "Oregon's Japanese in World War II," 165–66.

14. Major Axel V. Boldt, *Final Inspection: Audit of the Messes,* June 12, 1942, WCCA [Wartime Civil Control Authority] 319.1, cited in Pursinger, "Oregon's Japanese in World War II," 173–75.

15. Japanese chefs had been employed at the Arlington Club, University Club, and the Henry Thiele restaurant.

16. CWRIC, *Personal Justice Denied,* 135.

Chapter 27. Camp Tule Lake

1. The ten relocation centers were located at Manzanar, California; Tule Lake, California; Poston, Arizona; Gila, Arizona; Minidoka, Idaho; Heart Mountain, Wyoming; Granada, Colorado; Topaz, Utah; Rohwer, Arkansas; and Jerome, Arkansas. Daniels, *Concentration Camps,* 96.

2. The original plan of Milton Eisenhower, first director of the WRA, was to resettle evacuees voluntarily in the intermountain states, where they would be employed in public works projects, farming, and manufacturing. After opposition from those states' governors, however, the focus of the WRA became confinement rather than resettlement of the Japanese. CWRIC, *Personal Justice Denied,* 152, 155.

3. The 120,313 Japanese under WRA custody included 5,981 births, 1,579 seasonal workers, 1,275 institutionalized individuals transferred to the centers, 1,118 evacuated from Hawaii, and 219 voluntary residents. U.S. Department of the Interior, *The Evacuated People,* 8.

4. Michi Weglyn, *Years of Infamy: The Untold Story of America's Concentration Camps* (New York: Morrow Quill, 1976), 29.

5. *Tule Lake Interlude* (first anniversary edition of *Daily Tulean Dispatch*), May 27, 1943, 34.

6. *Daily Tulean Dispatch,* August 6, 1942, 2.

7. Residents were confined to only a small portion of the thirty-two-thousand-acre site.

8. Thomas and Nishimoto, *The Spoilage,* 28–29.

9. *Tule Lake Interlude,* May 27, 1943, 34.

10. Thomas and Nishimoto, *The Spoilage,* 29.

11. CWRIC, *Personal Justice Denied,* 158.

12. U.S. War Relocation Authority, *Questions and Answers for Evacuees* (Washington, D.C.: Government Printing Office, 1942), 2.

13. *Daily Tulean Dispatch,* September 16, 1942.

14. CWRIC, *Personal Justice Denied,* 163.

15. Ibid.

16. U.S. War Relocation Authority, *Myths and Facts about the Japanese Americans* (Washington, D.C.: Government Printing Office, June 1945), 45.

17. CWRIC, *Personal Justice Denied*, 160.

18. Thomas and Nishimoto, *The Spoilage*, 29.

19. In the coupon book in Mrs. Akiyama's possession, tickets were valued at one cent, two cents, five cents, and ten cents. Scrip books were issued in denominations of $2.25, $3.25, and $3.75. *Daily Tulean Dispatch*, November 12, 1942.

20. Ibid., July 30, 1942, January 1, 1943.

21. CWRIC, *Personal Justice Denied*, 146.

22. Kitagawa, *Issei and Nisei*, 80.

23. CWRIC, *Personal Justice Denied*, 166.

24. *Daily Tulean Dispatch*, May 5, 1943, January 1, 1943.

25. Ibid., August 17, 1942, September 4, 1942.

26. CWRIC, *Personal Justice Denied*, 168.

27. *Daily Tulean Dispatch*, October 7, 1942, March 9, 1943, March 25, 1943.

28. Fort Livingston in Alexandria, Louisiana, was a center operated by the Justice Department, where, at one point, 571 people of Japanese ancestry were held. Weglyn, *Years of Infamy*, 177.

29. George Akiyama noted, "At Camp Livingston, Louisiana, the Japanese interned were living in an army prison stockade fenced in. They were quartered in regular army barracks with army sleeping cots with a central recreation room and mess hall. The food was quite adequate and they had freedom to leave their sleeping quarters and spend time outside within the confines visiting friends or exercising. They were required to keep the grounds neat and clean, just like in an army camp."

Chapter 28. The Loyalty Questionnaire

1. CWRIC, *Personal Justice Denied*, 190; Daniels, *Concentration Camps*, 112–13.

2. CWRIC, *Personal Justice Denied*, 190.

3. Ibid., 194.

4. This was Mr. Tomita's interpretation of the question.

5. Thomas and Nishimoto, *The Spoilage*, 60.

6. Ibid., 57.

7. Ibid., 77–78.

8. Ibid., 105.

9. Daniels, *Concentration Camps*, 114.

10. Eventually 4,724 Japanese left as repatriates or expatriates, including 1,659 repatriated aliens accompanied by 1,949 U.S. citizens, almost all minors, and 1,116 expatriates, mostly *Kibei* (Nisei who spent their early years in Japan and returned to the United States). By 1959, 5,766 Japanese Americans had renounced their citizenship, 5,409 had requested citizenship be restored, and 4,978 had regained their citizenship. Wilson and Hosokawa, *East to America*, 232–33.

11. Daniels, *Concentration Camps*, 115.

12. Ibid., 114.

Chapter 29. Moving to Other Camps

1. Thomas and Nishimoto, *The Spoilage*, 104.

Chapter 30. The Work Release Program

1. CWRIC, *Personal Justice Denied*, 182; Thomas and Nishimoto, *The Spoilage*, 54.

2. CWRIC, *Personal Justice Denied*, 182; Wilson and Hosokawa, *East to America*, 217.

3. Sandra C. Taylor, "Leaving the Concentration Camps: Japanese American Resettlement in Utah and the Intermountain West," *Pacific Historical Review* 60 (May 1991): 177.

4. CWRIC, *Personal Justice Denied*, 183.

5. Taylor, "Leaving the Concentration Camps," 181.

6. Thomas and Nishimoto, *The Spoilage*, 55.

7. Idaho was outside the demilitarized zone.

8. CWRIC, *Personal Justice Denied*, 182.

9. *Daily Tulean Dispatch*, May 10, 1943.

Chapter 31. Camp Reflections

1. Mrs. Endow noted that her son's nature was to succeed. Later, he received honors for his many activities in school, and he eventually became a successful mechanical engineer.

2. "Alaska" was the name given to a distant section of the camp.

3. Kitano, *Japanese Americans*, 79.

4. Kitagawa, *Issei and Nisei*, 90–92.

5. Ibid., 89–90.

6. Amy Iwasaki Mass, "Psychological Effects of the Camps on Japanese Americans," in *Japanese Americans: From Relocation to Redress*, by Roger Daniels, Sandra C. Taylor, and H. L. Kitano (Salt Lake City: University of Utah, 1986), 160.

Chapter 32. Sons in the Military Service

1. Allan R. Bosworth, *America's Concentration Camps* (New York: W. W. Norton, 1967), 17.

2. Hosokawa, *Nisei*, 397.

3. Wilson and Hosokawa, *East to America*, 224–26; Harry K. Honda, "Mike Masaoka: The 'Go for Broke' Guy," *Pacific Citizen*, July 5, 1991, 3.

4. Bill Yamaki also had an early draft number. Eventually he entered officer's training school in Australia.

5. Bill Yamaki retired in 1977 after seventeen years of military and civil service. Among his appointments, he served at the Pentagon as chief of the Counterintelligence Branch, Intelligence and Security Division, and in the Office of the Assistant Chief of Staff for Intelligence, Department of the Army.

6. Kibi no Makibi from Kobi-gun in Okayama became the district chief for Shimotsumichi district. He lived between 693 and 775 and distinguished himself as a great diplomatic leader, leading missions to China during the Nara period.

He achieved the high rank of Minister of the Right and of second court rank, very high for one from the provinces and without noble blood.

7. Polly Timberman, "George Akiyama: 'Proving Ourselves,' " *Hood River News*, November 7, 1984, 11.

8. CWRIC, *Personal Justice Denied*, 256.

9. Bosworth, *America's Concentration Camps*, 13–14.

10. Hosokawa, *Nisei*, 409–10.

11. Ibid., 397–98.

12. Bosworth, *America's Concentration Camps*, 18.

13. Weglyn, *Years of Infamy*, 48–49.

14. CWRIC, *Personal Justice Denied*, 259.

15. Ibid., 258.

Chapter 33. The Anti-Japanese Campaign

1. *News*, February 16, 1945, 10. See also February 2, 9, 23, and March 23, 1945.

2. Editorial, *News*, January 1, 1943, 4.

3. *News*, January 8, 1943, 5; *Sun*, January 8, 1943, 1.

4. *News*, January 15, 1943, 6.

5. Ibid., January 29, 1943, 1.

6. Ibid., June 25, 1943, 6.

7. *Sun*, January 8, 1943, 1.

8. Editorial, *Sun*, April 1943, 4.

9. *News*, April 2, 1943, 8. Timothy Olmstead, in his analysis of two Oregon newspapers during the internment period, observed that the editor Hugh Ball had lived in Japan and had written about the wartime issues from a "more knowledgeable and objective point of view." Ball had campaigned against the spread of rumors and enabled the *Hood River News* to become a forum where the Japanese community could respond as well. Olmstead, "Nikkei Internment," 18–20.

10. Ibid., October 8, 1943, 1.

11. Ito, *Issei*, 692.

12. Prior to December 1, 1924, Japan conferred automatic citizenship to children born abroad to its citizens. After that date, citizenship was possible only if Japanese parents registered their children within fourteen days of birth. Those born before 1924 were also allowed to renounce their Japanese citizenship. Ichihashi, *Japanese in the United States*, 323. Despite these provisions of Japanese law, those born in the United States are, according to U.S. law, citizens unless they themselves take positive steps to renounce their citizenship.

13. American Legion Post No. 22, Hood River, Oregon, "A Statement on the Japanese" (Hood River, Oreg.: Post No. 22, 1945).

14. *News*, December 8, 1944, 8.

15. Ibid., December 29, 1944, 8.

16. Ibid.

17. Ibid.

18. Ibid., January 5, 1945, 8.

19. Ibid., January 19, 1945, 2.

20. *The Oregonian*, December 2, 1944, 1; *News*, December 8, 1944, 1.

21. Statement by Superintendent Frank H. Smith of the Board of Missions and Church Extension of the Methodist Church, *News*, January 5, 1945, 1.

22. *Sun*, January 12, 1945, 1.

23. *New York Herald Tribune*, December 15, 1944.

24. *The Oregonian*, December 15, 1944, 1.

25. *Sun*, December 29, 1944, 1.

26. *News*, January 5, 1945, 8, reprint of December 18, 1944, editorial in *Chicago Sun*.

27. *News*, December 29, 1944, 9.

28. *Argus Leader* (Sioux Falls, S.D.), December 6, 1944.

29. *Collier's*, January 20, 1945.

30. *Des Moines Register*, December 29, 1944.

31. Ed Sullivan, *New York News*, December 13, 1944.

32. Frank Sullivan, *PM* (New York), December 14, 1944.

33. *The Defender* (U.S. Army newspaper), cited in *Pacific Citizen*, February 17, 1945.

34. *The Stars and Stripes* (U.S. Army newspaper), January 5, 1945.

35. Stevens, "Free and Equal?" 17.

36. *News*, June 5, 1945, 9, reprint from *Daily Pioneer* (Mandan, N.D.), March 31, 1945.

37. CWRIC, *Personal Justice Denied*, 235, 15.

38. *News*, December 22, 1944.

39. Martha Ferguson McKeown, "Frank Hachiya: He Was an American at Birth—and at Death," *Sunday Oregonian*, May 20, 1945.

40. Budd Fukei, *The Japanese American Story* (Minneapolis: Dillon Press, 1976), 69; Hosokawa, *Nisei*, 414–15.

41. Editorial, *New York Times*, February 17, 1945.

42. Peggy E. Scripps, "Sgt. Hachiya, Spurned by Legion Post, Dies Hero's Death in P.I." *Honolulu Star Bullet*, February 15, 1945, 1; Joseph D. Harrington, *Yankee Samurai* (Detroit: Pettigrew Enterprises, 1979), 247–48.

43. On May 9, 1980, the central building at the Defense Language Institute, Presidio, San Francisco, was dedicated in Hachiya's honor. The new complex is the foreign language training base for intelligence personnel of all armed forces. Alan K. Ota, "Oregon War Hero Honored," *The Oregonian*, May 5, 1980; *News*, May 5, 1980, 1.

44. *The Oregonian*, February 17, 1945.

45. *Pacific Citizen*, February 24, 1945.

46. *News*, January 12, 1945, 1.

47. Oregon American Legion Department Headquarters, *Oregon Legionnaire* 27 (February 1945): 1.

48. The name of one of the sixteen servicemen, dishonorably discharged from the army for insubordination, was not replaced. Two other Nisei names apparently were not removed as had been intended. The *Hood River News* on December 15, 1944, reported that Isao Namba's name had been overlooked. According to an April 15, 1947, letter from Mrs. Max [Arline Winchell] Moore, local busi-

nesswoman, to Howard D. Samuel, the editor of *The Dartmouth*, Mamoru Noji's name was mistaken for a Finnish name and had not been removed.

49. *News*, January 26, 1945, 1; March 9, 1945, 1; April 13, 1945, 10.

50. Ibid., February 2, 1945, 6.

51. Ibid., February 9, 1945, 6.

52. Ibid., February 16, 1945, 10.

53. The book entitled *Once a Jap, Always a Jap* was written by T. S. Van Vleet and published by the Lomita, California, Post Veterans of Foreign Wars of the United States. *News*, February 23, 1945. "A Jap's a Jap" was an oft-quoted statement of General John DeWitt, commander of the Western Defense Command, in justifying military evacuation of Japanese. Thomas and Nishimoto, *The Spoilage*, 20.

54. *News*, February 23, 1945, 6.

55. Ibid., January 26, 1945, 10. Since Shoemaker's first ad was an open letter to Sherman Burgoyne, his signature was undoubtedly a play on Rev. Burgoyne's letter to the editor on January 5, 1944, signed "Yours for the American Way."

56. Moore, letter to Howard D. Samuel, 2.

57. U.S. War Relocation Authority, *Prejudice in Hood River Valley*, 13.

58. Editorial, *Sun*, January 5, 1945, 4.

59. Oregon Laws, 1945, Senate Bill 274, chapter 436, 787–89. The Alien Land Law was declared unconstitutional in 1947 in a suit filed on behalf of Etsuo Namba of Gresham and his Nisei son, Kenjin, in the Multnomah County Circuit Court. The Nambas sought to lease a sixty-two-acre farm and were represented in their successful case by Verne Dusenberry and Allan Hart. Pursinger, "Oregon's Japanese in World War II," 414–19. The state had ruled that the lease was invalid since no treaty existed between the United States and Japan. The court, however, declared the law illegal and an infringement on the equal protection provision of the Fourteenth Amendment. Wilson and Hosokawa, *East to America*, 280.

Chapter 34. Returning Home

1. *Time*, December 25, 1944, 14.

2. Ibid., March 19, 1945, 19.

3. Noda, *Yamato Colony*, 155.

4. Taylor, "Leaving the Concentration Camps," 188.

5. *Time*, April 16, 1945, 23.

6. *Time*, March 19, 1945, 19.

7. William L. Worden, "The Hate that Failed," *Saturday Evening Post*, May 4, 1946, 136.

8. Stevens, "Free and Equal?" 35.

9. *News*, January 12, 1945, 1.

10. U.S. War Relocation Authority, *Prejudice in Hood River Valley*, 14.

11. Sgt. Charles A. U'Ren, "Officer's Report: Japanese Situation, Hood River County," January 30, 1945, Sprague Manuscripts, Oregon Historical Society, Portland, Oreg.

12. The government report compared numbers of those Japanese known to have returned with figures in the 1940 census. U.S. Department of the Interior, *The Evacuated People*, 48, 46.

13. Daniels, *Asian America*, 242.

14. Tamura, "Grandma Noji," 109–12; *News*, January 19, 1945, 1.

15. *The Oregonian*, April 5, 1945, 6.

16. Mr. George S. Akiyama and Mr. Tomeji Katayama also returned with the Noji family to examine their own property.

17. CWRIC, *Personal Justice Denied*, 241.

18. U.S. War Relocation Authority, *Annual Report of the Director, WRA, to the Secretary of the Interior* (Washington, D.C.: Government Printing Office, June 1945), 276.

19. Taylor, "Leaving the Concentration Camps," 179.

20. The eldest of the seven was still in grade school, and the youngest was barely six years old. Mr. Kusachi's wife had died at Minidoka.

21. Trees were trimmed to allow sunlight through and to maximize growth of fruit and tree limbs.

22. The family was assisted by two other local Issei. Mr. Kamegoro Iwatsuki and his family also lived in the Kusachi home, for they were not yet able to regain their home. Mr. Riichi Kiyokawa was able to return to his home but could not recover his orchard at that time.

23. Attorney Gus Solomon was appointed to the Oregon District Court in 1949. He publicly opposed the Japanese internment and boycott of their produce and worked to defend them in the courts. Solomon died on February 16, 1987, at the age of eighty.

24. U.S. War Relocation Authority, *Final Report of the WRA Northwest Area Office: Evacuee Property Report* (Portland, Oreg.: WRA District Office, 1946), 4.

25. At that time, growers believed that loosening soil around trees would allow irrigation water to penetrate more easily into the ground, while also preventing ground cover from sapping valuable nutrients and allowing soil to retain heat during freezing temperatures. Turning the soil also simplified the job of digging irrigation ditches.

26. U.S. War Relocation Authority, *Final Report of the Area Attorney, Pacific Northwest Area* (Portland, Oreg.: WRA District Office, 1946), 10.

27. U'Ren, "Officer's Report"; Neuberger, "Their Brothers' Keepers," 27.

28. Dormant spray was sprayed on dormant trees during the spring to control disease and insects.

Chapter 35. The Hood River Community

1. Mr. Akiyama had been held for more than a year in Justice Department internment centers in three locations: Fort Missoula, Montana; Fort Sill, Oklahoma; and Fort Livingston, Louisiana.

2. George Akiyama, interview at Akiyama home, January 29, 1986; *The Oregonian*, December 23, 1945, 18.

3. Moore, Letter to Howard D. Samuel, 3.

4. Loftus, *Made in Japan*, 102.

5. Moore, "Hood River Redeems Itself," 316.

6. Statement by Mrs. Max [Arline Winchell] Moore in Richard L. Neuberger, "All Quiet on Hood River as Japs Return to Valley," *Sunday Oregonian*, June 16, 1946.

7. Stevens, "Free and Equal?" 36.

8. Officers were Avon Sutton, president; Wallace J. Miller, vice-president; Mrs. Carl Smith, secretary-treasurer; Mrs. Max Moore and Rev. Sherman Burgoyne, central committee. Mrs. Fannie Friedman of the district WRA office served as liaison. U.S. War Relocation Authority, *Final Report of Activities of the Portland, Oregon District Office* (Portland, Oreg.: WRA District Office, February 19, 1946), 10. Members included: Rev. and Mrs. Sherman Burgoyne, Mrs. Arline Moore, Mr. and Mrs. Avon Sutton, Fred Taylor, Mr. and Mrs. Carl Smith, Wallace Miller, J. R. Forden, A. L. Boe, R. J. McIsaac, Sydney Babson, Harold Shake, Gerhard Wertgen, Jim Willey, Ralph Lewis, Lafferty and Woods, Rev. and Mrs. Lloyd Thomas, Roy Webster, Norman Tucker, Joe Horn, Charles Sheppard, Martha McKeown, Mr. and Mrs. Bill Smullin, Mr. and Mrs. Pat Cosner, Mr. and Mrs. Harris Higgins, Mr. and Mrs. Glen Miller, Mr. and Mrs. Elmer Moller, Mr. and Mrs. Charles Fioretti, Mr. and Mrs. Harold McIsaac, Les Sherwood, Ida Mason, Pete Anderson, Ed Goetz, E. C. Smith, Mr. Rodamer, Clyde Linville, Kelly Brothers, June Haviland, Sheldon Laurence, and others (unidentified). "Japanese-American Research Project," Summary of the Activities of the League of Liberty and Justice by the Mid-Columbia Japanese American Citizens' League, copy in author's possession.

9. *News*, June 8, 1945, 9.

10. Ibid., May 25, 1945, 6.

11. Hood River League for Liberty and Justice, letter to local Japanese, June 8, 1945, copy in author's possession.

12. U.S. War Relocation Authority, *Final Report of Activities of the Portland, Oregon District Offce*, 10, 18.

13. Neuberger, "All Quiet on Hood River."

14. *News*, January 5, 1945, 8.

15. Ibid., March 16, 1945, 1.

16. Ibid., 8.

17. Ray Sato, letter to Linda Tamura, January 17, 1984; interview, August 3, 1984, Parkdale, Oregon.

18. Following his service in Hood River, Rev. Burgoyne was appointed to the Methodist church in tiny Shedd, Oregon, in 1947, but he declined and accepted a position with the Pacific Northwest Conference, serving a church in Spokane for one year. In 1948, he went to Portland as pastor of the Lents Methodist Church and in 1952 was transferred to the city's University Park Methodist Church. After retiring in 1957 with a heart condition, he died on February 4, 1964. "Official Supplement to the Journal of the Oregon Annual Conference of the Methodist Church," 1964, 100C.

19. *The Oregonian*, January 4, 1947, section 2, 3.

20. *New York Times*, February 14, 1947, 3.

21. Worden, "The Hate that Failed," May 4, 1946, 138. Although the article credited the quote only to "a militant lady" in Hood River, Mrs. Florence Olmstead, the daughter of Mrs. Moore (now deceased), admitted, "That sounds a lot like my mother," and said there was a strong possibility the family has some German blood. Another valley Nisei, Yuki Okimoto Sumoge, quoted in the first paragraphs of the article, also readily credited Mrs. Moore as a prominent and respected businesswoman who "cared enough and would have had the courage and conviction to take such a stand."

22. Stevens, "Free and Equal?" 37.

23. Hood River County Historical Society, *History*, 271.

24. *News*, January 12, 1945.

25. Ralph G. Martin, "Hood River Odyssey," *New Republic* 115 (December 16, 1946): 816.

26. Moore, Letter to Howard D. Samuel, 3.

27. U.S. War Relocation Authority, *Japanese Groups and Associations in the United States*, Community Analysis Report No. 3 (Washington, D.C.: Government Printing Office, March 1943), 3.

28. In 1981, Mr. Kusachi received the Sixth Class Order of the Sacred Treasure of the Emperor of Japan. He was cited in a newspaper article in his possession for serving almost twenty years as chair of the Hood River Japanese Society until its dissolution in 1973. The award recognized "his efforts in service of the Japanese American community and in promoting the area's Japanese American community."

Chapter 36. Compensation, Citizenship, and Redress

1. CWRIC, *Personal Justice Denied*, 118.

2. The Commission on Wartime Relocation and Internment of Civilians was established by Congress in 1980 to review circumstances surrounding Executive Order 9066 and its impact on U.S. citizens and resident aliens. It also reviewed directives of U.S. military forces requiring relocation and detention of U.S. citizens. Finally, it made recommendations based on its findings. CWRIC, *Personal Justice Denied*, 1, 118.

3. Ibid., 120.

4. Hosokawa, *Nisei*, 446.

5. CWRIC, *Personal Justice Denied*, 120.

6. Mary Chewning, "The Japanese Evacuation Claims for Oregon" (Master's thesis, Graduate Division of Holy Names College, August 1973), 120.

7. CWRIC, *Personal Justice Denied*, 121.

8. U.S. Department of the Interior, *The Evacuated People*, 64.

9. Chewning, "Japanese Evacuation Claims," 119.

10. CWRIC, *Personal Justice Denied*, 118.

11. "Oregon and Persons of Japanese Ancestry in World War II," Oregon State Archives, Salem, Oreg., in "Japanese-American Evacuation Claims, 1948–64," Marvin A. Pursinger file, MSS 183, Oregon Historical Society, Portland, Oreg.

12. Weglyn, *Years of Infamy,* 276. The figure $400 million dollars has been popularly cited as the amount of Japanese property losses during the war. The Federal Reserve Bank records show no documentation to support this, however; and Sandra Taylor refutes that figure now as "folk wisdom." Taylor, "Federal Reserve Bank," 29; Daniels, personal note.

13. Taylor, "Federal Reserve Bank," 30.

14. U.S. Department of the Interior, *The Wartime Handling of Evacuee Property* (Washington, D.C.: Government Printing Office, 1946, reprinted 1975), RG210-F6-2, National Archives, 3–4, cited in Taylor, "Federal Reserve Bank," 28.

15. Weglyn, *Years of Infamy,* 268. During the 1950s approximately 45,000 nonquota Japanese entered the United States. These provisions were legal through family reunification policies, the War Brides Act of 1945, the Alien Fiancees or Fiances Act of 1946, and the Refugee Relief Act of 1953. Daniels, *Asian America,* 306. In 1965, a bill signed by President Lyndon B. Johnson permitted 350,000 immigrants annually to be admitted, based not on their race, creed, or nationality but on their skills and relationships to those in the United States. Hosokawa, *Nisei,* 454–55.

16. Rev. Arthur Collins was the minister of the First Baptist Church and an instructor for the Japanese citizenship class.

17. The Alien Land Law of Oregon was challenged by attorney Verne Dusenberry, assisted by Allan A. Hart. The law was declared invalid by the Oregon Supreme Court in 1947.

18. CWRIC, *Personal Justice Denied,* Part 2: *Recommendations* (Washington, D.C.: Government Printing Office, 1983), 5.

19. Ibid., 6.

20. Ibid., 8–9.

21. *Pacific Citizen,* August 19, 1988, 1, 5.

22. Ibid., September 18, 1992, October 2, 1992; *The Oregonian,* September 30, 1989.

Chapter 37. Issei Reflect on Their Experiences

1. The Mid-Columbia chapter of the Japanese American Citizens' League (JACL) annually holds an Issei Appreciation Dinner and a Japanese community picnic, popular events for four generations of Japanese and an increasing number of Caucasian guests and members. In the past few years, with declining numbers of Issei and increasing ages of Nisei, the annual dinner has become a tribute to all Nikkei (those of Japanese ancestry who are not Japanese citizens).

Chapter 39. Issei Self-portraits

1. When Mrs. Noyori's son Mark was eighteen months old, he was rescued from a ditch by Mr. Edgar, a neighbor.

Chapter 40. Perspectives on the Hood River Issei

1. Roger Daniels, Sandra C. Taylor, and H. L. Kitano, *Japanese Americans: From Relocation to Redress* (Salt Lake City: University of Utah, 1986), 4.

2. John Modell, "The Japanese American Family: A Perspective for Future Investigations," *Pacific Historical Review* 37 (February 1968): 77.

3. Rohlen, *Japan's High Schools*, 53–54.

4. Kitano, *Japanese Americans*, 66; Ruth Benedict, *The Chrysanthemum and the Sword* (Boston: Houghton Mifflin, 1946), 101–2.

5. Mamoru Iga, "Japanese Social Structure and Sources," *Social Forces* 35 (March 1957): 275.

6. John C. Condon, *With Respect to the Japanese* (Yarmouth, Maine: Intercultural Press, 1984), 11.

7. Editorial, *Pacific Citizen*, June 9, 1989.

8. Mass, "Psychological Effects of the Camps," 161.

9. Ng, "Collective Memory, Social Networks, and Generations," 52.

10. CWRIC, *Personal Justice Denied*, 297–98.

Appendix B

1. Mr. J. W. Crites was the Hood River county school superintendent in 1925.

2. The minutes did not indicate the results, but subsequent classes were held in Issei homes.

3. Given names were not provided in the minutes and are included only when accessible.

Bibliography

American Legion Post No. 22, Hood River, Oregon. "A Statement on the Japanese." Hood River, Oreg.: Post No. 22, 1945.

Bauer, Helen, and Sherwin Carlquist. *Japanese Festivals*. Tokyo: Charles E. Tuttle, 1985.

Beardsley, Richard K., John W. Hall, and Robert E. Ward. *Village Japan*. Chicago: University of Chicago Press, 1959.

Beikoku Nikei-jin Hyakunen-shi [One Hundred Years of Japanese Americans]. San Francisco: Shin Nichibei Shimbun-sha, 1961.

Benedict, Ruth. *The Chrysanthemum and the Sword*. Boston: Houghton Mifflin, 1946.

Borton, Hugh, *Japan's Modern Century*. New York: Ronald Press, 1955.

Bosworth, Allan R. *America's Concentration Camps*. New York: W. W. Norton, 1967.

Buckner, Lindsay. Letter, July 23, 1986.

Burton, Margaret E. *The Education of Women in Japan*. New York: Fleming H. Revell, 1914.

Chamberlain, Basil Hall. *Things Japanese*. London: Kelly and Walsh, 1898; reprint Rutland, Vt.: Charles E. Tuttle, 1971.

Cherry, Kittredge. *Womansword: What Japanese Words Say about Women*. Tokyo: Kodansha International, 1989.

Chewning, Mary. "The Japanese Evacuation Claims for Oregon." Master's thesis, Graduate Division of Holy Names College, August 1973.

Commission on Wartime Relocation and Internment of Civilians. *Personal Justice Denied*. Washington, D.C.: Government Printing Office, 1982.

———. *Personal Justice Denied, Part 2: Recommendations*. Washington, D.C.: Government Printing Office, 1983.

Condon, John C. *With Respect to the Japanese*. Yarmouth, Maine: Intercultural Press, 1984.

Conroy, Hilary. *The Japanese Frontier in Hawaii, 1868–1898*. Berkeley: University of California Press, 1953.

Cramer, Jack. "We, Too, Please, Are 100 Per Cent Americans." Interview with Minoru Yasui. *Sunday Oregonian*, February 4, 1940, 5.

Daily Tulean Dispatch (Tule Lake Colony newspaper), 1942–43.

Daniels, Roger. *Asian America: Chinese and Japanese in the United States since 1850.* Seattle: University of Washington Press, 1988.

———. *Concentration Camps North America: Japanese in the United States and Canada during World War II.* Malabar, Fla.: Robert E. Krieger, 1981.

———. *The Politics of Prejudice.* Berkeley: University of California Press, 1962.

Daniels, Roger, Sandra C. Taylor, and H. L. Kitano. *Japanese Americans: From Relocation to Redress.* Salt Lake City: University of Utah, 1986.

Dunn, Charles J. *Everyday Life in Traditional Japan.* Tokyo: Charles E. Tuttle, 1969.

Embree, John F. *Suye Mura: A Japanese Village.* Chicago: University of Chicago Press, 1939.

Fiftieth Anniversary Program. Hood River, Oreg.: Japanese Methodist Church, May 1976.

Frank, Gerry. "Surprise! It's Friday Already and Time for Page in History." *The Oregonian*, July 26, 1991, 26.

Fujii, Toshimasu. "The Degree of Acculturation and Success Patterns in Three Generations of the Japanese Americans in the Portland Area." Master's thesis, Portland State University, 1980.

Fukei, Budd. *The Japanese American Story.* Minneapolis: Dillon Press, 1976.

Gee, Emma. "Issei: The First Women." In *Asian Women.* Berkeley: University of California Press, 1971.

Glenn, Evelyn Nakano. *Issei, Nisei, Warbride: Three Generations of Japanese American Women in Domestic Service.* Philadelphia: Temple University Press, 1986.

Guppy, Ruth M. "Japanese Hood River Story Echoes History." *Hood River News*, April 20, 1978, 2–4.

Hall, John Whitney. *Government and Local Power in Japan, 500 to 1700: A Study Based on Bizen Province.* Princeton, N.J.: Princeton University Press, 1980.

Hall, John Whitney, and Richard K. Beardsley. *Twelve Doors to Japan.* New York: McGraw-Hill, 1965.

Harrington, Joseph D. *Yankee Samurai.* Detroit: Pettigrew Enterprises, 1979.

Hirabayashi, Lane Ryo, and George Tanaka. "The Issei Community in Moneta and the Gardena Valley, 1900–1920." *Southern California Quarterly* 70, no. 2 (1988): 127–58.

History of Epworth United Methodist Church, Portland, Oregon. Translated by Yoshimi Kamano; additions by Rev. Shinya Maruya. Portland, Oreg.: Epworth Methodist Church, 1982.

Honda, Harry K. "Mike Masaoka: The 'Go For Broke' Guy." *Pacific Citizen*, July 5, 1991, 1–4, 9.

Hood River County Chamber of Commerce. *Brief Historical Sketches of Hood River County.* Hood River, Oreg.: Hood River Chamber of Commerce, n.d.

Hood River County Historical Society. *History of Hood River County.* Dallas: Taylor Publishing, 1982.

Hood River County Sun, 1941–45.

Hood River Glacier, 1919.

Hood River News, 1917–78.

Hosokawa, Bill. *Nisei: The Quiet Americans.* New York: William Morrow, 1969.

Ichihashi, Yamato. *Japanese in the United States.* Stanford, Calif.: Stanford University Press, 1932.

Ichioka, Yuji. "Amerika Nadeshiko: Japanese Immigrant Women in the United States, 1900–1924." *Pacific Historical Review* 49 (May 1980): 339–57.

————. *The Issei: The World of the First Generation Japanese Immigrants, 1885–1924.* New York: Free Press, 1988.

Iga, Mamoru. "Japanese Social Structure and Sources." *Social Forces* 35 (March 1957): 271–78.

Irons, Peter. *Justice Delayed: The Record of the Japanese American Internment Cases.* Middletown, Conn.: Wesleyan University Press, 1989.

Ishizuka, Karen C. *The Elder Japanese: A Cross Cultural Study of Minority Elders in San Diego.* San Diego: San Diego State University, 1978.

Issei Appreciation Committee. *Issei Pioneers in Oregon: A Short Subjective History.* Portland, Oreg.: Issei Appreciation Committee, September 1973.

Ito, Kazuo. *Issei: A History of Japanese Immigrants in North America.* Translated by Shinichiro Nakamura and Jean S. Gerard. Seattle: Executive Committee for Publication of Issei, 1973.

Japanese American Citizens' League. *Personal Justice Denied: Summary and Recommendations of the Committee on Wartime Relocation and Internment of Civilians.* San Francisco: Japanese American Citizens' League, 1983.

Japanese American Citizens' League, Mid-Columbia Chapter, Issei Story Committee (Mamoru Noji, chairman). "Japanese-Issei Story," Spring 1961. Hood River County Museum, Hood River, Oreg.

"Japanese-American Research Project." Summary of the activities of the League for Liberty and Justice by Mid-Columbia Japanese American Citizens' League. Undated, unauthored two-page paper. Copy in author's possession.

Japanese Farmers' Association of Hood River. Minutes, 1914–25. Translated by Yoko Gulde. Kusachi Family Collection.

Joya, Mock. *A Hundred Things Japanese.* Tokyo: Japan Publications Trading Company, 1975.

————. *Quaint Customs and Manners of Japan.* Tokyo: Tokyo News Service, 1951.

Kalish, Richard A., and Sharon Moriwaki. "The World of the Elderly Asian American." *Journal of Social Issues* 29, no. 2 (1973): 187–209.

Kataoka, Susan McCoin. "Issei Women: A Study in Subordinate Status." Ph.D. diss., University of California, Los Angeles, 1977.

Kawakami, K. K. *The Real Japanese Question.* New York: Macmillan, 1921.

Kikumura, Akemi. "The Life History of an Issei Woman: Conflicts and Strain in the Process of Acculturation." Ph.D. diss., University of California, Los Angeles, 1979.

————. *Through Harsh Winters: The Life of a Japanese Immigrant Woman.* Novato, Calif.: Chandler and Sharp, 1983.

Kitagawa, Daisuke. *Issei and Nisei: The Internment Years.* New York: Seabury Press, 1967.

Kitano, Harry H. L. *Japanese Americans: The Evolution of a Subculture.* Englewood Cliffs, N.J.: Prentice-Hall, 1976.

Knoll, Tricia. *Becoming Americans: Asian Sojourners, Immigrants, and Refugees in the Western United States.* Portland, Oreg.: Coast to Coast Books, 1982.

Lebra, Takie Sugiyama. *Japanese Women: Constraint and Fulfillment.* Honolulu: University of Hawaii Press, 1984.

Loftus, Mitzi Asai. *Made in Japan and Settled in Oregon.* Coos Bay, Oreg.: Pigeon Point Press, 1990.

Lukes, Timothy J., and Gary Y. Okihiro. *Japanese Legacy: Farming and Community Life in California's Santa Clara Valley.* Cupertino, Calif.: California History Center, 1985.

McKeown, Martha Ferguson. "Frank Hachiya: He Was an American at Birth—and at Death." *Sunday Oregonian,* May 20, 1945.

Martin, Ralph G. "Hood River Odyssey." *New Republic* 115 (December 16, 1946): 814–15.

Mass, Amy Iwasaki. "Psychological Effects of the Camps on Japanese Americans." In *Japanese Americans: From Relocation to Redress,* by Roger Daniels, Sandra C. Taylor, and H. L. Kitano. Salt Lake City: University of Utah Press, 1986.

Masumoto, David Mas. *Country Voices: The Oral History of a Japanese American Family Farm Community.* Del Rey, Calif.: Inaka Countryside Publications, 1987.

Matsumoto, Valerie. "Japanese American Women during World War II." *Frontiers* 8 (1984): 6–13.

Millis, H. A. *The Japanese Problem in the United States.* New York: Macmillan, 1915.

Mitson, Betty E. "Looking Back in Anguish: Oral History and Japanese American Evacuation." In *Voices Long Silent: An Oral Inquiry into the Japanese American Evacuation,* edited by Arthur A. Hansen and Betty E. Mitson. Fullerton: California State University, Fullerton, Oral History Program, 1974.

Miyamoto, S. Frank. "An Immigrant Community in America." In *East across the Pacific: Historical and Sociological Studies of Japanese Immigration and Assimilation,* edited by Hilary Conroy and T. Scott Miyakawa. Santa Barbara, Calif.: American Bibliographical Center Clio Press, 1972.

———. "The Japanese Minority in the Pacific Northwest." *Pacific Northwest Quarterly* 54 (October 1963): 143–49.

Modell, John. *The Economics and Politics of Racial Accommodation: The Japanese of Los Angeles, 1900–1942.* Urbana: University of Illinois Press, 1977.

———. "The Japanese American Family: A Perspective for Future Investigations." *Pacific Historical Review* 37 (February 1968): 67–81.

———. "Tradition and Opportunity: The Japanese Immigrants in America." *Pacific Historical Review* 40 (May 1971): 163–83.

Moore, Arline Winchell. "Hood River Redeems Itself." *Asia and the Americas* 6 (July 1946): 316–17.

———. Letter to Howard D. Samuel, Editor-in-Chief. *The Dartmouth* (Hanover, N.H.), April 15, 1947.

Nakane, Kazuko. *Nothing Left in My Hands: An Early Japanese American Community in Pajaro Valley.* Seattle: Young Pine Press, 1985.

Nakano, Mei. *Japanese American Women: Three Generations, 1890–1900.* Berkeley, Calif.: Mina Press, 1990.

National Japanese American Historical Society. *Americans of Japanese Ancestry and the United States Constitution: 1787–1987.* San Francisco: National Japanese American Historical Society, 1987.

Neuberger, Richard L. "All Quiet on Hood River as Japs Return to Valley." *Sunday Oregonian,* June 16, 1946.

———. "The Nisei Come Back to Hood River." *Reader's Digest* 49 (November 1946): 102–4.

———. "Their Brothers' Keepers." *Saturday Review of Literature* 29 (August 10, 1946): 5–6, 27–28.

Ng, Wendy Lee. "Collective Memory, Social Networks, and Generations: The Japanese American Community in Hood River, Oregon." Ph.D. diss., University of Oregon, 1989.

Noda, Kesa. *Yamato Colony: 1906–1960.* Livingston, Calif.: Japanese American Citizens' League, Livingston-Merced Chapter, 1979.

Noji, Toru. Letter, July 12, 1983.

Official Supplement to the Journal of the Oregon Annual Conference of the Methodist Church. Portland, Oreg.: Oregon-Idaho Conference Office, 1964.

Olmstead, Timothy. "Nikkei Internment: The Perspective of Two Oregon Weekly Newspapers." *Oregon Historical Quarterly* 85 (Spring 1984): 5–32.

Oregon American Legion Department Headquarters. *Oregon Legionnaire* 27 (February 1945).

Oregon Bureau of Labor. *Census: Japanese Population in Oregon.* Salem: State Printing Department, 1929.

Oregon, State of. *Report on the Japanese Situation in Oregon.* Salem: State Printing Department, 1920.

Ota, Alan K. "Oregon War Hero Honored." *The Oregonian,* May 5, 1980.

Pacific Citizen, 1945, 1988, 1992.

Pope, Clem. Interview, July 2, 1986, Odell, Oreg.

Pursinger, Marvin Gavin. "The Japanese Settle in Oregon: 1880–1920." *Journal of the West* 5 (April 1966): 251–62.

———. "Oregon's Japanese in World War II: A History of Compulsory Relocation." Ph.D. diss., University of Southern California, 1961.

Reischauer, Edwin O. *The Japanese.* Cambridge, Mass.: Belknap Press, 1981.

Rohlen, Thomas P. *Japan's High Schools.* Berkeley: University of California Press, 1983.

Ryder, R. W. "The Japanese and the Pacific Coast." *North American Review* 213 (January 1921): 1–15.

Sarasohn, Eileen Sunada. *The Issei: Portrait of a Pioneer, an Oral History.* Palo Alto, Calif.: Pacific Books, 1983.

Sato, Ray. Letter, January 17, 1984; interview, August 3, 1984, Parkdale, Oreg.

Schick, Lee, and Naomi Lee. *Asbury United Methodist Church, 1886–1986.* Hood River, Oreg.: Asbury Methodist Church, 1985.

Shibusawa, Keizo, ed. *Japanese Life and Culture in the Meiji Era.* Translated by Charles S. Terry. Tokyo: Toyo Bunko, 1958; reprint 1969.

Stearns, Marjorie R. "The History of the Japanese People in Oregon." Master's thesis, University of Oregon, 1937.

Stevens, Beatrice. "Free and Equal? The Japanese-Americans in Oregon." A unit of work for secondary schools prepared for the Workshop on Intercultural Education, Portland, Summer 1945. Oregon Historical Society, Portland, Oreg.

Straelen, H. V. *The Japanese Woman Looking Forward.* Tokyo: Kyo Bun Kwan, 1940.

Tamura, Linda. "Grandma Noji." Unpublished manuscript, August 1984.

Tateishi, John. *And Justice for All: An Oral History of the Japanese American Detention Camps.* New York: Random House, 1984.

Taylor, Sandra C. "The Federal Reserve Bank and the Relocation of the Japanese in 1942." *Public Historian* 5 (Winter 1983): 9–30.

——. "Leaving the Concentration Camps: Japanese American Resettlement in Utah and the Intermountain West." *Pacific Historical Review* 60 (May 1991): 169–94.

tenBroek, Jacobus, Edward N. Barnhart, and Floyd W. Matson. *Prejudice, War and the Constitution.* Berkeley: University of California Press, 1954.

Thomas, Dorothy Swaine, and Richard S. Nishimoto. *The Spoilage: Japanese American Evacuation.* Berkeley: University of California Press, 1946.

Timberman, Polly. "George Akiyama: 'Proving Ourselves,' " *Hood River News,* November 7, 1984, 11.

Tsutakawa, Mayumi, and Alan Chong Lau, ed. *Turning Shadows into Light: Art and Culture of the Northwest's Early Asian/Pacific Community.* Seattle: Young Pine Press, 1982.

Tule Lake Committee. *Kinenhi: Reflections on Tule Lake.* San Francisco: Tule Lake Committee, 1980.

Tule Lake Interlude (first anniversary edition of *Daily Tulean Dispatch*), May 27, 1943.

Umemoto, Ann. "Crisis in the Japanese American Family." In *Asian Women.* Berkeley: University of California Press, 1971.

United Methodist Church Journal and Yearbook. 133rd Session, California-Nevada Annual Conference. Dallas: TM/UMR Productions, June 1981.

U.S. Bureau of Agricultural Economics. *Japanese Farm Holdings on the Pacific Coast.* Berkeley: U.S. Department of Agriculture, December 1944.

U.S. Bureau of the Census, *Thirteenth, Fourteenth, Fifteenth, Sixteenth Census of the United States.* Washington, D.C.: Government Printing Office, 1910–40.

U.S. Department of the Interior. *The Evacuated People: A Quantitative Description.* Washington, D.C.: Government Printing Office, 1946.

U.S. War Relocation Authority. *Annual Report of the Director, WRA, to the Secretary of the Interior.* Washington, D.C.: Government Printing Office, June 1945.

————. *Buddhism in the United States.* Community Analysis Report No. 9. Washington, D.C.: Government Printing Office, May 15, 1944.

————. *Dealing with Japanese Americans.* Community Analysis Report No. 1. Washington, D.C.: Government Printing Office, October 1942.

————. *Final Report of Activities of the Portland, Oregon District Office.* Portland, Oreg.: WRA District Office, February 19, 1946.

————. *Final Report of the Area Attorney, Pacific Northwest Area.* Portland, Oreg.: WRA District Office, 1946.

————. *Final Report of the WRA Northwest Area Office: Evacuee Property Report.* Portland, Oreg.: WRA District Office, 1946.

————. *Japanese Groups and Associations in the United States.* Community Analysis Report No. 3. Washington, D.C.: Government Printing Office, March 1943.

————. *Myths and Facts about the Japanese Americans.* Washington, D.C.: Government Printing Office, June 1945.

————. *Prejudice in Hood River Valley: A Case Study in Race Relations.* Community Analysis Report No. 13. Washington, D.C.: Government Printing Office, June 6, 1945.

————. *Questions and Answers for Evacuees: Information Regarding the Relocation Program.* Washington, D.C.: Government Printing Office, 1942.

————. *Semi-Annual Report, January 1–June 30, 1945.* Washington, D.C.: Department of the Interior, 1945.

Weglyn, Michi. *Years of Infamy: The Untold Story of America's Concentration Camps.* New York: Morrow Quill, 1976.

Wells, Stanley. Interview at Dr. Wells's home, Hood River, May 7, 1986.

White, Merry. *The Japanese Educational Challenge.* Tokyo: Kodansha International, 1987.

Wilson, Robert A., and Bill Hosokawa. *East to America.* New York: William Morrow, 1980.

Worden, William L. "The Hate that Failed." *Saturday Evening Post,* May 4, 1946, 22–23, 137–38.

Yanagida, Kunio, ed. *Japanese Manners and Customs in the Meiji Era.* Translated by Charles S. Terry. Tokyo: Toyo Bunko, 1957; reprint 1969.

Yasui, Barbara. "The Nikkei in Oregon, 1834–1940." *Oregon Historical Quarterly* 76 (September 1975): 225–57.

Yasui, Maija. "Brothers' Store Rich Cultural Center." In *Panorama '91.* Hood River, Oreg.: Hood River News, April 17, 1991, 17–18.

Yasui, Ray T. Unabridged and unedited transcription of taped statement to Barbara Yasui regarding the Japanese in Hood River, Oregon, 1971. Ethnology Collection, MSS 1521, Oregon Historical Society, Portland, Oreg.

Yasui, Robert S. *The Yasui Family of Hood River, Oregon.* N.p.: Holly Yasui Desktop Publishing, 1987.

Yoshida, Yosaburo. "Sources and Causes of Japanese Emigration." *Annals of the American Academy of Political and Social Science* 34 (September 1909): 379–82.

Zich, Arthur. "Japanese Americans: Home at Last." *National Geographic* 169 (April 1986): 512–39.

Index

LINDA TAMURA is a professor of education and the chair of the Education Department at Pacific University in Forest Grove, Oregon, where she has taught since 1977. She is involved in multicultural school programs and Japanese American projects and has written articles and given presentations on those topics. Dr. Tamura grew up in Hood River, Oregon, and received her Ed.D. from Oregon State University, with a minor in anthropology.

University of Illinois Press
1325 South Oak Street
Champaign, Illinois 61820-6903
www.press.uillinois.edu